The 2016 American Presidential Campaign and the News

Lexington Studies in Political Communication

Series Editor: Robert E. Denton Jr., Virginia Tech

This series encourages focused work examining the role and function of communication in the realm of politics including campaigns and elections, media, and political institutions.

Recent Titles in the Series

The 2016 American Presidential Campaign and the News: Implications for American Democracy and the Republic. Edited by Jim A. Kuypers
A Rhetoric of Divisive Partisanship: The 2016 American Presidential Campaign Discourse of Bernie Sanders and Donald Trump. By Colleen Elizabeth Kelley
Studies of Communication in the 2016 Presidential Campaign. Edited by Robert E. Denton Jr.
The Monstrous Discourse in the Donald Trump Campaign: Implications for National Discourse. By Debbie Jay Williams and Kalyn L. Prince
The Political Blame Game in American Democracy. Edited by Larry Powell and Mark Hickson III
Political Campaign Communication: Theory, Method, and Practice. Edited by Robert E. Denton Jr.
Still Paving the Way for Madam President, Revised Edition. By Nichola D. Gutgold
James Farmer Jr.: The Great Debater. By Ben Voth
Persuasive Attacks on Donald Trump in the 2016 Presidential Primary. By William L. Benoit and Mark J. Glantz

The 2016 American Presidential Campaign and the News

Implications for American Democracy and the Republic

Edited by Jim A. Kuypers

LEXINGTON BOOKS
Lanham • Boulder • New York • London

Published by Lexington Books
An imprint of The Rowman & Littlefield Publishing Group, Inc.
4501 Forbes Boulevard, Suite 200, Lanham, Maryland 20706
www.rowman.com

Unit A, Whitacre Mews, 26-34 Stannary Street, London SE11 4AB

British Library Cataloguing in Publication Information Available

Library of Congress Cataloging-in-Publication Data

ISBN: 978-1-4985-6511-0 (cloth : alk. paper)
ISBN: 978-1-4985-6512-7 (electronic)

∞™ The paper used in this publication meets the minimum requirements of American National Standard for Information Sciences Permanence of Paper for Printed Library Materials, ANSI/NISO Z39.48-1992.

Printed in the United States of America

To

Stephen W. Braden

My friend; an original man, much missed.

Contents

1 The 2016 Presidential Campaign, the News, and the Republic 1
Jim A. Kuypers

2 Fact or Fiction: Defining Fake News During the 2016 U.S. Presidential Election 11
Abe Aamidor

3 The *Othering* of Donald Trump and His Supporters 31
Stephen D. Cooper

4 Donald J. Trump's Use of Twitter in the 2016 Campaign 55
Katherine Haenschen, Michael Horning, and Jim A. Kuypers

5 The Pundit Problem: A Look at Bias and Negativity in Cable News Coverage as the 2016 Election Came to a Close 77
Michael Horning

6 News Media Framing of the Donald J. Trump and Hillary Clinton 2016 Presidential Nomination Acceptance Speeches: Terministic Screens and the Discovery of the Worldview and Bias of the Press 101
Jim A. Kuypers

7 Social Media Candidate Attacks and Hillary Clinton's Failed Narrative in the 2016 Presidential Campaign 133
Stephanie A. Martin and Andrea J. Terry

8 Iconographic Tracking of Pepe the Frog Meme through the 2016 Presidential Campaign 155
Natalia Mielczarek

9 Entertainment News and Satire in the 2016 Presidential Election 181
Joseph M. Valenzano III and Chad Painter

10 Journalistic Hegemony of "Blue Privilege": Tracing the Use of Identity Politics Toward a Political Economy of News Coverage 203
Ben Voth

11 Sports Figures, Social Commentary, and the Role of Sports Journalism During the 2016 Presidential Election 223
Erin Whiteside

Index 243

About the Contributors 255

Chapter One

The 2016 Presidential Campaign, the News, and the Republic

Jim A. Kuypers

The general consensus among those concerned with political communication is that no modern presidential campaign has been so contentious and divisive as that between Donald J. Trump and Hillary Clinton. Americans, some in passing and others closely, watched and read daily about the rough and tumble of divisive partisan politics playing out in a strenuously fought presidential campaign. Their information was almost always from the same source: the news media. Which leads to this book. What role did the American news media play in the bitter presidential contest?

Obviously, it played a contested role. The Trump campaign repeatedly attacked the press for sloppy and biased reporting, with much of that coming from then candidate Trump himself in the form of stump speeches or Twitter declarations such as, "Dishonest media!"; "The media and establishment want me out of the race so badly"; "This election is being rigged by the media pushing false and unsubstantiated charges, and outright lies."[1] Long before winning the Republican nomination Trump made clear his feeling on the news media, calling *CNN*, for instance, "fake news." But even beyond that, he said of mainstream political journalists, "I do hate them. . . . Some of them are such lying, disgusting people. . . . (They're) among the most dishonest groups of people I've ever met."[2] The Clinton campaign, too, had issues with the news media, but of a different kind, that of charges of collusion to help her election prospects. This assertion, which gained increased attention after the Wikileaks email dump, dogged her throughout her campaign, and even to today.[3]

Complicating matters more, and lending strength to the charges of bias, many press outlets aggressively endorsed and defended Hillary Clinton during the campaign. For instance, after endorsing Hillary Clinton for president, the *New York Times* and the *Washington Post* published additional editorials attempting to make case for why Trump should not be president.[4] *USA Today,* which had never before endorsed a candidate for the presidency, wrote an editorial claiming Trump was "unfit for the presidency" and saying only about Clinton that the paper did "not have a consensus for a Clinton endorsement."[5] Eddie Scarry pointed out that many "media figures [were] actively lobbying their peers to challenge Donald Trump more aggressively when interviewing him or his surrogates, or even block Trump's campaign from gaining access to the press in some cases."[6]

Adding yet another level of complication, following the election many press outlets actually admitted to bias and attempted to justify it. For example, the *New York Times* penned an editorial where it admitted to its biased coverage and committed to "rededicate ourselves to the fundamental mission of Times journalism. That is to report America and the world honestly, without fear or favor."[7] Yet as pointed out by various media critics, "Had the paper actually been fair to both candidates, it wouldn't need to rededicate itself to honest reporting. And it wouldn't have been totally blindsided by Trump's victory."[8]

American political news journalism certainly played a controversial role in the 2016 election, and emerged from that event with the lowest credibility ratings on record. Entering the final leg of the campaign, only 18 percent of Americans possessed "a lot" of trust in the national news media.[9] Gallup asked the question in a slightly different way and found that in just one year, between September 2015 and September 2016, those Americans who had a "great deal" or "fair amount" of "trust and confidence in the media fell from 40% to 32%."[10] As of summer 2017, approximately "two-thirds of Americans say the mainstream press is full of fake news."[11] Of note is that as the news media continues its aggressive and negative reporting on President Trump,[12] Gallup reports that "Democrats' trust and confidence in the mass media to report the news 'fully, accurately and fairly' has jumped from 51% in 2016 to 72% this year—fueling a rise in Americans' overall confidence to 41%. Independents' trust has risen modestly to 37%, while Republicans' trust is unchanged at 14%." [13]

Some critics see the contested nature of news coverage in the 2016 election as a major event, the collapsing of American political journalism. Michael Goodwin, for instance, stated that,

> The shameful display of naked partisanship by the elite media is unlike anything seen in modern America.
>
> The largest broadcast networks—CBS, NBC and ABC—and major newspapers like the New York Times and Washington Post have jettisoned all

> pretense of fair play. Their fierce determination to keep Trump out of the Oval Office has no precedent.
>
> Indeed, no foreign enemy, no terror group, no native criminal gang suffers the daily beating that Trump does. The mad mullahs of Iran, who call America the Great Satan and vow to wipe Israel off the map, are treated gently by comparison.
>
> By torching its remaining credibility in service of Clinton, the mainstream media's reputations will likely never recover, nor will the standards. No future producer, editor, reporter or anchor can be expected to meet a test of fairness when that standard has been trashed in such willful and blatant fashion.[14]

Critic John Nolte goes further, arguing that the corruption of the American mainstream news media has actually destroyed America's crucial institutions.[15] Some in the news media, such as Gerard Baker, the editor in chief of the *Wall Street Journal*, have acknowledged trouble with the reportorial practices of their papers and are pushing back against the tide. Baker told his staff after an August 2017 Trump speech to "just stick to reporting what [Trump says] rather than packaging it in exegesis and selective criticism."[16]

Suffice it to say that a range of voices, including the media's own, have forcefully questioned the role that the mainstream news media played in the 2016 presidential election. It is the aim of this book to answer some of the questions surrounding its role in the 2016 campaign. Within, you will find ten additional chapters, each of which covers an issue of importance concerning the campaign coverage and analyzes some aspect of the news media coverage of the campaign. Areas covered include: fake news, media construction of the campaign personalities of Clinton and Trump, media bias, visual meme depictions of the candidates, identity politics as expressed through the news, Trump's tweets, entertainment news, social media as news, sports and political news, and others. The various chapters rely on insights generated through a variety of disciplinary perspectives including rhetorical, mass communication, media studies, journalism, and political communication. Although the book in its entirety will cover various areas of concern regarding media coverage of the campaign, each author comments directly upon implications for the American Republic and Democracy with respect to the situation explored in that author's chapter.

In "Fact or Fiction: Defining Fake News During the 2016 U.S. Presidential Election," veteran journalist and journalism scholar Abe Aamidor reminds us that an informed citizenry is essential to a functioning democracy. After all, he asks, how can voters make good choices on Election Day if they do not really know the facts? With that in mind, he notes that "fake news" was a main talking point of the media during the 2016 presidential campaign and its aftermath. This was especially true after a survey by the Internet news site *BuzzFeed* "claimed" that up to 75 percent of people who viewed a fake news headline tended to believe it. Later revelations about a virtual cottage industry for generating fake news stories out of Czechoslovakia only raised the level of concern. In his chapter, Aamidor briefly reviews the history of fake news in American politics and also investigates just how expansive the definition of "fake news" is. Carefully balancing examples from "the Right" and "the Left," Aamidor defines two broad types of fake news, and looks closely at the *BuzzFeed* report. He rounds out his chapter with a review of recent research that seeks to understand why people believe fake news, and looks at claims that fake news, including possible Russian hacking efforts, may have influenced the 2016 presidential election.

Media critic Stephen Cooper explores the notion of *othering*, a term often used to describe attempts to differentiate others from one's own group (usually in a negative way). In "The *Othering* of Donald Trump and His Supporters," Cooper takes a brief look at ways the eventual Republican nominee, and eventual forty-fifth President of the United States, was *othered* during the campaign by reporters and also by political commentators from both sides of the political spectrum. Cooper uses the term *othering* to mean efforts to stigmatize a public figure or group, rather than to critically examine that person's or group's positions on campaign issues. In his chapter, he examines some instances of attacks on Trump and his supporters that go beyond the customary rough-and-tumble of American politics. These examples are chosen both from the campaign and also from the first eight months of the Trump administration. Through his analysis he identifies particular features that indicate many attacks involve an "othering" process. Cooper argues that this reporting and commentary was a distressing and harmful turn in the political process, and also suggests the press has largely recast itself as an overt political actor, a process that has continued into the beginning of the new Trump administration. The implications of such practices for American democracy are discussed in the concluding remarks of the chapter.

In "Donald J. Trump's Use of Twitter in the 2016 Campaign," Katherine Haenschen, Michael Horning, and Jim A. Kuypers examine all of candidate Trump's Twitter tweets during the 2016 presidential campaign. These scholars correlate tweet popularity with retweets and media inclusion of particular tweets in various news reports. The chapter includes case studies looking at two of Trump's top ten tweets. The authors conclude that it was not so much the content of particular tweets that helped Trump obtain media coverage, but the sheer number of tweets and their personal nature that helped obtain coverage. Trump was "authentic" in his tweeting, and in stepping outside of the realm of the professional politician was able to attract followers and general press coverage, even as he sometimes attacked the press. The authors provide suggestions for future studies in the area of campaign tweeting.

In "The Pundit Problem: A Look at Bias and Negativity in Cable News Coverage as the 2016 Election Came to a Close," Michael Horning examines over three hundred thousand news references of Donald J. Trump and Hillary

Clinton in national news broadcasts during the campaign cycle. He notes that, leading up to the 2016 elections, media outlets were predicting that Hillary Clinton would win the presidency by a landslide. Yet as election returns came in, it became increasingly obvious that the media predictions had been wrong. These revelations come at a time when public trust in media had reached an all-time historical low. These missteps and other questionable media practices leading up to the national elections have caused many journalists to ask what they could have done differently in news coverage during the campaign. Horning looks at how national television news outlets covered Donald J. Trump and Hillary Clinton from the time of their nomination through the night of the presidential election. Of note is that Horning's study is driven by the differentiation between reporters, newscasters, and political pundits. He explores the total coverage for each candidate, the amount of time dedicated to fact versus opinion-based reporting, and the positive or negative mechanics of the coverage.

In "News Media Framing of the Donald J. Trump and Hillary Clinton 2016 Presidential Nomination Acceptance Speeches: Terministic Screens and the Discovery of the Worldview and Bias of the Press," I analyze the press coverage of those same speeches, looking for the worldviews of the mainstream press as expressed through its reporting on the speeches. Through dramatistical analysis of reportorial practices, I determine if the press exhibited worldviews similar to either of the candidates, and if the similarities/dissimilarities contributed to any form of media bias. To do this, I briefly share the worldviews expressed in the Clinton and Trump speeches. Then, bringing together the mainstream press responses to those speeches, I show the worldview of the press, demonstrating how the press echoed the worldview expressed in Clinton's address, but not that expressed in the Trump address. In the conclusion I discuss the findings in relation to various models of the press (libertarian, social responsibility, authoritarian) and the implications for press function within the American Republic.

Social media was often in the news, and often the source of news during the 2016 campaign. Stephanie A. Martin and Andrea J. Terry, in "Social Media Candidate Attacks and Hillary Clinton's Failed Narrative in the 2016 Presidential Campaign," acknowledge the prevalence of social media, and ask what kind of story it told? The authors argue that the social media campaigns of Clinton and Trump had less to do with policy than they did with how to articulate the American dream in the digital age. As the campaigns progressed, Clinton ceded the historical ground of her candidacy by failing to tell a story that mattered; Trump told a story with no plot, but that had a punchline that fit easily into 140 characters—"Make America Great Again" (MAGA!). This, the authors argue, gave Trump the upper hand, especially when it came to crafting an economic narrative for voters to follow. Focusing on the development of the campaign narratives on social media, the authors demonstrate how Trump presented 2016 as a ritual of "nostalgia" best understood as a statement of "normalcy": the abandonment of a culture of political correctness controlled by secular liberals insistent on mutating the American dream into an unrecognizable form. Trump promised to take on this PC culture, and his unorthodox use of social media was one way he proved his willingness to do so. Clinton, on the other hand, tried to perform the ritual of the election as an act of working together to be "stronger together," instead of rebuilding or, even, of celebration. Much of Clinton's campaign strategy appears to have been based in making the New York billionaire appear utterly unfit for office and a potential embarrassment to the nation, rather than making a case for the extension of Obama era policies and the adoption of her own.

There are moments of the unusual in any campaign season, and the 2016 race did not disappoint in that regard. Yet perhaps among the most unusual of moments occurred when a small green frog appeared on the meme scene. In "Iconographic Tracking of Pepe the Frog Meme through the 2016 Presidential Campaign," Natalia Mielczarek traces the rhetorical evolution of the once-obscure cartoon character, Pepe the Frog, from a fun Internet meme to a political argument and hate symbol during the 2016 presidential campaign. Through her explorations, Mielczarek illuminates how members of digital participatory culture appropriated the comic strip character over the years, and also traces how some white supremacists co-opted it as a mascot. She follows the development of the meme from association with Trump's campaign to mainstream news and the meme's appearance in the Clinton campaign. Mielczarek deftly shows how the Pepe the Frog meme elucidates a particular mode of political discourse in "remix" culture, a place where Internet users co-opt and rework culturally available content to create their own political statements and share them online. This grassroots approach to political participation draws attention to a still understudied phenomenon of Internet memes as vehicles for democratic expression in the American Republic. Through this case study, Mielczarek also illustrates how political campaigns deal with unwanted or harmful attention in the form of voter-produced messages and how mainstream media address such news developments as part of the election coverage.

Joeseph M. Valenzano III and Chad Painter explore the role of news entertainment programs and presidential campaigns in their chapter, "Entertainment News and Satire in the 2016 Presidential Election." As primary examples the authors use three satirical "news" sources: *Saturday Night Live*, *The Daily Show with Trevor Noah*, and *The Onion*. Specifically, the authors focus on coverage during four pivotal moments during the 2016 campaign: the September 26, October 9, and October 19 presidential debates, and the November 8 election. Using the lenses of social responsibility theory and satire as their theoretical grounding, Valenzano and Painter outline a theoretical conception of both, but note that both conceptions need to be expanded to include entertainment programming. They argue that because of the blurring boundaries between news and entertainment, the latter of which serves both the educational and informational needs of citizens, current conceptions of social responsibility theory are inadequate. *Saturday Night Live*, *The Daily Show*, and *The Onion* continue a long line of political satire that uses humor to express anger and pointedly criticize both politicians and traditional news media. It is clear from the 2016 election that entertainment media serve an important function in political discourse in terms of their ability to satirize both politicians and news programming. The positive and negative implications of this function for the future of American democracy are explored in concluding remarks of the authors.

In "Journalistic Hegemony of "Blue Privilege": Tracing the Use of Identity Politics Toward a Political Economy of News Coverage," Ben Voth begins by outlining the political left's conception of what they call "White Privilege," and then fleshes out a conception of "Blue Privilege," with "blue" denoting Democrat or liberal orientations and "privilege" referring to a status of symbolic privilege allowing an elite community to control meaning within a larger group. Of particular importance here is the symbolic placement and control of discrimination labels upon individuals. According to Voth, in a rhetorical hierarchy of political colors, blue is the highest order and can call into question all lower orders of color. In conventional views of current politics, the colorless group of whiteness is the most liable and regrettable of identity classifications. His analysis reviews how blue privilege operates to confer greater political power and ideological hegemony upon a narrow group that can be usefully compared to Plato's original vision of philosopher kings in *The Republic*—in Voth's argument, political progressives and the mainstream news media. Looking at the mainstream news media coverage of the 2016 election, Voth demonstrates how blue privilege assumed the absolute right to interpret meaning for all of America.

Erin Whiteside, in "Sports Figures, Social Commentary, and the Role of Sports Journalism During the 2016 Presidential Election," discusses how professional sports are often imagined as inherently apolitical, a cultural ritual which transcends difference, draws together diverse individuals, and provides a space for escapism. This definition has undergirded sports journalists' approach to covering their beat, and much sports coverage is defined by its lack of engagement with politics and related social issues. Whiteside points out how athletes, coaches, and others connected to sports have long adopted a similar posture and have pointedly avoided speaking out on such topics as a way to protect the brands they represent, a choice that simultaneously upholds the perceived social neutrality of sport in U.S. culture. However, during the 2016 election cycle, sports figures began engaging with social issues on which politicians were simultaneously addressing, putting sports journalists in an unfamiliar and perhaps uncomfortable position: How best to cover the intersection of sports and politics within a framework that has implicitly guarded against the acknowledgment of the latter? Noting that athletes in many ways represent adored cultural icons, Whiteside argues that by giving voice to key issues that dominated the political discourse, they offered the possibility that debates on politically- relevant topics might reach unique populations, or resonate in important ways through sporting discourse. This moment in sports and politics has raised important questions about the role of sports journalism in politics. Using the Colin Kaepernick controversy as a detailed case study, Whiteside examines how sports figures contributed to—and perhaps in some ways shaped—political discourse during the 2016 election cycle. She next explores the responsibility of sports journalists when sports figures make politics visible within sporting spaces. In doing so, she addresses the implications of reading news about social issues within the context of sports, and provides an argument for the conditions that give rise to socially just and ethically-sound sports journalism on political issues.

Together these chapters cover a wide range of issues related to the interaction of news media and the political campaign in 2016. Noteworthy in each is the author commentary on how press coverage of the presidential campaign has implications for the future of the American Republic and its democratic ideals. The chapters are designed to offer both sound arguments, and opinion based on those arguments, as a means to continue the conversation about the foundational function of the news media in a free society.

NOTES

1. Al Weaver, "2016 in Tweets from Donald Trump," *Washington Examiner*, December 30, 2016, http://www.washingtonexaminer.com/2016-in-tweets-from-donald-trump/article/2610574.

2. Rick Hampton, "Donald Trump Blasts the News Media That's Helped Him to Dominate GOP Field," *USA Today*, March 10, 2016, https://www.usatoday.com/story/news/politics/elections/2016/03/10/donald-trump-blasts-news-media-republican-new-york-times-des-moine-register/81576826/.

3. "BIAS ALERT: WikiLeaks Exposes Media's Secret Support of Clinton," *Fox News*, October 12, 2016, http://www.foxnews.com/politics/2016/10/12/bias-alert-wikileaks-exposes-medias-secret-support-clinton.html.

4. "Ed Boards Scramble to Undercut Trump Ahead of Debate, as Polls Show Dead Heat," *Fox News*, September 26, 2016, http://www.foxnews.com/politics/2016/09/26/ed-boards-scramble-to-undercut-trump-ahead-1st-debate-as-polls-show-dead-heat.html.

5. Editorial, "USA TODAY's Editorial Board: Trump Is 'Unfit for the Presidency,'" *USAToday*, September 29, 2016, https://www.usatoday.com/story/opinion/2016/09/29/dont-vote-for-donald-trump-editorial-board-editorials-debates/91295020/.

6. Eddie Scarry, "Media Defend Aggressive Standards for Covering Trump," *Washington Examiner*, August 30, 2016, http://www.washingtonexaminer.com/media-defend-more-aggressive-standards-for-covering-trump/article/2600486.

7. Editorial, "To Our Readers, from the Publisher and Executive Editor," *New York Times*, November 13, 2016, https://www.nytimes.com/2016/11/13/us/elections/to-our-readers-from-the-publisher-and-executive-editor.html?mcubz=0.

8. Michael Goodwin, "American Journalism Is Collapsing Before Our Eyes," *New York Post*, August 21, 2016, accessed July 27, 2017, http://nypost.com/2016/08/21/american-journalism-is-collapsing-before-our-eyes/.

9. "The Modern News Consumer," Pew Research Center, July 7, 2016, http://www.journalism.org/2016/07/07/trust-and-accuracy/.

10. Art Swift, "Americans' Trust in Mass Media Sinks to New Low," *Gallup* (September 14, 2016), http://news.gallup.com/poll/195542/americans-trust-mass-media-sinks-new-low.aspx.

11. Jonathan Easley, "Poll: Majority Says Mainstream Media Publishes Fake News," *The Hill*, May 24, 2017, http://thehill.com/homenews/campaign/334897-poll-majority-says-mainstream-media-publishes-fake-news.

12. Examples to follow in many of the chapters in this book.

13. Art Swift, "Democrats' Confidence in Mass Media Rises Sharply from 2016," *Gallup*, September 21, 2017, http://news.gallup.com/poll/219824/democrats-confidence-mass-media-rises-sharply-2016.aspx?g_source=Politics&g_medium=lead&g_campaign=tiles.

14. Michael Goodwin, "American Journalism Is Collapsing before Our Eyes," *New York Post*, August 21, 2016, accessed July 27, 2017, http://nypost.com/2016/08/21/american-journalism-is-collapsing-before-our-eyes/.

15. John Nolte, "How the Political Media's Corruption Destroyed America's Most Crucial Institutions," *Daily Wire*, November 7, 2016, http://www.dailywire.com/news/10555/how-political-medias-corruption-destroyed-americas-john-nolte#exit-modal.

16. Michael M. Grynbaum, "Wall Street Journal Editor Admonishes Reporters over Trump Coverage," *Wall Street Journal*, August 23, 2017, https://www.nytimes.com/2017/08/23/business/media/wall-street-journal-editor-admonishes-reporters-over-trump-coverage.html.

Chapter Two

Fact or Fiction

Defining Fake News During the 2016 U.S. Presidential Election

Abe Aamidor

"Fake news" became a topic of intense interest near the end of the 2016 Presidential election and in its aftermath, initially focusing on whether fake news helped elect Donald Trump. Examples of fake news that circulated during the 2016 campaign season abound, from "Pope Francis Shocks World, Endorses Donald Trump for President" to "George Soros Indicted for Election Hacking." Yet the issue exploded a month after the election when popular website *BuzzFeed* published a survey suggesting people believe fake news *more* than real news: "During these critical months of the campaign, 20 top-performing false election stories from hoax sites and hyperpartisan blogs generated 8,711,000 shares, reactions, and comments on Facebook," *BuzzFeed* reported. "Within the same time period, the 20 best-performing election stories from 19 major news websites generated a total of 7,367,000 shares, reactions, and comments on Facebook."[1] Alarming stuff; you don't know whom to believe. It's like a house of mirrors—what's real and what isn't? But are Americans as gullible as this and as other analyses seem to suggest? In this chapter we'll look more closely at the influential *BuzzFeed* report as well as try to understand what different people mean when they speak of "fake news." We'll also review some recent research that seeks to understand why people believe fake news, and we'll examine the role of bias in defining fake news. And, of course, we'll look at claims that fake news, including possible Russian hacks, may have influenced the 2016 presidential election.

WHAT IS FAKE NEWS?

Everyone knows what fake news is when it comes to the worst of the supermarket tabloids, an other-worldly experience of its own. Consider this one headline, "NASA Takes Photo of Ghosts in Space," from the front page of the *Weekly World News* on August 8, 1995. Similar stories that were published in supermarket tabloids include "Satan's Skull Found in New Mexico." There's also lots of Hollywood celebrity reporting, which may sometimes be true, but even that is understood as mostly gossip, that is, not real news. But if you know it's all fake in one way or another then it doesn't matter. No harm, no foul, as they say. Ditto for satire that always involves exaggeration, whether from an editorial cartoonist in your hometown newspaper or favorite late-night TV talk show host. You may or may not agree with what's being implied, but you know it's satire, not front-page news.

The definition of fake news as it applies to political discourse can be disputed, but the following is a particularly egregious example: the website abcnews.com.co, citing (AP) as its source, reported on November 17, 2016, that a thirty-seven-year-old man named Paul Horner revealed, "I was given $3,500 to protest Donald Trump's rally in Fountain Hills, Arizona. I answered a Craigslist ad about a group needing actors for a political event. I interviewed with them and got the part."[2]

The initial story was widely circulated on social media and then picked up by some established news media. Untold numbers of people may have believed the story to be true, but it eventually was exposed as a lie. For one thing, there was no real online news organization known as abcnews.com.co, a moniker that clearly was invented to deceive. And the reference to (AP) was not authentic, either. It simply mimicked an initialism that the real Associated Press often uses.[3] Other egregious fake news stories during the election campaign and in its aftermath were documented by CNN Money, as well as by others.[4]

Definitions of fake news as they relate to the 2016 election and its aftermath vary, but fall into two broad categories—one, that it's completely made-up stuff, events that never happened from phony sources that don't exist and are often promoted on social media or fringe websites. In general, that's what mainstream media and Democratic politicians alike mean when they allege something is fake news. A producer at CBS's *60 Minutes* newsmagazine revealed what he meant by fake news for its own in-depth report on the subject: "We weren't interested in doing a story about the fake news that is invoked by politicians against the media for stories that they don't like or for comments that they don't like," explained producer Michael Radutzky in a *60 Minutes Overtime* video. "We're using the term 'fake news' to describe stories that are provably false, have enormous traction in the culture, and are consumed by millions of people."[5] The long-established *U.S. News and World Report* newsmagazine concurs: "To be clear, fake news is just that: actually fabricated stories which are either wholly not ground in fact or work in enough falsehoods as to be misleading."[6] This, indeed, is what most mainstream journalists and academics mean by fake news—lies, basically. It is when the accuracy, truthfulness or veracity of a story is being challenged.

The other common definition of fake news is more likely to be found in conservative media—while acknowledging that lies and made-up stuff constitutes fake news, they include news that is allegedly not newsworthy to begin with (think of the old newspaper adage, "Dog bites man is not news, but man bites dog is"), or fake news is linked to allegedly deceitful editing wherein an excerpt from an interview is taken "out of context." Additionally, a story is alleged to be fake if it reflects political bias, particularly a left-leaning bias; is advocacy journalism or campaigning for this or that public policy; or if it's news based on anonymous sources. A good example of this notion of fake news occurred in the waning weeks of the 2016 campaign when Donald Trump was attacked for appearing to suggest that returning soldiers who suffered from PTSD were not "strong" or otherwise were the sort of people who "can't handle" the stress of war. Various headlines and stories excerpted those words from Trump's speech and many readers appeared outraged by Trump, as evidenced by the Comments sections that accompany so many online stories. Well, Trump said it, so it wasn't fake news in the sense that the CBS *60 Minutes* producer means, but Trump supporters howled that the reporting on his speech was indeed fake, meaning in the second sense of the word. Here's the full quote so you can decide for yourself: "When you talk about the mental health problems, when people come back from war and combat, and they see things that maybe a lot of the folks in this room have seen many times over—and you're strong and you can handle it—but a lot of people can't handle it."[7]

Fake news in this second sense may legitimately refer to bad journalism—or at least contested stories—but it does not necessarily mean a story called fake in this sense has been proven false and, to borrow from Shakespeare, there's the rub. One side, generally mainstream media or left-of-center pundits, say that only demonstrably false information counts as "fake" while others, generally right of center, say any biased reporting, out-of-context quotes, anonymous sources, and news deemed to be not actually newsworthy also is fake.

For instance, Sean Hannity, the popular *Fox News* host who's been the target of fake news allegations himself, slammed veteran TV journalist Ted Koppel for severely editing down a lengthy interview he gave in March 2017; Hannity demanded that the full interview be released so the audience could understand the give-and-take of the conversation for themselves. "Fake 'edited' news," Hannity wrote on his Twitter feed. "I did about a 45 minute interview with CBS. They ran less than 2. Why did Ted cut out my many examples of media bias?"[8] And the use of fake news as a substitute for either "not newsworthy," biased reporting or something based on anonymous sources has often been used by Donald Trump himself.[9] For example, when MSNBC's Rachel Maddow released Trump's 2005 federal tax return on live TV one evening early in 2017 the president tweeted that it was "fake news," but did not claim the document was false. This was at a time when many still were clamoring for Trump's most recent tax returns, which he had not released.[10]

The "fake but not necessarily false" and "not newsworthy" sense often employed by conservatives also showed up during the 2017 Congressional and special prosecutor investigations into possible Russian-Trump campaign links. Both the president and his supporters in and out of government said the real news was that anonymous sources were leaking confidential information about the investigations to media outlets; that's not the same as saying the leaks contained false information (though some Trump supporters also made that claim). Or, as an Associated Press writer contended in 2017, "To the White House and its supporters, the big story in Washington isn't the investigation into possible Trump campaign ties to Russia. It's about leakers working to undermine the president."[11]

As we move forward in this chapter keep in mind that we will be employing both senses of fake news—something that's demonstrably false, no better than a Martian invasion story, and stories that may very well be true, or contain elements of the truth, but which are denigrated as, essentially, not newsworthy, biased, taken out of context, or based on anonymous sources. We'll try to make clear in each case which sense is operative, something that is not always done elsewhere.

THE POT CALLED THE KETTLE . . .

Although it's usually supporters of Donald Trump and conservative media that are most likely to level the charge of fake news in the sense of "not newsworthy," "biased," or as something "taken out of context," it is mainstream media that is more likely to use the concept of fake news in the first sense described in this chapter, namely in alleging that some reports on conservative news sites and those further to the right, not to mention claims made by Donald Trump, are completely made-up stuff that can be demonstrably refuted.

The difference between "conservative" and "liberal" media[12] shows up in sharp relief in how each sometimes report the *same story. USA Today* did a careful analysis of the phenomenon in May 2017 when it analyzed coverage of initial reports that President Trump had shared classified information with the Russian foreign minister during a White House visit. The first news of the meeting was reported by the *Washington Post*; other media quickly picked up on it. For instance, this from *USA Today*:

> While CNN and MSNBC focused on the report . . . and the reaction from Trump's opponents, Fox News focused on a perceived hysteria among liberals. . . . Fox News ran a banner reading, "McMaster: *Washington Post* story on Russia meeting is false," while CNN's banner read, "Sources: Trump shared classified info with Russian foreign minister."
>
> On the Fox News website, the top story at 9:30 p.m. ET was about Hillary Clinton and the launch of her "Onward Together" PAC. The story about Trump was programmed beneath that under the headline, "It didn't happen": WH denies report Trump revealed classified info.[13]

The article was accurate, yet perhaps reflected its own bias—the article treated *Fox News* as the deviant outlet, and spent most of its space in an apparent effort to expose and deconstruct Fox, not the other outlets. This in itself suggested how something can be both true and fake at the same time, that is, fake in the second sense of the term used in this chapter.[14]

So far, we've mostly looked at the contentious debate over fake news in the weeks and months after the November 2016 election. This was done to clarify just what the allegation of fake news means to different people. In the following sections we will look more closely at the possible impact of fake news on the election itself, first by looking more closely at the influential *BuzzFeed* study that was released just days after the election, then a bit more closely at specific fake news stories and the evidence for Russian hacking during the campaign.[15]

WAS THE *BUZZFEED* STUDY VALID?

Use the word "study" and you have instant credibility. Scientists do studies; ordinary citizens just have opinions. It's known as framing bias—the word "study" implies objectivity, rigor, and effort, among other things. *BuzzFeed* referred to its blockbuster findings that were released on November 16, 2016, both as a study and an analysis, the latter being a term often used by media outlets for content that falls somewhere between "news" and "opinion." Yet some studies are better than others. The *BuzzFeed* study, to its credit, explained its methodology and acknowledged a few of its limitations, yet its findings were treated as gospel by numerous academics and journalists. *BuzzFeed* created lists of the URLs of what they called "known fake" websites, or hyperpartisan sites on the right and the left, and of more than one hundred pro-Trump sites run from Macedonia, which were widely believed to be fake news sites. Additionally, *BuzzFeed* created a list that included the websites of the *New York Times*, *Washington Post,* NBC News, *USA Today*,

Politico, CNN, *Wall Street Journal*, CBS News, ABC News, *New York Daily News*, *New York Post*, *BuzzFeed*, *Los Angeles Times*, NPR, *Guardian*, Vox, *Business Insider*, *Huffington Post*, and Fox News. The study covered a period of three months prior to the election and looked for shares and "engagement" of individual stories on Facebook. There was this critical caveat, often ignored when the *BuzzFeed* study's finding were reported by other media:

> It's important to note that Facebook engagement does not necessarily translate into traffic. This analysis was focused on how the best-performing fake news about the election compared with real news from major outlets on Facebook. It's entirely possible—and likely—that the mainstream sites received more traffic to their top-performing Facebook content than the fake news sites did. As the Facebook spokesman noted, large news sites overall see more engagement on Facebook than fake news sites.[16]

So, engagement does not mean traffic (we don't even know if suspect stories were shared to endorse them or to mock them), while traditional news sites such as NBC or the *Guardian* still are more likely to see more traffic on Facebook than fake news sites (whether or not their stories are shared). To this writer that's two major caveats, especially when we consider that at least 4.75 *billion* pieces of content were shared daily on Facebook as of May 2013, the most recent date for which such data are readily available according to a more recent analysis done by Zephoria Digital Marketing that cited Facebook's own internal statistics. As the number of "shares" in 2013 had increased by 94 percent over the figure for August 2012—nearly doubling in less than a year—we can assume that the number of shares by late 2016 (the time of the *BuzzFeed* study) were vastly greater yet.[17] The clear takeaway here is that Facebook is not a major source of news at all, and that both real news and fake news on Facebook are only tiny portions of that platform's engagement and traffic. This belies the notion that fake news of either variety described here had much effect on the 2016 presidential election, though it may be critical in a very close election.

There are additional problems with *BuzzFeed's* methodology. Virtually all of the nearly fourteen hundred daily newspapers in America and virtually every local TV station and "news radio" station have their traditional platforms where real news can be accessed directly, without recourse to Facebook, Twitter, and so on. These traditional news platforms were not studied at all. Simply put, people get their news from many more sources than Facebook.[18]

Additionally, people may share a news item on Facebook, but that does not necessarily mean either they or the recipients believe it. After all, I might claim on my Facebook page that I once dated Hillary Clinton (we are the same age and we both went to high school in the Chicago area so it's hypothetically possible), and such a post might cause lots of people to share it, but hardly anyone would believe it. *BuzzFeed* itself recognized this important limitation of its initial study and released a follow-up on December 6, 2016, that looked both at "recall" and "perceptions of accuracy" of fake news headlines and real ones. Respondents to an independent survey of more than three thousand Americans conducted by Ipsos Public Affairs on behalf of *BuzzFeed* found that respondents generally believed fake election news headlines they recalled, though they were (thankfully) more likely to believe real election news headlines they recalled. Republicans were more likely to believe fake news headlines they recalled than was the case for Democratic voters, however.[19] These findings might seem to support the initial *BuzzFeed* study's alarm bells as they relate to anyone believing fake news, yet only about 15 percent of all the people surveyed by Ipsos bothered to answer the questions about accuracy (belief that the fake news headline was accurate), a very low figure by survey standards, while only about half of all those surveyed bothered to answer the questions about recall, which is a mediocre figure at best.

The initial *BuzzFeed* poll had tremendous traction in late 2016 and into 2017 and was widely cited as proof that fake news may have tilted the election, especially given that Republicans were found to be more likely to believe fake news. Perhaps people liked the study because it provided at least some tangible evidence of the threat from fake news, confirming what they already suspected (for more on "confirmation bias" see below). More empirical research will need to be done before one can truly describe the impact of fake news on the election but one early study already has determined that some people even believe and recall stories that were never even published, posted, or broadcast in the first place, which speaks to the power of suggestion when you begin questioning people about various things.[20]

Another early study, this one by the Harvard-Harris Poll done exclusively for *The Hill* and released in May 2017, found that up to 65 percent of all Americans believe that even mainstream media publish fake news of either type identified in this chapter, at least some of the time. The summary of the Harvard-Harris Poll as published in *The Hill* was widely cited by other media, but not the original study, so it's not known what limitations the study had. As noted above, people are still far more likely to be exposed to news from mainstream and traditional news sites than from social media or what are sometimes denigrated as fake or hyperpartisan sites. We also must caution that a belief by 65 percent of respondents that all media are prone to publish or broadcast fake news some of the time is not the same as claiming they believe it's done all the time, that is, the poll results themselves may have been reported in such a way as to be alarmist.[21]

DUMB AND DUMBER

A subtext to the ongoing furor over fake news is the suggestion that conservative and right-wing voters are more susceptible to fake news, including the type that include demonstrably false claims. That certainly is the implication of the Ipsos study, cited above, as well as other studies that could be included here. The *Atlantic* magazine appeared to accept this stereotype, if that's what it is, and asked why it is so: "One of the few comforts liberals had in the aftermath of the election was the anecdotal reporting that fake-news purveyors found it easier to get conservatives to believe their baloney," the magazine wrote in 2017. "As one such fake-news entrepreneur, responsible for articles with headlines like, 'FBI Agent Suspected in Hillary Email Leaks Found Dead in Apparent Murder-Suicide' (said), 'We've tried to do [fake news with] liberals. It just has never worked, it never takes off. You'll get debunked within the first two comments and then the whole thing just kind of fizzles out.'"[22]

Well, not so fast. We'll address the incidences where liberals are likely to be had by fake news a little later in this chapter but for the moment let's assume that the *Atlantic*'s source is right, namely that Trump supporters (i.e., many Republicans and conservatives) were more likely to believe fake news (including the completely false variety), which would explain why so much fake news appears to have been targeted at them. The *Atlantic* had an answer that did not insult their intelligence, however, but one that is consistent with the well-known principle that people who are on high alert to threats are more likely to suspect or perceive those threats in the world around them.

The *Atlantic* wrote, "According to a study slated to be published in the journal Psychological Science, it might be true that conservatives are more likely to fall for false, threatening-seeming information, but it's not because they're dumb. It's because they're hyper-attuned to hazards in their world. If they spot a sign of danger, they figure trusting it is better than ignoring it." The study cited by The *Atlantic* and eventually published in *Psychological Science*, "Political Orientation Predicts Credulity Regarding Putative Hazards," was written by Daniel M. T. Fessler of the University of California, Los Angeles, and others.[23]

It's a kind of bias, but one based on experience in the world at large. Try this thought experiment: You're walking down a dark street at night in a strange part of town and you've recently read a story in the local newspaper about the rising crime rate in your city. Next, you hear a car screeching to a stop in the background, then a car door opens and you hear loud footsteps behind you. You'd be forgiven for thinking you're about to be robbed even if it's just a case of someone trying to get to the local drugstore to pick up a prescription before the place closes. Would this not be like Republican and conservative voters who are alarmed by any drug trade or human trafficking that's related to illegal immigration, hence they might be more likely to suspect even neutral reportage on immigration, than might be the case for some Democrats and Progressives who like to tout that America was built on immigration and that "no human is illegal."

Another type of bias that affects how we react to news is confirmation bias. According to *Psychology Today,* confirmation bias "occurs from the direct influence of desire on beliefs. When people would like a certain idea/ concept to be true, they end up believing it to be true. They are motivated by wishful thinking. This error leads the individual to stop gathering information when the evidence gathered so far confirms the views (prejudices) one would like to be true."[24]

Similarly, information that doesn't confirm one's bias is likely to be dismissed. This may be what is happening with some people who believe false stories or decry truthful information that doesn't confirm their biases. Though this phenomenon is often associated with Republican, conservative, or otherwise right-of-center voters, it may also explain why the so-called liberal media is quick to pick up unconfirmed stories before they've been vetted, that is, they suffer from their own biases.[25] Examples of specific fake news stories targeting liberal and left-of-center voters are given below, but a wide range of media outlets, including the *Christian Science Monitor*, *Slate*, *Los Angeles Times*, CBS's *60 Minutes* and many other outlets, all hardly right-wing or even conservative, have themselves noted the rise of fake news in both senses of the term targeting liberals mostly in the months *after* the election, which certainly is consistent with the Fessler study cited above—you're more likely to react to hazards you believe are imminent and liberals seemed to fear the worst after Trump won, just as conservatives fearing the worst about Hillary Clinton before the election swung to Trump.

In addition to confirmation bias, there is the theory of meta-beliefs, which are core beliefs an individual has that inform all other beliefs, and it is when information challenges meta-beliefs that new information is likely to be rejected. For example, the resistance to accepting evolutionary theory by some devoutly religious persons (Christian, Muslim, or Jewish) may be explained because it challenges their belief that God created the universe in just a few days. There's really no shortage of literature about either confirmation bias or meta-beliefs to explain how people can selectively choose information that reinforces what they already believe.

Furthermore, one might say there is an issue of "trust" for a lot of conservatives. They simply may not believe even true stories as reported in the mainstream media because they don't trust the sources. Put another way, they may not *know* that the *New York Times*, and so on, are lying, but they don't *believe* individual stories because they don't trust the outlet. That's what fake news means to these people. A Monmouth University Polling Institute report issued in March 2017 appears to support this view. Monmouth studied *ABC News*, MSNBC, and *Fox News* and found that Americans surveyed tended to believe *ABC News* more than either the right-leaning *Fox News* or the left-leaning MSNBC, that is, they know partisan reporting when they see it, which is good. Still, the study supported the belief that conservative and Republican voters tend to be less trusting overall even of putatively neutral or non-partisan media sites and outlets: "It is interesting that Democrats are more likely to give a credibility edge to an outlet that is seen as more mainstream over one whose political perspective is more in line with their own. Most Republicans, on the other hand, seem to assume that every source that isn't conservative must, by definition, have a liberal bias and is therefore *less trustworthy*. There doesn't seem to be a middle ground for them," said Patrick Murray, director of the polling institute.[26]

I'M FAKE NEWS? YOU'RE FAKE NEWS!

If all this looks like journalists and academics are picking on conservative and Republican voters it should be noted that both mainstream media and left-of-center voters have been had by fake news as well. For example, a substantial list of fake news articles aimed at liberals has been documented, such as a rumored new law to charge anti-Trump protesters with terrorism, a plan to turn the USS *Enterprise* into a floating casino, and even a claim that Vice President Mike Pence once avidly supported gay conversion therapy.[27] And Green Party candidate Jill Stein promoted a theory that Russian hackers manipulated the count in several states on election night to favor Trump and demanded a recount, a view that was spread on social media by her left-leaning supporters but for which the fact-checking site Snopes (and others) found no evidence.

And one particularly egregious election cycle fake news story promulgated in order to indict Donald Trump was a widely circulated rumor that multiple transgender teenagers had killed themselves in response to his election. A writer for the *Guardian*, perhaps the leading left-of-center publication in the English-speaking world, stated the rumor as fact, as did some lesser news organizations and websites. Most mainstream news sites either referred to "reports" of the suicides unchallenged, or alternatively quoted various suicide hotline operators who apparently had seen a spike in transgender phone calls at the time (but not suicides). Snopes, after investigating the reports, merely wrote that they were "unproven" and "unsubstantiated" rather than as "false," which perhaps is suggestive of their liberal bias in refusing to out-and-out condemn the anti-Trump reports.[28] As it turned out, the basis for the suicide rumors apparently were two Facebook posts that had been shared tens of thousands of times before being picked up by mainstream news media. None of this is to deny that bullied transgendered youth have, in fact, committed suicide over the years, but the linkage to Trump's election—the cause-and-effect that was insinuated—was fake in both senses of the word used in this chapter.[29]

LIES, DAMN LIES, AND *VRAN'YE*[30]

So far, we have dealt with, among other things, people who both access and believe fake news, and those outlets or platforms that promulgate such stuff, whether of the demonstrably false variety or the biased, anonymously sourced and "not newsworthy" kind. There are all sorts of fake news sites, of course, such as abcnews.com.co, and there are pranksters who may not realize their fictions are being taken seriously,[31] but which persons among the powerful and influential on the world stage have also been peddling "fake news?"

The hysteria, if that's the right word, often has been over Donald Trump's statements, claims and tweets, both before and after the election. He has made sensational claims—he saw "thousands" of Muslims in New Jersey celebrating the September 11, 2001, terrorist attacks;[32] three million undocumented immigrants voted in the presidential election; Ted Cruz's father was seen with Lee Harvey Oswald (John F. Kennedy's assassin), and other claims—yet it is he who has routinely called major media outlets "fake." A Canadian journalist, Donald Dale, counted fourteen "false claims" that Trump allegedly made in one March 2017 *Time* magazine interview alone, including the claim that he (Trump) had recently spoken to "25,000" supporters in Kentucky when the total capacity of the venue was 18,000—well, was that a lie or an exaggeration?[33]

Kellyanne Conway, the Trump administration counselor to the president, did not help the president when she defended his inflated estimate of the crowd that had witnessed his inauguration in January 2017 by claiming some people just have "alternative facts." Perhaps she was thinking of alternative hypotheses or alternative narratives, legitimate terms that are used in both scientific and political discourse, but it all added heat to the allegation that Trump (and his administration) lie, that is, that they're a source of fake news, not its victim.[34] Of course, Hillary Clinton dropped some whoppers during the 2016 campaign, as well. She claimed, for example, that U.S. prisons were overflowing with inmates largely because of marijuana convictions, which was a wild exaggeration; she claimed that she had landed under sniper fire during a visit to war-torn Bosnia when she was Secretary of State, which was false; and perhaps worst of all, she claimed that she had handled no classified documents on her private server that were marked as classified "at the time," a claim debunked by former FBI director James Comey because many of the emails in fact contained classified information and were marked as such "at the time," as he repeatedly stated during congressional hearings in the summer of 2016, even though he chose not to seek to indict her for mishandling the documents. So, did Hillary Clinton get more of a pass from the media during the campaign for her indiscretions than did Donald Trump for his? Certainly, Clinton's indiscretions were reported or we likely wouldn't know anything about them, but the question can then be restated as, "Were they under-reported?" Various surveys found that many Americans overall thought exactly that, namely that the media in the aggregate were softer on her than on Trump, though the findings somewhat break down on a Republican/Democrat and conservative/liberal divide.[35] If so—if Hillary Clinton did get more of a pass than did Donald Trump—it would suggest either that there is a liberal bias in the media after all or, arguably, that Trump made a greater number of false and egregious claims and statements during the campaign, which warranted harsher treatment by the media. (The latter point is the "equivalence" argument which states that demands for an even mix of positive and negative stories for both candidates makes no sense if one side or the other really is in fact worse than the other.)

Among the biggest controversies both during and after the November 2016 election concerned allegations of Russian interference. Their motive allegedly was to help Trump, who was seen as softer on Russian sanctions in the aftermath of the country's aggression in Ukraine and Syria, and who was popular in Moscow because of his criticisms of NATO, which Russia seems to see as an existential threat. Investigations into the extent of the alleged Russian hacking, and whether there was actual "collusion" between the Trump campaign and the Russians, were ongoing as this chapter was being written and likely won't be resolved for some time, if ever. What we can state here, though, is that allegations of Russian hacking have been made by independent sources worldwide and that Russia's capabilities and infrastructure to do so have been known for years and are credible.[36] But even here—even with a near consensus that Russian agents did seek to interfere in the 2016 election—there remained a kind of confirmation bias to quickly believe additional claims of interference that really were unfounded. Witness, for example, the forced resignations of three top CNN journalists in June 2017 after they reported that Congress was investigating "a Russian investment fund with ties to Trump officials." The story itself was retracted after it was disclosed that a single, anonymous source was the basis for the reporting, that is, fake news in the second sense of the term used in this chapter.[37]

Additionally, investigations into alleged Russian hacking have also targeted right-wing sites Breitbart News and InfoWars because of suspicions that they may have included some of the fake, Russian-sourced stories as part of their own alleged effort to influence the election. These investigations are ongoing as this chapter is being written.[38]

Another lingering controversy from the 2016 election campaign has been the death of former Democratic National Committee staffer Seth Rich, who was murdered early in the morning of July 10, 2016, outside his Washington home. Rumors began circulating after Rich's death that it was he who had leaked John Podesta's emails that embarrassed the Clinton campaign; Podesta was Clinton's campaign manager then. It was also suggested by some that Rich had given the emails to Julian Assange's Wikileaks organization, which then were passed on to Russia. Assange himself has hinted at the connection, even offering a reward for the capture of Rich's killer or killers. The conspiracy theory was widely denounced at the time and no evidence was produced to support it; Washington police declared the death had simply been the result of a botched robbery attempt though they provided no tangible evidence for their theory, either. The story lay mostly dormant until it was resurrected on May 16, 2017, by *Fox News* and further touted by popular *Fox News* host Sean Hannity—the labyrinthine conspiracy theory is just too complicated to review here but Rich's family denounced the reporting and *Fox News* quickly retracted the story.[39]

CONCLUDING THOUGHTS

Do some people get their news from Facebook "shares" or personal Twitter feeds and so on? Yes. Do some people believe everything they read? Yes. Can even a small disinformation campaign alter an election outcome, at least in a very close race? Yes. But do junk news and fake news carry anywhere near the weight that real news from credible organizations do—ones that fact-check, have access to troves of background information, and seek to contact either authoritative or impartial sources before jumping to conclusions? There's no reason to believe so, at least not yet.

More problematic is that many consumers of news just don't trust their sources of news anymore and that's the issue I want to explore a bit further in this section; a free press is critical to a functioning democracy and if people don't trust the press then our democracy will suffer. They see the media as too partisan, trying to lead opinion and not simply inform it. Let's explore their concern a bit. The author of this chapter is a former multiple-award-winning daily newspaper reporter in St. Louis, Indianapolis, and elsewhere, and I, just like many other veteran journalists, fancied myself as the eyes and ears of the reader. I could go places that my readers couldn't; I could ask the questions they might want to ask because I had access to important people that they probably didn't have; I was paid to dig for facts when they had neither the time, money, or resources to do so. However, I did not think of myself as an advocate or salesman for this or that cause, movement, party, or initiative, even ones I personally supported. Although complete objectivity probably is never attainable, it is always the goal and the closer one gets to that ideal the better. But if my readers no longer believed I was sincerely working for them, but instead only for my pet causes or political movements, or for the politicians or agencies or businesses I reported on, then I was sunk as a journalist. That's the trust issue in a nutshell and why so many people don't believe some of the stuff they see in print, on TV, or online. They don't believe journalists are working for them; rather they see us as salesmen and hucksters, as advocates and even propagandists for someone else or for other groups.

Yes, the public discourse on a host of issues has been weakened somewhat because some totally fake and demonstrably false news has been accepted by some voters, but also because some journalists and media outlets do seem to think their job is to advocate for certain causes, programs, and initiatives. For example, to actively counter racism and promote diversity; to counter xenophobia and promote immigration; to celebrate or promote gay rights as opposed to merely reporting on the gay rights movement. I am against racism, but am unwilling to tag anyone who decries the lack of fathers in the inner city or who calls for welfare reform a racist. I am against xenophobia (I'm the child of immigrants myself) but I'm unwilling to ignore the distinction between legal and illegal immigration. I believe in universal health care but don't like the complete absence of almost any media reporting on the poor lifestyle choices that lead to the majority of our health care costs, as well as the price gouging by health care providers, including non-profit hospitals and not just the big drug companies. I'm against Islamophobia but I don't believe in exaggerating the phenomenon in America any more than I believe in exaggerating the assault on Christian values in this country (both of which are done, I believe, by competing media outlets to pander to different audiences).

Various surveys over the years have shown that more journalists define themselves as liberal than conservative or identify more strongly with the Democratic Party than the Republican Party, though a large chunk always remains independent.[40] I don't think it should matter—journalists only need to define the issues and report the facts as well as they can and let the people decide for themselves. That's what I think a free press in a democratic nation does. Yet so much of our reporting is, in fact, tendentious. Let me give you just two examples, immigration and poverty. In the discourse over immigration reform, as it plays out in the media, there almost never is any acknowledgment that the United States adds more than *one million* "lawful permanent residents" and naturalized citizens combined in this country every year, year in and year out.[41] That's more legal immigration than any other country on Earth, though a few countries do have a higher percentage of legal residents added every year. Why is that vital information almost never included in stories about immigration? Every July 4 you'll see a few feel good features about a swearing-in ceremony for new citizens, but as part of the immigration debate itself you're more likely to find argumentative pieces that claim immigrants do the kinds of jobs "Americans no longer want to do" as a rationale for illegal immigration. Such stories, while partly true, represent a kind of campaigning for immigration reform. I've reported on the construction industry in America, particularly the lower end of that sector, such as framing, roofing, and bricklaying. Traditional workers in these semi-skilled areas, mostly white working class, have been widely displaced across the country by immigrants from Mexico and Central America, whether legal or illegal, because they work cheaper as well as do very good work, basically offering good value for money to contractors who hire them and consumers who ultimately foot the bill. It's not that American citizens don't want to do this work. I recall interviewing a former subcontractor whose small company did brickwork for new home builders in the Indianapolis suburbs. He was non-union yet he still could not successfully bid on jobs and pay his workers a wage they would accept in the face of immigrant competition, basically outsourcing American jobs by bringing the foreign workers here. In time his employees all quit, he dissolved his company, and he went back to laying bricks alongside the immigrants himself. What happened to his former employees? I think a lot of them became adamantly opposed to illegal immigration; I think a lot of them voted for Donald Trump and fake news had nothing to do with it. It's said that fake news moved a lot of voters into the Trump camp in 2016 but was it not also fake news to suppress so much relevant information about immigration for so many years?

Then there are the many articles about the notorious level of poverty in America and little feature stories about this or that program to help the poor, which is fair enough, but those stories overwhelmingly have focused on minorities in recent decades, not counting the occasional trailer park meth and opioid addict story, which often are demeaning. While it is true that blacks and Hispanics are twice as likely to live in poverty as whites, it is still the case that in terms of raw numbers more than half of all poor Americans are white.[42] Social scientists and media pundits have asked why working-class whites now vote so often for Republicans, the party of the rich, instead of the Democratic Party, the party of Franklin Delano Roosevelt and his grand coalition of blacks, women, Jews, Progressives, *and* working-class people? Well, this may be part of the answer, too—the Democratic Party and its standard bearer in 2016 paid far, far less attention to working-class people and poor whites than it did to other members of that "grand coalition." Only in the aftermath of the election, what must have been shocking to party leaders and media elites alike, did we see some soul searching about this glaring gap in the Democratic platform. Maybe ignoring the concerns of working class people and poor whites also constitutes "fake news," a sin of omission if not commission.

Ultimately, fake news is like testimony under oath in a court of law—we want the truth, the whole truth and nothing but the truth. When we don't get it we think the witness must be lying. I don't think it's a hard concept to grasp. How does the ordinary citizen survive in a world of fake news, then, when we don't get the story, the whole story, and nothing but the story? First and foremost, take personal responsibility to get the facts on your own. Do not trust any single source of information. If studies or reports are cited in an article and it's an important issue then find the original report or study and read it yourself. If you see an excerpt from an important speech or interview in a news article then find a transcript of the full speech or interview. On heavily politicized issues it's important to listen to other voices, even sit down with people you think you won't like and give them a fair hearing. And note that there are often more than just two ways of thinking about an issue, not just "liberal" and "conservative" but many shades of gray. These are all lessons one should have learned in a good undergraduate education.

I'd like to say I'm optimistic about getting Americans to think more critically about the news they follow, but I'm not. It's like lecturing people on the importance of keeping their weight down. Everyone already knows they should eat less and exercise more, but do they do it? Most don't, and to cite Shakespeare one more time, "There's the rub."

NOTES

1. Craig Silverman, "This Analysis Shows How Viral Fake Election News Outperformed Real News on Facebook," *BuzzFeed News*, November 16, 2016, https://www.buzzfeed.com/craigsilverman/viral-fake-election-news-outperformed-real-news-on-facebook?utm_term=.ueN7Y06xN#.qvrLrWzPA.

2. "Donald Trump Protester Speaks Out: 'I Was Paid $3,500 to Protest Trump's Rally,'" Unsigned and undated, http://abcnews.com.co/donald-trump-protester-speaks-out-i-was-paid-to-protest/. (The link was still up as of late July 2017.)

3. Louis Jacobson, "No, Someone Wasn't Paid $3,500 to Protest Donald Trump; It's Fake News," Politifact, November 17, 2016, at http://www.politifact.com/truth-o-meter/statements/2016/nov/17/blog-posting/no-someone-wasnt-paid-3500-protest-donald-trump-it/.

4. Ahiza Garcia and Justin Lear, "5 Stunning Fake News Stories That Reached Millions," *CNN Media*, November 2, 2016, http://money.cnn.com/2016/11/02/media/fake-news-stories/.

5. Lisa Orlando (editor), "What's 'Fake News'? 60 Minutes Producers Investigates," *60 Minutes Overtime*, March 26, 2017, http://www.cbsnews.com/news/whats-fake-news-60-minutes-producers-investigate/.

6. Robert Schlesinger, "Fake News in Reality," *U.S. News*, April 14, 2017, https://www.usnews.com/opinion/thomas-jefferson-street/articles/2017-04-14/what-is-fake-news-maybe-not-what-you-think.

7. You can find this quote easily via any online search engine—try it and you'll see that many stories and/or their headlines do seem to take the quote out of context with the apparent aim of demonizing Donald Trump. Other stories, usually sympathetic opinion pieces, complain that the "liberal media" have distorted Trump's words. It should be incontestable, though, that Donald Trump often speaks inelegantly, which makes him vulnerable to attack.

8. Jessica Chasmer, "Sean Hannity Blasts CBS for 'Fake Edited News' after Ted Koppel Interview," *Washington Times*, March 27, 2017, http://www.washingtontimes.com/news/2017/mar/27/sean-hannity-blasts-cbs-for-fake-edited-news-after/.

9. "Trump Attacks 'Fake News' Amid Russia Controversy That Now Includes Kirshner," *Fox News Politics*, (no byline), May 28, 2017, http://www.foxnews.com/politics/2017/05/28/trump-attacks-fake-news-amid-russia-controversy-that-now-includes-kushner.html.

10. Michael D. Shear, "Trump Calls 2005 Tax Return Release 'Fake News,'" *New York Times*, March 15, 2017, https://www.nytimes.com/2017/03/15/us/politics/trump-calls-2005-tax-return-release-fake-news.html?_r=0.

11. Jill Colvin, "To Trump Supporters, the Real Story Is about Leaks, Sabotage," *U.S. News*, May 19, 2017, https://www.usnews.com/news/politics/articles/2017-05-19/to-trump-supporters-the-real-story-is-about-leaks-sabotage.

12. Mainstream media (your daily newspaper; network television news; most cable news channels) are what conservatives mean by "the liberal media," while Leftist outlets such as the *Nation* magazine, DemocracyNow.org and others attack such mainstream media as "corporate-owned," both expressions meant to demean. But it's the same media! For more on this conundrum read Bernard Goldberg's "Bias" and Eric Alterman's "What Liberal Media?" side-by-side. See also Abe Aamidor, Jim A. Kuypers, and Susan Wiesinger, "Media Smackdown: Deconstructing the News and the Future of Journalism" (Peter Lang, 2013), especially chapters 6 and 7.

13. William Cummings, "How the Latest Trump Headlines Played Out in Conservative, Liberal Media," *USA Today*, May 15, 2017, https://www.usatoday.com/story/news/politics/onpolitics/2017/05/15/media-divide-washington-post-trump-russia-story/101733786/.

14. A note about our way of categorizing media outlets and politicians as either "conservative" or "liberal." These are very broad categories. A person might be liberal in terms of protecting the environment and abhorring climate change deniers, but might also be conservative in supporting stricter border control against undocumented immigrants. A newspaper might endorse three Democrats for separate races, but one Republican in another—at a minimum the newspaper is not being doctrinaire.

15. Facebook admitted to selling $100,000 in Internet ads to a Kremlin-connected troll farm during last year's U.S. presidential election. The ads, which the company did not previously reveal, could have been seen by tens of millions of Americans, which demonstrates well Facebook's potential for influencing the 2016 campaign. See Alyza Sebenius, "Should Facebook Ads Be Regulated like TV Commercials?" *Atlantic*, September 14, 2017, https://www.theatlantic.com/technology/archive/2017/09/facebook-ads-free-speech/539736/. Furthermore, Facebook announced in October 2017 that up to 126 million Americans "may have seen" Russian-backed election content. It's an ongoing story. Dylan Byers, "Facebook Estimates. . . ." *CNN Media*. http://money.cnn.com/2017/10/30/media/russia-facebook-126-million-users/index.html.

16. Craig Silverman, "This Analysis Shows How Viral Fake Election News Stories Outperformed Real News on Facebook," *BuzzFeed News*, November 16, 2016, https://www.buzzfeed.com/craigsilverman/viral-fake-election-news-outperformed-real-news-on-facebook?utm_term=.asLN2qAOa#.nmXwZpJPd.

17. "The Top 20 Facebook Statistics—Updated May 2017." Zephoria Digital Marketing, May 8, 2017, https://zephoria.com/top-15-valuable-facebook-statistics/.

18. *BuzzFeed's* spreadsheet for its original data analysis can be found at https://docs.google.com/spreadsheets/d/1ysnzawW6pDGBEqbXqeYuzWa7Rx2mQUip6CXUUUk4jIk/edit#gid=399992108. A sharply-worded rebuke of *BuzzFeed's* methodology, including its use of the term "engagements," can be found on the National Review at http://www.nationalreview.com/article/442291/buzzfeed-facebook-fake-news-study-methodology-questioned, though some will claim that the conservative magazine itself is not without bias.

19. Craig Silverman and Jeremy Singer-Vine, "Most Americans Who See Fake News Believe It, New Survey Says," *BuzzFeed News*. December 6, 2016, https://www.buzzfeed.com/craigsilverman/fake-news-survey?utm_term=.hgdynEaGO#.uqKX1p82B. (Chapter author's note: The headline for the report speaks of people who "see" fake news, while the report itself speaks of people who "recall" the fake news they saw; it's not the same thing. Was the headline deceptive?)

20. Hunt Alcott and Matthew Gentzlow, "Social Media and Fake News in the 2016 Election," *Journal of Economic Perspectives*, Vol. 31, No. 2, Spring 2017, page 226. (This paper

gives a historical overview of what has come to be called fake news and cites many additional studies.)

21. Jonathan Easley, "Poll: Majority Says Mainstream Media Publishes Fake News," *The Hill*, May 24, 2017, http://thehill.com/homenews/campaign/334897-poll-majority-says-mainstream-media-publishes-fake-news. Although *The Hill* links to the original study results, that study does not seem to report margins of error.

22. Olga Khazan, "Why Fake News Targeted Trump Supporters," *Atlantic/Science*, Feb. 2, 2017, https://www.theatlantic.com/science/archive/2017/02/why-fake-news-targeted-trump-supporters/515433/.

23. Daniel M. T. Fessler and Colin Holbrook, "Political Orientation Predicts Credulity Regarding Putative Hazards," accepted for publication in *Psychological Science*, accessed July 25, 2017, http://www.danielmtfessler.com/wp-content/uploads/2013/12/Fessler-et-al-in-press-Political-Orientation-Credulity.pdf.

24. Sharhram Heshmat, "What Is Confirmation Bias? Wishful Thinking." *Psychology Today*, April 23, 2015, https://www.psychologytoday.com/blog/science-choice/201504/what-is-confirmation-bias.

25. See especially Alex Berezow, "Liberals Are No Strangers to Confirmation Bias after All," *New Scientist*, April 28, 2017, https://www.newscientist.com/article/2129319-liberals-are-no-strangers-to-confirmation-bias-after-all/?utm_campaign=RSS%7CNSNS.

26. "POTUS Less Trusted Than Media, 'Fake News' Comes from All Sources," Monmouth University Polling Institute, March 29, 2017, https://www.monmouth.edu/polling-institute/reports/MonmouthPoll_US_032917/. With a margin of error of 3.5 percent and higher for subgroups, one should view the results of this study with reservations. Additionally, the polling organization Gallup has studied trust in the media for decades. They, too, report that trust in the media by both Democrats and Republicans has plummeted in recent years (after historic highs in the wake of the Watergate scandal of the early and mid-1970s), but that the decline has been greater among Republicans. See, "Americans' Trust in Mass Media Sinks to New Low," published September 14, 2016, during the height of the presidential election campaign, http://www.gallup.com/poll/195542/americans-trust-mass-media-sinks-new-low.aspx?version=print.

27. Andrew Stiles, "Heroism or Terrorism?" Nov. 18, 2016, www.snopes.com/law-charges-protesters-with-terrorism/ and "Shock Treatment," Oct. 26, 2016, www.snopes.com/mike-pence-supported-gay-conversion-therapy/.

28. "Election-Related Transgender Youth Suicides," Shopes.com, unsigned and undated, http://www.snopes.com/transgender-suicides-after-2016-election/.

29. Daniel Payne, "16 Fake News Stories Reporters Have Run since Trump Won," *Federalist*, Feb. 6, 2017, http://thefederalist.com/2017/02/06/16-fake-news-stories-reporters-have-run-since-trump-won/.

30. Russian for "lies."

31. See especially, Erik Hedegaard, "How a Fake Newsman Accidentally Helped Trump Win the White House," *Rolling Stone*, November 29, 2016, http://www.rollingstone.com/culture/news/how-a-fake-newsman-accidentally-helped-trump-win-white-house-w452488.

32. Donald Trump was perhaps most bitterly attacked for the claim that "thousands" of Muslims in New Jersey celebrated after the 9/11 attacks. He later amended his comment to claim he was citing a journalist who had allegedly made the claim initially, yet that initial media report merely claimed that authorities had detained a "number of people" suspected of celebrating the attacks. Some commentators nevertheless justified Trump's claim because there were verifiable reports that "some" people in New Jersey did celebrate; for example, see this report, "Exclusive: Some Jersey City Muslims Did Celebrate 9/11, Cop and Residents Say," posted December 21, 2015, at http://www.nj.com/news/index.ssf/2015/12/exclusive_jersey_city_cop_residents_say_some_musli.html.

33. Donald Dale, "Donald Trump Made 14 False Claims in His Time Interview on the Subject of Whether He Makes False Claims," Donald Dale's Twitter feed, March 23, 2017, and accessed May 26, 2017, at https://twitter.com/ddale8/status/844876675800227840.

34. See the original Conway interview with NBC's Chuck Todd at http://www.nbcnews.com/meet-the-press/video/conway-press-secretary-gave-alternative-facts-860142147643.

35. See in particular "News Coverage of the 2016 Election: How the Press Failed the Voters." Harvard Kennedy School: Shorenstein Center on Media, Politics, and Public Policy. December 7, 2016, https://shorensteincenter.org/news-coverage-2016-general-election/.

36. See, for example, Robert Windrem, "Timeline: Ten Years of Russian Cyber Attacks on Other Nations," *NBC News*: "Hacking of America," December 18, 2016, http://www.nbcnews.com/storyline/hacking-in-america/timeline-ten-years-russian-cyber-attacks-other-nations-n697111 and Massimo Calabresi, "Inside Russia's Social Media War on America," *Time* magazine, May 18, 2017, http://time.com/4783932/inside-russia-social-media-war-america/

37. Brian Stelter, "Three Journalists Leaving CNN after Retracted Article," *CNN Media*, June 27, 2017, http://money.cnn.com/2017/06/26/media/cnn-announcement-retracted-article/index.html.

38. Peter Stone and Greg Gordon, "FBI's Russian-Influence Probe Includes a Look at Breitbart, InfoWars News Sites," McClatchy DC Bureau, March 20, 2017, http://www.mcclatchydc.com/news/politics-government/white-house/article139695453.html.

39. David Weigel, "The Life and Death of the Seth Rich Conspiracy Theory," *Washington Post*, May 24, 2017, https://www.washingtonpost.com/powerpost/the-life-and-death-of-the-seth-rich-conspiracy-theory/2017/05/23/aba640c4-3ff3-11e7-adba-394ee67a7582_story.html?utm_term=.12f863f77548.

40. Lars Willnat and David H. Weaver, "The American Journalist in the Digital Age," School of Journalism, Indiana University, 2014, accessed July 28, 2017, http://archive.news.indiana.edu/releases/iu/2014/05/2013-american-journalist-key-findings.pdf.

41. See "Lawful Permanent Residents," Department of Homeland Security, accessed July 25, 2017, https://www.dhs.gov/immigration-statistics/lawful-permanent-residents; "LPR Table 8 to 11 Expanded," Department of Homeland Security, accessed July 25, 2017, https://www.dhs.gov/immigration-statistics/readingroom/LPR/request1; and "Naturalization Fact Sheet," U.S. Citizenship and Immigration Services, accessed July 25, 2017, https://www.uscis.gov/news/fact-sheets/naturalization-fact-sheet.

42. See "Who is Poor?" Institute for Research on Poverty, accessed July 25, 2017, http://www.irp.wisc.edu/faqs/faq3.htm. This report emphasizes relative probability, as is typical of most reports on poverty, but does not suppress data that show the majority of poor people in America are still white. It's mostly only when media report on welfare benefits and "food stamps" that they are likely to emphasize poor whites, i.e., proportionality and relative probability are out the window. See also, Arthur Delaney and Alissa Scheller, "Who Gets Food Stamps? White People, Mostly," *HuffPost*, Feb. 28, 2015, http://www.huffingtonpost.com/2015/02/28/food-stamp-demographics_n_6771938.html.

Chapter Three

The *Othering* of Donald Trump and His Supporters

Stephen D. Cooper

The 2016 presidential election was extraordinary in many respects. One was the way in which the Republican candidate and his supporters were disparaged in the establishment press. Although it is a truism that politics can often be rough (as in the sayings, "It ain't beanbag" and "It's a contact sport") and any apparent civility in the rhetoric is often just a mask in front of bare-knuckle tactics, many observers have noted that the 2016 election became especially rough.

Further, the attacks on candidate Donald Trump and his supporters came not only from political opponents—which would be expected—but also from those who identify themselves as conservatives, Republicans, or both. Under ordinary circumstances they would be expected to either be supportive of the party's candidate (whether enthusiastically or half-heartedly), or be mostly silent about their distaste for the candidate. That was not the case in this election; some of Trump's fiercest critics, both in the primary and in the general election campaign, were individuals and organizations one would expect to be at least nominally on his side.

In this chapter, I examine some instances of attacks on Trump and his supporters which go beyond the customary rough-and-tumble of American politics. These examples were chosen both from the campaign and also from the first eight months of the Trump administration. Through this analysis I identify particular features that indicate the attacks involve an "othering" process. First it is necessary to establish a working definition of "other" and "othering," as the application of the term has evolved considerably since its coinage in the philosophical dichotomy of self/other.

THE "OTHER" AND "OTHERING"

Both the noun and the verb are commonly used today inside and outside of university settings. Although speech having the effect of dividing people into opposing groups goes back as far as recorded history,[1] the term "Other" originated in theoretical exploration of the nature of self-awareness. Lately it has become a staple in social theory and critique. Along the way, in this migration from philosophy to sociology, the meaning (both denotation and connotation) seems to have shifted dramatically.

The Other is a key concept in phenomenology, explaining a human being's capacity to be aware both of oneself and of other human beings.[2] A number of different schools of phenomenology emerged in the nineteenth and twentieth century, but the project remained one of developing a theoretical understanding of human consciousness. In simple terms, one knows oneself in relation to other selves;[3] in that way, the Self and the Other are necessary ingredients to understanding experience. The appeal of the self/other dichotomy was that it refuted the possibility that the world (i.e., lived experience) existed only inside one's head (solipsism) without being forced into the position that only one world could possibly exist (positivism). Put concisely, "[t]he Other appears as a psychological phenomenon in the course of a person's life, and not as a radical threat to the existence of the Self."[4] In that context, the connotation is neutral; there is no moral wrong implied.

That application of the term, however useful it may be to understanding an individual's life world, does not readily scale upward to an understanding of social system features. As emphasis shifted in the twentieth century from philosophical exploration of consciousness and knowledge to sociological identification and critique of such issues as colonialism/imperialism, power, social class, gender relations, stereotyping, and inequality, the self/other dichotomy morphed into a negative denotation (dominator/dominated, "us versus them") carrying a negative connotation (doing so is a morally wrong act), and now is frequently invoked in a prescriptive context (one ought not do it or it is socially unjust). It seems clear this is the contemporary usage of the term *other*, as a few examples will illustrate.

It is not unusual today for credentialed academicians to place some of their work on personal web pages. A quote from a site called the Other Sociologist will provide an illustration of the self/other dichotomy in its contemporary usage as a conceptual tool for social critique:

> The idea of "otherness" is central to sociological analyses of how majority and minority identities are constructed. This is because the representation of different groups within any given society is controlled by groups that have greater political power. In order to understand the notion of The Other [capitals in original], sociologists first seek to put a critical spotlight on the ways in which social identities are constructed. . . .

> Social identities reflect the way individuals and groups internalize established social categories within their societies, such as their cultural (or ethnic) identities, gender identities, class identities, and so on. These social categories shape our ideas about who we think we are, how we want to be seen by others, and the groups to which we belong.[5]

The author makes explicit that she sees the value of the concept to primarily be its utility in activism intended to alter the existing social order: "The notion of otherness is used by sociologists to highlight how social identities are contested. We also use this concept to break down the ideologies and resources that groups use to maintain their social identities."[6]

Another example comes from a relatively new journal called *Othering and Belonging: Expanding the Circle of Human Concern*, associated with the Haas Institute for a Fair and Inclusive Society at UC Berkeley. An article in its inaugural issue declared that "The problem of the twenty-first century is the problem of 'othering.'" An indicator of the activist bent of this work is evident in the authors' definition of the verb form:

> We define "othering" as a set of dynamics, processes, and structures that engender marginality and persistent inequality across any of the full range of human differences based on group identities. While not entirely universal, the core mechanisms [that] engender marginality are largely similar across contexts. Dimensions of othering include, but are not limited to, religion, sex, race, ethnicity, socioeconomic status (class), disability, sexual orientation, and skin tone.[7]

Along the line of noticing how much the concept has changed over time, it is interesting that their definition centers not on the characteristics of a thing itself (social object, speech act, institutional feature, etc.), but on the social effects the thing is considered to produce.

Usage of the term has extended beyond the academic world. A personal web page defines it in this way:

> By "othering," we mean any action by which an individual or group becomes mentally classified in somebody's mind as "not one of us." Rather than always remembering that every person is a complex bundle of emotions, ideas, motivations, reflexes, priorities, and many other subtle aspects, it's sometimes easier to dismiss them as being in some way less human, and less worthy of respect and dignity than we are.[8]

The author describes his purpose:

> The concept behind this site, then, is that a) humans have an undeniable and insidious inclination to engage in "othering" through patterns for the purpose of self-preservation, and b) learning to avoid and counteract these thought patterns is integral to greatly reducing the world's hatred and suffering. Our

> intent is to raise people's consciousness about othering behavior, to make them more alert to these thought patterns, and to encourage alternative ways of addressing the problems that we often seek to avoid by dehumanizing any one group.[9]

It is noteworthy that the name of the site reflects the shift in meaning over time: There Are No Others. In the original sense of the term, the title is nonsensical, in that one cannot know oneself exists without knowing others.

For the purpose of this chapter, the challenge lies in the discriminant validity of the terms, *other* and *othering*. Of the huge amount of rhetoric in the political arena, both in the campaign and during the presidential administration, presumably some might constitute othering while the rest would not. Distinguishing one's candidacy, one's favored candidate, or one's identity group from different ones is othering in its initial meaning. Essentially, one differentiates one's position or preference from the alternatives, and—hopefully—provides a rationale for the preference. Accordingly, persuasive appeals can be couched in such terms. In my view, this is both legitimate and constructive in political discourse.

But attacks on the alternatives which demonize them or render them subaltern to the audience (in the sense of being inferior, not worthy of full social participation)[10] seem to me to be othering in the contemporary sense of being wrongful speech acts. As is usually the case, I am doubtful that a conceptual bright line can be drawn between the two. Nonetheless, the examples that follow strike me as fairly clear instances of Trump, his supporters, or both being othered (in the contemporary usage) during the 2016 election and the early period of the administration.

THE CAMPAIGN

It is to be expected that the major parties' presidential candidates will campaign vigorously for the office, and that the rhetoric they employ will include attacks on their opponents. Typically, such attacks focus on policy initiatives, empathy (specifically, lack of empathy) for various cohorts of citizens, temperament, or character traits. And, indeed, much of the 2016 campaign ran true to that expectation, on the part of candidates, their representatives and surrogates, and commentators.

What was non-routine was rhetoric so harsh as to dismiss the humanity of a candidate and supporters, and to suggest they were illegitimate participants in a democratic political process.

Even though her campaign quickly tried to walk it back, the comments of the Democrat candidate, Hillary Clinton, at a Manhattan fund-raiser on September 9, 2016, provide a clear example. In the transcript published by the *Los Angeles Times* most of Clinton's remarks are in keeping with traditional fund-raising pep talks to supporters: identifying harms her opponent's policies might create, invoking appeals to particular interest groups (in this case, LGBT), and raising doubts about her opponent's ability to handle the office of the president. This material drew no particular attention, nor did her request that audience members work phone banks and "if you know anybody who's even thinking about voting for Trump, stage an intervention."[11]

Embedded in this speech was the passage that rightly became controversial, in that it impugned the character of Trump supporters and pointedly excluded them from full political citizenship. Oddly, Clinton's remarks took this abrupt turn after an anodyne exhortation to her audience to not become "complacent" with the polling indicating she would win the election:

> We are living in a volatile political environment. You know, to just be grossly generalistic [sic; she presumably meant "to overgeneralize"], you could put half of Trump's supporters into what I call the basket of deplorables. Right? The racist, exist, homophobic, xenophobic, Islamophobic—you name it. And unfortunately there are people like that. And he has lifted them up. He has given voice to their websites that used to only have 11,000 people—now 11 million. He tweets and retweets their offensive[,] hateful[,] mean-spirited rhetoric. Now some of those folks—they are irredeemable, but thankfully they are not America.[12]

Having first accused a large portion of her opponent's supporters of moral failings—the "-isms" she listed—Clinton condemned them ("irredeemable") and excluded them ("not America"). In short, she othered them, to an audience of her supporters. She then proceeded to introduce Barbra Streisand as featured guest artist of the event, who performed a parody version of her hit "Send in the Clowns" with lyrics rewritten to identify Trump as the clown. The audience's reaction indicates it was well-received.[13]

The "basket of deplorables" comment was immediately seen as a gaffe, with the Trump campaign denouncing the insult and Clinton trying to walk back her disparaging reference to a large portion of his supporters and refocus the attack on the candidate, himself. In the original statement, "deplorable" was a noun, referring to Trump supporters; in the walk-back, it was an adjective referring to a Trump campaign strategy: "It is deplorable that Trump has built his campaign largely on prejudice and paranoia and given a national platform to hateful views and voices, including by retweeting fringe bigots with a few dozen followers and spreading their message to 11 million people."[14] It seems unlikely, however, that her comments at the fund-raiser were either intended for only a private audience or an off-the-cuff improvisation. *Los Angeles Times* reporting on the controversy states that the event was open to the press (hence the ready availability of a transcript and video), and that Clinton had used the word "deplorable" to describe at least some indefinite proportion of Trump's supporters before.[15]

Another surprising turn in the 2016 campaign was that two flagship conservative publications, the *National Review* and the *Weekly Standard*, maintained a #NeverTrump stance all the way to Election Day. It is customary for them to express preferences for a particular primary contestant and describe their objections to the others; after the primary concludes and the Republican Party has chosen its candidate, however, the publications do not actively undermine a candidate they previously disfavored. A few examples will illustrate how this election did not follow the template.

The editors of the *National Review* made no secret of their distaste for Donald Trump during the primary campaign. In their special "Against Trump" edition, a collection of essays opposing him as the potential party candidate, the editorial contained this particularly stinging characterization in its first paragraph:

> Donald Trump leads the polls nationally and in most states in the race for the Republican presidential nomination. There are understandable reasons for his eminence, and he has shown impressive gut-level skill as a campaigner. But he is not deserving of conservative support in the caucuses and primaries. Trump is a philosophically unmoored political opportunist who would trash the broad conservative ideological consensus within the GOP in favor of a free-floating populism with strong-man overtones.[16]

It is noteworthy that the magazine chose to devote an entire edition to opposing a single primary candidate; typically it would run articles analyzing the contestants for the nomination and eventually endorse one as the campaign wore on. The language choice in the above passage is also atypical: describing a candidate as "unmoored" and an "opportunist" pushes the outer limit of the refined tone of most writing in the magazine.

As a personal comment on this passage, I would express my doubt about there being a "broad conservative ideological consensus" within the Republican Party, which candidate Trump was likely to "trash." What comes to mind are periodic complaints about certain Republicans being "Republicans in Name Only" (a/k/a RINOs), and periodic primary challenges to incumbent Republicans; in any case, that the acronym has been commonplace in conservative political writing for a number of years is decent evidence that such intraparty consensus is a fantasy. In addition, it is not uncommon for Congressional Republicans to have difficulty in whip checks on controversial votes; this would not be the case if any broad ideological consensus did, in fact, exist and was accessible at crunch time on a difficult vote.

The *National Review* followed this with another issue, the cover of which displayed a caustic caricature of Trump with Chris Christie kissing his ring, and titled "The Clown Prince."[17] The theme had already appeared in an earlier issue, with roving editor Kevin D. Williamson contributing a piece titled, "Fifteen Elephants and a Clown"[18] (apparently a reference to the large initial field of Republican primary candidates), with the subtitle "The Donald's life has been seven decades of buffoonery" and closing with the comment, "He might have had any sort of life he chose, and Trump chose a clown's life."

Williamson did not confine his long-running diatribe to Trump himself. In the "Clown Prince" issue he had harsh words for an electoral cohort pundits were describing (and continued to describe) as Trump's base of enthusiastic supporters—white, working class voters who felt ignored in the political process. He pulled no punches, first asserting "In the story of the white working class's descent into dysfunction, they are the victims and villains both," following that with a reference to "the welfare dependency, the drug and alcohol addiction, the family anarchy—which is to say, the whelping of human children with all the respect and wisdom of a stray dog,"[19] and later closing the essay with a stinging summation:

> The truth about these dysfunctional, downscale communities is that they deserve to die. Economically, they are negative assets. Morally, they are indefensible. . . . The white American underclass is in thrall to a vicious, selfish culture whose main products are misery and used heroin needles. Donald Trump's speeches make them feel good. So does OxyContin. What they need isn't analgesics, literal or political.[20]

A *Washington Post* reporter interviewed *National Review*'s editor, Rich Lowry, about the magazine's decision to publish the Against Trump issue. Among other tidbits about the issue—including the disagreements among the editors and guest writers about their preferred candidate, and the anticipation they would be dropped from sponsoring one of the remaining Republican primary debates if they proceeded with plans to publish the Against Trump issue—Lowry responded to a question about why they decided to do it: "The most important thing is putting a marker down and saying, 'He's not one of us. He's not a conservative, and he's not what conservatism is.'"[21] Lowry did not use the actual word, but it seems fair to interpret this comment as an othering gesture.

Further examples of conservative pundits harshly denouncing Trump are plentiful. In a television appearance during the primary debate stage of the campaign Peter Wehner essentially described Trump as a demagogue:

> [Trump] is the most massively ignorant person ever to run for president and he cannot discuss public policy. So everything he's done from the day that he's gone in is to set up these debates that are on the ground of appealing to the darkest impulses of the country. That is what he relishes, and he wants to be in the gutter.[22]

For his part, Bill Kristol, editor of the *Weekly Standard*, was a consistently vocal critic of Trump, becoming an icon of the conservative branch of #NeverTrump through the primary campaign and even the general election campaign. It is striking that on the eve of the presidential election, he published a brief editorial reiterating his position.[23] After summarizing his career-long Republican bona fides, he described Trump as "a repulsive person, with dangerous prejudices, who's unfit to be President," and closed the piece with the #NeverTrump hashtag. It seems extraordinary that a self-identified party loyalist would openly wish for his party's defeat, and would do so in such harsh terms.

THE EARLY MONTHS OF THE TRUMP ADMINISTRATION

Traditionally, the general election is followed by a period of comparative quiet—that is, a lessening of the emotional intensity of the stretch of the campaign. Granted, one side will celebrate and express optimism about the future, while the other engages in post hoc analysis of its loss (possibly including some recriminations) and wax pessimistic about the consequences of the democratic choice. Nonetheless, the usual pattern as the next administration is formed, takes office, and begins to govern has long been termed the "honeymoon" period, in which overt partisanship is moderated (or, perhaps more accurately, masked for the time being) and criticism more measured. Quite simply, that was not the pattern in the 2016 election.

On the day after the election, the *New Yorker* ran an editorial attributed to the magazine's editor, David Remnick. It is remarkable for its relentlessly negative characterization of the election and the winning candidate. It begins with this:

> The election of Donald Trump to the Presidency is nothing less than a tragedy for the American republic, a tragedy for the Constitution, and a triumph for the forces, at home and abroad, of nativism, authoritarianism, misogyny, and racism. Trump's shocking victory, his ascension to the Presidency, is a sickening event in the history of the United States and liberal democracy.[24]

Remnick returned to this theme later in the piece: "Trump was not elected on a platform of decency, fairness, moderation, compromise, and the rule of law; he was elected, in the main, on a platform of resentment. Fascism is not our future—it cannot be; we cannot allow it to be so—but this is surely the way fascism can begin."[25]

Having raised various moralistic objections to the process (the laundry list of -isms and -ogys, above), Remnick damned Trump, the person, in no uncertain terms, describing him first alliteratively as "a twisted caricature of every rotten reflex of the radical right,"[26] and amplifying the point later in the piece with an indictment of Trump's character: "Trump [is] a flim-flam man who cheated his customers, investors, and contractors; a hollow man whose countless statements and behavior reflect a human being of dismal qualities—greedy, mendacious, and bigoted. His level of egotism is rarely exhibited outside of a clinical environment."[27]

In addition to accusations of character and personality defects, Remnick leveled the accusation that Trump had himself engaged in othering during the campaign. This passage is a good example of how the term is used in contemporary rhetoric, how it is axiomatic that othering is an illegitimate move, and how it is axiomatic that defending an othered group is presumptively a virtuous act:

> Trump is vulgarity unbounded, a knowledge-free national leader who will not only set markets tumbling but will strike fear into the hearts of the vulnerable, the weak, and above all, the many varieties of Other whom he has so deeply insulted. The African-American Other. The Hispanic Other. The female Other. The Jewish and Muslim Other.[28]

Remnick foresaw a dismal future, as one would expect; this passage moreover casts substantial doubt on the wisdom, and possibly character, of a large number of citizens: "That the electorate has, in its plurality, decided to live in Trump's world of vanity, hate, arrogance, untruth, and recklessness, his disdain for democratic norms, is a fact that will lead, inevitably, to all manner of national decline and suffering."[29]

The idea that the electorate made a bad choice of president was broadened, in a piece in *Foreign Policy* the next day. The problem was not simply an ill-considered choice; the problem was that the electorate is fundamentally incapable of making a good choice:

> OK, so that just happened. Donald Trump always enjoyed massive support from uneducated, low-information white people. . . . Last night we saw something historic: the dance of the dunces. Never have educated voters so uniformly rejected a candidate. But never before have the lesser-educated so uniformly supported a candidate. . . . Trump owes his victory to the uninformed.[30]

The "dance of the dunces" phrase is striking, as a disparagement of Trump's supporters. It is interesting that while it was not in the title or subtitle of the piece, it is part of its URL.

The author went on to argue that the electorate, in general, lacks enough knowledge to make an intelligent choice of leadership. This led him to speak favorably of alternatives to the current system of voting that "at least [take] seriously that universal suffrage and voter ignorance go hand in hand."[31] The pox-on-both-your-houses tone is evident in the close of the piece: "Trump's victory is the victory of the uninformed. But, to be fair, Clinton's victory would also have been. Democracy is the rule of the people, but the people are in many ways unfit to rule."[32] It is interesting to note that the piece begins as an explanation of Trump's surprising win (viz., his supporters are sufficiently ignorant of vital information relevant to their vote that they would be supporters), and eventually arrives at the position that since democratic choice, the process itself, suffers from an intractable problem, the only cure is a non-democratic process: "There is no real solution to the problem of political ignorance, unless we are willing to break with democratic politics."[33]

This position would appear in keeping with the postelection agitation for the Electoral College to nullify the actual electoral vote tally,[34] and with the advocacy for impeaching a president before his administration actually got up and running[35]—both unusual features of this election. It is also striking that it directly contradicts what has long been a cherished theme among intellectuals, that every citizen's vote be given equal weight and none should be excluded. Presumably the author would not wish the influence of his own vote to be diminished in the decision; an observer might well infer an implicit self/other dichotomy to underlie an essentially elitist position.

In the early days of the new administration a theme emerged that the efforts to implement campaign promises such as scaling back regulation, controlling illegal immigration, and taking tougher foreign policy stances were being undercut or at least sandbagged by career personnel in the respective units of the federal bureaucracy, individuals personally or professionally opposed to such changes. The term "deep state" came to be used as shorthand to denote this sort of organizational inertia. Bill Kristol used this term to express his continued opposition to the Trump presidency: "Obviously strongly prefer normal democratic and constitutional politics. But if it comes to it, prefer the deep state to the Trump state."[36] It is striking that just as he had hoped his party's candidate would lose the election, he wished his party's president would fail at implementing his policy initiatives. One can reasonably read this tweet to be a restatement that Trump was "not one of us."

The first-hundred-days review of a new administration is a tradition in political reporting, whatever one might think of the logical validity of an essentially arbitrary chronological benchmark. Although some pundits did temper their earlier criticism a bit, others chose to maintain the heat. In an op-ed, Peter Wehner reiterated his position that Trump was unqualified for office: "[T]hese developments paint a portrait of a man who was wholly unprepared to fulfill his primary job requirement—to govern competently and well."[37] In addition, he threw a jab at Trump's supporters: "In 2016, many voters saw ignorance not as something to be embarrassed about but as something to be celebrated."[38] Months later, Wehner still had not softened his stance appreciably:

> All of which brings us to Donald Trump, arguably the most disruptive and transgressive president in American history. He thrives on creating turbulence in every conceivable sphere. The blast radius of his tumultuous acts and chaotic temperament is vast. . . .
>
> His disordered personality thrives on mayhem and upheaval, on vicious personal attacks and ceaseless conflict. As we're seeing, his malignant character is emboldening some. . . .
>
> We have as president the closest thing to a nihilist in our history—a man who believes in little or nothing, who has the impulse to burn down rather than to build up.[39]

For his part, neither had David Remnick softened his denunciation of Trump; one might quip that such bipartisan agreement is rare in the pundit class. In his one-hundred-days essay Remnick maintained his negative assessment of Trump's character: "Impulsive, egocentric, and mendacious, Trump has . . . set fire to the integrity of his office. . . . Trump appears to strut through the world forever studying his own image. He thinks out loud, and is incapable of reflection. He is unserious, unfocussed, and, at times, it seems, unhinged."[40] Remnick continued his theme that a Trump presidency was a threat to the best aspects of the American political system, because of his character defects:

> The Trump Presidency represents a rebellion against liberalism itself—an angry assault on the advances of groups of people who have experienced profound, if fitful, empowerment over the past half century. There is nothing about Trump's public pronouncements that indicates that he has welcomed these moral advances; his language, his tone, his personal behavior, and his policies all suggest, and foster, a politics of resentment.[41]

Some in the pundit class ventured to strike a more conciliatory tone, only to be met with hostility from their audience. Online publication has facilitated direct comments from publishing outlets' consumers, and thus we can more readily get glimpses into the public mind. Nicholas Kristof made his own preference for progressive politics clear (and likewise made clear that his intent was to equip Democrat candidates to compete more effectively), but nonetheless wished to better understand the thinking of Trump supporters, especially those who might experience a personal cutback in government benefits as a result of the new administration's adjustments in funding. He seemed genuinely surprised at the reaction to an earlier column, describing the responses from the readers of the *New York Times* as "a torrent of venom":

> "I absolutely despise these people," one woman tweeted at me after I interviewed Trump voters. "Truly the worst of humanity. To hell with every one of them."

> . . . Another: "ALL [capitals in original] Trump voters are racist and deplorable. They'll never vote Democratic. We should never pander to the Trumpites. We're not a party for racists."[42]

On the *Power Line* blog, Steven Hayward collected additional reader responses to Kristof's repeated attempt to extend something of an olive branch, including these three:

> Just like the Klan and Aryan Nations filth, Republicans must be socially ostracized from coast to coast.
>
> Sorry, Nick. I've never met more ignorant and bigoted idiots than these people. Why be nice to them?
>
> No, Nick. You are way off base here. We are at war. A war against ignorance and bigotry.[43]

Clearly, these *New York Times* readers viewed Trump supporters as the Other group to their Self group.

The scorn for Trump supporters was not confined to the *New York Times* readership. *CNN* host Fareed Zakaria spoke of "the toxic energy on the far right" in much the same way in a *New Day* segment promoting his upcoming special show "Why Trump Won."[44] He got more specific, attributing Trump's election win to racism, sexism, homophobia, and xenophobia:

> And he [Trump] knew that the election of a black president had stirred a kind of racial animus among some people. . . . A real sense of cultural alienation that the older white, non-college educated Americans have [is] the sense that their country is changing because of immigrants. Because maybe blacks are getting—rising up to a kind of central place in society. Because of, you know, gays being afforded equal rights. Because of, frankly, a lot of working women.[45]

SOCIAL MEDIA AND POPULAR CULTURE

One would expect social media channels such as Twitter to foster a good amount of bashing. The limited character space and ease with which visual memes can be inserted inhibits nuanced and thoughtful exchange while facilitating telegraphic barbed comments—hardly a channel characteristic conducive to negotiating or even exchanging divergent views on substantive disagreements, while clearly fostering intemperate exchanges. Examples of othering moves abound, all across the political spectrum; it will be useful here to note a few as illustrations of the contempt for Trump and his supporters.

Social media celebrity Reign of April generated a lot of retweets and likes with the comment "Because, for some, the Confederacy isn't alt-history. It's right now." She included an image of the confederate flag with "Donald

Trump for President 2016" on the red field.[46] This tweet was part of her #NoConfederate hashtag campaign against a proposed HBO show, but it is of interest here as an example of visual rhetoric ostracizing Trump supporters. There had been some reporting of the confederate flag occasionally appearing at Trump rallies during the campaign[47] despite Trump's disavowal of it; April chose to include the image even though it was not directly relevant to the subject of her tweet, the HBO show, and the election was seven months in the past. It seems fair to see the visual juxtaposition of two different things (a battle flag from a civil war a century-and-a-half ago with a campaign slogan from the last election) as intended to suggest they both are the Other.

Media professionals have adopted Twitter as part of their routine, so it is unsurprising to find similar content from them. Referring to a Trump rally held in Huntington, West Virginia, on August 3, 2017, pundit Stuart Rothenberg tweeted the prejudiced remark, "Lots of people in West Virginia can't support themselves or speak English." When challenged on that, he maintained his stance, sharing his bigotry with this comment: "Of course they are hard-working. They mean well. Just close[d]-minded, provincial, angry & easily misled."[48] Also on Twitter, children's author J. K. Rowling described Trump as a "monster of narcissism."[49] What had set off Rowling's series of tweets excoriating Trump was a short video clip which she took to show him ignoring the outstretched hand of a child in a wheelchair; Rowling responded with "How stunning, and how horrible, that Trump cannot bring himself to shake the hand of a small boy who only wanted to touch the President."[50] A full-length recording of the event, however, showed that Trump had in fact paid a great deal of attention to the boy at the event. Moreover, the child's mother took to her Facebook page to rebut Rowling's mistaken impression: "If someone can please get a message to JK Rowling: Trump didn't snub my son & Monty wasn't even trying to shake his hand. (1. He's 3 and hand shaking is not his thing, 2. he was showing off his newly acquired secret service patch.)"[51] Rowling subsequently acknowledged her error and deleted the tweets, but did not recant her comments about Trump.[52]

In recent years many comedians have chosen to include politics or political figures in their material, but for the most part they would maintain a wry, satirical tone. Some changed their approach when dealing with Trump and his supporters, becoming far more aggressive and harsh in their material. For instance, Jim Carrey sent out a tweet about the Trump rally mentioned above: "Tonight in West Virginia @realDonaldTrump is expected to EAT A BABY on stage to the delight of his zombie base. #walkingdead."[53] He included a still image in the tweet, a line drawing caricature of Trump with a splotch of red on the mouth and chin. It seems fair to observe that, if this is humor, there is nothing subtle about it. Presumably Carrey believed his fans would find it amusing.

Sometimes when comedians attempt to seriously weigh in on political matters, there can be unintentional humor. This was the case with a pair of tweets from Chelsea Handler. In the first, she seemed to be concerned about a potential move toward authoritarianism in the Trump era: "What's happening in the state of Missouri [referring to the governor's decision to deploy state law enforcement resources in high-crime areas of St. Louis] is scary and unacceptable. If we don't speak up, this whole country could become a military state."[54] A few days later, she invoked the meme that Trump was mentally defective and called for the U.S. military to depose the president: "To all the generals surrounding our idiot-in-chief. . . [in original] the longer U wait to remove him, the longer UR name will appear negatively in history."[55] Presumably, Handler meant the two tweets unironically. Nonetheless, a number of observers took note of a contradiction. One paraphrased them in this way:

> America is in serious danger of becoming a military state.
> *Four days later*
> What America really needs is a good military coup.[56]

A vital aspect of the craft of comedy is to push the limit of acceptability without crossing over that limit. It seems that late-night host Stephen Colbert managed to just barely get away with a salty monologue addressed to Trump, personally. Saying he was mad at Trump for referring to CBS colleague John Dickerson's show as "Deface the Nation," Colbert began with a string of puns similar to Trump's (including "You're not the POTUS, you're the BLOATUS," "You're the Presi-Dunce," and referring to the Trump administration as "Disgrace the Nation") but then moved into some direct insults.[57] In the clip, the studio audience's enjoyment can be heard through the entire segment, but the climax of the monologue did become controversial: "Sir, you attract more skinheads than free Rogaine. You have more people marching against you than cancer. You talk like a sign-language gorilla who got hit in the head. In fact, the only thing your mouth is good for is being Vladimir Putin's cock holster."[58] The last sentence was considered by many to be homophobic;[59] Colbert found it necessary to express regret over his word choice, but stopped short of apologizing for his rude remarks to the president:[60]

> Now, if you saw my monologue Monday, you know that I was a little upset at Donald Trump for insulting a friend of mine. So at the end of that monologue I had a few choice insults for the President in return. I don't regret that. . . . So while I would do it again, I would change a few words that were cruder than they needed to be.[61]

Even less subtle than the caricature Carrey included in his tweet was a still photo Kathy Griffin created with celebrity photographer Tyler Shields and gave to the entertainment gossip outlet, TMZ.[62] Mimicking the composition and staging of ISIS beheading images, Griffin is shown holding up a theatrical prop severed head of Trump covered in blood, her expression deadpan as she looks into the camera lens positioned exactly perpendicular to the plane of her body. Part of the media package given to TMZ was a "making of" video. It seems apparent that Griffin expected this creation to be received favorably, but it proved to be a bit much for many people.[63] Met with an uproar rather than applause following the release of the photo, Griffin apologized and declared it had not been her intention to advocate Trump's assassination.

Neither Carrey's nor Handler's tweets seem to have generated any great amount of public attention, positive or negative. Both Colbert's rant and Griffin's photo did, however. Colbert benefitted, if anything.[64] Griffin suffered some negative consequence.[65] Of interest, here, is that whether one finds the examples humorous or offensive, the comedians' apparent intent was to please their respective audiences by othering Trump, his supporters, or both.

TRUMP'S PERSONALITY AND STATE OF MIND

During both the campaign and the start of the administration, some of the attacks on Trump centered on purported defects in his personality or mental health; that thread can be seen in a number of the examples mentioned above. Again, the attacks came from partisans on both the left and on the right. For instance, Eugene Robinson offered this take during the campaign:

> During the primary season, as Donald Trump's bizarre outbursts helped him crush the competition, I thought he was being crazy like a fox. Now I am increasingly convinced that he's just plain crazy. . . . At this point, it would be irresponsible to ignore the fact that Trump's grasp on reality appears to be tenuous at best.[66]

Robert Kagan, who left the Republican Party and endorsed Clinton in the 2016 election, described Trump during the campaign as "a man with a disordered personality."[67] Charles Blow added a racial twist to this theme, and claimed this explained Trump's appeal to his supporters:

> Trump is a mirror. He is a reflection of—indeed a revealing of—the ugliness that you [i.e., Trump supporters] harbor, only it is possible that you may have gone your life expressing it in ways that were more coded and politic. Trump is an unfiltered primal scream of the fragility and fear consuming white male America.[68]

Richard Kelsey had this to say, around the one-hundred-day mark of the administration: "It's hard being an American conservative right now. . . . The President of the United States is a nut job, to use his own phrase. He's stone-cold crazy. . . . [a] self-serving, crude, narcissistic, ego-maniac who is really an insecure man with the trappings of power."[69]

Amateur psychoanalysis is not all that rare in political talk, even if it does seem to have peaked in this election cycle. Speculation as to Trump's mental health was not confined to the pundit class, though, and that is an unusual feature. It is of particular interest given that in 1973 the American Psychiatric Association adopted an ethical tenet explicitly prohibiting its members from making such public statements, as practicing professionals. It became known as the "Goldwater rule,"[70] since it was included in the ethical code in response to psychiatrists participating in a magazine poll about Barry Goldwater's mental fitness for office during the 1964 presidential campaign. This appears in Section 7 of the code, and remains in effect:

> On occasion psychiatrists are asked for an opinion about an individual who is in the light of public attention or who has disclosed information about himself/herself through public media. In such circumstances, a psychiatrist may share with the public his or her expertise about psychiatric issues in general. However, it is unethical for a psychiatrist to offer a professional opinion unless he or she has conducted an examination and has been granted proper authorization for such a statement.[71]

Similar constraints (whether codified rules or guidance from the organization) apply to members of the American Psychological Association and the American Psychoanalytic Association.[72]

The rule generated periodic discussion but no particular controversy from its adoption until the 2016 campaign,[73] when some professionals began to assert that Trump's personality defects were evident in his public appearances, and that the purported mental health problems were so severe as to pose a danger to the country should he be elected. They justified the violation of the Goldwater rule on the grounds that their duty to warn the public overrode the ethical constraint against making public, remote (i.e., not based on personal contact with the individual), unauthorized diagnoses. This appears to be a considerable stretch of the traditional understanding of the duty to warn principle, which requires professionals to breach confidentiality when they are in possession of clinical information indicating an imminent danger to the public,[74] such as a patient of theirs they believed might become violent. In contrast, public statements that Trump had a defective personality would not be disclosing clinical details obtained in a private therapist/patient setting, but instead would be a diagnosis of mental illness based solely on transcripts and recordings of his public appearances and statements.

Nonetheless, this initiative outlived the campaign and, if anything, grew in the early period of the administration. The stated goal shifted from defeating a candidate to removing a sitting president from office. A report described a conference panel in this way:

> Donald Trump has a "dangerous mental illness" and is not fit to lead the US, a group of psychiatrists warned during a conference at Yale University. Mental health experts claimed the President was "paranoid and delusional," and said it was their "ethical responsibility" to warn the American public about the "dangers" Mr. Trump's psychological state poses to the country.[75]

In an earlier interview, one of the invited participants on that panel, Dr. John Gardner, had described his rationale for violating the Goldwater rule:

> The psychiatric interview is hardly the gold standard, by the way. If you have massive amounts of information about a person's behavior, that can be more accurate. And we have that. If the question is whether we can form a diagnosis from that information, I think it's clear that we can.
>
> In our field, we have a duty to warn. If a patient says they [sic] might harm someone, you're mandated by law to violate constitutionality [presumably he meant "confidentiality"] to warn that person. We're talking about a need to warn all people that this person [i.e., Trump] is a threat to world peace because of his psychiatric disorder.[76]

As one would expect, this theme was echoed in the popular press.[77]

FINAL COMMENTARY

Much of the political rhetoric in this campaign stayed within the traditional boundaries. The examples in the preceding sections were not intended to be broadly representative of the entire corpus of campaign rhetoric, but instead to illustrate a particular current in that flood, one that was out-of-the-ordinary for presidential election cycles. For instance, the examples described above of conservative pundits signing on to the #NeverTrump position should not be taken as evidence that establishment conservative pundits, as a unified sector of the political sphere, opposed Trump in the campaign and the early period of the administration. Defenses of Trump and empathy for his supporters appeared, and a particular theme in these is rebuttal to the "He's not one of us" running through the #NeverTrump writing during the campaign; this is especially true after the inauguration of the new administration, when it began to implement its promised policy and funding changes.[78]

Neither were the examples intended to make the case Trump, his supporters, or both, were the innocent victims of pernicious attacks from unprincipled enemies. It seems to me at least arguable that since the Trump campaign sometimes engaged in name-calling, it could be accused of othering, and it was a charge that was often vigorously leveled by critics of Trump and his campaign. That question is beyond the scope of this chapter—although it seems worthwhile to note in passing that the so-called "Muslim ban" executive order, often mentioned in accusations that Trump was engaging in othering, was actually not based on religion, but rather on the country of origin;[79] the way the controversy was short-handed in many press accounts and commentary as a "Muslim ban" essentially was a distortion.

Those disclaimers made, I believe the examples do show that in this campaign several prominent lines of attack against Trump or supporters can be reasonably seen as othering, do go beyond ad hominem, and are different in nature from the customary jousting in a political competition. As noted earlier, a bright line distinction between allowable attack rhetoric and objectionable attacks is difficult to make with regard to the issue of othering. Certainly, it is desirable for the candidates and any other participants in the political discourse to contrast their positions, preferences, and understandings of the current situation with that of their rivals; one would hope this might lead to a more informed electorate. This is othering in the traditional meaning, from phenomenology: one understands one's life world (self) in relation to that of others; it is to be expected that candidates would rally their supporters by contrasting "us" with "them" in a credo of core beliefs.

Name-calling is indeed an unpleasant feature of bare-knuckle politics; I am hard put to see such ad hominem tactics as constructive additions. But in my estimation the line is crossed from ad hominem into othering (in the contemporary sense of marginalization, delegitimation, rendering subaltern) when the speech acts primarily demonize the rival (or his supporters) as being less than human, or imply that the Other does not deserve full participation in the collective decision process we call elections, but, rather, deserves any and all abuse it receives. It is helpful to consider Jürgen Habermas's notion of the ideal discourse, and the conduct rules his student Robert Alexy developed as a way of implementing it:

> (3.1) Every subject with the competence to speak and act is allowed to take part in a discourse.
>
> (3.2) a. Everyone is allowed to question any assertion whatever.
> b. Everyone is allowed to introduce any assertion whatever into the discourse.
> c. Everyone is allowed to express his attitudes, desires, and needs.
>
> (3.3) No speaker may be prevented, by internal or external coercion, from exercising his rights as laid down in (3.1) and (3.2).[80]

I am under no illusion that human behavior is perfectible, either by persuasion or by regulation—but those rules seem constructive as guiding principles as to what is acceptable and what is not.

With that as a framework, it seems to me that the examples described in the preceding sections do cross a line between the traditional sense of othering (acceptable, potentially constructive) into the contemporary sense of othering as marginalization (unacceptable, damaging). Absent a proper clinical diagnosis, labelling Trump as insane or having a defective personality—and hence deserving exclusion from an election or removal from office—seems to violate the first rule; so, too, does stereotyping Trump voters as ignorant dupes too stupid to know what is in their best interest. Arguing that Trump raised problematics about issues that may not be problematized (i.e., it is impermissible to question trends considered by some to be evolution toward "social justice") seems to violate the second set of rules. Dismissing Trump's supporters as (to cut to the chase) white trash likewise seems to violate the second set of rules that they ought to be allowed to voice their personal concerns about the direction of the country and how it might affect their lives. Attempts to suppress speech supporting Trump by disrupting public events seems to violate the third rule. In short, the bar should be very high for would-be participants to be delegitimated and excluded—and such a move must be thoroughly grounded in factual evidence. Defending delegitimation requires much more than the interpretive assertion "But that's how good people like me see it; it's the only way a good person can see it."

On the face of it, it seems contradictory that many people who, themselves, decry othering (in its contemporary usage) engaged in othering Trump and his supporters in this election cycle. I have not seen an explicit justification of the apparent violation of what is otherwise treated as a categorical imperative,[81] beyond insinuating that this candidate and his supporters are such an egregious case they do not deserve the protection. This is similar to the explanation alt-left activist groups such as Antifa and By Any Means Necessary offer when questioned about their use of violence and fascist tactics to interfere with free speech.[82] Perhaps they are so certain their perspective on a political issue is just that their actions (speech, or physical) constitute "hating what is hateful and . . . loving what deserves love," as Alice Miller described recovery from childhood trauma.[83] But taking that position, itself, would constitute othering.

In addition to what appears to be a substantial threat to the traditional understanding of free speech and First Amendment rights (viz., leftist advocates justifying their use of street violence to disrupt the expression of political viewpoints they find repugnant[84]), there is a parallel concern that many journalists and media outlets have seemingly abandoned any pretense of impartiality in covering the election or the new administration. One veteran mainstream journalist worried, during the campaign, that his profession was making a fatal mistake by weakening its ethical tenet of objectivity in straight news reporting:

> Donald Trump may or may not fix his campaign, and Hillary Clinton may or may not become the first female president. But something else happening before our eyes is almost as important: the complete collapse of American journalism as we know it. . . .
>
> The shameful display of naked partisanship by the elite media is unlike anything seen in modern America. The largest broadcast networks—CBS, NBC and ABC—and major newspapers like the New York Times and Washington Post have jettisoned all pretense of fair play. Their fierce determination to keep Trump out of the Oval Office has no precedent.[85]

What prompted his concern was not just that the coverage seemed to heavily portray Clinton in a favorable light and Trump in an unfavorable light, but that some elite journalists had begun to openly justify taking sides. He pointed to a recent opinion piece in the *New York Times*:

> If you're a working journalist and you believe that Donald J. Trump is a demagogue playing to the nation's worst racist and nationalistic tendencies, that he cozies up to anti-American dictators and that he would be dangerous with control of the United State nuclear codes, how the heck are you supposed to cover him? . . .
>
> If you view a Trump presidency as something that's potentially dangerous, then your reporting is going to reflect that. You would move closer than you've ever been to being oppositional.[86]

Full exploration of those two corollary issues is beyond the scope of this chapter. Still, they deserve mention here as clear negative externalities of a recent trend in campaign rhetoric. The common thread is that behaviors long considered to be violations of law or professional ethics are starting to be justified (falsely, in my view) as virtuously confronting the Other.

Whatever the motivation or rationale, the othering of Donald Trump and his supporters seems to me to be a corrosive development in the last election, and it shows no sign of abating in the near future.

NOTES

1. James A. Mackin Jr., "Schismogenesis and Community: Pericles' Funeral Oration," *Quarterly Journal of Speech* 77(3) (1991): 251–262.

2. Richard Kilminster, "Phenomenology," in *The Blackwell Dictionary of Twentieth-Century Social Thought,* ed. William Outhwaite and Tom Bottomore (Cambridge: Blackwell Publishers, 1995), 460. See, too, John Torrance, "Phenomenology," in *The New Fontana Dictionary of Modern Thought,* ed. Alan Bullock and Stephen Trombley (London: Harper Collins Publishers, 2000), 645.

3. Roger Poole, "The Other," in *The New Fontana Dictionary of Modern Thought,* ed. Alan Bullock and Stephen Trombley (London: Harper Collins Publishers, 2000), 620.

4. "Other," *Wikipedia.org,* last modified May 9, 2017, accessed May 22, 2017, https://en.wikipedia.org/wiki/Other.

5. Zuleyka Zevallos, "What Is Otherness?," *The Other Sociologist,* October 14, 2011, accessed July 30, 2017, https://othersociologist.com/otherness-resources/.

6. Ibid.

7. John A. Powell and Stephen Menendian, "The Problem of Othering: Towards Inclusiveness and Belonging," *Othering and Belonging,* Issue One, accessed August 12, 2017, http://www.otheringandbelonging.org/the-problem-of-othering/.

8. James Norriss, "Othering 101: What Is 'Othering'?," *There Are No Others,* December 28, 2011, accessed August 12, 2017, https://therearenoothers.wordpress.com/2011/12/28/othering-101-what-is-othering/.

9. Ibid.

10. "Subaltern (Postcolonialism)," *Wikipedia.org*, last modified July 16, 2017, accessed August 25, 2017, https://en.wikipedia.org/wiki/Subaltern_(postcolonialism)/.

11. Seema Mehta, "Transcript: Clinton's Full Remarks as She Called Half of Trump Supporters 'Deplorables,'" *Los Angeles Times*, September 10, 2016, accessed May 22, 2017, http://www.latimes.com/nation/politics/trailguide/la-na-trailguide-updates-transcript-clinton-s-full-remarks-as-1473549076-htmlstory.html.

12. Ibid.

13. "Send In the Clowns—Trump Parody Barbra Streisand," accessed August 3, 2017, https://www.youtube.com/watch?v=35UjqvSubpA.

14. Amy Chozick, "Hillary Clinton Calls Many Trump Backers 'Deplorables,' and GOP Pounces," September 10, 2016, accessed May 22, 2017, https://www.nytimes.com/2016/09/11/us/politics/hillary-clinton-basket-of-deplorables.html?r=0.

15. Seema Mehta, "Is Clinton's 'Deplorables' Remark a Repeat of Romney's '47%' Comment? Maybe Not," September 10, 2016, accessed May 22, 2017, http://www.latimes.com/nation/politics/trailguide/la-na-trailguide-updates-transcript-clinton-s-full-remarks-as-1473549076-htmlstory.html.

16. "Against Trump," *National Review*, January 21, 2016, accessed August 2, 2017, http://www.nationalreview.com/node/430137/.

17. "The Clown Prince," *National Review*, March 28, 2016, accessed August 16, 2017, https://www.nationalreview.com/magazine/2016–03–28–0100.

18. Kevin D. Williamson, "Fifteen Elephants and a Clown," *National Review*, July 28, 2015, accessed August 2, 2017, http://www.nationalreview.com/421676/.

19. Kevin D. Williamson, "Chaos in the Family, Chaos in the State: The White Working Class's Dysfunction," *National Review*, March 28, 2016, accessed August 16, 2017, http://www.nationalreview.com/article/432876/donald-trump-white-working-class-dysfunction-real-opportunity-needed-not-trump.

20. Ibid.

21. Callum Borchers, "The Inside Story of National Review's Big Anti-Donald Trump Issue," *Washington Post*, January 22, 2016, accessed August 16, 2017, https://www.washingtonpost.com/news/the-fix/wp/2016/01/22/the-story-behind-the-national-reviews-big-anti-donald-trump-issue/.

22. "MSNBC Panel Rips Trump's 'Racist' Insinuation That Obama Supports Terrorism," *Mediamatters.com*, June 13, 2016, accessed August 7, 2017, https://www.mediamatters.org/2016/06/13/msnbc-panel-rips-trumps-racist-insinuation-obama-supports-terrorism/210920.

23. William Kristol, "#NeverTrump: A Final Word," *Weekly Standard*, November 7, 2016, accessed July 30, 2017, http://www.weeklystandard.com/nevertrump-a-final-word/article/2005275.

24. David Remnick, "An American Tragedy," *New Yorker*, November 9, 2016, accessed August 4, 2017, http://www.newyorker.com/news/news-desk/an-american-tragedy-2.

25. Ibid.

26. Ibid.

27. Ibid.

28. Ibid.

29. Ibid.

30. Jason Brennan, "Trump Won Because Voters Are Ignorant, Literally," *Foreign Policy*, November 10, 2016, accessed August 4, 2017, http://foreignpolicy.com/2016/11/10/the-dance-of-the-dunces-trump-clinton-election-republican-democrat/.

31. Ibid.

32. Ibid.

33. Ibid.

34. For instance: Peter Beinart, "The Electoral College Was Meant to Stop Men Like Trump from Being President," *Atlantic*, November 21, 2016, accessed August 7, 2017, https://www.theatlantic.com/politics/archive/2016/11/the-electoral-college-was-meant-to-stop-men-like-trump-from-being-president/508310/.

35. For instance: Vanessa Williams, "'Auntie Maxine' and the Quest for Impeachment," *Washington Post*, May 1, 2017, accessed 8/7/17, https://www.washingtonpost.com/politics/auntie-maxine-and-the-quest-for-impeachment/2017/4/29/.

36. Bill Kristol, "Obviously Strongly Prefer," February 14, 2017, accessed May 22, 2017, https://twitter.com/billkristol/status/831497364661747712.

37. Peter Wehner, "Mr. Trump Goes to Washington," *New York Times*, April 28, 2017, accessed August 7, 2017, https://www.nytimes.com/2017/04/28/opinion/donald-trump-goes-to-washington.html.

38. Ibid.

39. Peter Wehner, "Declaration of Disruption," *New York Times*, July 4, 2017, accessed August 4, 2017, https://www.nytimes.com/2017/07/04/opinion/trump-declaration-of-disruption.html.

40. David Remnick, "A Hundred Days of Trump," *New Yorker*, May 1, 2017, accessed August 4, 2017, http://www.newyorker.com/magazine/2017/05/01/a-hundred-days-of-trump.

41. Ibid.

42. Nicholas Kristof, "My Most Unpopular Idea: Be Nice to Trump Voters," *New York Times*, April 6, 2017, accessed August 4, 2017, https://www.nytimes.com/2017/04/06/opinion/my-most-unpopular-idea-be-nice-to-trump-voters.html.

43. Steven Hayward, "Democrats: The Party of Hate," *Power Line*, April 6, 2017, accessed April 6, 2017, http://www.powerlineblog.com/archives/2017/04/democrats-the-party-of-hate.php.

44. Don Surber, "CNN Still Does Not Understand Trump," *The Deplorable Don Surber*, July 31, 2017, accessed July 31, 2017, http://donsurber.blogspot.com/2017/07/cnn-still-does-not-understand-trump.html.

45. "New Day transcript," CNN.com, July 31, 2017, accessed August 9, 2017, http://www.cnn.com/TRANSCRIPTS/1707/31/nday.04.html.

46. April, "Because for Some," July 30, 2017, accessed August 4, 2017, https://twitter.com/ReignOfApril/status/891832703414403072.

47. Richard Fausset, "As Trump Rises, So Do Some Hands Waving Confederate Battle Flags," *New York Times*, November 18, 2016, accessed August 9, 2017, https://www.nytimes.com/2016/11/19/us/confederate-flag-trump.html.

48. "Helpful Context for Trump's Rally," August 3, 2017, accessed August 4, 2017, http://twitchy.com/brettt-3136/2017/08/03/helpful-context-for-trumps-rally-from-a-pro-west-virginians-are-angry-easily-misled-lots-dont-speak-english.

49. Christine Rousselle, "J. K. Rowling Still Hasn't Deleted Tweet Saying Trump Snubbed a Disabled Child," July 31, 2017, accessed July 31, 2017, https://townhall.com/tipsheet/christinerousselle/2017/07/31/jk-rowling-trump-tweet-n2362412.

50. Ibid.

51. Ibid.

52. Dan Bilefsky, "J. K. Rowling Apologizes for Anti-Trump Tweets (But Not to Trump)," *New York Times*, August 1, 2017, accessed August 9, 2017, https://www.nytimes.com/2017/08/01/books/uk-rowling-twitter-trump.html.

53. Jim Carrey, "Tonight in West Virginia," August 3, 2017, accessed August 7, 2017, https://twitter.com/JimCarrey/status/893162627550986240.

54. "Totally Coup-Coup," August 12, 2017, accessed August 12, 2017, http://twitchy.com/dougp-3137/2017/08/12/totally-coup-coup-this-chelsea-handler-inspired-shot-chaser-is-a-real-doozy.

55. Ibid.

56. Ibid.

57. "The Best of Stephen Colbert on Trump—'Cock Holster Joke,'" May 7, 2017, accessed August 17, 2017, https://www.youtube.com/watch?v=_I7duOJXMr8.

58. Ibid.

59. For instance: Mark Graham, "Stephen Colbert's Shocking Attack on Trump Concludes with a Homophobic Slur," May 2, 2017, accessed August 10, 2017, http://decider.com/2017/05/02/stephen-colbert-donald-trump-cock-holster/.

60. Tim Kenneally, "Read Stephen Colbert's Complete Comments on Trump 'Cock Holster' Joke," May 3, 2017, accessed August 10, 2017, http://www.thewrap.com/read-stephen-colberts-complete-comments-trump-cock-holster-joke.

61. "The Best of Stephen Colbert on Trump—'Cock Holster Joke,'" May 7, 2017, accessed August 17, 2017, https://www.youtube.com/watch?v=_I7duOJXMr8.

62. "Kathy Griffin Beheads Donald Trump," May 30, 2017, accessed August 7, 2017, http://www.tmz.com/2017/05/30/kathy-griffin-beheads-donald-trump-photo-tyler-shields/.

63. Herman Wong, "CNN Cuts Ties with Kathy Griffin amid Controversy over Comedian's Gruesome Anti-Trump Photo," *Washington Post*, May 31, 2017, accessed August 7, 2017, https://www.washingtonpost.com/news/arts-and-entertainment/wp/2017/05/30/kathy-griffin-apologizes-for-severed-donald-trump-head-photo-after-backlash/.

64. Laura Bradley, "Stephen Colbert Rides Trump Wave to Another Late Show Milestone," May 23, 2017, *Vanity Fair*, accessed August 10, 2017, https://www.vanityfair.com/hollywood/2017/05/stephen-colbert-late-show-ratings-tonight-show-donald-trump.

65. Herman Wong, "CNN Cuts Ties with Kathy Griffin."

66. Eugene Robinson, "Is Donald Trump Just Plain Crazy?," *Washington Post*, August 1, 2016, accessed August 11, 2017, https://www.washingtonpost.com/opinions/is-donald-trump-just-plain-crazy/2016/08/01/.

67. Robert Kagan, "There Is Something Very Wrong with Donald Trump," *Washington Post*, August 1, 2016, accessed August 11, 2017, https://www.washingtonpost.com/opinions/there-is-something-very-wrong-with-donald-trump/2016/08/01/.

68. Charles M. Blow, "Trump Reflects White Male Fragility," *New York Times*, August 4, 2016, accessed August 11, 2017, http://www.nytimes.com/2016/08/04/opinion/trump-reflects-white-male-fragility.html.

69. Richard Kelsey, "Trump Is Crazy and Gorsuch Is Not Enough," June 29, 2017, accessed July 28, 2017, http://committedconservative.com/2017/06/29/trump-crazy/.

70. "Goldwater Rule," *Wikipedia.org*, last modified July 26, 2017, accessed July 27, 2017, https://en.wikipedia.org/wiki/Goldwater_rule.

71. "The Principles of Medical Ethics with Annotations Especially Applicable to Psychiatry," *American Psychiatric Association*, 2013 Ed., accessed August 18, 2017, https://www.psychiatry.org/File%20Library/Psychiatrists/Practice/Ethics/principles-medical-ethics.pdf.

72. "Goldwater Rule," *Wikipedia.org.*

73. Benedict Carey, "The Psychiatric Question: Is It Fair to Analyze Donald Trump from Afar?," *New York Times*, August 15, 2016, accessed August 10, 2017, https://www.nytimes.com/2016/08/16/health/analyzing-donald-trump-psychology.html.

74. "Mental Health Professionals' Duty to Warn," *National Conference of State Legislatures*, September 28, 2015, accessed August 11, 2017, http://www.ncsl.org/research/mental-health-professionals-duty-to-warn.aspx.

75. May Bulman, "Donald Trump Has 'Dangerous Mental Illness,' Say Psychiatry Experts at Yale Conference," *Independent*, April 21, 2017, accessed August 10, 2017, http://www.independent.co.uk/news/world-0/donald-trump-dangerous-mental-illness-yale-psychiatrist-conference-us-president-unfit-james-gartner-a7694316.html.

76. Joshunda Sanders, "An Interview with Dr. John Gartner: 'We Have a Duty to Warn the World about Donald Trump,'" *Medium*, March 21, 2017, accessed August 18, 2017, https://

medium.com/the-fifth-estate/an-interview-with-dr-john-gartner-we-have-a-duty-to-warn-the-world-about-donald-trump-e1b54223c913.

77. Alex Morris, "Why Trump Is Not Mentally Fit to Be President," *Rolling Stone*, April 5, 2017. accessed August 18, 2017, http://www.rollingstone.com/politics/features/trump-and-the-pathology-of-narcissism-w474896 and Jeffrey Kluger, "Go Ahead, Psychiatrists: Diagnose Donald Trump," *Time*, July 26, 2017, accessed July 27, 2017, http://time.com/4872558/donald-trump-goldwater-rule/.

78. Roger Kimball, "Trump Critics Exude Desperate Political Nihilism," *American Greatness*, May 1, 2017, accessed May 8, 2017, https://amgreatness.com/2017/05/01/trump-critics-exude-desperate-political-nihilism/ and "The Nightmares and the Realities of Never Trump," *American Greatness*, May 17, 2017, accessed May 22, 2017, http://amgreatness.com/2017/05/17/nightmares-realities-never-trump/.

79. "Full Text of Trump's Executive Order on 7-Nation Ban, Refugee Suspension," CNN.com, January 28, 2017, accessed August 14, 2017, http://www.cnn.com/2017/01/28/politics/text-of-trump-executive-order-nation-ban-refugees/index.html.

80. Jurgen Habermas, *Moral Consciousness and Communicative Action* (Cambridge: MIT Press, 1990), 89.

81. "Categorical Imperative," *Wikipedia.org*, last modified July 24, 2017, accessed August 17, 2017, https://en.wikipedia.org/wiki/Categorical_imperative.

82. "'No Regrets' Organizer Calls for More Militant Protests," February 3, 2017, accessed August 14, 2017, https://www.youtube.com/watch?v=YPrRLyFTzSU.

83. Alice Miller, *The Drama of the Gifted Child* (New York: Basic Books, 1997), 114.

84. Thomas Fuller, Alan Feuer, and Serge F. Kovaleski, "'Antifa' Grows as Left-Wing Faction Set to, Literally, Fight the Far Right," *New York Times*, August 17, 2017, accessed August 21, 2017, https://www.nytimes.com/2017/08/17/us/antifa-left-wing-faction-far-right.html and Sara Ganim, "Unmasking the Leftist Antifa Movement," CNN.com, August 20, 2017, accessed August 21, 2017, http://www.cnn.com/2017/08/18/us/unmasking-antifa-anti-fascists-hard-left/index.html.

85. Michael Goodwin, "American Journalism Is Collapsing before Our Eyes," *New York Post*, August 21, 2016, accessed July 27, 2017, http://nypost.com/2016/08/21/american-journalism-is-collapsing-before-our-eyes/.

86. Jim Rutenberg, "Trump Is Testing the Norms of Objectivity in Journalism," *New York Times*, August 7, 2016, accessed August 18, 2017, https://www.nytimes.com/2016/08/08/business/balance-fairness-and-a-proudly-provocative-presidential-candidate.html.

Chapter Four

Donald J. Trump's Use of Twitter in the 2016 Campaign

Katherine Haenschen, Michael Horning, and Jim A. Kuypers

The 2016 presidential campaign was controversial in numerous ways, not the least of which were some aspects of social media use. *USA Today* reported that, "Social media has made a bigger impact in this election cycle than any other in history, both for breaking news and as a way for citizens to directly connect to candidates."[1] The traditional view of social media holds that it echoes or amplifies campaign communication, particularly that which is shared through more traditional mediums. However, developments during campaign 2016 suggest the need for emendations to that perspective. Our chapter examines one element that contributed to the controversy, that of Donald J. Trump's provocative and ultimately successful Twitter-based communication strategy. Twitter, a micro-blogging platform, allows users to post messages originally limited to 140 characters (now 280). Twitter users "follow" one another, which means they see their tweets in their Twitter feed on Twitter.com. Users can "retweet" others' posts to share them automatically into the feeds of their followers, or "favorite" a tweet. The platform also allows users to reply or tag other users by including an @ symbol before their username.

Trump registered with Twitter on March 18, 2009, with his first tweet on May 4, 2009, highlighting his upcoming appearance on the David Letterman show. He declared his candidacy on June 16, 2015, and quickly saw a dramatic increase in both followers and retweets. By Election Day, Trump had gathered over thirteen million followers, and used that platform to speak directly to his constituency, bypassing the traditional gatekeepers in the mainstream news media. In so doing, he was able to not only communicate directly to his supporters, but also to influence the agenda of the mainstream media and—some would argue—of the campaign for the presidency itself.

Unlike the other 2016 presidential candidates, who send quotes from press releases or hire campaign staff to craft their tweets, Trump's tweets are personal—and he writes a substantial portion of them himself. He uses his tweets as a means to provide voters with direct access to himself and often uses his tweets as personalized attacks on his opponents in real time. Several news reports and analysts have studied his accounts and noted that the tweets originate from several sources: some from an iPhone, others from an Android phone, and still others from Twitter ads and social media management platforms such as Hootsuite.[2] Through March of 2017, Trump typically used a Samsung (Android-based) phone, at which time he switched to an iPhone.[3] As a result, most analysts suggest that at least some of the content on Trump's account is managed by staffers and PR professionals who use it to speak to his base and to promote his agenda.[4] Notably, Trump's own missives are often the stuff of his in-the-moment, raw emotion. These tweets are then often retweeted by his followers, magnifying his Twitter presence exponentially.

This uncensored tweeting has been seized on by the news media since it provides fodder for news stories: raw emotions, conflict, and thoughts from a candidate without a committee filter. After the party nominating conventions and beginning in August, Trump had amassed over thirty thousand lifetime tweets to Clinton's seven thousand. Clearly, he had proficiency with this medium. He tweeted 1,453 times between July 19, 2016, the date of his nomination, and November 7, 2016, the day before the national election.[5] His tweets cover a range of material, from original content and stream of consciousness tweets, to retweeting his followers, sharing mainstream and alternative news articles (e.g., Breitbart, The Gateway Pundit), and promoting rally and campaign event information. What pulls all of this together is Trump's unique style of communication and ability to command attention.

Our analysis of these tweets proceeds in three parts. First, we examine relevant literature on Trump's use of Twitter, as well as research on the role of social media and Twitter in political campaigns. Next, we take a mixed-methods approach to analyzing Trump's Twitter output. We examine 1,453 Trump tweets spanning July 19 through November 7, 2016, and their intersection with press coverage of the campaign. Although only 12 percent of Trump's tweets directly referenced the media, these tweets had a statistically higher median number of retweets and favorites than non-media tweets. There is also a clear pattern in the volume of Trump tweets and media mentions. Subsequently, we perform a case study on the media coverage of two of Trump's key tweets, and demonstrate how the press treated Trump's digital utterances as statements in and of themselves, and wove them into traditional reporting on the events of the campaign. We conclude with an overall summary and suggestions for future research into Trump's tweets.

THE HYBRID MEDIA CAMPAIGN

One way of understanding Trump's use of Twitter to both respond to and drive media coverage of his campaign is through what Andrew Chadwick terms the hybrid media system.[6] He defines this system as one in which people "create, tap, or steer information flows in ways that suit their goals and in ways that modify, enable, or disable others' agency, across and between a range of older and newer media settings."[7] This system blurs the distinctions between "old" and "new" media, and emphasizes the interactions of communicators, audiences, and technologies. A political campaign that leverages these methods can thus be considered a hybrid media campaign.[8] Trump's simultaneous use of traditional and digital communication tools to drive the election news cycle makes his 2016 effort an example of such a campaign. In particular, Trump simultaneously engaged in traditional public relations tactics while also generating his own unique style of Twitter content that garnered the attention of both his supporters and the media.

This hybrid media framework has been applied by several scholars to explain the relationship between Trump and the press. Regina Lawrence and Amber Boydstun argue that it was Trump's entertainment value and ability to interest reporters that drove early coverage of his primary campaign when he was trailing in the polls.[9] Trump took advantage of the media's tendency to cover candidates who make controversial statements, thus ensuring him a place in the headlines. Others argue that it was specifically Trump's use of Twitter that enabled him to garner so much media coverage. For example, through a time-lagged analysis of Trump's tweets, Chris Wells and co-authors determined that supporters' retweets tended to attract media attention, and were a statistically significant predictor of news coverage.[10] Thus, Trump was able to use his own direct digital communication to shape narratives in the traditional press.

The relationship between Trump-as-candidate and the media remains complex. Julia Azari argues that the media, in performing its traditional role of spreading candidates' messages to the public, helped Trump during the nomination process by disseminating his message to Republican primary voters.[11] Given Trump's predilection for referring to mainstream journalism as "fake news," Juliane Lischka analyzed the *New York Times*'s response to these charges, which she suggests are considered a "badge of honor" within the industry.[12] She found that the *Times* attempted to delegitimize Trump's accusations of "fake news" through the use of moral evaluation, in which they suggest the claims undermine the role of journalism and damage trust in the news, which in turn harm our democratic society. Ultimately, as Lawrence and Boydstun state, more work is needed to understand the tenor and content of news coverage about Trump, as well as its role in reinforcing his supporters' attitudes regarding media bias.

TWITTER AS AN AGENDA-BUILDING MEDIUM

Much of the analysis of the interplay between candidates and the news media on Twitter has focused on the concepts of agenda-setting and agenda-building. At its simplest, the agenda-setting theory explains how the media decides what issues of the day to make salient to the public through what it covers and how much coverage is given; conversely, agenda-building theory concerns itself with the interplay between those covered by the news, and those that produce it.[13] Media agenda-building in particular focuses on efforts to influence media professionals, such as strategic communication campaigns, in an effort to raise the salience of an issue with the media itself. In this manner, Twitter can be used by candidates and campaigns as a public relations tool to shape news coverage, promote issues, and create impressions of support. Pamela Shoemaker and Stephen D. Reese describe such sources as extramedia influences on media content; in the case of campaign Twitter feeds, they can serve as an official source or statement from the candidate and thus make for content on which they can report.[14]

As such, analysis of Twitter as an agenda-building medium focuses on the campaign's efforts to shape issue coverage by the traditional media. Daniel Kreiss interviewed 2012 Obama and Romney campaign workers about how they used Twitter as a strategic communication tool, and ascertained that staff attempted to use the platform for agenda-building.[15] Both campaigns also tried to create favorable opinions of their candidates in response to journalists' use of the platform to gauge public sentiment. An analysis of tweets by 2016 presidential candidates found that candidate tweets predicted newspaper coverage on the economy, employment, foreign policy, and taxes, whereas newspaper coverage predicted candidate tweets on education, employment, health care, immigration, and national security.[16] A similar analysis of 2012 presidential primary tweets found that candidate and party tweets predicted newspaper coverage on six major issues; simultaneously, newspaper coverage also generally preceded candidates' Twitter discussion of those issues in the following days.[17] As such, candidates' use of Twitter in this context stands in contrast to social media as a whole: Jacob Groshek and Megan Clough Groshek found that trending topics on Twitter tend to follow traditional media, rather than drive the agenda of mainstream news coverage.[18]

WHAT TRUMP TWEETS

Both the press and academic scholars have examined the content of and strategy behind Trump's tweets. A comparative analysis of tweets from Trump and Clinton found that while Clinton's stream followed professional campaign norms, Trump's style was "amateurish yet authentic" and represents a new trend in political communication in which "professionalisation is challenged by amateurism."[19] Another comparison of Trump and Clinton's respective tweets finds that Trump was more likely to actively retweet his supporters' comments, and more prone to uncivil language.[20] In this manner, Trump's tweets find strategic accord with the medium itself: Brian L. Ott argues that Twitter privileges content that is simple, impulsive, and uncivil—and that Trump's digital output on the platform is characterized by all three of these attributes.[21]

The contents of Trump's tweets are generally described as self-focused, negative, and more uncivil than other candidates. Trump often uses negativity in his tweets to highlight a lack of strength in his opponent or to attack their character.[22] Sara Ahmadian, Sara Azarshahi, and Delroy L. Paulhus use text analysis software to evaluate Republican candidates' speeches and tweets and find Trump to score highest in terms of grandiose language, first-person pronouns, and informal communication styles.[23] Another analysis of all seventeen Republican candidates' Twitter feeds finds that Trump both sends and receives the most negative tweets, and is most likely to attack his opponents on the platform.[24] Using the Twitter platform as a way to distinguish between tweets by Trump himself and those posted by his staff, Brooke Auxier and Jennifer Golbeck argue that the president's tweets tend to be focused on himself or other individuals, and are more negative, angry, and anxious than those posted by staffers.[25] That said, Trump's Twitter feed also remained relatively on message throughout the campaign: Sam Petulla looked at over six thousand tweets from Trump and found that as a candidate he spent a great deal of his time focusing on his campaign theme of Make America Great Again.[26]

In this manner, Trump's use of Twitter to amplify his supporters and share uncivil discourse contrasts with the informal, yet professional, norms that shape how the medium is employed by campaigns. Most candidates use Twitter as a broadcast medium rather than engage in deliberation.[27] This is often due to the preponderance of harassment, trolling, and incivility in replies to tweets by candidates and elected officials.[28] Along these same lines, Daniel Kriess stated that due to internal approval processes, the 2012 Romney Twitter feed was often used to amplify press releases and other strategic communications.[29] Additionally, candidates and parties primarily use Twitter to promote their campaign activities and link to their websites; soliciting donations and engaging in policy discussions occur much less frequently.[30]

What remains largely under-analyzed is the interplay between Trump and the media on Twitter, something we address in our case studies below. As noted above, Wells et al. have argued that Trump used Twitter in an effort to seize control of the media cycle, since reporters would often cover his tweets that garnered the most attention from his followers. Ironically, at the time, Trump's campaign was caricatured in the press "as consisting of little more than large rallies, a Twitter account, and the free media that both engendered."[31] However, this impression ignores the impact of his followers. According to Persily, "The power of Trump's social-media account owed as much to its prominence in legacy media as it did to its propensity to 'go viral' online. Whether online, offline, in print, or on the air, Trump set the news agenda. Thanks in part to his followers' habit of retweeting him, his tweets dominated discussion of the election in every forum."[32] Furthermore, Trump's tweets were retweeted more often than Clinton's, and roughly 20 percent of his tweets were retweets of his supporters (although it remains unknown how many of these were automated, or "bot" accounts). Additionally, roughly half of the tweets contained links to news media, suggesting that as he was criticizing some reporting as "fake news," he was also driving traffic to coverage he found worthy of sharing.

The need for more analysis of Trump's use of Twitter in the 2016 campaign cycle and its function as a strategic communication tool motivates our own inquiry. We seek to discover what made Trump's tweets distinct during a tightly contested presidential race, and in particular, how his tweets engaged with mainstream news media coverage of the campaign. In conducting our study we considered the following research questions:

1. Which of Trump's tweets received the most "favorites"?
2. Which of Trump's tweets were most often retweeted?
3. Of all the tweets during the last six months of the election, how many tweets mentioned the media?
4. Did the tweets that mention the media differ in terms of favorites and retweets from those tweets that did not mention the media?
5. How did Trump's tweets influence media election coverage?

DONALD J. TRUMP'S CAMPAIGN TWEETS

The Trump Twitter Archive (www.trumptwitterarchive.com) has a database of Donald Trump's tweets that date as far back as 2009 when Trump joined Twitter. According to the website, out of the thirty-six thousand tweets Trump has made, the archive is nearly complete, containing all but four thousand of Trump's tweets. The archive is updated daily and is accessible to the public for download. Individuals who download the data set are provided with a link to the original tweets, the time and date of the tweet, and the number of individuals who favorited and retweeted the tweet.

Our sample begins on July 19, 2016, the day Donald Trump became the official nominee for the Republican Party, and runs through November 7, 2016, the day before the election. The total tweets in the dataset represent Donald Trump's activities on Twitter during these last six months of the election cycle. In that time, Trump tweeted 1,453 times.

Tweets for this analysis were collected from the Trump Twitter Archive on October 23, 2017, and downloaded to a CSV file, which was then imported to the SPSS statistical software program for analysis. In order to prepare the data, we first read through each of the tweets in the data set and identified any tweets that mentioned the media. These tweets consisted of generic references to "the media" (e.g. "The media and the establishment"), specific references to networks or newspapers (e.g. CNN or the *New York Times*), or references to media personalities (e.g. Sean Hannity). We considered the research questions posed above.

Trump's Most Retweeted and Favorited Tweets

The first research question looked at which tweets by Donald Trump received the most favorites. Table 4.1 shows the top five tweets ranked by the number of favorites each had received. Although three statements reference important events in the campaign (e.g. his nomination, his V.P.'s debate performance), two tweets involve important media events. Trump's most favorited tweet during the campaign was a response to accusations that Melania Trump had plagiarized part of her speech at the Republican National Convention from a speech given by Michelle Obama. In his tweet, Trump contrasted the media's coverage of Melania's speech to their coverage of Hillary Clinton's email scandal. The tweet seemed designed to portray a media that was fixated on trivial issues while simultaneously ignoring issues of substance. Trump's third tweet also referenced an important media event. In this instance, Trump simply provided a link to a video response containing his statement about a story that had appeared in the *Washington Post*. The story had made national attention and detailed an event in 2005 where Trump had a private conversation with Billy Bush from *Access Hollywood* while waiting for Trump to appear on the show. In the original video, Trump was caught on tape claiming to brag about committing sexual assault. In his tweet, he apologized for his comments and attempted to refocus the attention to his core issues (i.e. the economy, job growth, etc.), calling the video a distraction from these issues.

A second research question looked at the tweets which had received the highest number of retweets from other people on Twitter (table 4.2). In this instance, many of the tweets that were retweeted were similar to those that

Table 4.1. Top 5 Tweets, by Favorites Received

Date	Tweet	Total
7/20/2016	The media is spending more time doing a forensic analysis of Melania's speech than the FBI spent on Hillary's emails.	249249
7/19/2016	Such a great honor to be the Republican Nominee for President of the United States. I will work hard and never let you down! AMERICA FIRST!	129652
10/8/2016	Here is my statement. https://t.co/WAZiGoQqMQ	120244
10/5/2016	Mike Pence won big. We should all be proud of Mike!	120189
11/5/2016	MAKE AMERICA GREAT AGAIN!	115387

received high "favorite" ratings. The tweet with the highest number of retweets (120,661) was also the tweet that referenced the media's coverage of Melania Trump's plagiarism charges. In addition, Trump's video statement after the *Washington Post* released his conversation with Billy Bush was also heavily retweeted. Other tweets that received high numbers included references to campaign activities such as his slogan, his acceptance of the Republican nomination, and his choice of Mike Pence as a running mate.

We also explored how Trump dealt with the media on Twitter over the last six months of his campaign. Research question three looked at the frequency with which Trump tweeted about the media. Our results did show that surprisingly, references to the media were not as common in his tweets as references to other issues in the campaign. Specifically, of the 1,453 tweets made, 175 (12 percent) made reference to the media.

Engagement with Trump's Tweets about the Media

The fourth research question was interested in knowing if tweets that referenced media were favorited and retweeted more or less than other statements made by Trump. A Shapiro-Wilk test indicated that there were significant differences in the distributions of retweets and favorites, such that the assumption of normality was not met. As a result, in order to compare differences in the number of favorited tweets a non-parametric Mann-Whitney U test was used for our analysis. The results showed significant differences between tweets that mentioned the media and tweets that did not in terms of the numbers of "favorites" they received. Specifically, tweets that mentioned the media had significantly higher numbers (median = 29,378; mean rank = 873.4) of favorites than those that did not mention the media (median = 22,251; mean rank = 706.4), U = 86027.50 (Z = -4.94), $p < .001$.

Table 4.2. Top 5 Trump Tweets, by Retweets

Date	Tweet	Total
7/20/2016	The media is spending more time doing a forensic analysis of Melania's speech than the FBI spent on Hillary's emails.	120661
11/5/2016	MAKE AMERICA GREAT AGAIN!	59098
10/8/2016	Here is my statement. https://t.co/WAZiGoQqMQ	51891
7/19/2016	Such a great honor to be the Republican Nominee for President of the United States. I will work hard and never let you down! AMERICA FIRST!	41616
10/10/2016	RT @mike_pence: Congrats to my running mate @realDonaldTrump on a big debate win! Proud to stand with you as we #MAGA.	41496

A similar analysis was conducted to explore whether there were differences in the number of retweets that mentioned the media and those that did not. A Shapiro-Wilk's test of normality again indicated that there were significant differences in the distributions of the number of media and non-media retweets, so again a Mann-Whitney U test was used to analyze whether there were also difference between tweets that mentioned the media and tweets that did not in terms of the number of retweets. Similar to the previous findings, tweets about the media (median = 10,170; mean rank = 793.6) were also more likely to be retweeted than non-media tweets (median = 8,542; mean rank = 717.9), U = 100,170.00 (Z = -2.24), $p < .05$.

Trump Tweets and Media Coverage

Finally, our analysis considers the relationship between Trump's tweets and the amount of coverage he received on a given day in the news. Although the data here is merely exploratory, it examined whether increased activity on Trump's Twitter account resulted in more media attention. In order to answer this question, we used data from Google Trends. Google Trends allows users to search Google News feeds for the total number of mentions of a given set of keywords. In this case, we searched across the same time period mentioned above (July 19, 2016, to November 7, 2016) for any mentions of "Donald Trump" and "Twitter" in the news coverage. Figure 4.1 shows the total number of tweets by Donald Trump on each day with the total number of media mentions found in Google news on that same day. Results show a significant positive association between Trump's activity on Twitter and the mentions he received in the news, $r = .25$ $p < .01$ $N = 112$. Further implications of these findings are discussed in the conclusion.

CASE STUDIES: TWO OF TRUMP'S TWEETS

In this section, we take a closer look at the interaction between Trump's tweets and the mainstream news media. To do this, we examine in detail two popular tweets. The first tweet concerns Melania Trump's RNC convention speech, which was Trump's most favorited and retweeted tweet in our sample, and the top tweet with a media mention in terms of retweets and favorites. The second tweet concerns the fallout from Trump's *Access Hollywood* tape, which was Trump's eighth most retweeted and seventh-most favorited, as well as the second-most retweeted and favorited media tweet. We examine the news coverage given to the tweets in the *New York Times*, the *Washington Post*, *ABC News*, *CBS News*, *NBC News*, *CNN*, and *Fox News*.[33]

Melania Trump RNC Convention Speech Plagiarism

On the first night of the 2016 Republican National Convention, July 18, Melania Trump gave a speech which many immediately saw as containing two passages strikingly similar to that in a speech delivered by Michelle Obama on the first night of the 2008 Democrat National Convention. The Trump campaign initially denied that any part of the speech was "cribbed" or "plagiarized." The incident quickly became a topic of focus for the mainstream news media, with outlets devoting focused attention to it throughout the following day. It was soon demonstrated that several fragments of the

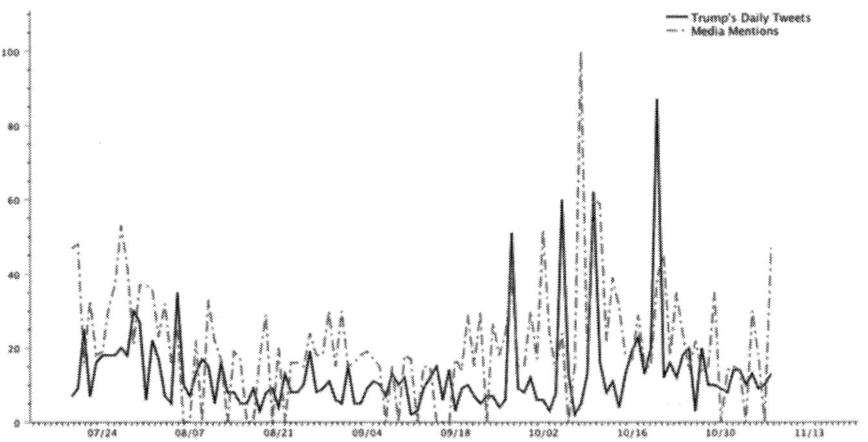

Figure 4.1. Timeline of Trump's Total Numbers Tweets and Total References to Trump in the News

speech bore a remarkable similarity to that of Michelle Obama's speech. For example, this passage from the speeches:

> Melania Trump:
> From a young age, my parents impressed on me the values that you work hard for what you want in life, that your word is your bond and you do what you say and keep your promise, that you treat people with respect. They taught and showed me values and morals in their daily life.[34]
>
> Michelle Obama:
> And Barack and I were raised with so many of the same values: like, you work hard for what you want in life, that your word is your bond, that you do what you say you're going to do, that you treat people with dignity and respect, even if you don't know them and even if you don't agree with them.[35]

The partial explanations from the campaign about the real similarities only kept the minor controversy alive, prolonging and increasing press scrutiny. For instance, campaign manager Paul Manafort stated Tuesday on CNN's *New Day*: "The speech was very effective and communicated those feelings. . . . The controversy you're talking about is not meaningful at all. She's not a candidate for office. She was expressing her personal feelings about her country and her husband and why he's best for the United States."[36] The next day Manafort admitted that Melania Trump's speech used "similar words" to Obama's and said, "I'm not lying about anything."[37] "The Republican National Committee also boosted the Trump campaign's defense, with its communications director Sean Spicer slapping down plagiarism charges by pointing to similar words and themes in everything from John Legend songs to 'My Little Pony.'"[38]

The convention and its orchestrated message was becoming tangled in the press obsession with Melania's speech and the Trump campaign's inability to present a satisfactory explanation. It was into this swirling press coverage that Trump tweeted:

> The media is spending more time doing a forensic analysis of Melania's speech than the FBI spent on Hillary's emails.[39]

According to *CNN*, "Donald Trump . . . pressed forward with the strategy of attacking the media as late as an hour before the campaign statement Wednesday. "The media is spending more time doing a forensic analysis of Melania's speech than the FBI spent on Hillary's emails," Trump said in a tweet.[40] Within a few hours this tweet was followed by the official campaign statement mentioned above:

> Longtime Trump organization staffer, Meredith McIver, said in a statement released by the campaign that she unintentionally included the passages after

> conversations with Melania about other speeches she admired. The aide offered to resign, a gesture candidate Trump rejected.[41]

By the next day the issue of the "borrowed" lines was generally forgotten as the press focused on Donald Trump's nomination acceptance speech and other aspects of the campaign, which likely had more to do with the forthright nature of McIver's admission and the focus on Donald Trump's speech than Trump's tweet.

Of note is that media coverage of Trump's tweet appears in a number of different contexts: opinion pieces, talk shows, and hard news stories. In general, two observations can be made in terms of how the press used Trump's tweet. First, the tweet was used as part of the controversy surrounding Melania's speech, which was a "lingering drama,"[42] that could "overshadow"[43] the day's events, and from which "fallout" could "upstage" speeches scheduled for Wednesday night.[44] It was also mentioned as part of the story involving Senator Ted Cruz's refusal to endorse Trump. Second, it was used as part of a conversational interaction between the press and other sources in describing the events of the convention. In short, "Trump himself addressed the controversy on Twitter, though he did not weigh in on allegations that his wife had borrowed language from the first lady's speech."[45]

Although a few press outlets seemed to accuse Trump of keeping the controversy alive,[46] in our opinion the tweet was used more as a statement from the presumptive presidential nominee to attack the media and Clinton than it was an attempt to keep the controversy alive. Its sticking power had more to do with Trump's ability to deflect and attack rather than any intentional timing. In terms of timing, it came just hours before the campaign released McIver's admission, which effectively ended the controversy, although coverage of her statement, and Trump's tweet, lingered into the next day, after which the press no longer covered this Trump tweet. The *Washington Post* provides a good example of how Trump's tweets are included as part of the conversation, writing of Cruz's refusal to endorse Trump:

> But the same speech will also offer Trump a prime chance to return to that old primary fight, and bash Cruz before an unprecedented audience. In the past, he has struggled to overcome that temptation. That continued Thursday. "Other than a small group of people who have suffered massive and embarrassing losses, the party is VERY united. Great love in the arena!" Trump tweeted Thursday morning. On the same day, Cruz defended his decision not to honor a pledge he made last year to honor the eventual nominee, whomever it may be. "The day that was abrogated was the day this became personal," he said.
>
> But there was also the lingering drama from the Monday address by Trump's wife, Melania, which included portions lifted from the speech Michelle Obama gave at the 2008 Democratic National Convention. In a statement . . . a staff member took responsibility for the insertion of the material and apologized. Shortly before the campaign distributed McIver's statement,

> Trump addressed the controversy via Twitter. . . . Multiple commentators and Trump opponents have said the duplication of the phrases amounts to plagiarism. "Good news is Melania's speech got more publicity than any in the history of politics especially if you believe that all press is good press!" he wrote in one message. And he attempted to shift blame to Clinton, writing, "The media is spending more time doing a forensic analysis of Melania's speech than the FBI spent on Hillary's emails."[47]

Other outlets followed this same conversational/source style, but the tweet is used more as part of the timeline. For instance, on *CNN*, Wolf Blitzer stated:

> The dam finally broke, and we got a fuller explanation as to how those portions from Michelle Obama's 2008 speech made her—their way into Melania Trump's 2016 speech, and it was a painful process. Even this morning on CNN's "NEW DAY," Chris Cuomo trying mightily to get campaign chairman Paul Manafort to fess up and explain what happened. Manafort was still insisting that no plagiarism had occurred and that only similar words were used from Michelle Obama's speech. And then Donald Trump put out this tweet at 11:30 this morning . . . "The media spends more time doing a forensic analysis of Melania's speech than the FBI spent on Hillary's emails." A good zinger. Perhaps should have been saved for his speech tomorrow night. But then about an hour after that, a statement came from . . . Marilyn McIver. She is a speechwriter for the Trump organization. She took responsibility for what happened.[48]

TRUMP'S *ACCESS HOLLYWOOD* TAPE

On October 7, 2016, the *Washington Post* published an article and accompanying video detailing a private 2005 conversation between Donald Trump and then *Access Hollywood* host Billy Bush having what reporter David Farenthold described as "an extremely lewd conversation about women."[49] One part of the conversation was of particular interest in later discussions about the tape: "And when you're a star, they let you do it," Trump says. "You can do anything." "Whatever you want," says another voice, apparently Bush's. "Grab them by the p—y," Trump says. "You can do anything."[50] Controversy erupted that day and continued into the second presidential debate between Trump and Hillary Clinton on October 9. Democrats and Republicans alike decried the statements, although Clinton declined to do so until the actual debate.[51]

On October 8, Republican politicians were described as being in a "growing revolt," against Trump with leaders such as John McCain quoted as saying they were withdrawing their support. "If you need any more proof of how serious the scandal is, a GOP official tells CNN there is now growing pressure for the RNC to dump Trump as the party's candidate and focus on saving Congress."[52] *CNN* also stated that, "Trump's campaign appeared to be deteriorating around him as the Republican Party descended in a state of chaos."[53] *NBC News* went further, stating that the tape had "left his campaign fighting for its life on Saturday morning."[54]

Trump told the *Washington Post* that he would never quit the race, even as the talk of Trump approving of sexual assault began to increasingly appear in news articles and stories. Trump later apologized for his comments, offering a ninety second taped apology late Saturday night in which he not only admitted to the comments and apologized but also reversed the charges, turning them to Hillary Clinton, essentially saying she enabled a man, Bill Clinton, who had "said far worse to me on the golf course":[55]

> I've never said I'm a perfect person nor pretended to be someone that I'm not. I've said and done things I regret and the words released today on this more than a decade old video are one of them. Anyone who knows me knows these words don't reflect who I am. I said it, I was wrong, and I apologize.
>
> I've said some foolish things but there's a big difference between the words and actions of other people. Bill Clinton has actually abused women and Hillary has bullied, attacked, shamed, and intimidated his victim. We will discuss this more in the coming days. See you at the debate on Sunday.[56]

The reactions, even after the apology, were coming from all quarters. Many Republicans stated they would no longer support his campaign, other Republicans called for his withdrawal from the ticket. Others denounced the comments, but did not withdraw support of his candidacy. The news media echoed accusations, and pushed speculations about his withdrawal from the race.

Melania Trump issued a statement in which she denounced the comments but forgave her husband and asked Americans to do as she did: "The words my husband used are unacceptable and offensive to me. This does not represent the man that I know. He has the heart and mind of a leader. I hope people will accept his apology, as I have, and focus on the important issues facing our nation and the world."[57]

Still, the press coverage continued, especially pushing a theme of Republican disunity and calls for Trump to quit: "'It's over'" *NBC News* quoted an anonymous Republican campaign strategist saying.[58] The "tape is threatening to decisively break Trump's support within the GOP."[59] The news controversy swirled, and leftist magazine *Mother Jones* labeled the entire exchange "Pussygate."[60]

Into this situation Trump tweeted:

> The media and establishment want me out of the race so badly—I WILL NEVER DROP OUT OF THE RACE, WILL NEVER LET MY SUPPORTERS DOWN! #MAGA[61]

Still the press relayed calls for Trump to quit the race, only once mentioning that it was establishment Republicans, and not the base that swept Trump into victory, that were calling for his removal. The press hyped the nature of these calls and the controversy: *CNN* stating that, "A campaign source this could be the death knell for Trump's presidential run."[62] *NBC News* stated, "Let's understand something: Trump is already likely to lose. The question now is how much damage will this do to the Republican Party. Already a parade of Republicans has either condemned Trump's comments, withdrawn their support completely, or called on him to step down as the nominee altogether."[63] *NBC News* stated that the Republicans are scrambling to determine a path forward for a campaign that appears to be in freefall.[64] The *Washington Post* wrote, "The Republican Party plunged into an epic and historic political crisis Saturday . . . as a growing wave of GOP lawmakers called on defiant . . . Donald Trump to drop out of the race."[65]

It was within this situation that Trump and Clinton clashed during the second presidential debate. Very early in the debate a moderator opined and asked Trump the following: "You described kissing women without consent, grabbing their genitals. That is sexual assault. You bragged that you have sexually assaulted women. Do you understand that?"[66] To which Trump replied:

> No, I didn't say that at all. I don't think you understood what was—this was locker room talk. I'm not proud of it. I apologize to my family. I apologize to the American people. Certainly I'm not proud of it. But this is locker room talk.
>
> You know, when we have a world where you have ISIS chopping off heads, where you have—and, frankly, drowning people in steel cages, where you have wars and horrible, horrible sights all over, where you have so many bad things happening, this is like medieval times. We haven't seen anything like this, the carnage all over the world.
>
> And they look and they see. Can you imagine the people that are, frankly, doing so well against us with ISIS? And they look at our country and they see what's going on.
>
> Yes, I'm very embarrassed by it. I hate it. But it's locker room talk, and it's one of those things. I will knock the hell out of ISIS. We're going to defeat ISIS. ISIS happened a number of years ago in a vacuum that was left because of bad judgment. And I will tell you, I will take care of ISIS.[67]

The story slowly faded after the second debate.

Once again we see the tweet by Trump, although so popular among his followers, and heavily used by the press, treated as part of the ongoing conversation about the situation. The tweet was inserted as if a personal response to an individual question from an individual journalist, and placed within the flow of events of a particular news story. In this manner, Trump's tweets provide an example of Chadwick's hybrid media system, in which distinctions between "old" and "new" media fall away as information flows across platforms and devices. Trump's tweets became part of the media conversation not because they were disseminated on Twitter, but because they were received as an official statement by a presidential candidate.

These case studies also shed light onto the findings of Wells and colleagues, who argue that retweets predict media coverage of Trump tweets. Here, we show that the media treated Trump's tweets as a quote, rather than as a digital artifact or technological novelty. As such, it is the content of Trump's tweets that mattered, not just the medium itself. Therefore, we suggest that the contents of Trump's tweets may also be a key factor in determining whether they make it into news coverage, in addition to the number of retweets they receive. Furthermore, the media tweets themselves have higher average engagement than tweets not pertaining to the media, which further contextualizes the findings by Wells and coauthors.

CONCLUSION

Based on our statistical analysis and close reading of news coverage surrounding two of Trump's most prominent tweets, we argue that it is not so much *how* Trump or the news media used his tweets as statements from a candidate that was unique; rather, it was how Trump broke the rules about what a candidate should or should not say, and in so doing used a deeply personal and authentic style of communication on Twitter to attract tremendous media and public attention, garnering tremendous numbers of retweets and favorites. In both case studies, the tweets were used by the press to personalize a Trump response as part of a media story. However, the press largely ignored responding tweets by supporters, thus leaving unacknowledged the many-to-many nature of the platform and Trump's unique style of retweeting their comments.

In looking at the content of Trump's tweets over the six months of his presidential campaign, we find that his tweets contain a general mix of comments directed toward the media itself and toward issues that were the focus of his campaign. We first observe that Trump's attacks on the media were a small part of his focus on Twitter. However, although Trump's tweets about the media only encompass 12 percent of his oeuvre, those tweets had a statistically higher median number of retweets and favorites. Our findings suggest that tweets about the media were thus disseminated more broadly and to a wider audience, and may have contributed to a perception that Trump tweeted extensively about and at the media. These tweets also likely garnered attention from media professionals themselves. Understanding why these tweets garnered so much attention is a subject for future inquiry. It is worth noting that Trump's confrontations with the media come at a time when public trust in the media has been steadily declining.[68] Researchers have argued that trust in journalism is necessary to link audiences with the press and that a lack of trust leads to the consumption of non-media sources and has been associated with increased partisan divides.[69] In this context, Trump's tweets targeting the media are an example of how a campaign can use existing tensions within democratic society to serve their own political ends. By undermining trust in media institutions, with or without just cause, campaigns tap into the existing public mistrust in the media, making it potentially easier for supporters to turn to other alternative, in our case, pro-Trump sources for information.

Our final research question examined the relationship between Trump's tweets and media coverage, and our findings suggest a clear positive relationship between the amount of activity on Trump's twitter account and the number of mentions he received in the media. These findings align with Wells et al., who explored a similar question but focused on Trump's twitter activity leading up to his nomination. In their research, they found that retweets of Trump's posts were a significant positive predictor of news stories and blog posts. Our results suggest a number of additional potential relationships between Trump and the media. First, they may indicate that Trump's activity on Twitter was successful in driving attention to his campaign, similar to the findings of Wells et al. Another interpretation may be that greater news coverage encourages Trump to become more active on Twitter, which was also reported in Wells and colleague's research. Although further analysis using more sophisticated modeling is merited to fully answer the question, the trend lines in figure 4.1 above does offer some insight, suggesting that higher peaks of activity by Trump are often followed by increased coverage in the media.

Our case studies also highlight the idea that Trump also uses Twitter to combat and redirect coverage in a way that serves his political interests. In both of our case studies we document how Trump takes issues in the news cycle that portray him negatively and redirects the focus in directions that works in his favor. In his tweets about Melania Trump, he refocuses attention on Hillary Clinton's emails and implies that the media is negligent in focusing on more substantive issues. When the *Access Hollywood* tapes are released, Trump reframes this as an attempt by the media to remove him from the race. This Media vs. Trump tactic seems to play well with his supporters who tweet and retweet such comments more often than other issues that Trump mentions in his campaign. Such tactics on the part of the Trump campaign, not only redirect negative coverage into a rallying cry for his base to combat media bias but also seem to delegitimize the media's neutral stance as merely a reporter of the news, making them instead complicit in attempts to undermine Trump's legitimacy as a presidential candidate. Few presidential candidates have dealt with the media in such a candid way, and perhaps this authenticity is what causes such tweets to garner so much attention.

LIMITATIONS AND NEXT STEPS

Although our preliminary analysis makes a contribution to understanding the relationship between Trump and the press on Twitter, we faced several methodological limitations in our study. First, the numbers of retweets and favorites were collected on October 23, 2017 and as such do not capture the volume of engagement at the time the tweet was made. Trump's tweets continue to circulate broadly, so it is probable that at least some of this engagement came after the time period in our study (July 19 through November 7, 2016). Additionally, Trump's twitter following of over forty-three million at the time of writing is known to contain a substantial number of automated, or "bot" accounts: according to the site TwitterAudit (www.twitteraudit.com), roughly 45 percent of his followers are fake. As such, these bots may have been programmed to amplify all or some of Trump's tweets, such as those about the media.

Further study of who (and what) are retweeting Trump's tweets is needed, to determine not only the influence of automated Twitter accounts but also whether members of the media themselves were prone to retweet Trump tweets about their industry. It stands to reason that professional journalists might be more likely to amplify Trump tweets about the media, and in so doing draw even more attention to them. In this manner, the press may have played a role in amplifying messages critical of their work, which paradoxically may have undermined public trust in the very work they do.

NOTES

1. Jefferson Graham, "Trump vs. Clinton: How the Rivals Rank on Twitter, Facebook, More," *USA Today*, August 4, 2016, https://www.usatoday.com/story/tech/news/2016/08/04/trump-clinton-social-media-twitter-facobook-youtube-snapchat/87974630/.

2. Andrew McGill, "A Bot That Can Tell When It's Really Donald Trump Who's Tweeting." *Atlantic*, March 28, 2017, https://www.theatlantic.com/politics/archive/2017/03/a-bot-that-detects-when-donald-trump-is-tweeting/521127/.

3. David Robinson, "Trump's Android and iPhone Tweets, One Year Later," https://www.r-bloggers.com/trumps-android-and-iphone-tweets-one-year-later/.

4. Ashley Feinberg, "How to Tell When Someone Else Tweets from @realDonaldTrump," *WIRED*, October 6, 2017, https://www.wired.com/story/tell-when-someone-else-tweets-from-realdonaldtrump/.

5. http://www.trumptwitterarchive.com/archive.

6. Andrew Chadwick, *The Hybrid Media System: Politics and Power* (Oxford: Oxford University Press, 2013).

7. Ibid, 4.

8. Regina G. Lawrence and Amber E. Boydstun, "What We Should Really Be Asking about Media Attention to Trump," *Political Communication* 34, no. 1 (2017): 150–153; Chris

Wells, Dhavan V. Shah, Jon C. Pevehouse, JungHwan Yang, Ayellet Pelled, Frederick Boehm, Josephine Lukito, Shreenita Ghosh, and Jessica L. Schmidt, "How Trump Drove Coverage to the Nomination: Hybrid Media Campaigning," *Political Communication* 33, no. 4 (2016): 669–676.

9. Lawrence and Boydstun, "What We Should Really Be Asking about Media Attention to Trump."

10. Wells et al., "How Trump Drove Coverage to the Nomination."

11. Julia R. Azari, "How the News Media Helped to Nominate Trump," *Political Communication* 33, no. 4 (2016): 677–680.

12. Juliane A. Lischka, "A Badge of Honor? How the New York Times Discredits President Trump's Fake News Accusations," *Journalism Studies* (2017): 1–18.

13. Roger W Cobb and Charles D. Elder, "Individual Orientations in the Study of Political Symbolism," *Social Science Quarterly* (1972): 79–90; Bryan E. Denham, "Toward Conceptual Consistency in Studies of Agenda-Building Processes: A Scholarly Review," *The Review of Communication* 10, no. 4 (2010): 306–323; Maxwell E. McCombs and Donald L. Shaw, "The Agenda-Setting Function of Mass Media," *Public Opinion Quarterly* 36, no. 2 (1972): 176–187.

14. Pamela Shoemaker and Stephen D. Reese, *Mediating the Message* (New York: Routledge, 2011).

15. Daniel Kreiss, "Seizing the Moment: The Presidential Campaigns' Use of Twitter during the 2012 Electoral Cycle," *New Media and Society* 18, no. 8 (2016): 1473–1490.

16. Bethany A. Conway-Silva, Christine R. Filer, Kate Kenski, and Eric Tsetsi, "Reassessing Twitter's Agenda-Building Power: An Analysis of Intermedia Agenda-Setting Effects during the 2016 Presidential Primary Season," *Social Science Computer Review* (2017): 1–15.

17. Bethany A. Conway, Kate Kenski, and Di Wang, "The Rise of Twitter in the Political Campaign: Searching for Intermedia Agenda-Setting Effects in the Presidential Primary," *Journal of Computer-Mediated Communication* 20, no. 4 (2015): 363–380.

18. Jacob Groshek and Megan Clough Groshek, "Agenda Trending: Reciprocity and the Predictive Capacity of Social Networking Sites in Intermedia Agenda Setting across Topics Over Time," *Media and Communication* 1, no. 1 (2013): 15.

19. Gunn Enli, "Twitter as Arena for the Authentic Outsider: Exploring the Social Media Campaigns of Trump and Clinton in the 2016 US Presidential Election," *European Journal of Communication* 32, no. 1 (2017): 50–61.

20. Jayeon Lee and Young-shin Lim, "Gendered Campaign Tweets: The Cases of Hillary Clinton and Donald Trump," *Public Relations Review* 42, no. 5 (2016): 849–855.

21. Brian L. Ott, "The Age of Twitter: Donald J. Trump and the Politics of Debasement," *Critical Studies in Media Communication* 34, no. 1 (2017): 59–68.

22. David Lazer and Oren Tsur, "I. You. Great. Trump: A Graphic Analysis of Trump's Twitter History, in Five Slides," *Politico Magazine*, June 2016, https://www.politico.com/magazine/gallery/2016/04/donald-trump-twitter-account-history-social-media-campaign-000631.

23. Sara Ahmadian, Sara Azarshahi, and Delroy L. Paulhus, "Explaining Donald Trump via Communication Style: Grandiosity, Informality, and Dynamism," *Personality and Individual Differences* 107 (2017): 49–53.

24. Just H. Gross and Kaylee T. Johnson, "Twitter Taunts and Tirades: Negative Campaigning in the Age of Trump," *PS: Political Science and Politics* 49, no. 4 (2016): 748–754.

25. Brooke Auxier and Jennifer Golbeck, "The President on Twitter: A Characterization Study of @realDonaldTrump," in *International Conference on Social Informatics*, pp. 377–390, Springer, Cham, 2017.

26. Sam Petulla, "One Year of Donald Trump's Tweets, Analyzed," *NBC News*, June 24, 2016, https://www.nbcnews.com/politics/2016-election/donald-trump-s-campaign-tweets-n593846.

27. Andreas Jungherr, "Twitter Use in Election Campaigns: A Systematic Literature Review," *Journal of Information Technology and Politics* 13, no. 1 (2016): 72–91; Yannis Theocharis, Pablo Barberá, Zoltán Fazekas, Sebastian Adrian Popa, and Olivier Parnet, "A Bad

Workman Blames His Tweets: The Consequences of Citizens' Uncivil Twitter Use when Interacting with Party Candidates," *Journal of Communication* 66, no. 6 (2016): 1007–1031.

28. Theocharis et al., "A Bad Workman Blames His Tweets."

29. Kreiss, "Seizing the Moment."

30. Jungherr, "Twitter Use in Election Campaigns."

31. Nathaniel Persily, "Can Democracy Survive the Internet?" *Journal of Democracy* 28, no. 2 (2017): 63–76, p. 64.

32. Ibid.

33. We found seventeen different news citations of Trump's Melania tweet and fifteen of his tape comments tweet. Although total news coverage of these events was considerably higher, we focus only on those reports that contained Trump's tweet.

34. "Melania Trump Speechwriter Admits 'Mistake' in Lifting Michelle Obama Lines," *Fox News* (July 20 2016), http://www.foxnews.com/politics/2016/07/20/melania-trump-speechwriter-admits-mistake-in-lifting-michelle-obama-lines.html.

35. Ibid.

36. Jeremy Diamond, "Trump Aide Offers Resignation in Melania Trump Plagiarism Incident," *CNN* (updated, 21 July 2016), http://www.cnn.com/2016/07/20/politics/trump-aide-offers-resignation-in-melania-trump-plagiarism-incident/index.html.

37. Ibid.

38. Ibid.

39. Donald J. Trump, Twitter Post, July 20, 2016.

40. Diamond, "Trump Aide Offers Resignation in Melania Trump Plagiarism Incident."

41. Jose A. DelReal, "Trump Aide, Acknowledging Plagiarized Lines in Speech, Contradicts Campaign's Initial Denials," *Washington Post* (July 20 2016), https://www.washingtonpost.com/news/post-politics/wp/2016/07/20/trump-aide-acknowledging-plagiarized-lines-in-speech-contradicts-campaigns-initial-denials/?utm_term=.af0dcd194761.

42. Karen Tumulty and Sean Sullivan, "Day 3 of Republican Convention: Pence Accepts Nomination; Sought-For Unity Falls Short," *Washington Post* (July 21 2016), https://www.washingtonpost.com/politics/day-3-of-republican-convention-pence-accepts-nomination-sought-for-unity-falls-short/2016/07/20/d592ff88–4e92–11e6-aa14-e0c1087f7583_story.html?utm_term=.01e8e65cd2a0.

43. Sean Sullivan and Isaac Stanley-Becker, "Pence, Cruz to Speak as Third Night of GOP Convention Kicks Off," *Washington Post* (20 July 2016).

44. Sean Sullivan and Isaac Stanley-Becker, "Cruz Offers Trump Congratulations—but No Endorsement—in Convention Speech," *Washington Post* (20 July 2016).

45. Sullivan and Stanley-Becker, "Cruz Offers Trump Congratulations."

46. Erik Wemple, "Trump Keeps Melania-Plagiarism Story Alive," *Washington Post*

47. David A. Fahrenthold, Philip Rucker, and Hose A. DelReal, "As Trump Prepares to Accept GOP Nomination, Party Unity Remains in Question," *Washington Post* (July 21, 2016).

48. Wolf Blitzer, et al., "Trump Makes Grand Return to Cleveland; Trump Staffer Takes Blame for Melania Speech; Eric Trump Previews Tonight's Speech; Sources: Trump Camp Reached Out to Kasich about V.P. Job; Day Three of Convention Focus on Making America First Again. Aired 5–6p ET," *CNN* (20 July 2016).

49. David A. Fahrenthold, "Trump Recorded Having Extremely Lewd Conversation about Women in 2005," *Washington Post* (October 7, 2016; updated October 8, 2016), https://www.washingtonpost.com/politics/trump-recorded-having-extremely-lewd-conversation-about-women-in-2005/2016/10/07/3b9ce776–8cb4–11e6-bf8a-3d26847eeed4_story.html.

50. Ibid.

51. Ali Vitali and Benji Sarlin, "Donald Trump Defiant as Top Republicans Flee Candidacy," *NBC News* (October 8, 2016), https://www.nbcnews.com/politics/2016-election/gop-piles-donald-trump-over-remarks-women-n662276.

52. "Trump to WSJ: Zero Chance I'll Quit; Trump Apologizes as Pressure Grows on RNC to Dump Trump; Melanie Trump Responds to Trump," *CNN* (October 8, 2016).

53. Jeremy Diamond, "Trump: 'Zero Chance I'll Quit,'" *CNN* (October 8, 2016).

54. Ali Vitali and Benjy Sarlin, "Donald Trump Defiant after Major Fallout Involving New Comments on Women," *NBC News* (October 8 2016), https://www.nbcnews.com/nightly-

news/video/donald-trump-defiant-after-major-fallout-involving-demeaning-new-comments-on-women-782026307948.

55. Aaron Blake, "Donald Trump Finally Said Something so Bad He Had to Apologize," *Washington Post* (October 8, 2016), https://www.washingtonpost.com/news/the-fix/wp/2016/10/07/donald-trump-finally-said-something-so-bad-he-had-to-apologize-kind-of.

56. Jeremy Diamond, "Trump: 'Zero Chance I'll Quit.'"

57. Ibid.

58. Vitali and Sarlin, "Donald Trump Defiant after Major Fallout Involving New Comments on Women."

59. Ibid.

60. Kevin Drum, "Pussygate Might Be the Final Straw for Donald Trump," *Mother Jones* (October 8, 2016), http://www.motherjones.com/kevin-drum/2016/10/pussygate-might-be-final-straw-donald-trump.

61. Donald J. Trump, Twitter Post, October 8, 2016.

62. Jeremy Diamond, "Trump to WSJ: Zero Chance I'll Quit; Trump Apologizes. . ."

63. Chuck Todd, "MEET THE PRESS for October 9, 2016, NBC," *NBC News* (October 9, 2016).

64. "All the Latest on the Trump Tape Fallout," *NBC News* (October 9, 2016), https://www.nbcnews.com/politics/2016-election/all-latest-trump-tape-fallout-n662461.

65. Jenna Johnson, Sean Sullivan, and Robert Costa, "GOP Consumed by Crisis as More Republicans Call on Trump to Quit Race."

66. "Transcript of Second Debate," *New York Times* (October 10, 2016). https://www.nytimes.com/2016/10/10/us/politics/transcript-second-debate.html.

67. Ibid.

68. Art Swift, "Americans' Trust in Mass Media Sinks to New Low," *Gallup.com*. Accessed November 30, 2017, http://news.gallup.com/poll/195542/americans-trust-mass-media-sinks-new-low.aspx.

69. Nikki Usher, "Re-Thinking Trust in the News," *Journalism Studies* 0, no. 0 (October 10, 2017): 1–15, DOI:10.1080/1461670X.2017.1375391.

Chapter Five

The Pundit Problem

A Look at Bias and Negativity in Cable News Coverage as the 2016 Election Came to a Close

Michael Horning

Although it seemed that a majority of the polling up until election night favored presidential candidate Hillary Clinton, many Americans were surprised when they turned on the news the next morning to discover that Donald Trump would be the forty-fifth president of the United States. In the coming weeks after the election, pundits and journalists alike would often turn the focus to themselves and ask where they had failed. *ProPublica*'s Alec MacGillis would write that there is a disconnect between national media and average Americans noting that "the media are so, so far removed from their country."[1] Meanwhile, Brian Stelter at *CNN* said, "This was a rural roar," and journalists on the coasts had a hard time hearing it.[2] Former *New York Times* executive editor Jill Abramson said, "I think there has to be more attention paid to the immense gulf between elites and the rest of the country, and that's going to be hard to report on because [mainstream news] institutions are obviously seen as pillars of what some people see as the elite."[3]

While the media continues to wrestle with this question, it is becoming increasingly obvious that journalists, pollsters, and pundits alike were not on the same page as at least half the country. One recent PEW study has suggested the lack of certain demographics that supported Trump may have been underrepresented in polling data, and that this explains why national media were so sure of his defeat. A second explanation is simply that respondents were hesitant to provide truthful responses to pollsters if they perceived that media and pollsters found their candidate socially undesirable.[4] Bolstering this idea, recent polls by the global research firm, Edelman, publisher of the annual Trust Barometer studies, have suggested that the vast majority of Trump voters expressed mistrust of the media.[5] Such levels of mistrust may have led some voters to avoid interactions with the media altogether, or created situations where citizens were less than truthful in interviews. Finally, some have suggested that journalists' reliance on pollsters and pundits caused them to become victims of their own pundit-filled filter bubbles that merely confirm their own biases.[6] For example, *Huffington Post*'s Ryan Grimm said that the media's reliance on experts such as Nate Silver was not based in fact but "merely political punditry dressed up as sophisticated mathematical modeling."[7]

The purpose of this study is to take a closer look at how the cable news media covered the 2016 election cycle with a focus on understanding what voters saw and heard as the election neared a close. Although both media accounts and researchers have suggested that this campaign was marked by a high degree of negativity that dismissed the possibility of a Trump victory, few studies have looked closely at the source of such negative coverage. The news industry today is not monolithic. It is comprised of a variety of experts including journalists and pundits who often find themselves providing commentary, analysis, and sometimes opinion. This research takes a careful look at these various news organizations and seeks to understand how each covered the election. An important question to ask is whether media were fair and balanced in their coverage of Trump and Clinton, and the extent to which that media coverage was provided by journalists or other media pundits who may have expressed favoritism toward one candidate or another. Finally, the study considers the tone of coverage and whether viewers saw overwhelmingly negative coverage of the candidates.

FAIRNESS AND BALANCE IN NEWS COVERAGE

It has been relatively common in recent elections for both campaign operatives and citizens to argue that the media have their own biases when it comes to election coverage. These claims were no different in the 2016 election cycle. For instance, in October 2016, the news site Politico released a poll that found that a majority of voters believed the media was biased against Trump.[8] A more recent poll by Rasmussen found that voters are mistrusting of polls themselves and feel that pollsters are out to stop the now elected president's agenda.[9] Donald Trump was himself one of the loudest critics during the campaign, stating once on Twitter, that "If the disgusting and corrupt media covered me honestly and didn't put false meaning into the words I say, I would be beating Hillary by 20%."[10] In some cases during the campaign Trump would find support for his concerns. As a case in point, in

October *CNN* reported that it had fired Donna Brazile as a political commentator after it was revealed that she gave debate questions to the Clinton campaign, leaving Bernie Sanders at a disadvantage. But while Trump and Trump voters may be skeptical of the media, Democrats have raised similar concerns. House minority leader Nancy Pelosi went on *CNN* shortly after the election and suggested that the press's constant coverage of Clinton's emails provided Trump with the edge he needed to win, and that they "were accomplices in the undermining of our elections."[11]

Although both political parties seem to see bias, it is more difficult to define and assess the extent to which bias is pervasive among the media. Decades ago Walter Lippmann suggested journalists have an obligation to fairly represent the truth. Being unbiased meant that a journalist would "confront the facts with a mind and with a heart that had no hidden entanglements."[12] Bill Kovach and Tom Rosenstiel have argued that being objective for a journalist should not be seen as a *product* of journalism but as a *process* for gathering facts. In their view, journalists avoid bias by demonstrating that their fact gathering process fairly and accurately represents the facts as they exist.[13] In their book *Four Theories of the Press*, Frederick Siebert, Theodore Peterson, and Wilbur Schramm have suggested that American media has practiced a "social responsibility" approach to covering news that avoids appearances of bias by providing multiple points of view on an issue. In this "marketplace of ideas" approach journalists should be fair and balanced in their coverage of individuals and controversies that arise.[14]

Studies that have looked at the question of media bias have had conflicting findings. Research by Frederick Fico and Stan Soffin that looked at how newspapers covered controversial issues found that both national and local newspapers were often biased in their use of sources and diverse points of view. Their findings showed that newspapers often provided more time in stories to one particular viewpoint.[15] This idea was also supported in the work of Jim A. Kuypers, which argues that media bias is often subtle.[16] In addition to a use of imbalanced sources, Kuypers also found that bias can be evident in how journalists select quotes that privilege a certain viewpoint, and that it can also be seen in how journalists choose to label people and news events (e.g. civil rights activists vs. advocates for leftist causes). In Kuypers's view these subtle choices collectively often reveal a media that is more sympathetic to liberal ideologies.

Research that has looked at the bias issue specifically as it relates to coverage of political campaigns has also had varied findings. Several academic studies conducted between 1960 and 1988 by Guido Stempel and John Windhauser found that newspapers provided relatively equal amounts of space and time to covering both Republican and Democratic presidential candidates, suggesting that both parties had a fair shot in expressing their views.[17] A recent study conducted by the *Washington Post* found that overall media coverage of the presidential campaign up through September of 2016 slightly favored Trump but that favoritism was small.[18] The same study also noted that while the *New York Times* coverage slightly favored Clinton it was only a moderate leaning and no more significant than *Fox News*' slight favoritism of Trump. This led the researchers to suggest that media coverage on the whole was fairly balanced but that there was some evidence to support certain media leaning one direction or another. Yet an analysis of the three major broadcast networks conducted by *The Media Research Center* found that media coverage of Trump and Clinton provided more airtime for Trump and that this coverage was overwhelmingly biased.[19]

Some researchers have reasoned that these types of conflicting findings stem from differing conceptualizations of bias. Kuypers, for example, notes that journalistic coverage can contain several types of bias.[20] As gatekeepers of information, journalists can privilege certain news over other content in the news cycle. In other instances, their coverage can focus on only two opposing viewpoints in a controversy. This tends to reduce issue complexity and often is dismissive of the numerous perspectives that surround an issue. In addition, the media often have a bias toward negative reporting. This tendency often downplays positive news events and constructs a worldview that is often depicted as much meaner than reality.[21] Dave D'Alessio and Mike Allen suggest that media can provide a coverage bias, a gatekeeping bias or a statement bias. Coverage bias, in their view, is focused on whether the media limit the amount of coverage one political party receives. Gatekeeping bias is focused more on selection of content and asks whether a news story provides favorability to one side of an issue. Statement bias is focused primarily on statements or non-verbal expressions made by journalists that convey an attitude of favoritism. In a meta-analysis of fifty-nine campaign studies that focused on bias in newspapers, magazines, and television and that spanned from 1958 to 1996, D'Alessio and Allen concluded that there were no significant observable differences in "the proportion of coverage, statement or gatekeeping bias favoring Democrats or Republicans."[22] The authors qualify this by noting that while several news organizations may lean left or right, the leanings of one group are offset by others, indicating no monolithic ideological direction. The research went further to note that analyses of television news, in particular, did indicate slight coverage bias and statement bias in favor of more liberal positions.

Given these prior findings, the current study looks at the bias question by examining three questions surrounding the bias debate. In order to address these questions, the study focused specifically on cable news coverage. While it is important to note that studies on bias have examined coverage in a variety of mediums (e.g. print, online, and television), cable news was ranked as the most helpful source for Americans in 2016 and is therefore an important way in which the public received its campaign news.[23] The first set of research questions in this study considers the amount of time cable news organizations dedicated to a particular candidate during the campaign and the degree to which network coverage expressed statements that indicated one particular point of view over another. The following research questions were explored:

RQ1: Did the networks differ in their overall amount of time spent on the campaign?

RQ2: Were the networks balanced in their coverage of the presidential candidates?

RQ3: To what extent were networks objective in their coverage of the presidential candidates?

MEDIA COVERAGE AND THE USE OF PUNDITS

In addition this study explored several questions related to the role of pundits in their coverage of the campaign. The use of pundits may impact how audiences perceive the extent to which a network is balanced and fair in its coverage of a campaign. Research suggests that the use of political pundits in news coverage has been steadily growing over the last one hundred years.[24] Although, much of what has been written about this rise of a pundit class has based this growth on qualitative observations about their increased presence, one study by David Hopmann and Jesper Strömbäck of Danish election coverage found partial support for this idea. They found that between 1994 and 2007 the growth of pundits was curvilinear with increases peaking in 2001 and then declining again in 2007.[25] While few studies have actually quantified this growth, there has been an assumption that the use of pundits became more prevalent as America moved into an industrial economy, which simultaneously saw the birth of television and radio and an increased interest in its uses for advertising and propaganda.[26]

As early as the 1920s, Walter Lippmann observed that politics was increasingly being shaped by "press agents" who sought to use the media to manufacture content. This new form of public relations in politics was a marked change in journalism from a focus on reporting about events to a greater reliance on news commentary and analysis.[27] Other researchers have suggested that pundits provide little in the way of actual useful information but instead the use of experts provide merely "spin" that support a favored candidate.[28] Such experts often come from a variety of backgrounds—academics, government agencies, or campaign operatives—and they appear in different types of political news genres (e.g., news, debates, commentary) as well as a variety of mediums (e.g., television, print, online).[29] Dan Nimmo and James Combs have argued that the use of pundits is now so common that they play a major role in opinion formation and agenda-setting to the extent that they constitute a fifth estate.[30]

The prevalence of pundits in print, television, and online has also been explained by various structural changes taking place in media. Erik Neveu has suggested that pundits are increasingly used because of the technical aspects of television.[31] Television is a fast-paced medium where news is often produced in "live" contexts. News packages are relatively short compared to other mediums such as print and therefore rely on sound bites and quick analysis over in-depth coverage. Television is also a ratings driven medium that must find ways to differentiate itself from other television content. In this context, pundits, who are often polished in both their appearance and delivery, are particularly well-suited for visual mediums. Fritz Plasser, however, suggests that changing economic shifts in newsrooms also explain the increased use of pundits.[32] Increased competition among networks, a reliance on ratings and the commercialization of media systems are primary causes. While Plasser also notes that the fast-paced, constant twenty-four hour news cycle often discourages in-depth analysis and relies on pundits to fill time slots with discussions about strategy rather than substance, he also notes that declining cuts in newsrooms have forced journalists to seek other ways to fill the news hole.

Regardless of the reasons, several scholars have been critical of the rise of punditry. Scholars have suggested that pundits create unnecessary tensions for viewers that lead to more partisan attitudes. Pundits can approach issues from a biased perspective. Their coverage and tone is increasingly combative and seeks to present views that are aligned primarily with the party line.[33] In this sense, citizens who are exposed to partisan news are less likely to experience in-depth news coverage but are also more likely to be exposed to news frames that seek to bolster a particular party platform in often highly combative and sometimes uncivil contexts. Some scholars have suggested that the rising tide of partisanship is in part due to a media system that privileges this type of uncivil, argumentative behavior over reasoned debate.[34]

Edward Herman and Noam Chomsky have argued that the increased use of pundits is problematic because their presence creates a misleading impression of balance.[35] In this view, "experts" and pundits are used by media to give the false impression of multiple viewpoints. Herman and Chomsky argue these viewpoints are in actuality carefully cultivated views that support the dominant ideologies in Anglo-American, classical liberalism. In their view, all pundits exist primarily to support existing political and market structures, thus limiting a true marketplace of ideas that might include other views (e.g., communism, socialism). In this sense, the use of pundits bolsters certain views while marginalizing those views of "dissident" voices and skews opinions in a "direction desired by the government and the 'market.'"[36]

Although much of the scholarship on pundits is from a critical perspective, some research has explored empirically the use of punditry in news programs. For example, a content analysis of cable TV, talk radio, and political blogs over a ten-week period found that "outrage discourse" was popular among these sites and even though both liberal and conservative oriented sites used similar discourse tactics, conservative media often used significantly more "outrage speech" than liberal media.[37] In an experiment conducted by Richard Forgette and Jonathan Morris that exposed subjects to high-conflict television news talk shows, the researchers found that individuals who were exposed to high-conflict shows were more likely to express distrust in political institutions (e.g., congress and the presidents) as well as lower levels of trust in the political system.[38] Still another study suggests that negative and hostile political television shows exacerbate political tensions between citizens. Diana Mutz's research found that when audiences viewed a political talk show with hosts that acted in an uncivil manner (e.g., rolling eyes, and aggressive talk), that participants were more likely to perceive those who stood in opposition to their own views as unworthy or illegitimate.[39] Taken together, these studies suggest that the use of pundits in some contexts can have disastrous consequences for a democracy. Viewers can, for instance, experience higher levels of mistrust, lower political efficacy, and more hostile attitudes toward their fellow citizens with opposing points of view. The findings suggest that citizens who consume partisan news that is hostile toward different points of view may move from mere disagreement with their political opponents to seeing their opponents as a type of tribal enemy.[40] Such ideological divides can increase hostility among fellow citizens and make it increasingly difficult for democracies that rely on consensus and compromise to function well.

Although several studies have suggested that the use of pundits in political talk shows leads to negative discourse, few studies have empirically measured how frequently pundits are used in political campaigns and the extent to which their coverage differs in tones from journalists. It is possible, in other words, that the frequent presence of pundits in campaign news coverage can lead to increased perceptions of media bias as they engage in partisan, hostile or combative coverage of the campaigns. As a result, this research considers the following:

RQ4: To what extent did journalists rely on pundits or other sources in their campaign coverage?

RQ5: What was the overall tone of that coverage and were there differences in tone for coverage of the two candidates?

Furthermore, this study considers whether pundits differed in their tone from journalists. Even as some reports have suggested that the 2016 campaign cycle was marked by a high degree of negativity, few researchers have looked more deeply at the sources of that negativity. One possibility is that both journalists and pundits were focused on negative content. Yet, prior studies have also shown that pundits often create tense, potentially negative news segments. As a result this study examines potential differences in tone between journalists and pundits as they covered the campaign. The following research question will be explored:

RQ6: Was the tone of the coverage different for journalists and pundits?

Finally, given that prior research has shown that pundits are often part of political campaigns and that many make appearances to support one candidate or another, this study expects to find that cable news segments with pundits will be more partisan in nature. Therefore the following hypothesis will be explored.

H1: Cable news segments with pundits will be less objective than news segments that contain only journalists.

METHOD

In order to answer the research questions, this study used a content analytic approach to analyze news segments of the three major cable news networks: CNN, Fox, and MSNBC. It used two sources for data collection. First, the TV News Archive is an online news site that archives local and national news broadcasts and contains closed captioning of each television program.[41] A second source, called the Television Explorer, which is part of the GDelt Project provides researchers with the ability to search the closed captioning provided by the TV News Archive for keywords.[42] While the TV News Archive has its own search capability, the Television Explorer Search Engine was used because it provided more sophisticated search features that allow one to search through the database for every mention of a key word. For example, a search across CNN during the month of November for the key words "Hillary Clinton" will return results with every single sentence that mentions Clinton during that month. These results return a nearly comprehensive set of results that include every mention of a candidate during a designated period of time. Such results can provide insights into the total amount of time (based on the number of mentions) a particular candidate was the focus of a particular news organization.

In order to collect this data set, all three networks, CNN, Fox, and MSNBC were searched during the last week of the election (November 1–8) using the keywords Hillary Clinton and Donald Trump. These searches returned links to 22,972 mentions of both Trump and Clinton during the last week of the election. This larger dataset was used to examine the total amount of coverage given to each candidate and identify potential differences in that coverage between networks. The last week of the election was chosen for analysis because it was the last opportunity for voters to learn about each political candidate. This particular election cycle was also marked by a large number of undecided voters who may have been tuned in as they made final decisions.[43]

The Television News Archive also returns hyperlinks that will allow researchers to link to specific locations in the news program and watch that content. These links provide an opportunity to analyze the context where the candidate was mentioned (e.g., mentioned by a journalist or pundit; tone of coverage). These hyperlinks take viewers to thirty-five seconds of video where each keyword is mentioned. These thirty-five second segments provided a standardized way of creating a unit of analysis that could be used for the content analysis portion of this research.

To create a subsample of the population dataset of 22,972 mentions, a random, stratified sample was used for additional analyses. In total, 1,011 news segments that were thirty-five seconds in length were analyzed for their content. A stratified sampling technique was chosen because initial analyses of the total population of mentions revealed that the three major networks differed in the proportionate number of overall mentions and in terms of their total mentions of each candidate (see below for details). As a result, the stratified sampling method was chosen to construct a sample population that had similar proportions to the larger population. For example, CNN was responsible for 43.6 percent of the 22,972 mentions of each Trump and Clinton. As a result, a similar percentage of the hyperlinks were randomly selected from the CNN list of mentions to construct a sample population that was proportionately similar to the larger population of new segments.

OPERATIONALIZATION AND RELIABILITY OF MEASURES

In order to analyze the content of the 1,011 news segments, a codebook was first constructed that provided definitions for each variable of interest. Initially, ten news segments were coded at the start of the analysis for initial refining of the codebook. In cases where confusion arose between coders, the codebook was revised to establish clearer standards for analysis. The following items were included in the analysis:

Which Cable News Network

Each segmented was coded for its network of origin—CNN, Fox, or MSNBC. Networks were clearly designated within the URL of each segment making this section of the coding matter of simply recording the network (e.g., www.archives.org/details/FOX . . .).

Type of Media Personality

After watching a news segment, coders identified each person in the segment (i.e., present/not present) and classified that individual as a journalist, a pundit, or a citizen. Each of these received a mark of present or not present. A journalist was defined as a person acting as the host of the news segment, a news anchor, or a reporter in the field covering an event. A pundit was defined as any type of guest appearing on the news segment who was acting in a professional capacity and providing facts, opinion, or analysis about the news topic. These could include individuals such as campaign operatives, politicians (other than those running for office), academics, or others offering professional insights into the campaign. These varying definitions of pundit have been applied by other researchers in this area.[44] A citizen was defined as an everyday person who was interviewed about the campaign. These often took the form of "person-on-the-street" interviews where journalists asked members of the public about their reactions to the events around the campaign. The data from this analysis was used to create four separate contexts for coverage which are explained further in the results section.

Candidates Covered

It was possible that within any given thirty-five second news segment, both candidates could also be mentioned in the coverage. As a result, each segment was also coded for each of the candidates covered. Three categories of Trump, Clinton, and Other (e.g., Gary Johnson) were identified as being present or not present. This data was used to identify and construct three types of news segments: those that included coverage of only Trump, only Clinton, or both Trump and Clinton.

Tone of Coverage

Each news segment was coded for the presence of negative, positive, and objective statements made about the candidates. Negative comments were operationalized as statements made about the candidates that were non-factual, opinion-based statements that expressed disparaging or condescending statements about a candidate (e.g., "Trump is just a horrible person," "Clinton is a disgrace to this country"). Coders were also told to distinguish between purely negative statements that expressed an opinion and statements that might reflect poorly on a candidate but that were factually based. For example, if a reporter mentioned that Hillary Clinton was under FBI investigation or if coverage focused on Trump's sexually explicit conversation with Billy Bush, coders were instructed to consider this as a fact-based statement. In other words, statements that could potentially paint a candidate in a negative light but that were about factual events were not included in the negativity measure. Instead, this measure focused purely on expressions of opinion stated by individuals in the segment that had no basis in fact. Positive statements were coded similarly in the sense that these were statements of opinion designed to express affirming statements about a candidate that were not based in fact (e.g., "Hillary Clinton is one of the finest candidates we've ever seen"). Finally, objectivity was defined as reporting that focused primarily on fact-based information about the campaign (e.g., "Clinton is ahead in the polls," "Trump gave a speech in Iowa that called for a stronger military").

Reliability Assessment

In order to establish the reliability of the items of interest two coders each analyzed 150 randomly selected news segments. This represents approximately 15 percent of the total sample, which is within the acceptable number of items necessary to establish reliability of the codebook.[45] Table 5.1 contains the specific results of the reliability analysis. Overall the average reliability was .77 using both Scott's Pi and Cohen's Kappa standards. However, one item (positive tone) was removed from the analysis due to a failure to reach acceptable minimum levels in standard practices.[46]

RESULTS

The first three research questions were designed to probe the degree to which cable news networks were balanced in their coverage of the candidates. The first research question looked at general trends in coverage and asked whether the networks differed in their overall coverage of the 2016 election. A one-sample chi-square test of each network's total mentions showed significant differences in proportions (see table 5.2), $\chi^2(2, N=22,972) = 1098.29$, $p < .001$. Specifically, CNN spent significantly more time (43.6 percent) on their

Table 5.1. Intercoder Reliability Scores

	% Agreement	Scott's Pi	Cohen's Kappa
Type of Media Personality			
Pundits	94.6 %	0.89	0.89
Journalists	98.0 %	0.85	0.85
Citizens	99.3 %	0.92	0.92
Tone of Coverage			
Negative	90.6 %	0.79	0.79
Positive	87.2 %	0.52	0.52
Objective	87.2 %	0.68	0.68

network discussing the candidates than both Fox (28.3 percent) and MSNBC (28.1 percent) did.

A second research question was designed to assess the balance of coverage on the networks and asked whether the cable networks spent similar amounts of time covering both Trump and Clinton. In order to answer this question, first a one-sample chi-square test of coverage of each of the candidates was employed to compare general trends in coverage of each candidate. The results showed significant differences, $\chi^2(1, N=22,972) = 177.27, p < .001$ in the total amount of coverage each candidate received. Specifically, Clinton received significantly fewer overall mentions (45.6 percent) than Trump (54.4 percent) indicating that overall coverage favored Trump in terms of the amount of coverage he received. To probe this question further, a 2x3 analysis of network by candidate was used to look at differences in coverage within each network. The results (see table 5.3) showed that compared to the other networks, Fox had slightly fewer mentions of Trump and more mentions of Clinton. CNN had the opposite with significantly more mentions of Trump and fewer mentions of Clinton than were expected. MSNBC's coverage of both Trump and Clinton did not significantly differ from what was expected, $\chi^2(2, N=22,972) = 94.37, V^* = .20, p < .001$.

The third research question focused on the degree to which networks demonstrated objectivity in their coverage. Overall the vast majority (84.9 percent) of the segments were coded as objective in their reporting. Further analysis of the networks did show some significant differences. Specifically, CNN (88.3 percent) practiced significantly more objectivity in its reporting in comparison to MSNBC (79.9 percent) with Fox news falling between the two networks (83.6 percent), $\chi^2(2, N=1,011) = 9.59, p < .01$.

The remaining research questions focused on the use of pundits themselves in campaign coverage. These questions were designed to probe the degree that pundits were used and whether their presence changed the dynamics of the coverage in term of its objectivity or negativity. The fourth research question looked first at whether journalists were primarily doing the reporting or whether they were also including others in their news segments such as pundits or citizens. In order to answer this question, the data included measures of the types of individuals in the segment (e.g., journalist, pundit,

Table 5.2. Percentage of total mentions for each candidate

Network		
FOX	MSNBC	CNN
28.3 $\%_a$	28.1 $\%_a$	43.6 $\%_b$

Note: Percentages with no subscript in common differ at P < .05 using Holm's sequential Bonferroni post hoc comparisons. $\chi^2(2, N=22,972) = 1098.29, p < .001$.

Table 5.3. Network coverage for each candidate

	Clinton	Trump	Total
FOX	31.1% $_a$	25.9% $_b$	28.3%
MSNBC	28.2% $_a$	28.0% $_a$	28.1%
CNN	40.7% $_a$	46.1% $_b$	43.6%
Total	100.0%	100.0%	100.0%

Note: Each subscript letter denotes a subset of Candidate categories whose column proportions do not differ significantly from each other at the .05 level using Bonferroni corrections.

citizen). In a few instances, the segment only included video footage from some other speaker such as b-roll footage of the candidate speaking at a campaign event. These individuals were placed in the category of "other." Each of these variables was used to create a new variable with the following categories: journalist only, journalist and pundit, journalist and citizen, and other. For example, if a segment was coded as having both a journalist and a pundit present in the segment, this received a code of journalist and pundit.

A single-sample chi-square test was conducted on these four categories to determine whether there were differences in the types of individuals used in each segment. The results of this test showed that the most significant differences were between the "Journalist Only" category and the "Journalist and Citizen" and "Other" categories. In addition, there were significant differences between the three categories of "Journalist and Pundit," "Journalist and Citizen," and the "Other" categories (see table 5.4). In other words, the news segments showed that roughly equal amounts of news time were spent between journalists only (45.6 percent) and journalists and pundits in their segment (47.5 percent), while journalists included citizens far less often (4.2 percent) than the other groups.

The fifth research question looked at the overall tone of coverage and whether it differed for Trump or Clinton. The majority of news segments coded were not negative (71.9 percent). Furthermore, a 2x2 chi-square was employed of candidate (Trump or Clinton) by negativity (present vs. not present) to look at whether the negative coverage was more directed toward Trump or Clinton. Results showed no significant differences in terms of negative coverage between the two candidates, $\chi^2(2, N=1{,}009) = 4.22$, $p = .12$. In other words, among the negative coverage that existed, it was relatively equally distributed among both candidates.

While research question 5 looked specifically at whether the tone of the coverage was negative and if that tone was more negative for Trump or Clinton, the last research question asked whether that negative coverage might be due to the presence of journalists, pundits, or other media personal-

Table 5.4. Percentages of each type appearing in a news segment

Media Personality			
Journalist Only	Journalist and Pundit	Journalist and Citizen	Other
$45.6\%_a$	$47.5\%_a$	$4.2\%_b$	$2.8\%_b$

$\chi^2(3, N{=}1011) = 751.79, p < .001$

ities. In order to answer this research question a 2x3 chi-square test was employed between media personalities (e.g. journalist only, journalist and pundit, etc.) and tone (present, not present). The results (see table 5.5) indicated that among those segments that were coded negative, those segments that contained both journalists and pundits were significantly more negative than segments that only contained journalists, $\chi^2(3, N{=}22{,}972) = 41.9$, $V^* = .20$, p < .001. The segments coded "other" were also significantly more negative than both. This finding was not surprising, given that most of these "other" segments contained partisan b-roll coverage of the candidate or other advocates working the campaign trail.

Finally, the last section of analysis explored a hypothesis. It was expected that news segments that contained pundits would be less objective than those that included journalists only. Not surprisingly 2x3 chi-square test of media personality by objectivity (table 5.6) showed that journalists remained most objective when they were reporting alone (90.9 percent) or interviewing citizens (88.1 percent), but when journalists worked with pundits, news segments took on a significantly less objective tone. While the majority of the news segments were coded as objective (82.1 percent), this number was significantly lower in contexts where journalists worked with pundits to provide analysis or commentary on the campaign, χ^2 (3, N=1,011) = 85.35, $V^* = .29$, p < .001.

CONCLUSION

This research set out to better understand how journalists and pundits covered the 2016 election as it neared its end. It first began by looking at questions of balance. Overall, the findings show that there were differences in the amount of time candidates dedicated to the campaign coverage. CNN had significantly more mentions than the other two networks, indicating that in the last week of the campaign the network spent more time covering both Trump and Clinton. A closer look at the data shows that while the network did spend more time in their coverage focused on Trump, this coverage was somewhat balanced by Fox's greater emphasis on Clinton. Furthermore, the bulk of that coverage was relatively objective with CNN having coverage

Table 5.5. Comparison of negative tone in news segments

% of Negative Tone by Media Personality					
	Journalist Only	Journalist and Pundit	Journalist and Citizen	Other	Total
Present	19.3%$_a$	34.4%$_b$	31.0%$_{abc}$	60.7%$_c$	28.1%
Not Present	80.7%$_a$	65.6%$_b$	69.0%$_{abc}$	39.3%$_c$	71.9%
Total	100%	100%	100%	100%	100%

Note: Each subscript letter denotes a subset of Candidate categories whose column proportions do not differ significantly from each other at the .05 level using Bonferroni corrections. $\chi^2(3, N{=}22{,}972) = 41.9$, $V^* = .20$, $p < .001$

that was rated as mostly objective while MSNBC was the network that seemed to practice the least objectivity.

The findings have several implications. First, we can see that cable news media didn't favor one candidate or another if you look at the networks as a whole. However, in looking at the sheer amount of coverage, CNN was by far the network that obsessed the most about the campaign. It spent a significantly greater amount of its airtime covering the campaign than the other networks, and it also spent more of that time focused on Donald Trump. In looking further at this data, we see that the majority of CNN's coverage was rated as objective and most of that coverage was not coded as negative. However, among that content coded as negative, more of (about 36 percent) that negativity was directed at Trump, while 20.6 percent was directed at Clinton.[47] Taken as a whole, we can see that the CNN network did seem to spend a great deal of time on the campaign, and in those times when the coverage turned negative it did focus more on negative coverage of the Republican candidate. We can also see similar patterns at MSNBC. Here the majority of the coverage was also coded as objective, but the content that was coded as negative tended to focus on Trump (40.8 percent) rather than Clinton (11.3 percent). However, when we compare these results to Fox news, we see that this network, while spending less time on the campaign, tended to spend more of that time on Clinton. While the majority of this coverage was also not coded as negative, when this network did focus on the negative, more of that coverage (39.1 percent) was about Clinton than Trump (16.7 percent).

If we consider the notion of balance and fairness as part of the question of whether a network is biased, we can see from this data, that during the last week of the election, audiences were exposed to content that was relatively objective in its coverage. If we also look at the three networks as a whole, we can see that Trump did receive somewhat slightly more negative coverage than Clinton from the networks on two of the three networks. This lends

Table 5.6. Media personality and objectivity

% of Objectivity by Media Personality

	Journalist Only	Journalist and Pundit	Journalist and Citizen	Other	Total
No	9.1%$_a$	17.9%$_b$	11.9%$_{ab}$	71.4%$_c$	15.1%
Yes	90.9%$_a$	82.1%$_b$	88.1%$_{ab}$	28.6%$_c$	84.9%
Total	100%	100%	100%	100%	100%

Note: Each subscript letter denotes a subset of Candidate categories whose column proportions do not differ significantly from each other at the .05 level using Bonferroni corrections. $\chi^2(3, N=1,011) = 85.35$, $V^* = .29$, $p < .001$

some support to claims by Trump surrogates that the media coverage toward Trump was more negative; however, this may be qualified by data that shows that the vast majority of the content viewers received was focused on objective reporting and that it is likely that viewers at Fox would have been more likely to be exposed to less negative coverage of Trump overall. Several scholars[48] have found in previous campaign coverage that the media on the whole were relatively balanced in their coverage; the findings here lend additional support to these claims but do provide some additional insights by suggesting that among the coverage that was negative, the negative coverage was focused more on the Republican candidate. This aligns somewhat with Kuypers's prior work which looked at several case studies of specific press coverage of political events. Kuypers concluded from his analysis that while the press does not reliably embrace liberal ideas, it also consistently rejects conservative positions.[49] These findings also align more closely with prior research conducted by Stephen Farnsworth and Robert Lichter. In an analysis of campaign coverage in the 1980s, the researchers found that negative coverage was slightly more directed toward Republicans. They concluded that "Democrats did not always get better press than Republicans, but Republican candidates never got much better press than Democrats."[50] This led the authors to conclude that claims of an ideological tilt on the part of the networks cannot be dismissed outright, but that negativity is not simply a product of an ideological bias but perhaps an artefact of newsroom culture itself that has a propensity to focus on negative news.

The last week of election coverage also does not support popular claims that media coverage collectively favored one candidate over the other. Shortly before the close of the elections Gallup reported that 52 percent of the voters thought that media favored Clinton during the campaign, while less than 8 percent thought it favored Trump. While the question is broadly stated, it stands in stark contrast to these current findings which show that an analysis of the coverage during approximately the same time period of the poll did not reflect these biases. This current research aligns with prior studies that have also found that biases in the media, while occasionally present, have been minimal.[51] Still, while most empirical research hasn't detected a strong presence of bias, the public seems to remain increasingly sure that it exists.

There are several possible explanations for why public opinion diverges from these findings. For example, publics may be responding to negative news coverage that is perceived as privileging one candidate over another. While the current study found less negativity in the reporting, it only focused on the last week of the election. Other studies that have focused on coverage earlier in the election have found that coverage to be overwhelming negative.[52] Shorenstein data, for example, found that coverage of Trump was initially positive at the start of the campaign but that it became negative as other Republican candidates dropped out. Public perceptions of campaign coverage may take into account this earlier coverage.

The second part of this study also attempted to offer some additional insights into the ways that pundits may play a role in public perceptions of news negativity and bias. Initial analyses found that news coverage relied on using pundits (47.5 percent) in their coverage slightly more than journalists alone (45.6 percent). In other words, viewers who turned on their televisions to learn about the election stood a fairly good chance of watching a TV segment that involved a pundit. Furthermore, when these segments contained pundits, they were more likely to take on a negative tone and less likely to be objective. Brian Gervais has found that viewing uncivil dialogue also leads audiences to engage in their own uncivil discourse. Diana Mutz's research is perhaps even more alarming, demonstrating that when viewers watch pundits engage in aggressive dialogue that this heightened arousal increases viewer's aggression toward the other side.[53] The fact that newsrooms seem to be increasingly reliant on pundits and that they are more likely to engage in negative types of reporting may be creating additional tensions for viewers and legitimizing uncivil discourse between citizens as dialogue spills into the workplace and on social media. Negativity has also been found to have an effect on how individuals process information messages. Prior studies have suggested that negative valenced messages increase attention to messages, and are easier for audiences to comprehend and recall.[54] In light of these prior findings, negative news coverage, even in smaller doses may be more memorable leading audiences to overestimate the degree of negativity actually found in the coverage.

This current study, along with prior findings, suggests that when networks use pundits who are both biased and negative, audiences may be more likely to ascribe their attitudes to the network itself. Such activities may undermine newsroom credibility and could be pushing away certain viewers. Research suggests that partisans in particular are averse to watching content that doesn't align with their ideological views.[55] Shanto Iyengar and Kyu Hahn, for example, found that Republicans gravitated to news that was attributed to Fox news while avoiding CNN and NPR while Democrats took the opposite position.[56] In a survey of the 2004 elections Stroud found that as Republicans and Democrats continued to watch news through the election cycle, they increasingly expressed interest in news sources that aligned with their ideological preferences. In other words, as the election neared an end, audiences selectively exposed themselves to news that was more likely to bolster their existing points of view. This behavior is not unusual among partisans and has been documented in other studies.[57] This finding is particularly concerning given research that suggests that as audiences selectively expose themselves to news, the likelihood that they adopt more extreme partisan points of view increases.[58]

In short, the use of pundits creates a context ripe for criticism particularly by partisan viewers and opens a network up to claims of bias. Their presence on news segments allows partisans to engage in a sort of confirmation bias. When the use of pundits favors one candidate over the other, such "endorsements" may be perceived by the viewing public as the news network's support for a particular candidate, particularly since negative segments are often coupled with the presence of journalists and pundits together. In best case scenarios, pundits who espouse a viewpoint that is in agreement with a partisan simply serve as echo chambers that reaffirm ideological points of view. Either way, this increased presence of pundits and their tendency toward negativity may exacerbate existing political tensions among viewers, raising questions about their usefulness in a democracy that functions often on compromise and consensus.

LIMITATIONS OF THE CURRENT STUDY

With that said, this study should be understood in light of certain limitations. For example, while the study notes the potentially negative impact of pundits, some research has found that in certain civil contexts that audiences have benefitted from pundits. These studies are still quite limited and few studies overall have fully explored the ways that pundits might make their own unique contributions to democracy. It should also be noted here that there are limitations to the data. This research only coded for the presence of negative opinions rather than negative, fact-based statements. This was done in part because it is much more difficult to ascribe a motive to negative coverage based in fact. A report, for example, that focusses on Hillary Clinton's use of a private email server may be perceived as overly hostile, negative coverage by those who supported Clinton and yet be perceived positively by those who see journalists as exposing inappropriate conduct on the part of a government official. The same coverage may be perceived as a statement of objective fact by journalists. This may explain why these findings stand in contrast to other studies that have found negative coverage in political campaigns to be steadily on the rise.[59] It is likely that other studies will find more negative coverage if negative news is defined more broadly. It should also be noted that this narrow definition of negative news doesn't take into account the appropriateness of negative fact-based coverage. For example, if a news organization continues to run negative, fact-based stories long after they have entered the news cycle, such actions may be construed as a negative bias by some audiences. Further studies would need to look more closely at such questions to fully answer questions about how newsrooms handle negative news.

It is also worth observing that these subtle differences mentioned above also point to a need for researchers to develop a clearer conceptualization of negativity. There has been a general consensus among researchers that news in general often focusses on the negative.[60] This is sometimes seen in a tendency for news to focus on topics such as crime, personal tragedy, and government corruption, so it is not surprising to see some studies find negativity to be a focus in campaigns. These findings, however, often use such data to imply a particular favoritism toward one candidate or another, when there are numerous possible motives for these types of news (e.g., journalist tendencies to focus on the negative, greater audience attention to negative news). Further studies should move beyond negative, positive, objective paradigms and seek to understand motives behind such reporting choices. This research takes a step in that direction by coding only those statements that had no clear basis in factual events but it does not fully explain why journalists choose some negative coverage over others.

Furthermore, the findings here do not suggest that pundits are the entire cause of all of the public perceptions of bias in the media, but the study does indicate perhaps a future direction for research. The data here demonstrates that pundits are at least associated with more negative biased content, and that their associations with newsrooms as "experts" may explain some of the reasons why the public sees so much bias in the media. While many journalists may see clear lines of distinction between the editorial side and the opinion side of news, publics may make no such distinction. Future studies should seek to understand whether pundits and their opinions are viewed separately from journalists as audiences view their involvement in news content.

No one study can fully capture the varied and often seemingly schizophrenic decisions made by the media as they covered both Trump and Clinton campaigns. However, this study attempts to provide some insight into why publics seem so sure that the media has their own political favorites. Part of that public perception may be self-inflicted by news networks as they reach for opportunities to cut through the proverbial noise and bring more audiences to their programs. As pundits continue to become nearly as common as journalists themselves, newsrooms may consider how their presence might undermine newsroom credibility. That is not to say that formats with pundits cannot be informative, but in their current state, they are more likely to continue to contribute to our contentious politics.

NOTES

1. Dylan Byers, "How Politicians, Pollsters and Media Missed Trump's Groundswell," CNNMoney, November 9, 2016, http://money.cnn.com/2016/11/09/media/polling-media-missed-trump/index.html.

2. Tim Franklin and Mullin Benjamin, "How the Media Missed President Trump, and What Comes Next for Journalism," *Poynter*, November 10, 2016, https://www.poynter.org/2016/how-the-media-missed-president-trump-and-what-comes-next-for-journalism/438665/.

3. Joe Pompeo et al., "What Went Wrong? Eleven Takes from Media Veterans," *Politico*, November 10, 2016, http://politi.co/2fERfJB.

4. Andrew Mercer, Claudia Deane, and Kyley McGeeney, "Why 2016 Election Polls Missed Their Mark," Pew Research Center, *Why 2016 Election Polls Missed Their Mark*, (November 9, 2016), http://www.pewresearch.org/fact-tank/2016/11/09/why-2016-election-polls-missed-their-mark/.

5. Mathew Ingram, "Most Trump Supporters Don't Trust the Media Any More," *Fortune*, accessed July 31, 2017, http://fortune.com/2017/02/01/trump-voters-media-trust/.

6. Jack Shafer and Tucker Doherty, "The Media Bubble Is Real—And Worse than You Think," *Politico Magazine*, June 2017, http://politi.co/2q0ZmYh.

7. Mark Joyella, "How Donald Trump's Win Made Pollsters, Pundits and Journos All Big Losers," *AdWeek*, November 11, 2016, http://www.adweek.com/tv-video/how-donald-trump-s-win-made-pollsters-pundits-and-journos-all-big-losers-174573/. Grimm later retracted these statements after a debate over the matter with Silver.

8. Nolan D. Mccaskill, "Poll: Majority of Voters Believe Media Biased against Trump," *Politico.com*, October 19, 2016, http://politi.co/2el8Vgf.

9. "Voters Don't Trust Polls, See Anti-Trump Bias," *Rasumssen Reports*, May 5, 2017, http://www.rasmussenreports.com/public_content/politics/general_politics/may_2017/voters_don_t_trust_polls_see_anti_trump_bias.

10. Donald J. Trump, "Trump Tweet," *Twitter.com*, August 8, 2016, https://twitter.com/realDonaldTrump/status/764803159692836864.

11. Ian Schwartz, "Pelosi: 'The Press Were Accomplices in the Undermining of Our Election,'" *RealClear Politics*, March 6, 2017, http://www.realclearpolitics.com/video/2017/03/06/pelosi_the_press_were_accomplices_in_the_undermining_of_our_election.html.

12. Walter Lippmann, "The Press and Public Opinion," *Political Science Quarterly* 46, no. 2 (1931): 2, doi:10.2307/2142743.

13. Bill Kovach and Tom Rosenstiel, *The Elements of Journalism : What Newspeople Should Know and the Public Should Expect* (New York: Three Rivers Press, 2007).

14. Fred S. Siebert, Theodore Peterson, and Wilbur Schramm, *Four Theories of the Press* (Urbana: Univ. of Ill., 1978).

15. Frederick Fico and Stan Soffin, "Fairness and Balance of Selected Newspaper Coverage of Controversial National, State, and Local Issues," *Journalism and Mass Communication Quarterly* 72, no. 3 (September 1995): 621–33, doi:10.1177/107769909507200312.

16. Jim A. Kuypers, *Press Bias and Politics: How the Media Frame Controversial Issues* (Greenwood Publishing Group, 2002).

17. Guido H. Stempel, "The Prestige Press Covers the 1960 Presidential Campaign," *Journalism Quarterly* 38, no. 2 (June 1961): 157–63, doi:10.1177/107769906103800201; Guido H. Stempel and John. W. Windhauser, "The Prestige Press Revisited: Coverage of the 1980

Presidential Campaign," *Journalism Quarterly* 61, no. 1 (March 1984): 49–55, doi:10.1177/107769908406100107; Guido H. Stempel and John W. Windhauser, "Coverage by the Prestige Press of the 1988 Presidential Campaign," *Journalism Quarterly* 66, no. 4 (December 1989): 894–919, doi:10.1177/107769908906600418.

18. John Sides, Analysis, "Is the Media Biased toward Clinton or Trump? Here Is Some Actual Hard Data," *Washington Post*, September 20, 2016, sec. Monkey Cage Analysis Analysis Interpretation of the news based on evidence, including data, as well as anticipating how events might unfold based on past events, https://www.washingtonpost.com/news/monkey-cage/wp/2016/09/20/is-the-media-biased-toward-clinton-or-trump-heres-some-actual-hard-data/.

19. Rich Noyes, "MRC Study: Documenting TV's Twelve Weeks of Trump Bashing," *NewsBusters*, October 25, 2016, https://www.newsbusters.org/blogs/nb/rich-noyes/2016/10/25/mrc-study-documenting-tvs-twelve-weeks-trump-bashing.

20. Jim A. Kuypers, "Issues of Bias in the News Media," in *Media Smackdown: Deconstructing the News and the Future of Journalism*, ed. Abraham Aamidor, Susan Wiesinger, and Jim A Kuypers (Peter Lang, 2013), 127–154.

21. George Gerbner and Larry Gross, "Living with Television: The Violence Profile," *Journal of Communication* 26, no. 2 (1976): 172–194, doi:10.1111/j.1460–2466.1976.tb01397.x.

22. Dave D'Alessio and Mike Allen, "Media Bias in Presidential Elections: A Meta-Analysis," *Journal of Communication* 50, no. 4 (December 1, 2000): 133–156, doi:10.1111/j.1460–2466.2000.tb02866.x.

23. Jeffrey Gottfried et al., "The 2016 Presidential Campaign—a News Event That's Hard to Miss," Pew Research Center's Journalism Project, February 4, 2016, http://www.journalism.org/2016/02/04/the-2016-presidential-campaign-a-news-event-thats-hard-to-miss/. Note that cable news was ranked as more helpful than other sources of news (e.g., network news, radio, national newspapers).

24. David Nicolas Hopmann and Jesper Strömbäck, "The Rise of the Media Punditocracy? Journalists and Media Pundits in Danish Election News 1994–2007," *Media, Culture and Society* 32, no. 6 (November 1, 2010): 943–960, doi:10.1177/0163443710379666; David Weaver, Maxwell McCombs, and Donald L. Shaw, "Agenda-Setting Research: Issues, Attributes, and Influences," *Handbook of Political Communication Research* 257 (2004).

25. Hopmann and Strömbäck, "The Rise of the Media Punditocracy?"

26. Dan D. Nimmo and James E. Combs, *The Political Pundits* (Westport, CT: Greenwood Publishing Group, 1992).

27. Brian McNair, *Journalism and Democracy: An Evaluation of the Political Public Sphere* (London: Routledge, 2000).

28. Hopmann and Strömbäck, "The Rise of the Media Punditocracy?"; Anders Horsbøl, "Experts in Political Communication: The Construal of Communication Expertise in Prime Time Television News," *Journal of Language and Politics* 9, no. 1 (April 2010): 29–49.

29. Horsbøl, "Experts in Political Communication: The Construal of Communication Expertise in Prime Time Television News."

30. Nimmo and Combs, *The Political Pundits*.

31. Erik Neveu, "Four Generations of Political Journalism," in *Political Journalism: New Challenges, New Practices*, ed. Raymond Kuhn, Routledge/ECPR Studies in European Political Science (London: Routledge, 2003), 22–45.

32. Fritz Plasser, "From Hard to Soft News Standards?: How Political Journalists in Different Media Systems Evaluate the Shifting Quality of News," *Harvard International Journal of Press/Politics* 10, no. 2 (April 1, 2005): 47–68, doi:10.1177/1081180X05277746.

33. Diana C. Mutz and Byron Reeves, "The New Videomalaise: Effects of Televised Incivility on Political Trust," *American Political Science Review* 99, no. 1 (February 2005): 1–15, doi:10.1017/S0003055405051452.

34. Daniel M. Shea and Morris P. Fiorina, *Can We Talk? The Rise of Rude, Nasty, Stubborn Politics*, 1st edition (New York: Pearson, 2012).

35. Edward S. Herman and Noam Chomsky, *Manufacturing Consent: The Political Economy of the Mass Media*, reprint edition (New York: Pantheon, 2002).

36. Ibid., 23.

37. Sarah Sobieraj and Jeffrey M. Berry, "From Incivility to Outrage: Political Discourse in Blogs, Talk Radio, and Cable News," *Political Communication* 28, no. 1 (February 9, 2011): 19–41, doi:10.1080/10584609.2010.542360.

38. Richard Forgette and Jonathan S. Morris, "High-Conflict Television News and Public Opinion," *Political Research Quarterly* 59, no. 3 (September 2006): 447–456, doi:10.1177/106591290605900312.

39. Diana C. Mutz, "Effects of 'In-Your-Face' Television Discourse on Perceptions of a Legitimate Opposition," *American Political Science Review* 101, no. 4 (November 2007): 621–635, doi:10.1017/S000305540707044X.

40. Jonathan Haidt, *The Righteous Mind: Why Good People Are Divided by Politics and Religion*, reprint edition (New York: Vintage, 2013).

41. See https://archive.org/details/tv.

42. See http://television.gdeltproject.org.

43. "An Unusual Number of Voters Are Still Undecided," *The Week*, November 5, 2016, http://theweek.com/speedreads/659904/unusual-number-voters-are-still-undecided.

44. Nimmo and Combs, *The Political Pundits*; Eric Alterman, *Sound and Fury: The Making of the Punditocracy* (Cornell University Press, 1999).

45. Kimberly A. Neuendorf, *The Content Analysis Guidebook* (Thousand Oaks, California: Sage, 2002).

46. Ibid.

47. These numbers reported only include content that was coded as "present" for negativity.

48. Sides, Analysis, "Is the Media Biased toward Clinton or Trump?"; Stempel, "The Prestige Press Covers the 1960 Presidential Campaign"; Stempel and Windhauser, "The Prestige Press Revisited"; Stempel and Windhauser, "Coverage by the Prestige Press of the 1988 Presidential Campaign."

49. Kuypers, *Press Bias and Politics*.

50. See page 53, Stephen Farnsworth and Robert Lichter, "The Handbook of Election News Coverage around the World," in *Trend in Television Network News Coverage of U.S. Elections* (New York: Routledge, 2008), 42–57.

51. D'Alessio and Allen, "Media Bias in Presidential Elections."

52. "Research: Media Coverage of the 2016 Election," Shorenstein Center, September 7, 2016, https://shorensteincenter.org/research-media-coverage-2016-election/; in Campaigns et al., "News Coverage of the 2016 General Election: How the Press Failed the Voters," Shorenstein Center, December 7, 2016, https://shorensteincenter.org/news-coverage-2016-general-election/.

53. Bryan T. Gervais, "Following the News? Reception of Uncivil Partisan Media and the Use of Incivility in Political Expression," *Political Communication* 31, no. 4 (October 2, 2014): 564–583, doi:10.1080/10584609.2013.852640; Mutz, "Effects of 'In-Your-Face' Television Discourse on Perceptions of a Legitimate Opposition."

54. Maria Elizabeth Grabe and Rasha Kamhawi, "Hard Wired for Negative News? Gender Differences in Processing Broadcast News," *Communication Research* 33, no. 5 (October 1, 2006): 346–369, doi:10.1177/0093650206291479; Paul Freedman and Ken Goldstein, "Measuring Media Exposure and the Effects of Negative Campaign Ads," *American Journal of Political Science*, 1999, 1189–1208; Robin L. Nabi, "A Cognitive-Functional Model for the Effects of Discrete Negative Emotions on Information Processing, Attitude Change, and Recall," *Communication Theory* 9, no. 3 (1999): 292–320.

55. Natalie Jomini Stroud, "Media Use and Political Predispositions: Revisiting the Concept of Selective Exposure," *Political Behavior* 30, no. 3 (September 1, 2008): 341–366, doi:10.1007/s11109–007–9050–9; Natalie Jomini Stroud, "Polarization and Partisan Selective Exposure," *Journal of Communication* 60, no. 3 (September 1, 2010): 556–576, doi:10.1111/j.1460–2466.2010.01497.x.

56. Shanto Iyengar and Kyu S Hahn, "Red Media, Blue Media: Evidence of Ideological Selectivity in Media Use," *Journal of Communication* 59, no. 1 (March 1, 2009): 19–39, doi:10.1111/j.1460–2466.2008.01402.x.

57. For examples see Lauren Feldman, "Partisan Differences in Opinionated News Perceptions: A Test of the Hostile Media Effect," *Political Behavior* 33, no. 3 (September 1, 2011): 407–432, doi:10.1007/s11109–010–9139–4.

58. Iyengar and Hahn, "Red Media, Blue Media"; Pietro S. Nivola and David W. Brady, eds., *Red and Blue Nation? Characteristics and Causes of America's Polarized Politics* (Stanford, CA: Washington, DC: Brookings Institution Press, 2006); Cass R. Sunstein, *Republic.com 2.0* (Princeton: Princeton University Press, 2007).

59. Farnsworth and Lichter, "The Handbook of Election News Coverage around the World"; "Research."

60. Gerbner and Gross, "Living with Television: The Violence Profile"; Grabe and Kamhawi, "Hard Wired for Negative News?"

Chapter Six

News Media Framing of the Donald J. Trump and Hillary Clinton 2016 Presidential Nomination Acceptance Speeches

Terministic Screens and the Discovery of the Worldview and Bias of the Press

Jim A. Kuypers

How has America come to a point where the chief strategist of the president of the United States, *in public* and to their faces, allegedly calls a press line of mainstream journalists the "opposition party, all lined up,"[1] and the president of the United States, Donald J. Trump tweets, "The FAKE NEWS media (failing @nytimes, @NBCNews, @ABC, @CBS, @CNN) is not my enemy, it is the enemy of the American People!"? Of course, Republican presidents have long known and shared *in private* that the press was at best unfriendly and at worse, as noted by President Richard M. Nixon, "the enemy."[2] Yet how did we move from private complaining to public denouncing? And why was the press response to President Trump's tweet and Bannon's alleged remark to not question its own contribution to conditions allowing for such comments, but rather to complain about them? Are such press complaints warranted, or do Bannon and President Trump have grounds for their claims?

In "The Presidential Nomination Acceptance Speeches of Donald J. Trump and Hillary Clinton: Terministic Screens and Antagonistic World-views,"[3] I wrote about the worldviews expressed by the candidates through their respective convention speeches. In this chapter I analyze the main-stream news media coverage of those same speeches, looking for press worldviews as expressed through its reporting on the speeches. After the speeches were delivered I began collecting the press responses, focusing on hard news print and broadcast stories, editorials, and opinion essays.[4]

Looking over the collected examples, I was struck by the stark difference in reporting on the two candidates, and how this difference suggested a movement away from a Libertarian/Socially Responsible model of the press. To demonstrate this change, in the pages that follow I briefly share with you the worldviews expressed in the Trump and Clinton speeches, and also show the worldview of the press. This worldview in some ways explains the difference in coverage, and also illuminates the "opposition" of which Bannon spoke. The remainder of this chapter is divided into four sections: First, I review how the terms used by the candidates and the press can be analyzed for worldviews; second, I present a brief synopsis of the results of an analysis of the speeches of both candidates; third, I specifically examine the press responses for worldviews; finally, I present examples of press bias and how the worldview of the press and its actions constitutes a major break from a socially responsible press.

WORLDVIEWS?

The term *worldview* denotes a particular philosophical underpinning to one's perception and expression of the world as shared through one's discourse. Although there are a multitude of studies exploring the worldviews of individuals, no such studies exist in which the worldviews of the news media have been explored.[5] In this chapter I use a dramatistic perspective to guide my analysis of the news responses to the speeches of each candidate. I examine these responses as a composite narrative, looking for areas in which individual news reports overlap or coalesce,[6] thus allowing for the determination of a worldview. By carefully examining the language choices made, we can discover where key terms coalesce, forming terministic screens; these screens in turn may allow us to discover the underlying Motive, the worldview that influences the discourse.

Kenneth Burke wrote of terministic screens that, "even if any given terminology is a *reflection* of reality, by its very nature as a terminology, it must be a *selection* of reality; and to this extent it must function also as a *deflection* of reality."[7] The words we use every day act to highlight some aspects of our reality over others. Importantly, from an interpretive point of view, "whatever terms we use . . . constitute a . . . kind of screen [and this screen] directs [our] attention to one field rather than another."[8] This directing of attention is both inducement and determinant, and such screens are often powerful in shaping our perceptions. Important to this study, they are also "indicative of the internal thinking of the communicator [for the nature] of our terms affects the nature of our observations, in the sense that the terms direct the attention to one field rather than to another. Also, *many of the 'observations' are but implications of the particular terminology in terms of which the observations are made.*"[9]

Although terministic screens surround a multitude of different concepts,[10] they also coalesce around elements of the Burkeian pentad.[11] In this sense, descriptions of acts, agents, and so on, can in some ways be viewed as terministic screens.[12] As I have written elsewhere:

> [D]iscovering terministic screens allows us to track pentadic elements—act, scene, agent, agency, purpose—and better understand the larger, and sometimes background understanding of a situation expressed by the communicator. By examining the key terms and phrases used, we can answer very real questions concerning the nature of the observations "implicit in the terminology" chosen. We can discover how the terminologies direct attention to affect a particular quality of observation. Moreover, by determining the nature and inner workings of the terministic screens operating, we can shed insight into the Motives, or underlying worldviews.[13]

In pursuing such an investigation, I do not search for obvious terms of the pentad (this is a description of a "scene," and this is a description of an "agent," and so on). Instead, I "look for ways in which . . . statements direct attention to particular pentadic terms, characterize those terms, and characterize terministic relationships."[14] As Clarke Rountree argued: we "must take care to look not simply for terms that are 'scenic' (or 'purposive' or 'agency-related,' etc.) on their face, but for those that *function* within a particular grammar of motives as 'scene' (or 'purpose' or 'agency,' etc.)."[15] I examined press reports for "the actual grammatical functions of terms for motives, not just their superficial connection to a terministic source."[16]

WORLDVIEWS IN THE NOMINATION ACCEPTANCE SPEECHES OF TRUMP AND CLINTON

What follows is a brief summary of the main elements in the nomination acceptance speeches of Trump and Clinton.

Trump: An Interanimation of Purpose and Act

Trump focused on crime, immigration, the economy, and foreign affairs/terrorism, presenting a scene of chaos and danger for individual Americans, a scene to which he links Hillary Clinton as both causal agent and potential future agent if elected; from this scene emerges a uniting of Trump's purpose for running for president as well as proposed future acts if elected president.

Importantly, neither Trump's purpose or proposed acts dominates the speech; rather, each influences the other, eventuating in an interanimation that invites audience participation in a higher and larger vision for America, a vision that is both anti-collectivist and anti-globalist.

In order for the acts Trump proposes to alter the present scene, he must win the election; yet, to many in the electorate, he is the mysterious other—billionaire, reality TV star, real estate mogul, and former owner of the Miss Universe and Miss USA pageants. Mystery, however, becomes the ground for discovery.[17] Trump invites transcendence of the estrangement between a person of great wealth and a great mass of people of lesser wealth, as the latter recognizes in him their champion-herald, their "voice." Trump's use of the term "we" conjoins "the people" with their "voice." Thus unified, Trump/citizens become *we*, the people, who begin to take the actions that will transcend the present dangerous scene; first, by rejecting one of its causal agents (i.e., Clinton), and second, by empowering themselves, as individuals, to work together, in unity with him directing their message to a tone-deaf Washington to essentially get out of the way so *the people* can act[18] to produce a resurgent America. Individual votes become part of the larger purpose of empowering the voice of the people. Once elected, that voice will direct individual actions that serve the greater *purpose* of making America "great again." His envisioned acts suggest a philosophical realism. The sense of realism, applied to the scene in his speech, allows him to promise that he will remove impediments to individual actions, and to reduce government to its essential role of protector of safety so individuals may act to produce wealth. Capitalism is emphasized here through the promotion of the rights of individuals and the placing of freedom, opportunities, and responsibilities for wealth-creation in their hands, rather than under the control of government, and by promoting "America First," rather than a vision of globalism. Trump's vision allows one to work for oneself—individualism—and in so doing, to work for America.

Clinton: The Co-mingling Of Agency and Agent

Clinton's speech involved an interanimation of agency with agent, with Clinton playing both roles. As agency/agent, Clinton acts for those who support her, those who have joined with her in her policy endeavors. Americans who are "with her" are the *agency* through which she is able to act as *agent* for continuation of Obama policies. In contrast with Trump acting on behalf of *individual* Americans, Clinton describes a Collective of like-minded others who are "with her," imbuing that Collective with agent-like qualities when it supports her in her proposed acts; however, this Collective also operates at the level of Clinton's agency though which she will act for change.

Clinton's underlying stress on agent suggests a philosophical idealism. As agent, she stresses not the reality of the scene today, but rather *ideas* about the present scene and future acts that she describes. Yet, Clinton does not present herself as a fully autonomous agent in the world, but rather as part of the Collective of like-minded others, part of the agency through which America is rescued. Thus, agency "becomes the focus of the entire means-ends relationship."[19] We more readily understand agency/agent Clinton's speech viewed in this manner; in so doing, we have a better understanding of her view of the function of government and the Collective as a means to the end of social justice and, ultimately, Socialism, in as much that those who are not part of the Collective—"Wall Street," corporations, the wealthy—are relegated to an agency for Clinton as she becomes an agency for the goals of the Collective. Corporations and others who produce wealth are to become servants of the federal government to enable social justice.

THE PRESS WORLDVIEW: DONALD J. TRUMP

The press coverage of Donald Trump's speech[20] overwhelmingly consisted of an interanimation of agent-scene.

Agent Trump

The terms used to focus our attention on the nature of the agent—Trump—were primarily generated from the words of the press instead of from the actual words of Trump. Seemingly the most favored line of the press was, "Beginning on January 20th, 2017, safety will be restored," Trump proclaimed. And, "Nobody knows the system better than me, which is why I alone can fix it." To which the reporter added, "The authoritarian overtones were neck-prickling."[21] Authoritarian was just one aspect of press imposition of its own views upon the speech. Specific terminology to describe Trump included describing the speech as "the evidence of his own unsuitability";[22] calling him "Belligerent and erratic,"[23] a "businessman and reality star with no political experience,"[24] and "divisive . . . like the man in the high castle."[25] The *Washington Post* (*WP*) stated that, "He will run as a hard man, a tough, nationalist authoritarian for whom order is paramount. And he will advance his case by offering a dismal and profoundly gloomy account of what he called 'a moment of crisis for our nation.'"[26] The *New York Times* (*NYT*) wrote that Trump was a "hard-liner," and that he "offered himself as an all-powerful savior."[27]

ABC News (ABC) asserted that Trump "painted a dark picture of an America beset by threats both at home and abroad and he presented himself as the savior."[28] Worrying that Trump was not self-effacing enough, the *NYT* stated:

> "It was Donald J. Trump's best chance to escape his own caricature. He did not. Mr. Trump decided . . . that he was not interested in revealing himself to America with disarming tales of his upbringing, hard-earned lessons from his tumultuous career or the inner struggles masked by his outward pomposity. Mr. Trump sounded much like [an] unreflective man. . . . For those grasping for new signs of humility, generosity and depth, Mr. Trump offered the thinnest of reeds. [H]e portrayed himself, over and over, as an almost messianic figure prepared to rescue the country from the ills of urban crime, illegal immigration and global terrorism."[29] For many in the press, Trump's speech was simply a "messianic portrayal of himself."[30]

This interpretation was linked with a single sentence recontextualized by the press.

The "I Alone" Agent

Trump contrasted himself to Hillary Clinton, from which the press produced a continuously reverberated soundbite: "Nobody knows the system better than me, which is why I alone can fix it." Approximately half of all press reports relayed this quote, yet ignored both the context (expanded upon below) and the delivery with disarming smile and slight laugh. The press instead focused on describing Trump negatively: "This notion of him alone as being able to fix some of the problems he describes also shed some of the humility he might have wanted to [cultivate]. But what it lacked was a sense of who he is . . . and a sense of getting beyond the notion of a strong man. There is chaos. I am strong man. I will fix it. Really? Well how?"[31] Like other outlets, Fox News (FN) also presented more of Trump's "I" statements than his "We" statements, but with an important distinction: "My pledge reads I'm with you, the American people. I am your voice. I am with you. . . . Nobody knows this system better than me, which is why I alone can fix it. My opponent asks certain supporters to recite a . . . loyalty pledge. It reads, 'I'm with her.' I choose to recite a different pledge. My pledge reads 'I'm with you, the American people.'"[32]

Scene

For the press, the speech "was very dark [and] scary."[33] Trump "painted . . . a grim picture of America, one stalked by crime, threatened by terrorism and struggling to maintain order."[34] He "painted a dark picture of an America beset by threats both at home and abroad and he presented himself as savior."[35] It was a "relentlessly foreboding speech."[36]

The *WP* made a point of cherry-picking establishment GOP representatives to help frame the speech as dark:

> Others simply saw Trump's speech as an exceedingly dystopian commentary. . . . This from a former speechwriter for George H. W. Bush. "This is a very dark and frightening speech." And this from an aide to the two Bush presidents and Ronald Reagan: "This is a remarkably dark/bleak speech. No uplift; almost purely negative." On CNN, GOP consultant and Jeb Bush ally Ana Navarro was equally blunt. "That disgusting speech . . . does nothing than bring out the DARKNESS in America." Top Mitt Romney aide Stuart Stevens was not converted. "Before going to bed, make sure you practice duck and cover. They are here." Ditto Mike Murphy . . . McCain and Jeb Bush [supporter]. Great @murphymike line: "I didn't know we lived in Gotham City."[37]

The accounts of agent Trump were solidly intertwined with his depiction of the American scene in his speech. The press reported what Trump said, but in such a way as to push beyond the troubled scene Trump was relaying, and then downplay or minimize its potential effect. In short, 1.) Trump said things were *bad*;[38] 2.) the press reported Trump said things were *extremely bad*; 3.) the press would then say things really were actually *pretty good*. This reportorial practice served to vitiate the need for Trump's proposed policy actions, and also to highlight the agent Trump *created by the press*. The scene created by the press was one overwhelmingly radical, dark, and dystopian; Trump was "tapping into the economic anxiety of the country, painting a rather bleak picture of the United States right now."[39]

For instance, CNN stated that, "Donald Trump . . . paint[ed] a dire picture of America in crisis, citizens in danger, the economy . . . a disaster, lawlessness in the streets, immigrants flooding the borders and driving down wages all threatening American peace and prosperity. Listen. TRUMP: Our convention occurs at a moment of crisis for our nation. The attacks on our police and the terrorism of our cities threaten our very way of life. Any politician who does not grasp this danger is not fit to lead our country."[40] The building of the scene as dark was relentless: "He said he would be the law and order candidate, and depicted, again, a nation that he said was rampant with lawlessness."[41] "So . . . Donald Trump gives us a . . . speech that's basically all negative, not just doom and gloom, but antiHillary, antiObama, not a lot of positive ideas, not a lot of policy plans. . . ."[42] He "painted such a grim picture of America. [V]ery short on hope and a litany of themes about where America is heading and all of it in the wrong direction."[43]

Minimization

When the press was presented with alternate interpretations and hard facts about the speech that contradicted its interpretation, it minimally reported or ignored them. Thus, those who would say that Trump's speech conveyed "the reality of what's happening in this country [so] it wasn't dark, it was reality"[44] were simply drowned out by the collective weight of press oversubscription to a dark, unrealistic interpretation of the speech. For example, from a CNN Political commentator: "this disgusting speech that we heard tonight . . . that does nothing but bring out this darkness in America. It is terrifying."[45] The "core of the message was dark and it was confrontational and it was divisive on street crime, on undocumented immigration, on terrorism."[46] ABC suggested that something was wrong with you if you supported Trump; someone could only imagine Trump in the Oval Office "if you're angry. If you're upset, if you're dislocated, disconnected in some way, you found lots of things to like in that speech."[47]

Even as it sought to overstate the strength of Trump's claims, the press also sought to undercut them. For instance, the implications of the scene Trump created were minimized through making it seem as if the public was imagining it: "people *have this feeling that* there aren't as many good jobs."[48] And another example: "Trump took real challenges and recast them in terms that were not only exaggerated but also apocalyptic."[49] In short, the press said that Trump framed things darker than they were, but then it framed the scene as even darker than Trump stated, and then sought to *minimize* belief in this scene, thus obviating the need for a Trump presidency. When Trump surrogates were stressing similarities to FDR, for example, the press was fixated on comparing Trump to Richard Nixon: "But you know, in 1968 for Nixon, we were in the middle of the period which the violent crime rate actually doubled from 1960 to 1970. Since 1991, even with the uptick in murders in some cities in the last year, the violent crime rate is half of what it was in 1991 to today. You think of how often people are killed by undocumented immigrants, I mean, the fact the two of the three examples they [Trump's speech] had were car accidents, kind of give you a sense—[CNN Host]: [Yes,] Not violent crimes."[50]

A CNN contributor imagined what President Obama might say in reply to Trump's assertion that the "number of new illegal immigrant families who have crossed the border so far this year already exceeds the entire total from 2015. They are being released by the tens of thousands into our communities with no regard for the impact on public safety or resources. [CNN contributor]: So that is the kind of rhetoric we expect . . . President Obama to be asked to respond to today. . . . We expect the President is likely to bring up statistics [suggesting] that illegal immigration to the US is at its lowest level since the 1970s."[51] The press was especially sensitive to issues of immigration, almost always ignoring Trump's differentiation between legal and illegal immigration. For instance, CNN stated that, "when he talked about immigration, everything he talked about immigration is actually wrong. Immigration is at a net negative right now."[52]

Of course, the above ignores that Trump was speaking specifically of illegal immigration, and also ignores the dozens of published sources he cited for his information. Yet press comments attempted to minimize the effectiveness of the scene Trump was depicting. CNN was particularly flagrant in its conflation of illegal and legal immigration: He "was taking a very hard line as he's done all primary season on *immigration*. Listen to the hard line he took by saying that the country's *immigrants*, the problem with *immigration*, is leading to the economic problems that are happening here in this country. TRUMP: Americans want relief from uncontrolled immigration, which is what we have now. Communities want relief, yet Hillary Clinton is proposing mass amnesty, mass immigration, and mass lawlessness."[53] The press ignored the specific citation of sources in Trump's speech and the readily available facts showing that almost 50 percent of legal immigrants are on some form of federal assistance, and almost 62 percent of illegal immigrants are on some form of welfare.[54] They also ignored the disproportionate amount of crime in the United States committed by illegal aliens who, although making up roughly 3 percent of the U.S. population, represent some 11 to 15 percent of the U.S. jail population.[55]

Illegal immigration was only part of the scene described by Trump. CBS provides an example of the press minimizing his claims about crime: "'But here [we] will honor the American people with the truth, and nothing else.' The truth, as Trump saw is, included [sic]: a spike in violent crime rates in the U.S., a 50 percent rise in police officers killed in the line of duty since last year, and a plunge in average household income. In short: America is in dire straits. (In fact, violent and property crime has been falling for decades in the U.S., according to Politifact. The number of police officers barely rose eight percent since 2015, according to the National Law Enforcement Officers Memorial Fund.)"[56] Yet, Trump did not claim violent crime was up overall, just that violence had increased, and that the murder rate in American cities had increased.

In another example of minimization, this one on trade, CNN cherry-picked one item in a list Trump gave, and then tried to discredit that one item in order to diminish the impact of the entire statement: Trump "vowed to stop 'China's outrageous theft of intellectual property, along with their illegal product dumping, and their devastating currency manipulation,' and vowed to renegotiate trade deals with Beijing." And then the singling out: "China has long been a favorite target for Trump, he has blamed Beijing repeatedly for America's woes. However, a CNN Reality Check found that many of his arguments were out of date or wrong, particularly regarding alleged currency manipulation."[57] Yet the "reality check" did not examine all aspects of trade with China, and glaringly ignored Chinese control of U.S. debt and currency manipulation *upward*,[58] again, serving to minimize the problem Trump cites in his speech.

A Few Words on Purpose and Act

Why Trump is doing what he is doing was an important part of his speech, yet not at all for the press. The *NYT* provides a cogent example of this: "How did a braggadocious Manhattan billionaire with a history of dodgy business deals convince 13 million people feeling battered by a changing world that he is their solution? Chutzpah, reality TV and a hyperactive Twitter account are part of the answer." Mr. Trump offered no solutions beyond his messianic portrayal of himself. "Every day I wake up determined to deliver a better life for the people all across this nation that have been neglected, ignored, and abandoned," he says in advance excerpts from his speech. He is a "crude, boastful, force[ful]" man.[59] The press misses, in the very quote presented above, a glimpse of the purpose, calling it messianic, even as they call a similar statement from Clinton a mere week later laudatory. Other than the occasional insertion, the press leaves out concerns of purpose.

With a scene of the nature described by the press, the need to explore acts becomes meaningless since Trump's acts are directed to, in the eyes of the press, non-existent or overly-exaggerated problems. The proposed policy acts were minimally described when compared to the focus on agent and scene, and when they were described, they were presented as essentially promises without detail: "It was a speech, [said CNN], that was full of promises. [He] made many promises to the audience there but critics also pointing out that there weren't many specifics there."[60]

THE PRESS WORLDVIEW: HILLARY CLINTON

Press reports concerning Clinton's description of the condition of the country and world closely matched her assertions. Her depiction of the scene, explained below, was reported as essentially correct. Reporting stressed Clinton's depiction of America and shared the presentation of a morbid future scene should Trump win the presidency. Thus, we have Clinton describing everything as "pretty good," intimating that we need only continue the Obama administration's policies to continue the positive growth in American social and economic outcomes. The essential quote is relayed here by FN: "'I don't' think President Obama and Vice President Biden get the credit they deserve for saving us from the worst economic crisis of our lifetime. Our economy is so much stronger than when they took office. Nearly 15 million new private sector jobs, 20 million more Americans with health insurance, and an auto industry that just had its best year ever."[61]

CNN extended Clinton's assertion of an economic recovery, with analysts saying they believed she reached out to those "populous forces that have really driven our politics with anger and anxiety the cycle [sic] *despite the economic recovery*, and she is squaring the circle effectively and saying if you're angry about the economy, if you're frustrated with Washington . . . implicitly *that's a Republican problem* and [Clinton] can help address that."[62] A FN contributor highlighted the press's depiction of Clinton's sense of everything is pretty good: "[S]he made a great effort to draw clear distinctions about how we have two different world views. One in which we are stronger through our diversity. We are inclusive, we are forward looking, we are optimistic, we believe this country is the greatest country on earth. [With Trump,] all you heard was negativity. Talking down the economy. Talking down our military, talking down our veterans, complaining."[63]

The *WP* summed up well the overall thrust of press reporting in this area: "Clinton had to avoid being Pollyannish at a time many people *think* America is on the wrong track, but yet provide a contrast with Donald Trump's dystopian view of the nation. 'We are clear-eyed about what our country is up against,' she said. She acknowledged how chaotic the world is. 'Anyone reading the news can see the threats and turbulence we face. . . .' She dwelt on what is good about America—our values, our strong military, our diversity. It was the America . . . Trump left out of his dark vision."[64] This was a sentiment repeated by many in the press: "Judging by their convention speeches, Donald Trump and Hillary Clinton live in different countries. Trump described a weakened America that faces mounting threats. Clinton painted a strong nation, lifted by its diversity."[65]

Act with a Purpose within the Scene

Within this "pretty good" scene, Clinton's speech acted to accomplish several goals, and these goals were described by the press in general ways. In terms of sheer numbers, (32 of 52 press reports) there was the act of Clinton being the first female presidential nominee of the Republican or Democratic Party: "Hillary Clinton is the first female nominee of a major American political party, and she would love for you to vote for the first female president."[66] However, these instances functioned as historical footnote rather than Clinton's act in her speech. The actions entailed in Clinton's speech intermingled with its purpose: accept the nomination and reintroduce herself to America; attack Donald Trump; unify Sanders supporters and others into her campaign.

For instance, the *WP* wrote the speech "was designed to reintroduce her to a country that already had lived through decades of her in the public eye."[67] On attacking Trump the *WP* wrote: "Clinton mentioned Trump by name 21 times and in other ways plenty of other times. Her comments were often brutal and made for TV—sound bites with real bite."[68] Unlike with Trump, little was said about actual policy proposals in the speech. When the press did mention policy aspects, Clinton was essentially presented as President Obama's third term: "It was a powerful speech in which she combined the personal with policy, a vigorous defense of the Obama record with an insistence that she would take on problems left unsolved and injustices that still needed righting."[69] The act of unification was in a majority of press comments. NBC reported that "The 'stronger together' theme helped Clinton reach out to embrace Bernie Sanders supporters with one arm and Republicans wary of Donald Trump with the other. [She] seamlessly marr[ied] a progressive agenda with small-c conservative values. Clinton said, 'now let's go out there and make it happen together.'"[70] The *WP* highlighted that Clinton stressed that, "We have to decide whether we're going to work together, so we can all rise together. *We* will rise to the challenge, just as *we* always have."[71] This act of unifying, along with attacking Trump, was the strongest underlying factor in terms of act. Although mentioned by all news agencies, *WP*, FN, and CNN mentioned this attack line in almost all of their respective coverages: "Clinton attacked Trump, questioning his temperament: 'Ask yourself: Does . . . Trump have the temperament to be Commander-in-Chief? [He] can't even handle the rough-and-tumble of a presidential campaign. He loses his cool at the slightest provocation. A man you can bait with a tweet is not a man we can trust with nuclear weapons.'"[72]

When looking for the web of terms that form a screen of sorts, it is crucial that one looks at how terms function in their interrelationships, and not focus on total numbers of words. It is how a given term operates to reflect, deflect, or select aspects of our reality that is important. It is in this light that an analysis of the Clinton coverage found a dominance of terms working to highlight agent and agency elements.

Agent/Agency Conflation

Overwhelmingly the press presented a distinct conflation of *agent* Clinton with Clinton as the *agency* of change. Of course, this subtle interanimation of agent/agency did not occur in isolation; it was situated within a dual scene, mentioned above, that functioned to ground one's understanding of the agent/agency. As agent, Clinton is the first female candidate for president, a policy wonk who "loves to go into the weeds on policy."[73] She is "forceful, cogent, and clear,"[74] competent, unifying, humble, determined, confident, and positive.[75] Importantly, she is not Donald Trump—divisive, unqualified, and ill-tempered. The contrast with the way the press treated Trump as agent and Clinton as agent is striking: "Declaring that the United States is at 'a moment of reckoning,' Clinton promised that 'progress is possible' and offered herself as a fearless executive who would get the job done. She also warned against what she considers the dangers represented by Republican nominee Donald Trump, who she said would usher in 'midnight in America.'"[76]

Clinton addressed pre-existing criticisms of herself in her speech, and the press extended her defenses. The *NYT*, for instance, asked the country to trust her, going so far as to redefine the meaning of trust. Asserting that she is ready for the job, the paper claimed that enemies had built a "scaffold of assumptions" about her motives, so she offered a "firm and extensive counterargument: A succession of senior government position, deep dives in the intricacies of policy and high-stakes international negotiations [that] have prepared her for the presidency in ways that . . . Trump cannot possibly match. Besieged by lingering doubts about her honesty, Mrs. Clinton made the case for *a different kind of trust . . . not the textbook definition*, but a more pragmatic faith in her judgment, experience, temperament and priorities."[77] Even when the press admitted to the boilerplate nature of Clinton's speech, it depicted her in laudable ways: "The speech didn't really show us a side of Clinton we didn't know," Chris Cillizza argues on *The Fix*. "'No one questions her long record of fighting for progressive policy. No one doubts her comprehensive knowledge of issues.' [I call] Clinton a winner because the speech was exactly who she is: 'A worker, a nose-to-the-grindstone churner who never, ever stops. That is, at heart, her strongest attribute as a candidate.'"[78]

"We" versus "I Alone"

The press constructed Clinton agency is presented as a means to a better scene and avoiding a (press constructed) worse scene. It is also a way of unifying with Sanders's supporters, which involves an even larger unification with like-minded others, eventuating in a "Collective" of sorts. This is the "we" of which Clinton and the press speaks.[79] The contrast of "we" with the Clinton/media constructed Trump "I alone" is striking, and was among the most frequent of themes mentioned by the press: "[S]he put her finger on the most frightening element of Trump's appeal: 'Our founders fought a revolution and wrote a Constitution so America would never be a nation where one person had all the power.' It is fair to say that the founders would have held the main thesis of Trump's candidacy—the promise of a man on horseback to save a frightened and supine nation—in utter contempt."[80] "Clinton emphasized the word 'we.' Nobody knows the system better than me,' Trump said last week in Cleveland, 'which is why I alone can fix it.' Americans don't say: 'I alone can fix it,' Clinton countered. . . . 'We say: "We'll fix it together.' 'I am your voice,' Trump said. 'We will rise to the challenge,' Clinton said."[81]

For the press, construction of "Trump's use of 'I' and Clinton's use of 'we' sen[t] deliberate messages to voters."[82] In his acceptance speech, though, Trump specifically stated, "Who would have believed that when we started this journey . . . last year we—and I say 'we' because we are a team," and also used the term "we" sixty-four times. Moreover, he even had an interview July 24 on *Meet the Press* (NBC News) during which he was asked about his use of the term "I" referred to above:

> CHUCK TODD: One of the phrases you used, "I alone can fix it." And to some people, that sounded almost too strong-mannish for them. Do you understand that criticism and what do you make of it?
>
> DONALD TRUMP: [P]art of it was I'm comparing myself to Hillary. And we know Hillary. . . . Her record has been a disaster. And I am running against Hillary. It's not like I'm running against the rest of the world. I know people that are very, very capable that could do a very good job, but they could never get elected. They wouldn't know where to begin. But for governing, they would be good. I'm running and, you know, against one person.[83]

This interview was given four days before Clinton's speech. Thus, even if one were to ignore the context in Trump's speech, it is beyond doubt that Clinton *and the press* were deliberately perverting the meaning of Trump's comment. The press instead pushed the "we" of collectivism in Clinton's address, and dismissed Trump as a strongman.

As the *WP* reported, "Clinton counts on her belief that the public is looking for results and therefore a candidate who has real policy proposals, not sweeping promises. She says that, in the end, voters will reject a candidate who says that 'I alone can fix it,' as Trump put it so directly. . . . Her philosophy is the opposite, summed in the title of the book she wrote years ago and invoked again Thursday night, that it takes a village and not a strong man. 'No one gets through life alone,' she said."[84] Most outlets highlighted this collective means of embracing progressive values, or, as the *WP* stated, a "liberal communitarianism."[85]

According to the *NYT*, she "fashioned herself as 'a progressive who likes to get things done.'"[86] As has been discussed elsewhere,[87] the push toward collectivism is engaged as the agency through which agent Clinton will be able to promote the progressive agenda she promises in her speech, a feat not unnoticed by the press: "At a moment when political discourse is divisive and dark, Mrs. Clinton acknowledged stiff challenges but summoned optimism in her call . . . for Americans to work together. 'America is once again at a moment of reckoning . . . Bonds of trust and respect are fraying,' she said. 'We are clear eyed about what our country is up against. We will rise to the challenge, just as we always have.'"[88] This position was summed up well in these oft repeated lines in news reports: "We have to decide whether we're going to work together, so we can all rise together."[89] And specifically to Sanders's supporters: "I want you to know, I've heard you. Your cause is our cause."[90]

As pointed out by the *WP*, "Clinton embraced the communitarian theme, signaling that her 'Stronger Together' slogan would remain at the heart of her campaign. 'None of us can do it alone. That's why we are stronger together.' And she underscored the other side of that catchphrase by warning that Trump would divide the nation. 'It's truly is up to us. We have to decide whether we're going to work together so we can all rise together.'"[91]

For the press, "It was a speech that ratified the progressive thrust of the party's platform and its move in a more progressive direction."[92] Clinton presented progressive policy proposals, "ticking through a litany of policy promises," and attempted to build a coalition of disparate voters, even reaching out to Independents and Republicans dissatisfied with Trump: "An underlying theme of Clinton's address was that progress can be achieved only if people work together, a direct rebuke to Trump's pledge that he alone can fix what ails the nation."[93]

This notion of the collective rests on another assumption, that of Americans making a shared sacrifice, whether or not they wish to do so. As pointed out by the press, "Hillary Clinton delivered an argument for her candidacy that kept coming back to her campaign's simple theme: that progress requires shared sacrifice, in contrast to Donald Trump's claim that 'I alone can fix it.'"[94] This idea, of shared sacrifice (including increasing taxes by 1.1 trillion over ten years, although that remained unmentioned by the press here),[95] and of working together was pushed well by the press: "The 'stronger together' theme helped Clinton reach out" to both Sanders's supporters and Republicans who disliked Trump. "'Whatever party you belong to, or if you belong to no party at all, if you share these beliefs, this is your campaign,' she said. Her inclusive vision of America . . . left little room for Donald Trump's 'bigotry and bombast.'"[96] "Mr. Trump has urged voters to trust him alone to fix what ails the nation. On Thursday night, Mrs. Clinton rejected that argument, promising, 'We will fix it together.' Her message: Do not trust her alone. Trust 'us.'"[97] Trust the collective.

TERMINISTIC SCREENS AND THE PRESS WORLDVIEW

In the original speeches, the terministic screens were such that Trump reflected a purpose/act mix and Clinton reflected an agency/agent mix. The press reporting was only substantially different with regard to Trump, with reporting showing a strong terminological underpinning of agent/scene, whereas the reporting of Clinton's speech demonstrates a press focusing on agent/agency. Clinton's speech—agency/agent—is not exactly the same as the press's agent/agency. The press response is indicative of a cult of personality, one that places the primary stress on the nature of the agent as something around which the collective forces of the agency coalesce.

Press on Trump: Agent/Scene

An agent/scene stress evinces a philosophical idealism operating within the discourse. Idealism here consists of "any theory which maintains the universe to be throughout the work of reason and mind."[98] This idealism is any "system of thought . . . in which the object of external perception is held to consist, either in itself, or as perceived, of ideas."[99] Richard E. Crable and John J. Makay write about this from a rhetorical angle, stating, "the featuring of a term implicitly *features the motives within that term*. Thus, idealism features 'agent' because the idealist believes that the agent's purposive motion is controlled by the agent's attitudes, values, opinions, and prejudices."[100] And thus the *idealism of the press* is revealed here through the press constructed *anti-ideal* agent Trump.

Importantly for us here, "the unadulteratedly idealistic philosophy starts and ends in the featuring of properties belonging to the term, *agent*. Idealistic philosophies think in terms of the 'ego,' the 'self,' the 'super-ego,' consciousness, 'will'. . . . [V]ariants in esthetic theory stress such terms as 'sensibility,' 'expression,' 'self-expression,' 'consciousness'" and so on.[101] Seeing idealism's strong link with agent, Burke suggested that idealism, important for our understanding of the press response to Trump's speech, "leads readily into both individual and group psychology."[102] The press savaged Trump, creating a creature so vile that nobody with a moral conscience could support him, even if one were to believe the scene at its worse.

Of course, scene is usually a container for the action in a given situation. In our case, though, the press presented minimal acts for its audience to consider. Scene was instead used as a means to highlight the unsuitable nature of the agent. The minimization of the scene by the press served to highlight Trump, constructed as messianic and simply lying about the American scene, as a delusional candidate unsuitable for the office of president. Texts that emphasize scene often have a materialistic influence; they "emphasize the power of the surrounding environment or the coercive power of circumstance."[103] Thus, with the press focus on scene we have a type of materialism operating in the news reports. Materialism is "that metaphysical theory which regards all the facts of the universe as sufficiently explained by the assumption of body or matter, conceived as extended, impenetrable, eternally existent, and susceptible of movement or change of relative position."[104] It is "the theory which regards all the facts of the universe as explainable in terms of matter and motion."[105] As I have written elsewhere:

> "*action* is reduced to *motion* when scene dominates. In this sense, only the material is significant; that which is observable, touchable, and measurable takes precedence is over other concerns. This materialistic motive also allows pressure to be placed upon those interpellated within the scene. We are a part

> of that which is occurring, but we are not necessarily able to remove ourselves from it."[106]

By examining how the press describes the scene, we can access the degree to which scene reveals the thoughts of the press pertaining to how the scene will control Trump's actions. Ryan Erik McGeough and Andrew King address the potentially deterministic nature of such discourse:

> Texts that emphasize scene downplay free choice and emphasize situational determinism. They tend to emphasize the power of circumstances over individual choice. Clarence Darrow excused the behavior of many criminals by arguing that they were victims of bad heredity and merciless environment. Supporters of social welfare programs point to bad schools and failing local economies as reasons that such programs are needed. Speakers who advise accommodating to circumstances emphasize the deterministic power of scene.[107]

Of course, the press did not accurately relay Trump's depiction of scene, but instead presented a harsher reality, and then sought to minimize that reality as untrue. In short, the conditions of the American scene as reported by the press, were also enervated by the press, negating any deterministic pressure. Thus, no such scene, no need for Trump.

Press on Clinton: Agent/Agency

A philosophical pragmatism often underpins discourse when terminological screens suggest a primacy of agency; such texts are "concerned with practical consequences or values."[108] Bernard Brock, Robert L. Scott, and James Chesebro, writing of William James, who said that "pragmatism is 'a method only,'" state that "he goes on to indicate that *consequence, function, what it is good for,* and *the difference it will make to you and me* are pragmatic evaluations. However, pure pragmatism goes beyond James to transcend purpose, as in the applied sciences, when the method is built into the instrument itself. At this point agency becomes the focus of the entire means-ends relationship."[109] The press coverage of agency/agent Clinton can be handily understood in this manner. For the press, Clinton is the agency *through whom* the collective will be led into progressive social policy. But what happens when agency is influenced by agent?

Clearly the press highlighted Clinton's role as agent, stressing her qualifications even to the point of explaining away her flaws. When terminological screens so stress agent, one often sees a philosophical idealism underpinning the discourse. Recall from above that idealism points to an agent's actions being controlled by that agent's "attitudes, values, opinions, and prejudices."[110] In our case, the press highlighted extensively Clinton's progressive values while concomitantly asserting its attitudes and opinions concerning her ability to be president.

This becomes pertinent for us here as "Idealistic philosophies think in terms of the 'ego,' the 'self,' the 'super-ego,' 'consciousness,' 'will.' . . . [V]ariants in esthetic theory stress such terms as 'sensibility,' 'expression,' 'self-expression,' 'consciousness,'" and so on.[111] Understanding idealism's strong link with agent, important for our understanding of the press coverage of Clinton's speech, "leads readily into both individual and group psychology."[112] In her speech, Clinton did not present herself so much as a fully autonomous actor as she situated herself as part of the Collective; and here the press most closely aligned themselves with Clinton since in their presentation of her they stressed agent Clinton in her ability *as agency* (Collective) to achieve the progressive political program.

Consubtantiality, or, The Press is with Her

It is obvious from the press coverage of Trump that it was *in*consubstantial with him. The press does, however, become one with substance with Clinton. Through its lockstep reporting of her speech, the press demonstrates that it is consubstantial with Clinton's thinking, with the worldview she expressed in her speech.

That the worldview expressed by Clinton and the press are so close in composition is cause for concern. The tendency would be for those consubstantial with each other to see reality in much the same manner, and with the press, to report the same as true. Of note is that only FN challenged the general thrust of the news coverage. *Although FN did present the same material that the other major sources covered*, the organization also brought in information that the other news organizations did not, and had a more balanced terminological dispersion (elements of the pentad, and so on) than did the other press agencies; thus, a more balanced exploration of the themes in the speeches were had than with the other press outlets. And therein lies the crux of the issue. The terminological screens of the press prevented it from fairly and accurately covering both candidates. The implications for this are stunning when considering the power of terminological screens to select, reflect, and deflect our attention from one aspect of reality toward another. Moreover, recall that such screens are "indicative of the internal thinking of the communicator" and affect the very "nature of our observations." Or as Burke puts it, "*many of the 'observations' are but implications of the particular terminology in terms of which the observations are made.*"[113] In short, such strong consubstantiality between Clinton and the press could naturally lead the press to pro-Clinton coverage on issues and events.

PRESS COVERAGE AND BIAS DURING AND AFTER THE CAMPAIGN

Press practices during and after the campaign suggests the consubtantiality is so strong that the press actually acted in an unethical manner when covering the candidates. The Society of Professional Journalists (SPJ) suggests four key elements as the foundation of ethical journalism, two of which are particularly relevant here:

1. Seek Truth and Report It. Ethical journalism should be accurate and fair.
2. Minimize Harm. Ethical journalism treats sources, subjects, colleagues and members of the public as human beings deserving of respect.[114]

In existence since 1922, the American Society of Newspaper Editors statement of principles is similar to the ethical code of the SPJ. Articles 1 and 4 are particularly relevant here:

> ARTICLE I: The primary purpose of gathering and distributing news and opinion is to serve the general welfare by informing the people and enabling *them to make* judgments on the issues of the time.
>
> ARTICLE IV: Every effort must be made to assure that the news content is accurate, free from bias and in context, and that all sides are presented fairly. Editorials, analytical articles and commentary should be held to the same standards of accuracy with respect to facts as news reports.[115]

The Associated Press Media Editors Statement of Ethical Principles states specifically that "The newspaper should strive for impartial treatment of issues and dispassionate handling of controversial subjects.[116]

Yet the above was not what we saw with coverage of the convention speeches, and I wondered whether the worldview that allowed for such biased coverage would continue throughout the campaign.[117] In the end, and looking only for the most blatant examples, I collected 494 examples of what I considered mainstream news media bias either *for* Hillary Clinton or *against* Donald Trump (I did not find it to be the other way around). What follows are just a few examples of these pro-Clinton/anti-Trump actions:

> A study of the evening news casts of ABC, CBS, and NBC found that between 7/29/16 and 10/20/16 there were 623 negative statements [roughtly 90 percent] about Trump compared to only 63 positive statements.[118] "Comparatively, seventy-one percent of the coverage of Mr. Obama during the 2008 campaign was positive or neutral, with only 29 percent negative."[119]

CNN played *eighteen* DNC-produced "video montages and anti-Donald Trump featurettes . . . totaling 62 minutes . . . of air time—all during their prime time coverage . . . of the political confab. By contrast, CNN only played *three* of the Republican convention's videos, which added up to 14 minutes and 17 seconds of air time over four nights. The network skipped playing the GOP's videos on the Benghazi terror attack scandal and on the Fast and Furious gunrunning scandal."[120]

New York Times tech columnist Farhad Manjoo [called] on Google to "fix" its search engine results to hide evidence of Hillary Clinton's failing health.[121]

Media organizations such as Google, CNN, PBS and the *New York Times* donated "to [the] Clinton Foundation [then] downplay[ed] the Clinton Foundation scandal."[122]

The "FBI found extensive evidence Hillary emails violated federal records laws," yet this was minimally reported in the mainstream news.[123]

Wikileaks revelations concerning Clinton campaign emails showed a direct link to 38 journalists from ABC News, Bloomberg, CBS, CNN, *Daily Beast*, GPG, *Huffington Post*, *More*, MSNBC, NBC, *New Yorker*, the *New York Times*, *People*, Politico, VICE, VOX, and others who were providing the Clinton campaign with special privileges and favoritism,[124] including advanced "notice of debate questions, the promise of positive coverage, and even editorial control over stories."[125]

The *NYT* refused to report on the revelation that "85 of 154 people who got an audience with Hillary Clinton while she led the State Department had donated to her family charity."[126] CNN actually castigated the AP for publishing the story.[127]

The MSM virtually ignored that newly "released emails [from the Wikileak dump] suggest a senior Hillary Clinton aide stage-managed her first hearing on the Benghazi terrorist attack by feeding specific topics Clinton wanted to address to Democratic Sen. Robert Menendez, who at the time was acting chairman of the Foreign Relations Committee."[128]

The MSM downplayed Clinton saying, "'you can put half of Trump supporters into what I call the basket of deplorables. Right? Racist, sexist, homophobic, xenophobic, Islamaphobic, you name it. . . .'" Some major news networks even condoned the remarks.[129]

CNN was caught grossly oversampling Clinton supporters to make it look as if Clinton won the October 9 debate.[130]

Leaked emails showed that the "chairman of Univision, Haim Saban, [secretly] pressured Hillary Clinton's presidential campaign to attack Donald Trump more fiercely on immigration . . ." a story virtually ignored by the mainstream news.[131]

In exchange for access to Clinton, the *New York Times* allowed Clinton to veto any of reporter Mark Leibovich's story on her.[132] Same type of arrangement from *Politico* reporter Glenn Rush, who "apologized to campaign chairman John Podesta for writing a 'shitty' story that embarrassed the operation."[133]

CNBC chief Washington correspondent and *New York Times* political writer John Harwood . . . is shown in [email] leaks giving advice to the Clinton campaign . . . as is *The Boston Globe*'s op-ed editor Marjorie Pritchard.[134]

A *Washington Post* reporter gave former White House Senior Counselor John Podesta advance reassurance she was withholding information about his ethically compromising financial links to a Democratic mega-donor.[135]

As of October 2016, journalists financially contributed to Clinton's campaign at a rate of almost 27 to 1 over Trump.[136]

NBC/Survey Monkey, ABC News Tracking, Reuters/IPSOS, CBS News/NY Times/SSRS, all polling on issues related to Hillary Clinton and the campaign, had employee political donations going upwards of 96% to candidate Clinton.[137]

Undercover video footage suggests that both the "Clinton Campaign [and the] DNC coordinated with organizations to incite violence at Trump events," a revelation receiving virtually no press coverage.[138]

"The FBI's probe into pay-for-play schemes at the Clinton Foundation and the State Department has been far more expansive than anyone reported so far and has been going on for more than a year. FBI sources even warned there could be indictments down the road." Other than FN, virtually no mainstream news coverage of this explosive revelation.[139]

Glenn Greenwald, a liberal journalist from *The Intercept* stated, "The U.S. media is essentially 100 percent united, vehemently, against Trump, and preventing him from being elected president. I don't have an actual problem with that because I share the premises on which it is based.[140]

In a story "about a man who saved a baby from a hot car, CNN's Headline News . . . chose to censor the Good Samaritan's 'Trump for President 2016' T-shirt on air."[141]

Politico co-founder Jim VandeHei stated that the, "number of mainstream media reporters who are out there expressing their explicit opinions, that tend to be decisively pro-Hillary and anti-Trump, to me is scary."[142]

CNN claimed Trump called for 'racial' profiling" when he never did.[143]

Third debate moderator Lester Holt, who aggressively interrupted and challenged Trump (approximately 41 times) and did not treat Clinton in the same manner (approximately 7 times), received praise from the MSM for his aggressive questioning, except from those who criticized him for not being aggressive enough.[144]

During the debate in St. Louis, "moderators Raddatz [and] Cooper interrupt, talk over and even debate Trump."[145] The same treatment was not given to Clinton.

In response to Trump's election win, an MSNBC host stated live to viewers, "You're not having a terrible, terrible dream. Also you're not dead and you haven't gone to hell."[146]

The press virtually ignored discovery of an audio tape of Hillary Clinton proposing in 2006 to rig the Palestinian election.[147]

The *Washington Times* released a special report on stories of Clinton's "pay to play" scandals that the news media had either downplayed or ignored: "Clinton State Dept. approved transfer of 20 percent of U.S. Uranium to Russian Government, as Clinton Foundation took in $145 million in donations from investors of the deal"; "Clinton ally aided the wife of an FBI agent who was investigating Mrs. Clinton's email server"; "Bill Clinton gets $1 million birthday present from Qatar for 5 minute meeting request"; "Hillary Clinton's State Dept. Gave Clinton Foundation Donors Weapons Deals."[148]

Within three weeks after "the Democratic National Committee emails were leaked . . . three people associated with the DNC [had] been found dead under what could be questionable circumstances." The press refused to investigate the potential relationship.[149]

The press ignored the story that the head of a for-profit university that donated close to "$5 million to the Clinton Foundation was rewarded with an invite to a high-profile State Department dinner at the request of then-Secretary of State Hillary Clinton." Shortly after, Bill Clinton was signed on as an honorary chancellor to the university and received $17 million over 5 years.[150]

The press virtually ignored the Wikileaks revelation of an email by Clinton aid Huma Abedin that it "was HRC's idea" for the King of Morocco to pay $12 million into the Clinton Foundation in exchange for then Secretary of State Clinton to speak at a meeting of the Clinton Global Initiative in Morocco.[151]

The examples are legion, and I could easily cite several hundred more that occurred during the campaign. The point is the potential link with unethical reportorial habits and the press over-identification with Clinton. I suggest that the strong consubstantiality results in bias for Clinton and against Trump; Trump's faults are magnified and Clinton's minimized. Moreover, the press is so consubstantial with Clinton that it actually attempts to explain away its bias against Trump. For instance, the *New York Times* made the intellectually vacuous argument that reporters could ignore objectivity and discriminate against Trump because he is "an abnormal and potentially dangerous candidate."[152] The *New York Post* pointed out that "The largest broadcast networks—CBS, NBC and ABC—and major newspapers like the New York Times and Washington Post have jettisoned all pretense of fair play. Their fierce determination to keep Trump out of the Oval Office has no precedent. The shameful display of naked partisanship by the elite media is unlike anything seen in modern America."[153]

Writers from the Vox, Bill Moyer's website, the *Atlantic*, and others seemed in agreement; that is, journalists who personally oppose Trump have an obligation to "throw out the textbook" when covering him, according to *New York Times*'s media critic Jim Rutenberg. Moreover, journalists assert that because *they* feel Trump "is a mortal danger to this country" they are actually being responsible journalists by actively opposing him.[154] Such thinking is in direct opposition to the very norm of reportorial ethics the press purports to embrace, and instead announces political subjectivity as norm: "good press if I agree with you, bad if I don't." This became so extreme that some "media figures [were] actively lobbying their peers to challenge . . . Trump more aggressively when interviewing him or his surrogates, or even block Trump's campaign from gaining access to the press."[155] As Howard Kurtz pointed out, "This is about the mainstream media's reporters, editors and producers, whose credo is supposed to be fairness. And now some of them are flat-out making the case for unfairness—an unprecedented approach for an unprecedented campaign."[156] And it shows no signs of abating following the election. According to NBC News, the "Pew Research Center, in a content analysis of the early days of the Trump presidency, found that 62 percent of the coverage was negative and only 5 percent was positive. In contrast, President Barack Obama's coverage in early 2009 was 42 percent positive and 20 percent negative, the study said."[157]

ACCOUNTABILITY, CONSUBSTANTIALITY, AND THE ATTACK ON THE AMERICAN REPUBLIC

The press was consubstantial with Clinton's worldview, one whose values are rooted in both the Democratic National Committee's platform and progressive politics. Part of this might be due to the political leanings of the press. Studies have demonstrated the overwhelmingly left-of-center, progressive composition of mainstream journalists, and have also shed light on journalists' reportorial hostility toward conservatives and Republicans.[158] But we need to be open to the possibility that shared worldviews contributed to this as well; that in as much as it was consubstantial with Clinton the press was working (consciously or not) on its own behalf in helping her and hurting Trump. That the press here is consubstantial with Clinton (or perhaps so inconsubstantial with Trump) is certainly one explanation for why it was able to so easily ignore its social responsibility to remain neutral during the campaign, and instead act to help candidate Clinton. The press voluntarily became, in practice, an extension of her campaign.

That press reporting so closely comports with the worldview of Clinton takes it away from its self-declared ethical norms, and also away from a libertarian/social responsibility model of the press. That reporting so closely aligned with what Clinton was saying leads toward the conclusion that the press has, consciously or not, subordinated itself to those views, adopting *in practice* a model of press functioning that seems to blend the old Soviet model and an authoritarian model of press production. Willingly and intentionally in some cases, the press morphed into a self-controlled authoritarian style model of news production; thus, in some ways, the media here acted as an arm of the Clinton campaign, grounded in progressive ideology. The press acted to serve the needs of its worldview, which was one with Clinton's. Taken further, one could say that "our national media now sees itself as part of the government, and as a consequence, the media's mission to hold institutions accountable has been dropped entirely in favor of relentless agenda-pushing"; and this goes a long way toward explaining its favoritism toward Clinton.[159] And perhaps its hostility toward President Trump.

Certainly, the worldview of the press in some ways explains the press bias I detected, and also explains how the press abrogated its social mandate as the fourth estate watchdog and morphed into a new model of news production; thus it, in some ways, exemplified the "opposition" of which Bannon spoke. In 2002 I wrote that, "by its political composition and its biased reportorial practices, the press not only breaks its own code of ethics, it functions as an anti-democratic institution since it undermines the very democratic ideals it professes to uphold."[160] I see no reason to change that assessment. If anything, the press is now *openly* taking sides in partisan political concerns, slowly rending the very fabric of our Republic.[161] Such raw partisan shaping of political news has come back to haunt the mainstream press; American's trust in the news media is at a historic low.[162] Voters don't trust news media fact-checking.[163] A majority of Americans believe it was the media, not the Russians, that [were] attempting to influence the 2016 election.[164] A majority of voters believe the press was and is biased against Trump.[165] Alarmingly, voters are mistrusting of polls themselves and feel that pollsters are out to stop the now elected president's agenda.[166] The American mainstream news media, in terms of political reporting, is seen as partisan, unethical, and untrustworthy. It has only itself to blame.

NOTES

1. Francesca Chambers, "Trump's Chief Strategist Steve Bannon Strolls by White House Reporters, Says It's 'The Opposition Party, All Lined Up,'" *DailyMail.com*, February 15, 2017. http://www.dailymail.co.uk/news/article-4229064/Bannon-trolls-White-House-reporters-opposition-party.html.

2. "Inside Trump's Nixonian Strategy to Make the Media the Enemy," *MSNBC* (February 17, 2017). http://www.msnbc.com/the-last-word/watch/inside-trump-s-nixonian-strategy-to-make-the-media-the-enemy-880058435528.

3. Jim A. Kuypers, "The Presidential Nomination Acceptance Speeches of Donald Trump and Hillary Clinton: Terministic Screens and Antagonistic Worldviews," *Political Campaign Communication: Theory, Method and Practice.* Robert E. Denton Jr., ed. (Lanham, MD: Lexington Books, 2017): 141–168.

4. News sources included the following: *Washington Post*, *New York Times*, *ABC News*, *CBS News*, *NBC News*, *CNN*, and *Fox News*. Unless otherwise noted, all documents were obtained through Lexis-Nexus.

5. A few unpublished studies apply the pentad to news reports, but do not explore the worldviews of the press. For instance, Burkean pentadic ratios and framing analysis have been examined in María José Canel and Mario García Gurrionero, "Framing Analysis, Dramatism and Terrorism Coverage: Politician and Press Responses to the Madrid Airport Bombing," *Communication and Society* 29(4), 133–149. These researchers use the term motive as synonymous with a communicator's purpose. See, too, John Marlier, "Fifteen Minutes of Glory: A Burkean Analysis of Press Coverage of Oliver North's Testimony," *Political Communication and Persuasion* 6.4 (1989), 269–288. Kevin R. McClure does explore terminological screens and the news media in "Media Coverage of Natural Disasters: Pentadic Cartography and the Case of the 1993 Great Flood of the Mississippi," *KB Journal* 8.1 (2012), http://kbjournal.org/mcclure_media_coverage_natural_disasters. Kathryn M. Olson looks at how form functions across a series of news articles in "The Function of Form in Newspapers' Political Conflict Coverage: The *New York Times*' Shaping of Expectations in the Bitburg Controversy," *Political Communication* 12 (1995): 43–64.

6. For examples of composite narratives see: Jim A. Kuypers, Marilyn J. Young, and Michael K. Launer, "Composite Narrative, Authoritarian Discourse, and the Soviet Response to the Destruction of Iran Air Flight 655," *Quarterly Journal of Speech* 87.3 (2001): 305–320; and Jim A. Kuypers, "From Chaos, Community: The Crisis Leadership of Virginia Tech President Charles W. Steger," *The American Communication Journal* 9.1 (2007) http://acjournal.org/journal/2007/Spring/articles/leadership_crisis.html.

7. Kenneth Burke, *Language as Symbolic Action: Essays on Life, Literature, and Method* (Berkeley: University of California Press, 1966), 45.

8. Ibid., 49.

9. Ibid., 46.

10. For example, see Adriana Angel and Benjamin Bates, "Terministic Screens of Corruption: A Cluster Analysis of Colombian Radio Conversations," *KB Journal* 10.1 (2014).

11. Richard Bello, "A Burkeian Analysis of the 'Political Correctness' Confrontation in Higher Education," *Southern Communication Journal* 61 (1996): 243–252. If you are unfamiliar with the Burkean pentad, see Ryan Erik McGeough and Andrew King, "Dramatism and Kenneth Burke's Pentadic Criticism," *Rhetorical Criticism: Perspectives in Action*, 2nd ed. Jim A. Kuypers, ed. (Lanham, MD: Rowman and Littlefield, 2016), 147–165; Kenneth Burke, *A Grammar of Motives*, (Berkeley: University of California Press, 1969); Kenneth Burke, *A Rhetoric of Motives* (New York: George Braziller, Inc., 1955).

12. Burke, *A Grammar of Motives*, 199.

13. Jim A. Kuypers, "The January 1832 Debate on Slavery in Virginia: Clashing Scenes and Terministic Screens," *KB Journal* 12.2 (2017). http://kbjournal.org/kuypers_1832_debate_on_slavery. Quote found in Burke, *Language as Symbolic Action*, 47.

14. Clarke J. Rountree III, "Coming to Terms with Kenneth Burke's Pentad," *American Communication Journal* 1, no. 3 (May 1998), http://ac-journal.org/journal/vol1/iss3/burke/rountree.html.

15. Ibid.

16. Ibid.

17. Burke, *A Rhetoric of Motives*, 115.

18. Donald J. Trump: "Address Accepting the Presidential Nomination at the Republican National Convention in Cleveland, Ohio," July 21, 2016. Online by Gerhard Peters and John T. Woolley, *The American Presidency Project*. http://www.presidency.ucsb.edu/ws/?pid=117935. Emphasis mine for these and all subsequent italicized instances of "we."

19. Bernard Brock, Robert L. Scott, and James Chesebro, "Rhetorical Criticism: A Burkeian Approach Revisited," *Methods of Rhetorical Criticism: A Twentieth-Century Perspective* 3rd ed. (Detroit: Wayne State University Press, 1990), 189.

20. There were forty-eight Trump and forty-six Clinton and press reports and broadcasts used for this chapter, almost all of which were generated using the search terms "Trump" or "Clinton," "nomination," and "speech" in Lexis Nexus.

21. Ruth Marcus, "Donald Trump Just Set the Table for Clinton; Now All She Has to Do Is Lay Out an Appetizing Agenda," *Washington Post Blogs*, July 22, 2016.

22. Ibid.

23. Editorial, "Mr. Trump's Apocalypse Now," *Washington Post* (July 22, 2016).

24. Dan Harris, "Trump's Big Night; Speech at RNC," *Nightline* (ABC News), July 22, 2016.

25. Alisyn Camerota, Chris Cuomo, Phil Mattingly, Ron Brownstein, Maeve Reston, David Gregory, Jason Carroll, "Donald Trump Accepts Republican Nomination; Ivanka Trump Appeals to Women in Speech," *Early Start* (CNN), July 22, 2016.

26. E. J. Dionne Jr., "Trump's Acceptance Speech: Seeking Victory by Scaring the Country to Death," *Washington Post*, July 22, 2016.

27. Patrick Healy and Jonathan Martin, "Trump, as Nominee, Vows: 'I am Your Voice,'" *New York Times*, July 22, 2016.

28. Harris, "Trump's Big Night."

29. Michael Barbaro, "Failed Chance to Humanize Outsize Image," *New York Times*, July 22, 2016.

30. Editorial, "Donald Trump's Campaign of Fear," *New York Times*, July 22, 2016.

31. Camerota, Cuomo, Mattingly, Brownstein, Reston, Gregory, Carroll, "Donald Trump Accepts Republican Nomination."

32. Maria Bartiromo, Dagen McDowell, John Roberts, Cheryl Casone, Jeff Flock, "Donald Trump Accepts Republic Nomination; GOP Convention Ends," *Mornings with Maria* (FOX) (July 22, 2016). A notable exception to this was CBS running a single story in which this quote was featured, but removed from the "I alone" statement. See, Reena Flores, "Donald Trump Offers Dark Vision of America in GOP Convention Speech," *CBSNews.com*, July 22, 2016. http://www.cbsnews.com/news/donald-trump-gop-convention-speech/.

33. Camerota, et al., "Donald Trump Accepts Republican Nomination."

34. Charlie Rose and Gayle King, *CBS This Morning*, July 22, 2016.

35. Harris, "Trump's Big Night."
36. Ibid.
37. Aaron Blake, "Trump's Speech Was Either Reagan 2.0 or the Death of the GOP, Depending on Your Republican; Donald Trump's Ability to Divide the GOP Persists," *Washington Post Blogs*, July 22, 2016. Internal quotation marks added by author.
38. Of note is that Trump cited each of his assertions, using some 282 endnotes to cite sources primarily reported from the very press agencies denying the veracity of the assertions he made in his speech. No mention of his citation of sources was mentioned.
39. John Berman, Christine Romans, Manu Raju, Ben Ferguson, John Pillips, Maria Cardona, Josh Rogin, "Donald Trump Accepts Republican Nomination; Clinton to Unveil Running Mate Today," *Early Start* (CNN), July 22, 2016.
40. Ibid.
41. Ibid.
42. Ibid.
43. Rose and King, *CBS This Morning*.
44. Anderson Cooper, John King, Wolf Blitzer, Dana Bash, Jake Tapper, "Donald Trump Accepts Presidential Nomination; Trump's Speech Examined," *CNN Live Event/Special*, July 22, 2016.
45. Cooper, et al.
46. Camerota, et al.
47. Harris, "Trump's Big Night."
48. John Berman and Christine Romans, "Trump Accepts Party's Nomination; Examining Trump Acceptance Speech," *Early Start* (CNN), July 22, 2016.
49. Editorial, "Mr. Trump's Apocalypse Now."
50. Camerota, et al., "Donald Trump Accepts."
51. Zain Asher, Phil Mattingly, Jason Carroll, Athena Jones, Chris Moody, Ian Lee, Ben Wedeman, Joe Johns, "Reviewing Donald Trumps' Speech; Ivanka Trump Speech Examined; Mexican President Meeting with President Obama; Turkish President Cracks Down on Opposition; Iraqis Flee Mosul," *IDESK* (CNN), July 22, 2016.
52. Berman, et al., "Donald Trump Accepts."
53. John Berman and Christine Romans, "Trump Accepts Party's Nomination; Examining Trump Acceptance Speech," *Early Start* (CNN), July 22, 2016.
54. Steven A. Camarota, "Welfare Use by Legal and Illegal Immigrant Households," Center for Immigration Studies, September 9, 2015. https://cis.org/Welfare-Use-Legal-and-Illegal-Immigrant-Households
55. Hans A. von Spakovsky and Grant Strobl, "What the Media Won't Tell You about Illegal Immigration and Criminal Activity," The Heritage Foundation, March 13, 2017. http://www.heritage.org/immigration/commentary/what-the-media-wont-tell-you-about-illegal-immigration-and-criminal-activity; Steven A. Camarota and Jessica Vaughan, "Immigration and Crime," Center for Immigration Studies, November 18, 2009, https://cis.org/Report/Immigration-and-Crime; Hans Von Spakovsky, "Crimes by Illegal Aliens, Not Legal Immigrants, Are the Real Problem," *The Hill*, April 4, 2017, http://thehill.com/blogs/pundits-blog/immigration/327229-crimes-by-illegal-aliens-not-legal-immigrants-are-the-real.
56. Reena Flores, "Donald Trump Offers Dark Vision of America in GOP Convention Speech,"*CBSNews.com*, July 22, 2016, http://www.cbsnews.com/news/donald-trump-gop-convention-speech/.
57. James Griffiths, "World Reacts to Donald Trump's Acceptance Speech," CNN, July 22, 2016, http://www.cnn.com/2016/07/22/politics/donald-trump-rnc-speech-world-reacts/index.html.
58. See, for instance, https://www.forbes.com/sites/johnmauldin/2017/01/12/chinese-currency-manipulation-could-become-a-global-problem-in-2017/#2ae5c4334fd9.
59. Editorial, "Donald Trump's Campaign of Fear."
60. George Howell, Tal Kopan, Shasta Darlington, Clare Sebastian, Nic Robertson, Frida Ghitis, Ben Wedeman, Alexandra Fields, Matt Rivers, Kate Riley, Claire Sebastian, Christine Brennan, "Donald Trump Accepts Presidential Nomination; Brazil Foiled . . . Olympic," *CNN Newsroom*, July 22, 2016. In fairness, the CNN political reporter, Tal Kopan, did admit that a

nomination acceptance speech might not be the place for such details, but his was the exception to prove the rule of press coverage.

61. Eric Bolling, "Clinton Fires Away at Trump during Acceptance Speech; Trump vs Clinton Now Begins," *The O'Reilly Factor*, Fox News Network, July 29, 2016.

62. Alisyn Camerata, Chris Cuomo, Joe John, Dick Gregory, Juana Summers, John Avlon, "Examining Hillary Clinton's Acceptance Speech," *CNN: New Day*, July 29, 2016. Emphasis mine.

63. Bolling, "Clinton Fires."

64. Jennifer Rubin, "Did Hillary Clinton Close the Deal?" *Washington Post Blogs: Right Turn* (July 29, 2016). Emphasis mine.

65. Danielle Paquette, "The Central Difference between Hillary Clinton and Donald Trump Comes Down to Two Words," *Washington Post Blogs*, July 29, 2016.

66. Aaron Blake, "Welcome to the Next, Most Negative Presidential Election of our Lives," *Washington Post Blogs: The Fix*, July 29, 2016.

67. Peter Marks, "A Slick Production Fit for Broadway," *Washington Post*, July 29, 2016.

68. Blake, "Welcome to the Next."

69. Jennifer Rubin, "Republican's Wishful Thinking: Enough Already," *Washington Post*, July 29, 2016.

70. Alex Seitz-Wald, "On Historic Night, Hillary Clinton Favors Pragmatism Over Flair," *NBC News*, July 29, 2016. http://www.nbcnews.com/storyline/2016-conventions/historic-night-hillary-clinton-favors-pragmatism-over-flair-n619476.

71. Dan Balz, "Clinton Doubles Down on Hope," *Washington Post*, July 29, 2016.

72. Jennifer Rubin, "Did Hillary Clinton Close the Deal?" *Washington Post Blogs: Right Turn*, July 29, 2016.

73. James Hohmann, "The Daily 202: Hillary Clinton Tries to Be All Things to All People at Democratic Convention," *Washington Post Blogs*, July 29, 2016.

74. Seitz-Wald, "On Historic Night."

75. Brooke Baldwin, Jeff Zeleny, Jackie Kucinich, John Avalon, Jason Carroll, "Hitting Trail; Presidential Race; Trump on Twitter," *CNN Newsroom*, July 29, 2016. See, too, for examples, Balz; Rubin; Lee.

76. Philip Rucker and Anne Gearan, "Clinton Offers an Optimistic Vision for the Future; Her Historic Speech Highlights Diversity and Opportunity," *Washington Post Blogs*, July 29, 2016.

77. Michael Barbaro and Amy Chozick, "Asking the Public to Set Doubts Aside and Put Faith in Competence," *New York Times*, July 29, 2016. Emphasis mine.

78. Hohmann, "The Daily 202."

79. Of this "we" I write at great length in Kuypers, "The Presidential Nomination Acceptance Speeches of Donald Trump and Hillary Clinton."

80. Michael Gerson, "Clinton vs. Trump: A Choice Between the Uninspiring and the Unfit; I Get That Inspiration Is Not Hillary Clinton's 'Thing,' but She Missed a Key Moment to Go After Donald Trump," *Washington Post Blogs*, July 29, 2016.

81. Paquette, "The Central Difference."

82. Ibid.

83. Chuck Todd, "Meet the Press—July 24, 2016," *Meet the Press*, July 24, 2016. http://www.nbcnews.com/meet-the-press/meet-press-july-24–2016-n615706.

84. Balz, "Clinton Doubles."

85. Gerson, "Clinton vs. Trump."

86. Patrick Healy and Amy Chozick, "Clinton Warns of 'a Moment of Reckoning,'" *New York Times*, July 29, 2016.

87. Kuypers, "The Presidential Nomination Acceptance Speeches of Donald Trump and Hillary Clinton."

88. Editorial, "Hillary Clinton Makes History," *New York Times*, 29 July, 2016.

89. Dan Balz, "Clinton Doubles Down on Hope," *Washington Post*, July 29, 2016.

90. Healy and Chozick, "Clinton Warns."

91. E. J. Dionne Jr., "Clinton Takes the Fight to Trump," *Washington Post Blogs*, July 29, 2016.

92. Ibid.
93. Gerson, "Clinton vs. Trump."
94. Seitz-Wald, "On Historic Night."
95. Neil Irwin, "How Hillary Clinton and Donald Trump Differ on Taxes," *New York Times*, August 12, 2016. https://www.nytimes.com/2016/08/13/upshot/how-hillary-clinton-and-donald-trump-differ-on-taxes.html and http://www.atr.org/full-list-hillary-s-planned-tax-hikes.
96. Seitz-Wald, "On Historic Night."
97. Barbaro and Chozick, "Asking the Public."
98. Burke, *A Grammar of Motives*, 171.
99. "Idealism," *Oxford English Dictionary*, New Edition, http://dictionary.oed.com.
100. Richard E. Crable and John J. Makay, "Kenneth Burke's Concept of Motives in Rhetorical Theory," *Today's Speech* (Winter 1972), 14.
101. Burke, *Grammar of Motives*, 171.
102. Ibid., 172.
103. McGeough and King, 153.
104. Burke, *Grammar of Motives*, 131.
105. Ibid.
106. Jim A. Kuypers, "From Science, Moral Poetics: Dr. James Dobson's Response to the Fetal Tissue Research Initiative," *Quarterly Journal of Speech* 86.2 (2000), 154–155.
107. McGeough and King, 156.
108. "Pragmatic," *Oxford English Dictionary*, New Edition, http://dictionary.oed.com.
109. Brock, Scott, and Chesebro, 189.
110. Richard E. Crable and John J. Makay, "Kenneth Burke's Concept of Motives in Rhetorical Theory," *Today's Speech* (Winter 1972), 14.
111. Burke, *Grammar of Motives*, 171.
112. Ibid., 172.
113. Burke, *Language as Symbolic Action,* 46.
114. Code of Ethics, Society for Professional Journalists, http://www.spj.org/ethicscode.asp.
115. American Society of Newspaper Editors Statement of Principles, http://asne.org/content.asp?pl=24&sl=171&contentid=171.
116. For the complete listing of the Statement of Ethical Principles, see http://www.apme.com/?page=EthicsStatement
117. There are numerous types of biases, and also numerous ways of detecting bias. For examples of these see, Denton, Robert E. and Jim A. Kuypers, *Politics and Communication in America: Campaigns, Media, and Governing in the 21st Century*, (Carbondale, IL: Waveland Press, 2008): 111–125, and also Aamidor, Abe, Jim A. Kuypers, and Susan Wiesinger, *Media Smackdown: Deconstructing the News and the Future of Journalism* (New York, Peter Lang Publishing, 2013), 127–154, and Kuypers, Jim A., *Press Bias and Politics: How the Media Frame Controversial Issues* (Westport, CT: Praeger, 2002).
118. Rich Noyes, "MRC Study: Documenting TV's Twelve Weeks of Trump Bashing," *MRC Newsbusters*, October 25, 2016, https://www.newsbusters.org/blogs/nb/rich-noyes/2016/10/25/mrc-study-documenting-tvs-twelve-weeks-trump-bashing.
119. Kelly Riddell, "A Biased Media in Action," *Washington Times* (September 29, 2016), http://www.washingtontimes.com/news/2016/sep/29/media-double-standard-revealed-in-trump-16-vs-obam/.
120. Matthew Balen, "UPDATED: CNN Plays SIX Times More Convention Videos from Dems than GOP," *MRC Newsbusters*, July 28, 2016, https://www.newsbusters.org/blogs/nb/matthew-balan/2016/07/28/cnn-plays-five-times-more-videos-dems-gop-during-conventions. Emphasis mine.
121. Patrick Howley, "New York Times Tech Columnist Calls on Google to Hide Hillary Health Info," *Brietbart*, August 21, 2016, http://www.breitbart.com/2016-presidential-race/2016/08/21/nyt-tech-columnist-calls-google-suppress-hillary-health-info/.
122. Liz Crokin, "Media Orgs Donate to Clinton Foundation Then Downplay Clinton Foundation Scandal," *Observer*, August 29, 2016. http://observer.com/2016/08/media-orgs-donate-to-clinton-foundation-then-downplay-clinton-foundation-scandal/.

123. Kellen Howell, "FBI Found Extensive Evidence Hillary Emails Violated Federal Records Laws," *Circa*, September 1, 2016, https://www.circa.com/story/2016/09/01/fbi-found-extensive-evidence-hillary-emails-violated-federal-records-laws.

124. Glenn Greenwald, "Exclusive: New Email Leak Reveals Clinton Campaign's Cozy Press Relationship," *The Intercept*, October 9, 2016, https://theintercept.com/2016/10/09/exclusive-new-email-leak-reveals-clinton-campaigns-cozy-press-relationship/ and "The Podesta Emails," https://wikileaks.org/podesta-emails/ and Jack Shafer, "WikiLeaks and the Oily Washington Press," *Politico*, October 18, 2016, http://www.politico.com/magazine/story/2016/10/john-podesta-emails-wikileaks-press-214367.

125. "BIAS ALERT: WikiLeaks Exposes Media's Secret Support of Clinton," *Fox News*, October 12, 2016, http://www.foxnews.com/politics/2016/10/12/bias-alert-wikileaks-exposes-medias-secret-support-clinton.html.

126. "BIAS ALERT: *New York Times* Finds Latest Clinton Foundation Bombshell Unfit to Print," August 24, 2016, http://www.foxnews.com/politics/2016/08/24/bias-alert-new-york-times-finds-latest-clinton-foundation-bombshell-unfit-to-print.html; "AP: Many Donors to Clinton Foundation Met with Hillary Clinton at State Department," *CBS News*, August 23, 2016, http://www.cbsnews.com/news/ap-many-donors-to-clinton-foundation-met-with-her-at-state/.

127. "BIAS ALERT: CNN Host Grills AP Boss for Publishing Clinton Exposé," *Fox News*, August 29, 2016, http://www.foxnews.com/politics/2016/08/29/bias-alert-cnn-host-grills-ap-boss-for-publishing-clinton-expos.html.

128. Catherine Herridge and Pamela K. Browne, "Clinton Aide Stage-Managed Benghazi Hearing Questions," *Fox News*, September 6, 2016, http://www.foxnews.com/politics/2016/09/06/wired-it-emails-suggest-clinton-aide-stage-managed-benghazi-hearing-questions.html.

129. Howard Kurtz, "Media Rip Hillary's Handling of Health, but Not Attack on Trump Backers," *Fox News*, September 14, 2016, http://www.foxnews.com/politics/2016/09/14/media-rip-hillarys-handling-health-but-not-attack-on-trump-backers.html.

130. Paul Joseph Watson, "CNN Rigs Its Own Poll Again to Claim Clinton Won the Debate," *Infowars*, October 10, 2016, https://www.infowars.com/cnn-rigs-its-own-poll-again-to-claim-clinton-won-the-debate/.

131. Mark Hensch, "Report: Univision Chief Urged Clinton Camp to Hit Trump, Hacked Emails Show," *The Hill*, October 10, 2016, http://thehill.com/blogs/ballot-box/presidential-races/300332-univision-chief-urged-clinton-camp-to-hit-trump.

132. Brendan Kirby, "New York Times Gave Hillary Veto Power," *Lifezette*, February 23, 2017, http://www.lifezette.com/polizette/new-york-times-gave-hillary-veto/.

133. Evan Gahr, "No Consequences from Media Peers for Reporters Caught Colluding with Hillary," *Observer*, October 24, 2017, http://observer.com/2016/10/no-consequences-from-media-peers-for-reporters-caught-colluding-with-hillary/.

134. Alex Pfeiffer, "Hill's Shills: Leaks Have Exposed Journalists in Clinton's Corner," *Daily Caller*, October 11, 2016, http://dailycaller.com/2016/10/11/hills-shills-leaks-have-exposed-journalists-in-clintons-corner/.

135. Mark Tapscott, "Washington Post Reporter Spiked Info about Podesta Conflict of Interest," *Daily Caller*, October 11, 2016, http://dailycaller.com/2016/10/11/washington-post-reporter-spiked-info-about-podesta-conflict-of-interest/.

136. Dave Leventhal and Michael Beckel, "Buying of the President: Journalists shower Hillary Clinton with Campaign Cash," The Center for Public Integrity, October 18, 2016, https://www.publicintegrity.org/2016/10/17/20330/journalists-shower-hillary-clinton-campaign-cash.

137. Leon Sculti, "Presidential Pollsters' Political Contributions: Heavily for Hillary Clinton," *Heat Street*, November 4, 2016, https://web.archive.org/web/20170706041953/https://heatst.com/politics/presidential-pollsters-political-contributions-heavily-for-hillary-clinton.

138. Tim Haines, "James O'Keefe: Clinton Campaign, DNC Coordinated with Organizations to Incite Violence at Trump Events," *Real Clear Politics*, October 17, 2016, https://www.realclearpolitics.com/video/2016/10/17/new_okeefe_video_clinton_campaign_dnc_coordinated_with_organizations_to_beat_up_trump_supporters.html.

139. Brent Bozell and Tim Graham, "Bozell and Graham Column: Network Blackout Exposes Corrupt Media," *MRC Newsbusters*, November 3, 2016, https://www.newsbusters.org/

blogs/nb/tim-graham/2016/11/03/bozell-graham-column-network-blackout-exposes-corrupt-media.

140. Isaac Chotiner, "Is the Elite Media Failing to Reach Trump Voters?" *Slate*, July 28, 2016, http://www.slate.com/articles/news_and_politics/interrogation/2016/07/glenn_greenwald_on_donald_trump_the_dnc_hack_and_a_new_mccarthyism.html.

141. "BIAS ALERT: HLN Blurs Out Retired Officer's Trump 2016 Shirt," *Fox News*, September 1, 2016, http://www.foxnews.com/politics/2016/09/01/bias-alert-hln-blurs-out-retired-officers-trump-2016-shirt.html.

142. Duane Patterson, "Politico Co-Founder Jim VandeHei on the MSM Anti-Trump Bias in 2016," *Hugh Hewitt*, September 9, 2016, http://www.hughhewitt.com/politico-co-founder-jim-vandehei-msm-anti-trump-bias-2016/.

143. "CNN Claims Trump Called for 'Racial' Profiling," *Fox News*, September 20, 2016, http://www.foxnews.com/politics/2016/09/20/cnn-claims-trump-called-for-racial-profiling-didnt.html.

144. Heat Street Staff, "Lester Holt: The Third Debater?" *Heat Street*, September 26, 2016, https://web.archive.org/web/20170705093418/http://heatst.com/politics/lester-holt-the-third-debater/.

145. Dan Gainor, "In St. Louis, Moderators Raddatz, Cooper interrupt, Talk Over and Even Debate Trump," *Fox News*, October 10, 2016, http://www.foxnews.com/opinion/2016/10/10/in-st-louis-moderators-raddatz-cooper-interrupt-talk-over-and-even-debate-trump.html.

146. Joe Barnes, "'Meltdown of the Night' Bitter News Anchor Bemoans Trump's Election Success," *Express* (UK), November 10, 2016, http://www.express.co.uk/news/world/730317/us-election-donald-trump-hillary-clinton-msnbc-coverage-rachel-maddow.

147. Ken Kurson, "2006 Audio Emerges of Hillary Clinton Proposing Rigging Palestine Election," *The Observer*, October 28, 2016, http://observer.com/2016/10/2006-audio-emerges-of-hillary-clinton-proposing-rigging-palestine-election/.

148. Kelly Riddell, "The Clintons' Top 10 Pay-to-Play Scandals," *Washington Times*, October 24, 2016, http://www.washingtontimes.com/news/2016/oct/24/clintons-top-10-pay-play-allegations/.

149. Rachel Alexander, "Clinton Body Count or Left-Wing Conspiracy? Three with Ties to DNC Mysteriously Die," *Townhall*, August 9, 2016, https://townhall.com/columnists/rachelalexander/2016/08/09/clinton-body-count-or-leftwing-conspiracy-three-with-ties-to-dnc-mysteriously-die-n2203000.

150. Bob Fredericks, "Clinton Donor Got State Department Invite—and Bill Got $17M," *New York Post*, October 28, 2016, http://nypost.com/2016/10/28/clinton-donor-got-state-department-invite-and-bill-got-17m/.

151. Ed Henry, "Abedin Implicated Clinton in Foundation Trade-Off with Morocco Amid $12 Million Commitment," *Fox News*, October 20, 2016, http://www.foxnews.com/politics/2016/10/20/abedin-implicated-clinton-in-foundation-trade-off-with-morocco-amid-12-million-commitment.html.

152. Jim Rutenberg, "Trump Is Testing the Norms of Objectivity in Journalism," *New York Times*, August 7, 2016, https://www.nytimes.com/2016/08/08/business/balance-fairness-and-a-proudly-provocative-presidential-candidate.html?_r=0.

153. Michael Goodwin, "American Journalism Is Collapsing before Our Eyes," *New York Post*, August 21, 2016, http://nypost.com/2016/08/21/american-journalism-is-collapsing-before-our-eyes/.

154. Rutenberg, "Trump is Testing."

155. Eddie Scarry, "Media Defend Aggressive Standards for Covering Trump," *Washington Examiner*, August 30, 2016, http://www.washingtonexaminer.com/media-defend-more-aggressive-standards-for-covering-trump/article/2600486.

156. Howard Kurtz, "Media Justify Anti-Trump Bias, Claim He's Too 'Dangerous' for Normal Rules," *Fox News*, August 9, 2016, http://www.foxnews.com/politics/2016/08/09/media-justify-anti-trump-bias-claim-hes-too-dangerous-for-normal-rules.html.

157. Claire Atkinson, "Trump's Right: His Media Coverage Is Mostly Negative," *NBC News*, October 2, 2017, https://www.nbcnews.com/politics/donald-trump/trump-s-right-his-media-coverage-mostly-negative-n806681.

158. See Kuypers, *Partisan Journalism*; Kuypers, *Press Bias and Politics*; Aamidor, Kuypers, and Wiesinger, *Media Smackdown* for examples of this.

159. John Nolte, "How the Political Media's Corruption Destroyed America's Most Crucial Institutions," *Daily Wire*, November 7, 2016, http://www.dailywire.com/news/10555/how-political-medias-corruption-destroyed-americas-john-nolte#exit-modal.

160. Kuypers, *Press Bias and Politics.*

161. I am not alone in this assessment. See, Michael Goodwin, "American Journalism Is Collapsing before Our Eyes," *New York Post*, August 21, 2016, http://nypost.com/2016/08/21/american-journalism-is-collapsing-before-our-eyes/ and Nolte, "How the Political Media's Corruption."

162. Benjamin Mullen, "Gallup: Trust in Media Is at All-Time Low," *Poynter*, September 14, 2016, http://www.poynter.org/2016/gallup-trust-in-media-is-at-all-time-low/430342/.

163. "Voters Don't Trust Media Fact-Checking," *Rasmussen Reports*, September 30, 2016, http://www.rasmussenreports.com/public_content/politics/general_politics/september_2016/voters_don_t_trust_media_fact_checking.

164. "Most Say Media, Not Russians, Tilting the Election," *Rasmussen Reports*, October 18, 2016, http://www.rasmussenreports.com/public_content/politics/general_politics/october_2016/most_say_media_not_russians_tilting_the_election.

165. Nolan D. Mccaskill, "Poll: Majority of Voters Believe Media Biased against Trump," *Politico.com*, October 19, 2016, http://politi.co/2el8Vgf.

166. "Voters Don't Trust Polls, See Anti-Trump Bias," *Rasumssen Reports*, May 5, 2017, http://www.rasmussenreports.com/public_content/politics/general_politics/may_2017/voters_don_t_trust_polls_see_anti_trump_bias.

Chapter Seven

Social Media Candidate Attacks and Hillary Clinton's Failed Narrative in the 2016 Presidential Campaign

Stephanie A. Martin and Andrea J. Terry

The day after her unexpected loss to Donald J. Trump, Hillary Clinton addressed her supporters from the New Yorker's Grand Ballroom in New York City. In a nod to bipartisanship, she was dressed in a deep purple shirt.[1] She used her remarks to both acknowledge the disappointment of her defeat and, it seemed, to embrace one last time the historicity of her candidacy. Recalling her concession speech in the 2008 primary to then-Senator Barack Obama, Clinton acknowledged that while she had "still not shattered that highest and hardest glass ceiling . . . someday someone will and hopefully sooner than we might think right now." Clinton also took time to encourage the girls in her audience, recognizing her role as a standard bearer for females across the country, even in the face of disappointment. "And to all the little girls who are watching this," she said, "never doubt that you are valuable and powerful and deserving of every chance and opportunity in the world to pursue and achieve your own dreams."[2]

Some had criticized Clinton for waiting until the day after the election to offer her public concession. After all, she had called Donald Trump in the early morning hours to concede, but refused to appear before her supporters gathered at the Javits Center in New York, sending only her campaign manager John Podesta to address the crowd. But *Washington Post* columnist Jena McGregor suggested that another reason for Clinton's delay might have been to make sure as many young people—young girls—as possible would see what she had to say:

> Certainly, anyone could have watched a video later online of the speech had it been delivered in the middle of the night, on that vast stage, under that still intact glass ceiling. Yet the importance of the message, and who it was aimed at in particular, allowed for the composure and restraint that was required at such a pivotal and historic moment, even in her loss. And delaying it allowed its message to break through in ways that might have gotten lost in the early morning hours.[3]

The notion that Clinton's message to females across the country about their own potential, as well as the idea that Clinton's message about her own historicity as a candidate, could only "break through" in her concession speech the next morning is startling to imagine. Although Clinton had never encouraged anyone to vote for her because she was a woman—as Kari Anderson writes, to have done so would have been akin to asking to be laughed out of the race[4]—Clinton often made mention of her gender, in both coded and overt ways. For example, in her acceptance speech at the Democratic National Convention, Clinton said, "Tonight, we've reached a milestone in our nation's march toward a more perfect union: the first time that a major party has nominated a woman for president. Standing here as my mother's daughter, and my daughter's mother, I'm so happy this day has come. Happy for grandmothers and little girls and everyone in between. . . . When there are no ceilings, the sky's the limit." She talked often on the campaign trail about her own mother, how much it meant that she was born on the same day the Nineteenth Amendment was passed, and how much progress had been made in the years since.

However inspirational it may have been to some, the narrative of female achievement was but one of many Clinton advanced in the race. Like so many of the messages she tried, it never quite seemed to "break through"; instead it was lost in a surfeit of other narratives and stories—especially attacks on her opponent, Donald Trump. Indeed, among the many mistakes of her campaign, the failure to forward a compelling and cohesive narrative is among the most glaring.

This did not mean that Clinton did not try and try mightily. As we argue in this essay, the confluence of the digital environment of the 2016 race and constraints imposed by Clinton's gender made maintaining a clear message nearly impossible. Even so, this failure of narrative proved catastrophic. In hindsight, if the 2016 race turned on anything, it turned on competing notions about the American story, what it means to belong in the United States, and what citizens owe to their country. Both Clinton and Trump made calls to citizens on this front. On one side was Donald Trump, who said he would "Make America Great Again," invoking a slogan that many said suggested nostalgia for an era gone by, imagined American exceptionalism as intertwined with White hegemony, and tapped into deep-seated anger and disappointment in some parts of the electorate.[5] This clarity of narrative forced

Clinton to craft her message in response to Trump rather than tell her own tale, and to continuously frame her opponent as an unsuitable president who posed a danger to the nation. She urged the citizenry to be "Stronger Together." This "narrative-in-response" tactic by Clinton and her team is evidenced by the fact that the majority of her social media activity took the form of attack—more, indeed, than did Trump's, even though he had the reputation in the race for going negative.[6] It is also made clear by the fact that her motto only makes sense in retort to her opponent's—something she admits was part of her strategy in her memoir.[7]

In this chapter, we primarily consider the narrative(s) that emerged from Clinton throughout her campaign. This will require paying some attention to Trump's campaign rhetoric, but that is not the focus here. Rather, that is our foil. We argue that Trump told voters a clearer, more digestible story, and this story helped push him over the finish line, while Clinton came up short. To be clear, we do not argue that Clinton *should* have won or that she would have made the better president. We do, however, acknowledge that her loss came as a surprise, as the polls and pundits leading up to the election indicated she had more paths to victory than did Trump. Nonetheless, and as scholars primarily interested in campaign rhetoric and campaign narrative, we think her loss is in many ways more predictable than it seemed when it first happened. Through analyzing both Clinton's digital media strategy and several of her most important speeches, we show how the Democratic nominee ended up with a campaign narrative that tried to be collective, inclusive, invested in the American dream, and out to spotlight average voters instead of the candidate herself; but that instead wound up being muddled, attack-oriented, and vague. This allowed Trump the space to continue pressing a line that was both implicit and self-evident—Make America Great Again—but also easy to attach to, while also applying one's own individual meaning. As Kenneth Burke explains, we are persuaded by those with whom we can be made to identify, and we are most easily made to identify with those who have messages we can understand.[8] In 2016, the candidate with a clear, understandable message, was Trump. Our task here is to explain why Clinton came up short.

TELL EVERY STORY: REVIEWING THE LITERATURE

It is no aphorism to say that the Internet has fundamentally changed American politics, including presidential politics. In 1992, when William Jefferson Clinton ran for the nation's top job, the White House did not even have email. That would come in 1993.[9] At first, not everyone was convinced that the technology would prove transformative. In 1999, political science professor Richard Davis wrote that "the internet [would] not lead to the social and political revolution so widely predicted" because only the most civically-motivated would use the new technology to engage the public sphere.[10] He was wrong. By the time George W. Bush took office in 2001, he expressed regret that being president meant he would have to be more careful online, and send fewer emails.[11] In 2008, Barack Obama leveraged the innovations of Howard Dean's 2004 Internet primary campaign, and ran to become the first social media president. He struggled to give up his BlackBerry phone when he took office, eventually earning the nickname, BlackBerry One.[12] By 2012, Obama sat for an "ask me anything" chat on Reddit, while the Romney campaign joined Pinterest and had Ann Romney post pictures, recipes, and other personal items. The candidates wanted to be everywhere to reach as many voters as they could—even if they had to sacrifice some of their most intimate spaces to do so.[13]

Given this 24/7, user-driven digital environment, by the time the 2016 presidential contest came around the rules of campaign communication seemed under constant revision. What remained unchanged, however, was the power of political narrative. In 1987, using Ronald Reagan's success as a master communicator as an example, William Lewis applied narrative theory to the field of presidential rhetoric. In so doing, Lewis explained how the best political speakers tell stories that motivate action. This means that the public sphere is not merely a place where problems are posed and solutions are offered, but it is a space of activity with both actors and reactors.[14] That is, stories are not merely useful for giving humans good reasons about life, in general, as Walter Fisher so famously argued, but are also essential for giving voters good reasons to support certain candidates, take on certain worldviews, and remain committed to certain causes. Among the most important stories politicians tell are myths, including the myth of the American dream. When it comes to myths, the point for hearers is not usually whether the myth is factually *true* in all its parts. Rather, the point is one of narrative fidelity: Is the story *true enough*, which is to say, "*true to life*?"[15]

The distinctions between true, true enough, and true to life ran through the narrative formulations of both the Trump and the Clinton campaigns, usually to the detriment of the Democratic nominee, as we will describe below. The trouble with distinction became especially problematic as the Internet worked to simultaneously amplify and distort campaign communications. That is, social media did not merely influence the 2016 election; 2016 *was* a social media election.[16] Moreover, as simplistic as it sounds, because Clinton is a woman, she had to run as a female candidate. Scholars have made clear how female contenders for all public offices, and especially the presidency, have to contend with a different set of rules than do men. As Clinton became the first woman to be officially nominated for the nation's highest office, the question of her gender, and how to negotiate it as part of her narrative strategy within an online environment, became difficult, to say the least.

First, the technology question: the online environment has transformed how presidential campaign messages are constructed and disseminated.[17] Social media, digital messaging, daily news cycles, and active online communities make it all but inevitable that presidential campaign communications will become fragmented, necessitating progressively simpler and repetitive posts. This creates another inevitability—a superfluity of messages from candidates and their campaigns. Although more voters than ever are online,[18] most are unlikely to attend to ongoing descriptions of a candidate's positions. In his discussion of presidential rhetoric, Stephen Heidt explains that "the scene for presidential speech has become overwhelmed by a glut of messages, the result of which manifests in a public sphere increasingly noted for [citizen] attention deficit and [the] inability to process even the simplest messages.[19] Because of this, voter opinion comes together in haphazard form, as individuals interact with bits and pieces of messages, cobbling together a pastiche of images and storylines that comprise their understanding of candidates. This condition applies even more so to presidential campaigns: the advertisements, social media posts, debates, news coverage, and a torturously long campaign cycle all contribute to a cacophonous rhetorical scene in which candidates must fight to get their messages through.

Second, as a woman, Clinton had to work even harder to be heard and taken seriously inside this cacophonous, fragmented system. Unlike men, Susan Fiske of Princeton has found that women who represent themselves in typically feminine ways are often viewed as warm and welcoming, but not as capable. On the other hand, women who perform in more masculine ways—say, as athletes, or who identify as queer, or who take on roles as business professionals, or who dare to run for office—may be viewed as capable, but not as warm and welcoming. Women really cannot have it both ways.[20] This is a depressing finding, given that twenty years have passed since Kathleen Hall Jamieson released *Beyond the Double Bind*, in which she argued that while the females among us often *have* been historically caught between impossible social constructs (including silence and shame; femininity and competence; aging and invisibility; among others) women were making progress in overcoming these dichotomies.[21] In fact, writes Karrin Vasby Anderson, women in politics still face an uphill climb. While Clinton's loss to Trump was "perhaps the biggest political upset in U.S. history," and while many blame her failure on scandal, a poor relationship with the press, an "underwhelming presence on the stump," or her status as a "political insider in a year of change,"[22] the question of her gender cannot be discounted. Anderson further explains, "The contention that Clinton was the wrong candidate for a 'change' election. . . obscures another, more important, insight—not that Clinton was the wrong woman for the presidency in 2016, but that *every* woman is the wrong woman—and will be until cultural understanding of the presidency changes."[23] It is this insight that drives much of our analysis with regard to how Clinton crafted her narrative. In navigating her status as a female nominee, Clinton had to stand out front as the candidate, but not too far out front, lest she look like she was in it merely for herself and personal ambition. This required her to find a way to both occupy center stage and stand to the side, even as she surfaced as a candidate. She needed a campaign narrative that both recognized her history, her success, and her status as a female in the race, but she also needed to "cultivate an image of competence and leadership without being labeled a 'bitch.'"[24] We argue this ultimately led to message confusion, and a tendency on the part of her campaign to change messages too much. This narrative problem was worsened still by the fact of the ever-present digital campaign. To highlight how this messaging problem took shape in the election, we consider a small sample of Clinton's digital videos, as well as two of her most important speeches—her official announcement speech, given on June 13, 2015, and her speech at the Democratic National Convention, given on July 28, 2016.

CLINTON EMERGES AS A CANDIDATE: EARLY CAMPAIGN COMMUNICATIONS

It is impossible in the space of one chapter to exhaustively analyze Clinton's entire 2016 corpus of speeches and online videos. However, based on our review of Clinton's speeches and campaign videos posted on Facebook and Twitter, it is apparent that two of the Democratic nominee's early digital spots and her first major speech suggest the kind of narrative Clinton and her team initially planned to develop over the course of the campaign. The first of these was her announcement video, and the second was the "Fighter" campaign ad, which originally appeared on Facebook and YouTube. Once we have briefly described the imagery and messaging of these two early digital efforts, we will offer more generalized thoughts about how her campaign narrative ultimately drifted from its early formulation, and became garbled as the candidate's attention turned more toward attacking Trump and his fitness for office.

All candidates, even those who are well known, must pass through a period of presidential surfacing, and Clinton was no exception.[25] In her 2017 memoir about the campaign, she wrote that early polling had indicated that while voters knew who she was and even liked her, many also said they weren't sure about her accomplishments beyond being "an extension of Bill Clinton or Barack Obama."[26] This meant Clinton needed to reintroduce herself, as well as become more trustworthy to voters. As the double-bind scholarship had predicted, Clinton's own campaign research and internal polling revealed doubts among voters that she wanted to be president as an act of national service, rather than for power or other personal gain. "I was determined to change that perception," Clinton wrote. "The reason I had gotten into public service was to make life better for children and families, and now it was my job to make sure people understood that."[27]

Whether or not this is a truthful or merely self-serving recollection of Clinton's entry and early thoughts about the 2016 race—and particularly the relationship and conversation she would need to have with the American public—is not important to this analysis. However, that Clinton and her team may have felt obliged to underscore her call to duty before other possible campaign narratives and, in fact, may have felt compelled to deemphasize the candidate's own personal story for fear of seeming too self-important, is reflected in the rhetoric of the campaign's surfacing period.

THE TWO VIDEOS

Clinton formally announced her bid for office via a web video in April 2015.[28] This video announcement included a series of people talking about their new endeavors, such as starting a business, sending a child off to kindergarten, getting married, or finally training the dog to stop eating the trash. When Clinton appeared about halfway through the video, she was standing outside her personal home in Chappaqua, New York, dressed with a bipartisan touch in a red shirt and a blue blazer, and smiling under the bright sunshine. "I'm getting ready to do something, too," she said casually. "I'm running for president." The whimsical tone worked to undersell the gravity of her announcement, a framing that was enhanced by the everyday, relatable endeavors the diverse cast of Americans in the video said they were embracing. Her new project was more or less like theirs, she implied, nothing to get too worked up about. The cast of Americans also allowed Clinton to place herself in a position of support. She was running for the people in the video and to help ensure their success, as well as for the viewer who was watching. "Everyday Americans need a champion," she said. "And I want to be that champion." To do this, she would be "hitting the road to earn your vote. Because it's your time."

The invocation of "your time" as a surfacing phrase was noteworthy because it captured Clinton's opening bid to cast her candidacy for 2016 in the public imagination by decentering herself and invoking the primacy of the citizen-listener-viewer. This work to craft a de-centering narrative continued with a second video, "Fighter," which the campaign released to coincide with her official announcement speech at Four Freedoms Park in Manhattan. However, in Fighter, the message was more serious and framed Clinton's successes as always in the service of others. Clinton did not seek the spotlight. Rather, she sought to be of use and in this seeking found herself in leadership roles. To make this point even clearer, Clinton did not do all the talking in the video. As with the announcement video, much of it was done by others—this time by people whose lives had been touched by her public service: "Before Secretary of State, Senator, First Lady of the country, she was just a caring, young, bright, creative student, who cared about children and those left behind," said Marian Wright Edelman, founder of the Children's Defense fund. "There are no miracles in all this. It's hard work. It's sticking with it. It's perseverance. And over the years, she has made a cumulative . . . significant difference."

The Fighter video put forth that it was this grit and determination that Clinton would bring to the presidency, to continue her fight for children, and all other Americans who found themselves "left behind." Just as she had spoken out for women's rights in China; just as she had turned her defeat in the push for universal healthcare into CHIP, the Children's Health Insurance Program; and just as she stood by the first responders from 9/11; so she would continue the fight for those in need as president. Although the video was about Clinton's work in the public sphere, its meaning was found in the lives of those she had touched. That is, the two videos we consider here can be read as a kind of set. In both videos, real people—real Americans and real voters—were featured. They all mattered to Clinton, whether their projects were seemingly mundane, like training the dog, or a matter of life and death, such as ensuring medical care for vulnerable children. All were welcome on Clinton's campaign, and all were part of the public she hoped to serve. Unstated but implied in this developing narrative was the idea that by electing Clinton, all citizens would have a better chance to achieve their (American) dreams, and all would have a place to serve.

This "Fighter" storyline was consistent throughout the first part of her campaign, as Clinton focused on the issues for which she had historically fought, developing a "narrative logic that emphasize[d] the connection between character and action."[29] The central idea was to allow viewers—voters—to link Clinton's character with the American ideals of hard work, perseverance, and upward mobility. It was a campaign story that drew on the myth of the American dream, with Clinton representing its possibilities on a triple front: she had done it; she had spent a lifetime working to make it more accessible to vulnerable populations including women, children, immigrants, those who identify as queer, and racial minorities; and she would continue to do the same as president. Missing, however, was a sense of action. That is, her articulation of the narrative did not fully resonate with the existing myth of the American dream, because there was a problem with audience identification in Burkean terms. The American dream is active; it is "up by the bootstraps;" in community it requires a sense of the "can do" together. Although the idea of Clinton "fighting for us" described Clinton's role as a candidate, there was absent in its formulation an active role for the American people. As Lewis explained in his discussion of the power of political narrative, the best story tellers are the ones who instantiate the audience as players who must carry the project forward. One of the more successful aspects of Reagan's narrative was his ability to tell the story *of* the American people *to* the American people in a way that gave them a clear sense of their role, along with a sense of ownership in both the past and the future.[30]

Along these lines, Trump's campaign reiterated the idea that he and his supporters could "Make America Great Again." This phrase invoked nostalgia for a bygone era of imagined "greatness" and endowed the voter with a sacred charge to protect. It made sense, appealed to a preexisting narrative, and offered its adherents a specific and active role in fulfilling its promises. Clinton's "Fighter" narrative, by contrast, lacked narrative coherence, or failed to "hang together" in a way that resonated with existing conceptions of the American dream.[31] Instead, the "Fighter" narrative tried to leverage Clinton's past success into justification for future service. Because she had been able to accomplish acts for others before, she would be able to do it again, leading to communal achievement and a better America. The necessary path toward justice would come through electing her president. Left unstated and unclear, however, was a call to citizen action. Instead, in the summer of 2015, Clinton continued to rely on the iconography of a blue H made with a red arrow running through, suggesting that she would push the country forward, and a rhetoric personal service, each of which she carried into the first major rally of the campaign.

THE ANNOUNCEMENT SPEECH

Two months passed between the release of Clinton's announcement video and her official announcement speech. In the interim, Clinton went on a "listening tour" through Iowa and parts of New Hampshire. She appears to have also used this time to hone a narrative that deemphasized her personal motivations for being in the race and so her own personal history.[32] Even so, in the beginning, her story was still more evident to her candidacy than it would later become. Perhaps this is because Donald Trump had yet to enter the race.

Clinton gave her announcement speech on June 13, 2015, at Roosevelt Island in New York City.[33] On the one hand, the speech was relatively unremarkable as far as political rituals go. Clinton used her remarks to situate herself as an American with an American story to tell. This meant that while she is the wife of a former president—an obvious fact to most—she is also the granddaughter of a factory worker and the daughter of a small business owner. However, these small bits of biographical information were hardly the meat of the speech. Instead, as was true of her campaign announcement video, Clinton used much of the speech to highlight "every American" and the "basic bargain" of citizenship where, "If you do your part, you ought to be able to get ahead." In highlighting "you," "every American," and this "bargain," Clinton's words again had a deemphasizing effect—she was not the story; rather, those she was "running for" were. In fact, even though the speech did include biographical bits of information, she only spoke in the first person to communicate those political achievements that most people already knew, illustrating the kind of president she intended to be. "I'll always stand my ground when I must," she said. "That's something I did as Senator and Secretary of State—whether it was working with Republicans to expand health care for children . . . or pass a treaty to reduce the number of Russian nuclear warheads that could threaten our cities." For other parts of her story, particularly where she wanted to draw attention to her character, she pointed to the arc of her family's history, especially that of her mother and father. Her words seemed aimed to persuade listeners that they could trust she was a person of character and strength, because the people who had made her were, too. This technique allowed Clinton to implicitly acknowledge the many criticisms she faced over the years, including criticisms about her ethics and principles, and then dismiss them without giving a direct response:

> I think you know by now that I've been called many things by many people—"quitter" is not one of them. . . .
>
> Like so much else in my life, I got this from my mother.
>
> When I was a girl, she never let me back down from any bully or barrier. In her later years, Mom lived with us, and she was still teaching me the same lessons . . . she would remind me why we keep fighting, even when the odds are long and the opposition is fierce.
>
> I can still hear her saying: "Life's not about what happens to you, it's about what you do with what happens to you"—so get back out there.[34]

Here, near the end of the speech, Clinton began to gesture toward the historical nature of her candidacy as a woman running for president, who, if elected, would be the first female American to hold the nation's top office. However, she kept her mother at the center of this history, rather than highlight herself, rhetorically connecting the best of her mother's life story with the history of America, writ large:

> She lived to be 92 years old, and I often think about all the battles she witnessed over the course of the last century—all the progress that was won because Americans refused to give up or back down. . . .
>
> The story of America is a story of hard-fought, hard-won progress. And it continues today. New chapters are being written by men and women who

> believe that all of us—not just some, but all—should have the chance to live up to our God-given potential . . .
>
> I wish my mother could have been with us longer. I wish she could have seen Chelsea (Clinton's daughter) become a mother herself. I wish she could have met Charlotte (Clinton's granddaughter). . . .
>
> An America where a father can tell his daughter: yes, you can be anything you want to be. Even President of the United States.[35]

For Clinton, this final line in the speech is clearly self-referential. And yet, when she spoke of her father earlier in the speech, she made no mention of having ever heard similar words of support, but only talked about how her dad had worked hard to build his business and provide his family with a solid, middle-class life. As such, Clinton *could* be the girl who would grow up to be president, or she could not. Instead, the girl could be the listener's daughter, sister, niece, cousin, or the offspring of a cherished friend. As such, once again Clinton seems to be refracting herself into a spirit of the American dream, while also again leaving an implicit but unstated—inactive—role for the American people. Moreover, although Clinton lived through important history (she was born during both the Civil Rights movement and the Women's movement, was a child during the Cuban Missile Crisis and some of the worst years of the Cold War, participated in the Watergate investigation, to say nothing of her time as First Lady, Senator, and Secretary of State), she highlighted instead her mother's life, and her birth that coincided with the passing of the Nineteenth Amendment.

What this shows, we argue, is how the Clinton campaign was already struggling with the multivariate factors of how to position herself as a woman and not a man; as motivated by an instinct for service and not power; as interested in sharing the spotlight and the journey (and the work) with the American people; and to do it all in speeches and videos with memorable sound bites that would translate in the digital age. Like all candidates, Clinton had to participate in the surfacing rituals required for being taken seriously by voters as a contender in the race. Clinton was also already well-known, but only in particular kinds of ways. Some saw her as an extension of her husband or part of the Obama team. Others wondered if she were corrupt or in it only for herself, and so were on the fence. Still others loved her, and wanted her to win. Because of all this, Clinton's deep political history was already muddling her message, even as she struggled to develop a narrative that situated voters as important and tell her own story, all while avoiding perceptions of over confidence or personal ambition.

This problem with diluted messages and lost meaning would only grow in the months to come as Donald Trump entered the race and commanded the media's attention—both social and mainstream—and became the target of both Clinton's ire and a central part of her developing narrative. Soon she found herself in the position of responding to Trump rather than extending her own narrative.

TRUMP ENTERS, CLINTON RESPONDS

Donald Trump joined the presidential field on June 16, 2015. Immediately the tone of the race shifted, as Trump declared that many Mexican immigrants were rapists, drug dealers, and criminals.[36] His incendiary rhetoric would grow from there, and before long he had denigrated nearly everyone, including the disabled, women, Gold Star families, and more. These "strategems based in hate"[37] earned widespread condemnation, including from Clinton and her team. Almost as soon as he became a candidate, a significant amount of Clinton's attention was redirected toward attacking Trump, which gave her less time to refine and advance the "Fighter" narrative. In particular, Clinton put out numerous videos criticizing Trump's fitness for office, his suitability as a role model, and his disparaging remarks regarding Latino/a immigrants. Among the most talked about of these ads came out just before the Republican National Convention in July, 2016, and aired on broadcast networks as well as online. This ad, titled "Role Models," broke with the archetypical negative ads that frame "the bad guy candidate in a black-and-white photo as a gravel-voiced narrator lists concerns about his record."[38] The ad was similar to another one that had run earlier in the campaign, called "Speak," and that had used similar rhetorical and visual strategies. However, "Speak" was funded by Priorities USA, a Super PAC that supported Clinton, and not the campaign itself.[39]

In both "Speak," and "Role Models"—and more ads to follow—the soundtrack for the ad was, quite literally, that of Donald Trump. He was heard reciting his own words. The trick, however, was framing them either to come from the lips of one of his targets (in the case of "Speak," women he was denigrating) or, as in "Role Models," to reveal their effects on vulnerable children watching the television as Trump spoke in interviews and at rallies and press conferences. In the ad, children stood by the television, watching and listening silently as Trump bragged about being able to "stand in the middle of Fifth Avenue and shoot somebody and not lose any voters; watching a young Latina girl see him call Mexican immigrants "rapists" and criminals; and then watch still more children of all races take in the Republican nominee's infamous impression of a disabled reporter, among other remarks.[40] The ad was extremely effective. The *New York Times*, *Time*, the *Los Angeles Times*, and *Politico* all listed it as among the best political ads of the 2016 cycle, across all races, including presidential, congressional, and gubernatorial.[41] On July 21, 2016—the day before the Democratic Convention opened in Philadelphia—a writer for the American Marketing Association wondered if the spot would end up being as historic as was Reagan's "Morning in America" from 1984.[42] If Clinton was drifting from her original narrative, perhaps using Trump's words against him would be an effective rhetorical strategy.

In any event, by the time of the July Democratic Convention in Philadelphia, Clinton had a growing number of messages in play. The early "Fighter" narrative that invited listeners to join Clinton on the campaign journey, see themselves in her struggle, and trust her with their aspirations for the American dream persisted across her speeches. However, always present, too, was the rhetorical effort to decenter herself and her own story in favor of allowing others to champion her or creating space for voters to share the narrative and so the campaign fight. In part, this made sense. For one thing, women in general and women candidates, in particular, tend to think and speak more collectively than do men.[43] Nonetheless, it also created a kind of rhetorical muddling. Finally, there were the constant attacks on Trump, which were even present in the Clinton team's campaign motto—"Stronger Together," which first appeared in May 2016.

Understanding "Stronger Together" required first knowing about, and then rejecting, Trump's own campaign call. This worked to the GOP nominee's advantage, because every "Stronger Together" utterance referred back to "Make America Great Again," along with its ubiquitous Twitter hashtag #MAGA. Equally problematic, the "Stronger Together" message was less rhetorically generative than was the MAGA message because it failed to call voters to specific action, in the ways Lewis describes is true of the most effective political narratives. With MAGA, there was a clear and active role: one's vote for Trump was a vote to restore the country to a presumed state of previous prominence. Clinton's message was looser: "Stronger Together," but with whom and for what?

Clinton spoke on the last night of the convention, as is traditionally the case for these campaign rituals. Earlier speakers had included Elizabeth Warren, Bernie Sanders, and Michelle Obama on Monday night; Bill Clinton on Tuesday night; and Barack Obama on Wednesday night. President Clinton and both Obamas were especially noteworthy in their praise and defense of the Democratic nominee. However, they, too, gestured to how Hillary's longstanding presence on the national stage had the unfortunate effect of erasing some of the luster from her candidacy. "Because of Hillary Clinton, my daughters and all our sons and daughters now take for granted that a woman can be president of the United States," Mrs. Obama said.[44] It had almost become too easy. The next night Bill Clinton added a story about how when he proposed to Hillary he told her she really should not marry him, but ought to run for office instead. It was that line, he claimed, that finally got her to visit Arkansas, eventually marry him and begin the journey so many Americans had watched them live out.[45] President Obama was the most direct in defense. “Look, Hillary’s got her share of critics. She’s been caricatured by the right and by some folks on the left; accused of everything you can imagine,” he said. “She knows she’s made mistakes. . . . And if you’re serious about our democracy, you can’t afford to stay home just because she might not align with you on every issue. You’ve got to get in the arena with her, because democracy isn’t a spectator sport. America isn’t about ‘yes he will.’ It’s about ‘yes we can.’”[46]

In invoking “yes we can,” Obama was, of course, reaching back to his own historical campaign in 2008, and to create the same sense of shared mission and required action in the Clinton campaign that had motivated his supporters then. His words lent unstated credibility to Clinton’s “together” calls, setting the stage for Clinton’s own speech. She appeared wearing a white pantsuit, a gesture to the suffragettes who paved the way for her candidacy. Clinton’s speech, too, embraced what she had accomplished as a woman in particular, and the strength of women in general. The theme of motherhood ran throughout her remarks. Her daughter introduced her. In the speech itself, Clinton spoke of being a mother, about the influence of her own mother, and about becoming a grandmother. “Standing here as my mother’s daughter and my daughter’s mother, I’m so happy this day has come,” she said. “I’m happy for grandmothers and little girls and everyone in between. I’m happy for boys and men. Because when any barrier falls in America, it clears the way for everyone.” Throughout this speech, Clinton drew attention to her life spent working on children’s issues—in some ways unsurprising, we should add, that the first female nominee for president should also identify so strongly with children—as well as created identification and so unity with her audience. “It’s true, I sweat the details of policy” she said. “Because it’s not just a detail if it’s your kid, if it’s your family. It’s a big deal. And it should be a big deal to your president, too.”[47]

But for many of the claims, invitations, and admonitions that Clinton made, there was a stated or implied attack on Trump. Only a few minutes into the speech, the Democratic nominee recounted the history of Philadelphia, as the place where the Declaration of Independence was signed and the Constitution was debated and drafted. As was true then, she continued, the United States again found itself “at a moment of reckoning.” This reckoning was as rhetorical as it was literal, and it could be summarized with the words of her campaign slogan, and whether or not “we will all work together so we can all rise together.” The alternative was to believe Trump’s claim that he “alone,” could “fix it.”

Throughout the speech, as a leader and proposed president, Clinton tried to position herself as Trump’s opposite. Where he was intolerant, she was kindhearted and merciful. Where he was miserly, she was munificent. Where he wanted war, she sought peace. Where he took credit, she shared responsibility and trust. This nod toward shared responsibility and credit was, again, a rhetorical strategy to involve her audience as collaborators in her campaign, while distancing them from Trump. Perhaps this is the goal of almost all convention speeches. However, in Clinton's case the job was especially important because she carried the added burden of being a presidential contender with a deep history who the public still claimed *they didn't really know*. Clinton's speech thus worked to present her as a serious candidate with extensive policy knowledge; it also drew together her personal commitments, like her family, with her political ones, like a lifetime spent working on women's and children's issues.

Even so, unlike Trump's nomination acceptance speech, Clinton's lacked the narrative takeaway for audience members to hear and remember. In his speech, Donald Trump's penultimate line was that his campaign would "Make America Great Again." Likewise, Clinton, mentioned her own slogan in her speech, and did so three times. But unlike Trump's slogan, "Stronger Together" could never stand on its own. In the first case, it was the nation's founders who "embraced the enduring truth that we are stronger together." The second time she said it, she claimed it was not just a lesson from history, or a slogan, but a guiding principle for building an inclusive economy. And the last time she said it, near the end of her speech, she followed with more injunctions about looking to the future and building for tomorrow because "when we do, America will be greater than ever!"

There was nothing Trump-like in her final call for greatness, and this is not our point. Rather, we suggest that her call to be "stronger together" always required more explanation, attacks and counterattacks, along with stories about Clinton that were supposed to invite the audience into her narrative—and so her campaign—without allowing her to become too much of the story. "Stronger Together" was always a call to embrace diversity *and* join the work of the American project *and* reject the divisive, offensive campaign of Donald Trump. So even a successful, inspirational speech like Clinton gave at the DNC—and most pundits agreed that the speech was very good—could only do so much, because the narrative remained unclear.

As the campaign moved forward into the fall, Trump continued to supply the Clinton campaign with ample opportunities to attack him. Indeed, our analysis of Clinton's video postings on Facebook shows that Clinton's attacks increased in frequency, to the point that Trump was always present, even when he was not being overtly discussed: for example, between October 1 and November 8 (Election Day), Clinton's team posted fifty-eight videos directly attacking Trump. Another twenty-seven videos during this same time frame forwarded Clinton's policy proposals and discussed her character as responses to Trump. Most of these ads featured the phrase, "what's at stake," implicitly comparing Clinton's views on the environment, religious and racial tolerance, women's rights, queer rights, and more to those of the Republican nominee. For example, a video posted October 30,

2016, featured Clinton delivering a stump speech in Daytona, Florida. In this video clip, Clinton frames her views in opposition to Trump, stating that in the election, "everything we care about is at stake." "Fighting climate change is at stake. LGBTQ rights are at stake. Equal pay for women is at stake."[48]

By framing the discussion in terms of what's "at stake" and discussing the issues frequently referenced in her attack ads, Trump is ever-present in Clinton's rhetoric, the antithesis to her candidacy. He is present not only in the ads where Clinton, herself speaks, but also in those of her surrogates: Michele Obama, Barack Obama, and Joe Biden are all featured in videos using the same kind of framing. The result was a campaign where Clinton's policies, knowledgeable and nuanced though they were, never truly seemed like her own, but only existed *in response* to Trump.

Among the best of the attack ads was "Mirrors," which was rhetorically very similar to both "Speak" and "Role Models."[49] It, too, went after the Republican nominee, and used clips from Trump's own speeches, narrated in his own voice. The content of the video included shots of girls from varying ethnic backgrounds somberly looking at themselves in mirrors, the reflection of a television screen, and their cell phone cameras. Interspersed with these images were clips of Trump insulting women, calling them "fat," "ugly," "flat-chested," and "slob." The video closed as Howard Stern asked Trump, "So you treat women with respect?" and Trump responded, "No, I can't say that, either." The final shot was of white text on a black screen and the words, "Is this the president we want for our daughters?"[50]

The "Mirrors" advertisement debuted in September 2016 and was reposted seven times on Clinton's campaign Facebook page during the months of September, October, and November. Each time the video was posted, it was reframed for the audience, with descriptions such as "Imagine a president who said these things," "Our daughters deserve better," and "Is this the president we want for our daughters?"

The strategy of this video, as with "Role Models," "What's at Stake," and many others, seemed to be that public backlash against the inherently offensive nature of Trump's rhetoric would do the work of making the argument for Clinton and against Trump. In reality, Clinton's attack videos may have detracted from her more nuanced message and made it impossible for enough voters (or the right voters) to hear much of anything besides "Make America Great Again." In employing this strategy, Clinton's videos frequently called Trump out by name. The "Role Models" video was captioned, "Our children are watching, Donald." A video responding to Trump's criticism of Clinton was captioned, "Saw your speech, Donald. About that 'woman card.'" A video in response to the first debate read, "Donald just criticized me for being prepared for the debate." And yet another video posted in October responding to Trump's "nasty woman" comment was captioned, "Get this Donald: nasty women are smart, nasty women are tough, and nasty women vote." In each of these examples (which are but a small sampling of a much larger corpus of videos), Clinton's message became increasingly reactive rather than proactive. Ironically, one of the earliest videos in the campaign was a clip of Clinton being interviewed by Jimmy Fallon. It was posted on January 15, 2016. Here, Clinton said, "I'll tell you what: Donald J. Trump's a lot more obsessed with me than I am with him."[51] All in all, this turned out not to be the case.

CONCLUSION

By now it is cliché to write that the outcome of the 2016 presidential election was surprising. The campaign itself disrupted norms of political communication, as two of the most well-known, and least well-liked nominees in history vied for the nation's highest office. Polls and pundits across the spectrum predicted Hillary Clinton would win.

But she did not. Since her loss became clear in the early morning hours of November 9, 2016, those same pundits, along with academics, the political class, and members of the general public have been trying to figure out what happened. No doubt, there are many explanations. What we have suggested, however, is that Clinton's campaign was complicated by two major issues: the female presidentiality paradox and the rapidly changing environment of the social media political campaign. The confluence of these two factors made it difficult, if not impossible, for Clinton to advance a clear and compelling campaign narrative that included an active role for voters. Because Clinton could not be *too* center stage for fear of feeding accusations of ambition or power-grabbing, her campaign rhetoric worked to decenter her as the candidate and in so doing, diluted her message. As the campaign wore on, Clinton's team foregrounded Trump via attack ads, with the inconvenient effect of spreading his message at the expense of her own. In fact, as Jennifer Stromer-Galley and her team at Illuminating 2016 make plain, Clinton and her team actually launched more online attacks than did Trump in 2016.[52] We suggest this resulted in a narrative-in-response, not a narrative-in-itself, for the Democratic nominee. That is, she seemed more interested in contradicting Trump than forwarding a clear and compelling political narrative, a necessity in a "change" election.

As scholars continue to reflect on the 2016 presidential election, there are a number of issues that merit further consideration. First, the development of the "social media election" has created an environment in which candidates must continuously craft messages to stay in the news cycle. For Clinton, this environment of continuous message making muddled her narrative, as she attempted to decenter herself and instead focused on attacking Trump. This created the second issue that should be further considered: the shifting expectations for narrative in the social media campaign. If candidates must continuously post items in order to stay in the news cycle, then the core narrative of the campaign must be prominent in those stories and advertisements. Otherwise, the campaign narrative will be lost in the overabundance of campaign messages. In Clinton's campaign, we see a clear example of this. In attempting to stay on top of the news cycle, her campaign videos increasingly referenced information about Trump. Eventually, as was clear in her convention address, the attacks on Trump overwhelmed her early "Fighter" narrative, instead of shifting toward "Stronger Together," a clear rhetorical referent to Trump's "Make America Great Again." Of course, we cannot say with any certainty what *could* have happened, had Clinton employed a simple, active, repetitive narrative, but there is something to be said for the stark contrast between Clinton's near-constant, nuanced reinvention and Trump's simple, repetitive refrain.

If Lewis is right and the best political narratives make use of myth, calling the American electorate to action, then it is equally important to consider what kinds of narratives and attendant campaign slogans have a chance in the glut of competing messages during a campaign. Certainly short, active messages that are easily folded into national and individual stories will be more effective. Although we did not discuss his campaign strategy in detail, Trump's "Make America Great Again" drew from the existing mythic narrative of American Exceptionalism. This campaign slogan was active, giving individuals a distinct role, and tapped into a shared understanding of the need to protect the United States' status as a moral and economic force. In comparison, Clinton's "Stronger Together" seemed passive, did not tap into any clear myths, and always required further explication. Additional scholarship on the role of the active mythic narrative in the social media presidential campaign would shed further light on this issue.

NOTES

1. Hillary Clinton, *What Happened* (Kindle Edition) (New York: Simon & Schuster, 2017), loc 293. When mixed together, blue and red make purple.

2. "Remarks in New York City Conceding the 2016 Presidential Election," in *The American Presidency Project* (Santa Barbara: The American Presidency Project, November 9, 2016).

3. Jena McGregor, "Hillary Clinton Didn't Give Her Concession Speech on Election Night. Now We See One Reason Why," *Washington Post*, November 9, 2016.

4. Karrin Vasby Anderson, "Every Woman Is the Wrong Woman: The Female Presidentiality Paradox," *Women's Studies in Communication* 40, no. 2 (2017): 134.

5. While Donald Trump did do marginally better with Black and Latino voters in 2016 than had Mitt Romney in 2012 (8 percent and 28 percent to 6 percent and 27 percent respectively) the Republican Party has a longstanding problem attracting minority voters. Alec Tyson and Shiva Maniam, "Behind Trump's Victory: Divisions by Race, Gender, Education," Pew Research Center, November 9, 2016, http://www.pewresearch.org/fact-tank/2016/11/09/behind-trumps-victory-divisions-by-race-gender-education/; Jens Manuel Krogstad and Mark Hugo

Lopez, "Hillary Clinton Won Latino Vote but Fell Below 2012 Support for Obama," Pew Research Center, November 29, 2016, http://www.pewresearch.org/fact-tank/2016/11/29/hillary-clinton-wins-latino-vote-but-falls-below-2012-support-for-obama/. In addition, Michael Kazin, a leading historian of American populism, distinguishes between the populist left and the populist right in the United States. The populist tradition on the American right, he argues, "is narrower and more ethnically restrictive. For most of U.S. history, it meant only citizens of European heritage—'real Americans,' whose ethnicity alone afforded them a claim to share in the country's bounty. Typically, this breed of populist alleges that there is a nefarious alliance between evil forces on high and the unworthy, dark-skinned poor below—a cabal that imperils the interests and values of the patriotic (white) majority in the middle." Our claim is *not* that *all* Trump supporters were inherently racist. Rather, we posit that as a rhetorical matter, the slogan "Make America Great Again" included this kind of populism as one possible meaning, and was open to this kind of interpretation. Michael Kazin, "Trump and American Populism: Old Whine, New Bottles," *Foreign Affairs* 95, no. 6 (2016), 17. Also see *The Populist Persuasion* (Ithaca: Cornell University Press, 1998).

6. Jennifer Stromer-Galley and a team of researchers collected all of the social media messages they could gather, especially from Twitter and Facebook, and archived them at their site, illuminating2016. A longitudinal and in-depth study of their data shows that the Clinton campaign was more frequently negative, although Trump may have personally sent out more "mean" tweets. illuminating2016, "Candidate Total Messsage Activity," Syracuse University School of Information Studies, http://illuminating.ischool.syr.edu/#/platforms/1,2/dates/2016–11–01,2016–11–08/candidates/10,5/types/8&9,5&6.

7. Clinton, *What Happened* (Kindle Edition), loc 3513.

8. Kenneth Burke, *A Rhetoric of Motives*, 1st ed. (New York: Prentice Hall, 1950).

9. Stephen A. Smith, "Technological Transformations and Timeless Truths: The Press and the Presidency in a Social Media Age," in *Columns to Characters: The Presidency and the Press Enter the Digital Age*, ed. Stephanie A. Martin (College Station, TX: A&M Press, 2017), 120.

10. Richard Davis, *The Web of Politics: The Internet's Impact on the American Political System* (New York: Oxford University Press, 1999), 168.

11. Of course, the Internet did not invent an "intimacy" phenomenon. First there was radio and then, even more famously, television, especially daytime talk TV.

12. Stephanie A. Martin, "Introduction," in *Columns to Characters: The Press and the Presidency Enter the Digital Age*, ed. Stephanie A. Martin (College Station, TX: A&M Press, 2017), 15.

13. Tom Price, "Social Media and Politics," *CQ Researcher* 22, no. 36 (October 12, 2012). Of course, the Internet did not invent an "intimacy" phenomenon. First there was radio and then, even more famously, television, especially daytime talk TV. See Shawn Parry-Giles and Trevor Parry-Giles, "Political Scopophilia, Presidential Campaigning, and the Intimacy of American Politics," *Communication Studies* 47 (Fall 1996), (emphasis added).

14. William F. Lewis, "Telling America's Story: Narrative Form and the Reagan Presidency," *The Quarterly Journal of Speech* 73 (1987).

15. Ibid., 288 (italics ours).

16. John Allen Hendricks and Dan Schill, "The Social Media Election of 2016," in *The 2016 US Presidential Campaign*, ed. Robert E. Denton Jr. (London: Palgrave MacMillan, 2017), 121.

17. Scholars have discussed at length the effect of the Internet and social media on presidential campaigns. Among the best book-length treatments of the role of the data, the Internet, and social media on politics and campaigning are Jennifer Stromer-Galley, *Presidential Campaigning in the Internet Age* (New York: Oxford University Press, 2014). And Daniel Kreiss, *Prototype Politics: Technology-Intensive Campaigning and the Data of Democracy* (New York: Oxford University Press, 2016).

18. A 2016 Pew Research Center Study found that 86 percent of Americans are on the Internet, and most also use social media. Of those who are online, 80 percent use Facebook, 32 percent use Instagram, 31 percent use Pinterest, 24 percent use Twitter, and 29 percent use LinkedIn. Shannon Greenwood, Andrew Perrin, and Maeve Duggan, "Social Media Update

2016: Facebook Usage and Engagement Is on the Rise, While Adoption of Other Platforms Holds Steady," (November 11, 2016), http://www.pewinternet.org/2016/11/11/social-media-update-2016/. More than three-quarters of Americans also have smart phones. Lee Raine and Andrew Perrin, "10 Facts about Smartphones as the iPhone Turns 10," (2017), http://www.pewresearch.org/fact-tank/2017/06/28/10-facts-about-smartphones/.

19. Stephen Heidt, "The Presidency as Pastiche: Atomization, Circulation, and Rhetorical Instability," (Michigan State University Press, 2012), 623.

20. Susan T. Fiske, "Managing Ambivalent Prejudices," *The ANNALS of the American Academy of Political and Social Science* 639, no. 1 (2012).

21. Kathleen Hall Jamieson, *Beyond the Double Bind: Women and Leadership* (New York: Oxford University Press, 1995).

22. Anderson, 132.

23. Ibid. The question arises as to whether men do not face similar constraints to their subjectivity. We argue that they do not, and that this is especially true for cisgender, heteronormative, White men. Moreover, this is not only true for liberal candidates, like Clinton, but holds true for conservatives, as well, and is about whether women can ultimately be *elected* president, given cultural constraints, not whether they will be called to run or whether citizens can (hypothetically) *imagine* a woman as president. As Anderson and Kristina Horn Sheeler write in *Woman President: Confronting Post Feminist Political Culture*, "No one blanched when, for a few weeks in 2011 . . . Michele Bachmann led the Republican pack after garnering the allegiance of the conservative Tea Party constituency. Notably, however, that support vanished the moment that Texas governor Rick Perry entered the race and put a more masculine face on conservative bone fides that matched Bachmann's. By December 2011, Bachmann had been dismissed by pundits as an 'afterthought' and a 'saucer-eyed looney tune.' The *Washington Post* declared her presidential hopes 'all but counted out.' Like Clinton and [Sarah] Palin before her, Bachmann felt the sting of backlash." Kristina Horn Sheeler and Karrin Vasby Anderson, *Woman President: Confronting Postfeminist Political Culture*, ed. Karrin Vasby Anderson, 1st ed.. ed. (College Station, TX: A&M University Press, 2013).

24. Karrin Vasby Anderson, "'Rhymes with Rich': 'Bitch' as a Tool of Containment in Contemporary American Politics," *Rhetoric and Public Affairs* 2, no. 4 (1999).

25. Judith S. Trent, "Presidential Surfacing: The Ritualistic and Crucial First Act," *Communication Monographs* 45, no. 4 (1978).

26. Clinton, *What Happened* (Kindle Edition), loc 948.

27. Ibid., loc. 951.

28. "Hillary Clinton's 2016 Presidential Campaign Announcement," April 12, 2015.

29. Lewis, "Telling America's Story," 283.

30. Ibid., 284.

31. Walter R. Fisher, "The Narrative Paradigm: An Elaboration," *Communication Monographs* 52 (December 1985).

32. In contrast, Marco Rubio, for example, began his speech announcing his presidential bid by claiming his Cuban heritage and situating it into the broader American narrative. Jeb Bush began his announcement speech by criticizing Democrats and then saying, "The question for me is: What am I going to do about it?" And Chris Christie's speech began with extensive remarks about his family, followed with reflections about his accomplishments as New Jersey governor.

33. Hillary Clinton, "Remarks in a Campaign 'Kickoff' Speech in New York City," in *The American Presidency Project* (Santa Barbara, CA: The American Presidency Project, June 13, 2015).

34. Ibid.

35. Ibid.

36. Donald Trump, "Remarks Announcing Candidacy for President in New York City," Hillary Clinton, "Remarks in a Campaign 'Kickoff' Speech in New York City," in The American Presidency Project (Santa Barbara, CA: The American Presidency Project, June 13, 2015).

37. Stephanie A. Martin and Rita Kirk, "The Dark Power of Words: Strategems of Hate in the 2016 Presidential Campaign," in *The 2016 Us Presidential Campaign: Political Communication and Practice*, ed. Robert E. Denton Jr. (London: Palgrave Macmillan, 2017).
38. Seth Stevenson, "Hillary Clinton's Ads Are Using Trump's Words against Him in an Ingenious Way," *Slate.com*, July 14, 2015, http://www.slate.com/blogs/the_slatest/2016/07/14/hillary_clinton_s_role_models_ad_is_extremely_effective.html.
39. Priorities USA, "Speak."
40. Hillary Clinton, "Role Models."
41. Michael Barbaro, "The Best (and Worst) Campaign Ads So Far," *New York Times* September 6, 2016. Ryan Teague Beckwith, "Watch the 10 Most Notable Campaign Ads of 2016," *Time,* November 3, 2016. Doyle McManus, "The Best Political Ads of the 2016 Campaign," *Los Angeles Times* October 26, 2016. Daniel Strauss, "16 Ads That Mattered in 2016," *Politico* (November 6, 2016), http://www.politico.com/story/2016/11/2016-election-best-campaign-ads-230789.
42. Sarah Steimer, "Could Clinton's 'Role Models' Spot Be as Historic as 'Morning in America'?," *Marketing News Weekly*, July 21, 2016. https://www.ama.org/publications/eNewsletters/Marketing-News-Weekly/Pages/clinton-role-models-spot-historic-as-morning-in-america.aspx.
43. It is an imperfect book but, of course, one good place to begin looking into the differences between men's and women's language patterns is Robin Tolmach Lakoff, *Language and Woman's Place* (New York: Harper & Row, 1975).
44. Michelle Obama, "Michelle Obama's Entire Democratic Convention Speech," CNN, http://www.cnn.com/2016/07/26/politics/transcript-michelle-obama-speech-democratic-national-convention/index.html.
45. William J. Clinton, "Transcript: Bill Clinton's DNC Speech," http://www.cnn.com/2016/07/27/politics/bill-clinton-speech-transcript/index.html.
46. Barack Obama, "Remarks at the Democratic National Convention in Philadelphia, Pennsylvania," July 27, 2016. Online by Gerhard Peters and John T. Woolley, *The American Presidency Project*, http://www.presidency.ucsb.edu/ws/?pid=118049.
47. Hillary Clinton, "Address Accepting the Presidential Nomination at the Democratic National Convention in Philadelphia, Pennsylvania," July 28, 2016. Online by Gerhard Peters and John T. Woolley, *The American Presidency Project*, http://www.presidency.ucsb.edu/ws/?pid=118051.
48. Hillary Clinton, "Education Is at Stake," (October 30, 2016).
49. "Mirrors," (July 14, 2016). Priorities USA. Clinton, "Role Models."
50. Ibid.
51. Monica Alba, "Hillary Clinton: Trump Is 'More Obsessed with Me Than I Am with Him,'" *NBC News* (January 15, 2016), https://www.nbcnews.com/politics/2016-election/hillary-clinton-touts-exciting-race-her-selfie-prowess-fallon-n496866.
52. Illuminating 2016, http://illuminating.ischool.syr.edu/#/candidate/10.

Chapter Eight

Iconographic Tracking of Pepe the Frog Meme through the 2016 Presidential Campaign

Natalia Mielczarek

Comic artist Matt Furie's cousin Dave used to "drop trau" in elementary school to urinate, a habit that fascinated the artist then and one that ultimately made him famous a couple of decades later. Furie's 2005 comic strip *Boy's Club*, first published on MySpace, featured a group of best friends: anthropomorphized animals and monsters living a rather stereotypical youth. They ate pizza, played video games, and got stoned on occasion. In one of the scenes, Pepe the Frog, a hunter green amphibian with wide red lips, mimicked cousin Dave's bathroom routine saying, "Feels good, man."[1]

The moment and the one-liner jumped platforms around 2008 to become an Internet meme, a piece of digital content that shares common characteristics and gets replicated and manipulated as it spreads online from user to user.[2] Its iterations placed Pepe in various situations—mourning passage of time, staring smugly at the viewer, or screaming into the camera—and functioned as reaction shorthand for the connected public to comment on the everyday.[3]

By 2014, Pepe jumped again and surfaced on mainstream social media platforms, with dedicated pages on Tumblr, Instagram, Reddit, and Facebook,[4] all of which are known for cultivating memes and other visual content. By Tumblr's own calculations, the frog was the most popular meme of 2015 on the site. As Pepe infiltrated pop culture, he even showed up in social media posts of some celebrities. Singer Katy Perry, for instance, tweeted a crying Pepe in November 2014 to comment on her jet lag after traveling to Australia. Rapper Nicki Minaj posted a Pepe meme on Instagram a month later. In a response to a meme request from a follower, the fast food chain Wendy's tweeted the brand's mascot in a Pepe likeness in January 2017, eliciting much criticism online.[5] Wendy's representatives deleted the tweet saying they were not aware of the political connotation of the meme.

Pepe's journey in remix culture, in which participating members of the public appropriate already existing content to create and share their own takes on reality,[6] does not diverge from the typical trajectory of an Internet meme theorized in media studies in recent years; that is, until 2015 and 2016. It is then that the silly cartoon character became an object of contestation and political warfare that played out on social media and in mainstream press. The green frog transformed from a pop prop deployed by Internet users to talk about their lives to a classified symbol of hate that made a cameo appearance in the 2016 presidential elections, alleging links between the Republican candidate and white supremacy. It is that space—both temporal and digital—that is at the heart of this chapter. The aim here is to analyze what happened during that window when various groups online, including the legacy media and the 4chan and Reddit communities, weaponized the meme to define and share their interpretations of the frog, exposing the fluidity and volatility of meaning in remix culture and the role that mainstream media and politicians play in shaping it.

REMIX CULTURE AND MEMES

Before tracing these milestones in Pepe's digital life, a quick look at the context of meme production and circulation is in order. In digital participatory culture,[7] producers and consumers of cultural content meld into one—called the "produsers";[8] they simultaneously create, consume, re-create and distribute content, effectively participating in meaning co-creation with each other.[9] Much of this cultural collaboration happens on message boards such as Reddit and 4chan, two prominent platforms at the center of this study. Both are forums for public discourse on a wide array of topics with varying levels of civility, ranging from friendly and intellectual, to threatening and openly hostile.[10] Users' anonymity on both sites shapes in part the tone of the discourse, emboldening some to engage in vitriol without revealing their identity.[11]

The "ordinary participation through everyday cultural production"[12] happens in non-elite, non-vertical environments of information production, allowing for self-representation and presence of diverse and often alternative voices in the public discourse.[13] Such was the case with Pepe the Frog when it changed hands and meanings as it circulated cyberspace and multiplied through iterations of the meme.

The practice of remixing is not a new concept as "culture itself is, and has always been, remix. . . . This remix potential is now amplified by technology."[14] The produsers filter content through their own experiences, ideologies, and needs to coauthor *their* takes on reality—and share them digitally with others, who do the same, fueling an ongoing cultural production of meaning that brings together the familiar with the novel.[15]

Internet memes are among the most popular artifacts of digital participatory culture, produced through the vernacular creativity of the masses.[16] Considered ubiquitous online, memes have become a lingua franca[17] of remix culture, a "fundamental feature of socially and technologically propagated knowledge."[18] As they multiply and spread online, memes retain some elements of the original template that they replicate—the likeness of Pepe, for example—but also mutate from it to create its new versions. In effect, an Internet meme becomes a "hub for further creative activity,"[19] a collection of iterations that shares some features in common but also introduces new elements that alter the content and interpretation.

In addition to serving as communicative tools, memes are crucial in "forming and signifying communal belonging."[20] Their circulation may seem random and rather chaotic online, but their produsers and disseminators use them to address a familiar community that speaks a common language and understands the functions memes serve in remix parlance—humor, social commentary, political dissent and social justice, but also marginalization and discrimination against certain groups.[21] In short, memes can unite people and designate the *in* crowd, but they can also alienate and target those deemed *outsiders* by their produsers, a trend explored through the Pepe example later in this chapter. In some cases, Internet memes have become tools of subcultural trolling[22] that produce "highly crude, cynical, and irreverent content, aiming to provoke and shock for the sake of humor,"[23] sometimes crossing the line to aggression and even harassment.

ICONOGRAPHIC TRACKING AND PEPE MEMES ONLINE

Images rarely end their lives at publication. They circulate on and offline across various platforms, making appearances in newspapers, magazines, television, on t-shirts, mugs, social networking sites, postcards, and textbooks. Some garner extra attention as iconic photographs that summarize events for generations.[24] They may go dormant, only to resurface again in new contexts at different points in time, acquiring fresh meanings and functions for their users.[25] Such was the case with Pepe, who started out as a cartoon character in a fairly obscure comic strip and ended up as a contested hate symbol. How the frog went from subcultural visual shorthand deployed to comment on the everyday to a stand-in for white supremacy and a signifier for a specific group of Trump's constituencies is the overarching question that drives this chapter.

The answers emerge through the use of iconographic tracking,[26] a qualitative visual analysis approach designed to trace the "open-ended rhetorical becomings"[27] of images as they interact with other images and audiences in their continued post-production lives. In addition to revealing changes in Pepe's meanings, functions, circulation, and composition, tracing the frog's rhetorical transformation helps to understand the roles that mainstream media, politicians, subcultural online communities, and regular people played in these transfigurations.

Iconographic tracking's main goal is to establish the whereabouts of an image as it traverses cyberspace, appears across various platforms and gets reappropriated along the way, creating new meanings and functions. The aim here was not to document every iteration of the Pepe meme or account for every platform that hosted it, but rather to retrace the critical moments in Pepe's journey as they registered in mainstream media and among subcultural communities online, paying attention not only to the changing iterations of the original Pepe but also to the narratives around them. The method allows us to pursue those avenues freely, without preconceived constraints as to where the searches *should* start and stop, and without anticipated results as to what the newly discovered meanings, functions, and uses *ought* to signify. Instead, the approach lets these elements emerge from the ground up, by following links that surface through searches and discovering meanings that naturally come to surface through analysis.

Given the churning nature of the Internet and anonymity of interactions online, it is crucial to acknowledge that attempts to establish a truly precise chronology of Pepe's perceived downfall in mainstream media and to vet the credibility of statements made by 4chan and Reddit users were challenging and impossible, respectively. Claiming that a news outlet was the first or the only one to publish a story amid the onslaught of online content is always risky, hence the extra caution with such pronouncements here. Further, 4chan, for example, does not maintain archives as the site erases content throughout the day, making it impossible to access older posts unless otherwise stored by third parties. The unconfirmed identities of 4chan and Reddit users—almost all 4chan community members are anonymous (they use the default username Anonymous), and Reddit users typically rely on made-up monikers—combined with the propensity of subcultural Internet users to embellish, fabricate, and manipulate content[28] further complicated the work. As such, even though espoused political views on both message boards were taken at face value, their authenticity and sincerity could not be verified.

Working within those constraints, the study relied on iconographic tracking to chart out when, where, and how Pepe memes registered in mainstream media as well as on social media, with particular focus on Reddit, 4chan, and Twitter platforms known for curating memes. More specifically, the news media searches combined general Google and Google Images searches (keywords "Pepe the Frog") with targeted searches of online portals of ABC News, NBC News, CBS News, Fox News, CNN, the *New York Times*, the

Wall Street Journal, the *Washington Post*, *Wired*, and *Politico*. Those outlets were chosen as representative mainstream news sources known to cover general and political news and Internet culture/technology.

Tailored searches of Reddit, 4chan, and Twitter (using the same keywords) yielded numerous conversation strands that covered the timeline of the campaign and the postelection period. A handful of sites offered access to curated 4chan archives, some of which captured fragments of exchanges surrounding Pepe's meaning and perceived ties to white supremacy groups. The bulk of cited 4chan discussions, however, came from periodic real-time searches of the site during the researching and writing stages of the chapter, given the ephemeral nature of this particular message board. Because of the sheer volume of conversations about Pepe on the three social media sites, limited access to 4chan's curated archives, and the site's self-cleaning feature, the chapter offers snapshots of public discourse surrounding Pepe at different moments in time, not exhaustive "gavel-to-gavel" coverage.

Additionally, the pop culture site Know Your Meme, which describes itself as a repository of prominent Internet memes and their cultural histories, served as another source of information about the Pepe meme and its uses and circulation online. The site also provided links to various Pepe meme sites, which, in turn, led to others, and so on, allowing for a degree of triangulation.

PEPE ENTERS THE MAINSTREAM

Anonymous or not, Internet users loved Pepe. By 2014, the frog ventured outside his long-term digital home of 4chan's image boards and Reddit threads, having circulated through social media platforms and appearing in feeds of some pop culture celebrities, thus gradually building up his fame toward becoming a mainstream Internet sensation. This digital crosspollination was much to the chagrin of 4channers and Redditors, who by then had long adopted and claimed Pepe as *their* meme and icon, an association that would drive their reclamation efforts of the popular character in 2016 and 2017.

Pepe's first memetic association with the-then Candidate Trump, some believe, took place in July 2015 when the Malaysian artist Maldraw posted an image of smug Pepe—a version of the meme with a smirking Pepe that initially appeared on 4chan around 2011—as the Republican presidential candidate.[29] With the signature orange wave of hair, Trump Pepe stands in front of a fence on the U.S.-Mexico border, smirking into the camera; a handful of Mexican characters look at Pepe from behind the demarcation line. The image—and, more importantly, the association between Pepe and Trump—took root on 4chan, Reddit, and Twitter, with some adopting Pepe and Trump Pepe as their avatars, thus perpetuating the connection further. It is impossible to say whether those Internet users were indeed Trump supporters who used the meme to signify their political leaning or simply deployed the meme as a joke or commentary. One popular place where Pepe did seem to become the equivalent of Trump's backing was *The _Donald* subreddit, a thread on Reddit devoted to the Republican candidate, Clinton bashing, ultra conservative, and often racist, remarks.

Trump himself retweeted a Pepe meme in October 2015; the image displays the frog as Trump, running for the presidency. It was a non-event in the mass media, registering no apparent coverage or commentary, since Pepe had not yet been associated with white supremacy in mainstream culture, thus soliciting little interest as an otherwise benign cartoon character. Pepe's creator, Matt Furie, interpreted Trump's posting of his frog as a typical example of remix culture when talking with a *New York Magazine* reporter in 2016: "I'm sure it was just a young Republican dude posting it to appeal to smug Trumpies. It was just as amusing as anything else stupid on the Internet."[30] Furie neither linked Pepe to a particular ideology nor ascribed white supremacy sentiments to Trump.

Such neutral interpretations of Pepe and his rhetorical powers in the mainstream did not last long. By late 2015, Pepe memes became angrier and politicized, transforming the goofy character into an aggressive, bullish, and racist frog.[31] In some of them, Pepe morphed into Hitler, donning the Führer's signature skinny mustache accompanied by hateful rhetoric. In others, he was a Nazi solider waiting at the gates to Auschwitz. Although, according to some Internet users, quite visible on 4chan, Reddit, Twitter, and Facebook, this transformation went largely unreported in mainstream media—and to no surprise. As mentioned, Pepe had functioned as communicative shorthand primarily *outside* the mainstream culture, still circulating parts of 4chan and Reddit away from the pop culture limelight and only beginning to make inroads into Twitter and other social media as memes tend to do. Also, such metamorphoses of memes—even those that take on hateful rhetoric—are part and parcel of remix culture, not exceptions that would typically warrant news coverage, even if they did make it to the top of a news cycle.

What is more, when one takes into account the nature of some of the platforms that perpetuated the new wave of Nazi Pepes, they are simply on par for the course. Both 4chan and Reddit largely follow the "lulz logic": the creating of vile, often racist, misogynistic, or otherwise offensive content for the sake of amusement and deriving pleasure from someone else's pain.[32] Such exploitative content designed to wreak havoc by targeting members of mainstream culture—known as "normies" in Reddit and 4chan parlance—has the makings of subcultural trolling; it weaponizes memes to "poke and prod their targets until they draw metaphorical blood,"[33] an idea to which we will return later in this chapter when talking about efforts to reclaim Pepe. This is not to suggest, however, that the Nazi Pepe meme creators and fans merely engaged in potty Internet humor. Some surely did subscribe to the racist, anti-Semitic, and abusive narratives, linking the frog with extremist politics and Donald Trump to express their political beliefs and support for their presidential candidate. Some, however, may have jumped on the white supremacy bandwagon out of spite and a lulzy sense of humor.

By January 2016, as Pepe continued to make his way through social media as an avatar, he piqued the curiosity of a handful of mainstream journalists. One of them, Jay Nordlinger from *National Review*, asked on Twitter: "Does anyone know what that green face is that 'alt' and 'cuck' people put in their avatars and their other images?" Nordlinger's question suggests that he spotted a trend on social media: those who expressed ultra-conservative and alt-right sentiments also used Pepe as their profile pictures. But his inquiry into "that green face" was also telling for another reason; it showed his outright unfamiliarity with the symbol itself. The Twittersphere obliged, responding with links to Pepe memes, explanations, and political banter. Several answers zeroed in on Pepe's connection to white supremacy, suggesting that the link between the two was familiar to Twitter users despite mass media's lack of visible coverage of the issue at that time.

The public finally did learn about Pepe's white supremacy ties and alleged connections to Trump from a May 2016 article, in which a *Daily Beast* reporter quoted anonymous, self-identified white supremacist Twitter users who talked about an organized effort online to connect the frog with extremist rhetoric and to voice support for candidate Trump.[34] The exposé was among first such mainstream media accounts that linked Pepe to white supremacy and the Republican candidate, establishing the controversial association in the popular culture, one that Trump's Democratic opponent would soon advance and one that the mainstream news media would subsequently solidify and recirculate for months to come.

It is worth noting that one of the interviewed Twitter users in the *Daily Beast* article, with Twitter handle @JaredTSwift, later told *New York Magazine* that he had made up the story and called it a prank.[35] A Twitter user with the same handle posted a few weeks before the story was published: "We need to make meme Pepe into a Nazi icon so that SJWs stop using him. This is our greatest task."[36] The posts point to a concerted effort on the part of a group to turn Pepe into a white supremacy symbol to reclaim him from—in Reddit and 4chan vernacular—the social justice warriors (SJWs), aka, the normies. Two months later, someone with the same Twitter handle tweeted: "I have no idea how this right-wing parody account got so big. I'm just a snarky Marxist who's good at staying in character."[37] It is difficult to assess the sincerity and accuracy of @JaredTSwift's claims, especially in light of the *New York Magazine*'s story (the account has since been disconnected). Whether perceived credible or not, a handful of Swift's followers credited him with Pepe's mainstream debut. Twitter user David Williams (@NagatronTV) tweeted at Swift: "Uhh @JaredTSwift am I hallucinating or did you just troll your way into the election?"[38] Swift had no comment.

Some Reddit users marked Pepe's appearance in mainstream media with self-congratulatory satisfaction, though meme crossover from subcultural image boards such as Reddit to the mainstream typically signifies the end of a joke on the anti-normie platforms.[39] Still, some celebrated Pepe's arrival in the mainstream as a testament of Reddit's power to set the agenda for the mainstream press. Reddit user FillMemesWithCreams, for instance, posted a screenshot in September 2016 from MSNBC with various Pepe memes, noting, "Pepe hits mainstream media." The post elicited more than 570 comments, including one from user Assy-McGee: "we did it Reddit," clearly taking credit on behalf of the Reddit community for pushing a meme popular on the fringes of the Internet into the limelight.

The Plot Thickens: Pepe (Re)Enters Both Presidential Campaigns

The notion of Pepe as a white supremacy mascot used by Trump supporters and embraced by Trump himself was only to be reinforced and cemented in the coming months. In a September 9, 2016 speech, Hillary Clinton called half of Trump voters a "basket of deplorables"—racist, sexist, homophobic, and more—sparking enthusiasm among her legions and outrage among her opponents, who felt insulted. But not everyone remained hurt for long. Donald Trump Jr. reappropriated Clinton's word and released a doctored poster of the 2010 movie *The Expendables* the following day, switching out the Hollywood superheroes for his father's likeness and other prominent Trump supporters, including Pepe the Frog, New Jersey Governor Chris Christie, former New York City Mayor Rudi Giuliani, and more. The name of this crew: The Deplorables.

This time, the act of posting a Pepe meme by a Trump did ignite a media furor as it happened in the midst of ongoing public chatter about the candidate's alleged flirtations with his white supremacy supporters. Mainstream news outlets, from CBS News to CNN, jumped on the story, explicitly making connections between Pepe and white supremacy, commenting on the candidate's son's deployment of an already loaded symbol during the campaign. A day later, Clinton advanced the narrative in a Pepe primer posted on her campaign page. The Q&A format explained to the presumed unaware voter the significance of the frog and its ties to Trump, suggesting the Republican candidate's connections to an extremist ideology. "Trump has retweeted his white supremacist supporters with regularity, but the connection between the alt-right and his campaign continues to strengthen," part of the primer read, referencing the right-wing, ultra conservative Trump supporters with nativist tendencies. "Now white supremacists have given Pepe the cartoon frog some Trump hair—and the candidate's own son says he is 'honored to be grouped with' him. This is horrifying." Clinton's message was not hard to read: Trump, via the association with Pepe and his son's use of the frog now branded a racist symbol, was a deplorable, too.

Less than two weeks later, the Anti-Defamation League classified Pepe the Frog as a symbol of hate, alongside swastika, the Ku Klux Klan robes and the Confederate flag. The organization did acknowledge that most of Pepe memes and uses did not have racist or anti-Semitic connotations, and that it was crucial to look at the context within which the cartoon character was used. But, the League argued, the bigoted Pepe had proliferated the Internet and was doing damage. In fact, the League teamed up with Furie in a #Save-Pepe campaign on social media to reclaim the symbol from white supremacists. The effort encouraged people to create positive images of Pepe to turn the tide online.

Some Redditors did not take Pepe's classification as a hate symbol well. They vented online, often claiming that the League's decision showed lack of basic understanding of remix culture on the part of the mainstream, including the liberals. Their political affiliations were not explicitly stated. In general, Reddit users tend to be young, male, and "self-identify as liberal at higher rates than the overall public."[40] More specifically, close to half of Reddit users claims to be liberal (as compared with approximately 20 percent of the American public who identifies as liberal), 13 percent say they are conservative, and 39 percent report being moderate. Close to half of Reddit users also self-identify as "heavy" Internet users who are online almost all the time.[41]

User Templar_Knight08 vented nine months after the League's announcement, echoing a common sentiment among scores of Reddit users:

> How the fuck is this even possible? Am I wrong in assuming that MILLIONS of people around the world use Pepe every single day? And that out of all of the millions of Pepes and RarePepes out there, these guys just happened to find the rarest of RarePepes that not even an image search could turn up many examples of. Have some people used Pepe in ways which people might define as offensive? Sure. But so has ALMOST EVERY OTHER FUCKING MEME OUT THERE! The point of memes is that that [sic] they are a joke about a situation. Pepe is a joke. And Pepe didn't ask for this. Its [sic] insane and completely out of touch with the concept of memes and their usership [sic].[42]

Others proposed conspiracy theories on the part of Clinton and the so-called "liberal media," suggesting that the controversy around Pepe was manufactured. User KaineDame wrote: "Funny Pepe memes can be used in any way people desire. It so happens that Pepe was used far and wide in good fun against mainstream news narratives, some people even used Pepe to support Trump! Some people found this so threatening that they had to label Pepe a white supremacist symbol. It's pathetic when you think about [it]." Farther in the same thread, other Redditors chimed in, pondering why Pepe was singled out of all the memes to be designated a hate symbol. User FMantothemax responded, "Because it was used by Trump or one of his sons in a tweet. Before it was even labeled a white supremacist symbol I'm pretty sure."[43] Redditor State_ added, "To push a narrative so the media can spin it all day,"[44] revealing a cynical and distrustful attitude of the subcultural Internet users toward the mainstream press and its ascribed objectives to destroy the conservative viewpoint.

WAS PEPE A SYMBOL OF WHITE SUPREMACY?

Various theories circulated mainstream media, Reddit, and 4chan, speculating not only whether Pepe truly turned into a bigot but whether his transformation was a part of a concerted effort to push the white extremist agenda into the limelight or to hijack the presidential election. As mentioned, a handful of anonymous Twitter sources who self-identified as white supremacists told a *Daily Beast* reporter of a movement online to support Trump and bring their ideas into the mainstream, claims later retracted by those sources and further disputed by a few journalists who cover digital culture. The lulz logic of message boards such as 4chan and Reddit, combined with past examples of similar meme hijackings and the tinkering nature of remix culture, suggest that for some, Pepe's racist bastardization may have had more to do with subcultural trolling and performance in remix culture than with genuine expression of extremist ideology by white supremacists (or the Republican presidential candidate).[45] That is not to dismiss the idea that some of those who coopted Pepe as a white supremacy mascot could have genuinely espoused the racist ideology.

But to arrive at this idea, it is essential to understand the nature of subcultural trolling, which reigns on both of the message boards of interest and relies on memes as a common language of remix culture. Subcultural trolls self-identify as such, and their online activity is motivated by the logic of lulz, a modification of the Internet shorthand "lol"—laugh out loud. Subcultural trolls position themselves vis-à-vis mainstream culture, which they generally define as the corporate mainstream born out of capitalism and consumerism, and perpetuated by the entertainment industry.[46] In other words, they oppose the mainstream order of things that they claim has been imposed on the masses, automatically designating much of mainstream culture a target of their "lulz economy"[47]—pranks, hoax, hacking, and ridicule. In their cynicism and suspicion of the dominant corporate ideology—they regard mainstream culture as cancer—trolls "believe that nothing should be taken seriously, and therefore treat public displays of sentimentality, political conviction, and/or ideological rigidity as a call to trolling arms,"[48] unleashing "lulzy mayhem"[49] in the "culture of automatic dissent."[50] The attacks are often strategic and run a gamut, from innocuous jokes to exploitative campaigns, some of which border on the illegal. Their goal is to expose, humiliate, provoke, and punish—all for a mean-spirited chuckle. Trolls "function as cultural dung beetles"[51] that feed off of such cultural "waste," emboldened by anonymity online, where almost all activity is faceless and nameless. With the help of such disguise, trolls and pranksters have been known to invent their narratives, experiences, opinions, and even gender online, all in pursuit of a joke—the more outrageous, the better. On 4chan, for example, men frequently pose as women and paddle stories of traumas such as rape and other abuse to justify offensive behavior.[52]

But as much as trolls seem to despise mainstream culture and media, they also maintain a symbiotic relationship with both.[53] That is because "for trolls, media attention paid to their activities simply makes the lulz louder and sweeter."[54] The dynamic fuels a self-perpetuating cycle where "trolls needed the media to become hysterical, and the media needed trolls to terrorize, each side benefited from the overreaction of the other."[55] Such seems to have been the case with Pepe: some meme creators transformed a benign frog into a Nazi sympathizer, ratcheting up the outrage by—from the normie perspective—desecrating a likable cartoon character for no apparent reason but to incite hatred and stir the proverbial pot. By trolling standards, this was a feat. The mainstream media, with the help from Hillary Clinton and online speculations, latched onto the chatter and alleged connections between the re-made Pepe, white nationalism, and Donald Trump and churned the story for days, sealing Pepe's dominant narrative as a frog gone bad. The mainstream culture's disgust with Pepe has since lingered, gesturing to the agenda-setting powers of legacy media, which will be explored in the latter part of the chapter.

As the frog's newly created negative connotation erased its past as a goofy amphibian for the mainstream media consumers, Reddit and 4chan users recognized the change and its sweeping effects on pop culture. Reddit user ZorbaTHut's wrote in early 2017: "The last game I worked on actually removed an about-to-be-released ingame emoticon because it was a Pepe reference. The funny part was that we all agreed it was ridiculous and that Pepe wasn't a racist frog, we just didn't want to end up in the crosshairs of the news system."[56] Which is exactly what happened to the Spanish clothing line Zara in April 2017 when it came out with a denim skirt that displayed appliqué likeness of Pepe. Following a public outcry on social media—it started with a single tweet—the company pulled the skirt from circulation and denounced any links to Pepe's Nazi ideology.[57] The mainstream media coverage of the event reiterated Pepe's white supremacy connections, further perpetuating the negative association in the mainstream, much of it through providing Pepe's background that chronicled his demise.

Pepe's imposed right-wing ideology surely elicited a chuckle among trolls and some tech journalists, a few of whom called it a quintessential lulz shortly after Pepe's classification by the ADL.[58] Turning Pepe into Hitler fits the lulz logic of subcultural trolling: outrageous, offensive, hurtful, and subversive, all for the smug entertainment of the troll and fellow "lulzers." Its racist overtones and transgressive tactics echo prior pranks, including the now legendary Habbo Hotel trolling raid in 2006, during which Anonymous members—4channers who did not use their names—took over a virtual space for children and teens, turning their avatars into swastikas and picket lines.[59] In both cases, the disruption seems pointless from a normie perspective, but for trolls, the teen site was just too mainstream and needed to be denigrated, disrupted, and ultimately squashed. In Pepe's case, putting a funny frog with hateful ideology and linking it to the Republican presidential candidate—especially that he and his son had already deployed Pepe during the campaign—produced a combustive combination so outrageous that it captured the attention and imagination of the mainstream news cycle and audiences for days, and intermittently ever since. But there was another dimension to this association that registered in some news accounts: if people who used Pepe to denote their white supremacy leanings were indeed self-proclaimed Trump supporters, the candidate and his son's use of the frog no longer looked benign.

It is that juxtaposition—a seemingly innocuous teen website taken over by human swastikas and a cartoon character with extremist symbolism—that is designed by the lulz logic to shock, disrupt, and rattle the status quo. Similarly, trolls attacked memorial sites on Facebook, posting offensive comments in a dedicated space of mourning.[60] The viciousness of the deed was immediately apparent and hurtful, especially to the parents, family members, and friends of the dead. From the trolls' perspective, the lulz had a point beyond being a silly prank: it exposed perceived inauthenticity of those who posted condolences even though they did not know the dead.[61] In another contradictory logic of lulz, authentic vulnerability gets mocked, but inauthentic vulnerability, as in this case, also becomes a target. The trolls then often function as bullies who control the virtual playground, rhetorically beating up the rest of the kids and taking over the toys—all for the lulz.

Such subversive humor—making a mascot racist or offending mourners—epitomizes trolling as "lulz-oriented actions [that] puncture the consensus around our politics and ethics, our social lives, and our aesthetic sensibilities,"[62] calling into question mainstream values, customs, and points of view. Contemporary trolls are "provocateurs and saboteurs who dismantle conventions while occupying a liminal zone."[63]

Some media writers and pundits suggested at the time that trolls who turned Pepe into a Nazi were motivated by pranking and lulz, rendering their action apolitical. But given the ideological origin of subcultural trolling and its vehement objection to the status quo, desecrating a beloved cartoon or taking over a virtual memorial—such as breaking taboos to create outrage and moral panic—seems to be about more than just a chuckle. Such anti-establishment sentiments are indeed political and, in the case of 4chan, gave rise to Anonymous, the global network of activists and hackers who have been known to disrupt norms through pranks, hacks, and lulz on a massive scale. Such actions are counter-cultural, rooted in an ideological objection to anything normie, thus being, in fact, deliberately political.[64] What is more, both 4chan and Reddit users distinguish themselves from the mainstream culture also through nomenclature and rules of communicating online—the logics of the boards—clearly drawing the line between *us* and *them*.[65]

RECLAIMING PEPE ONLINE AND IN THE MEDIA

In early October 2016, a handful of YouTube celebrities created a four-minute video (which included an original Pepe song), debunking the amphibian's racist and anti-Semitic character. One by one, the personalities told the public that "many unfair assumptions, outright lies, and nasty rumors have been made about our good friend," referring to the frog. Their tone was mocking seriousness, with funerary music playing in the background. The YouTube personalities called ADL's decision to list Pepe as a hate symbol "a mistake" and argued that Pepe was "a symbol of joy, of happiness, of friendship," talking about a fictional character as if he were a person. In a direct plea to the viewers, the artists said: "You and I cannot let reckless politicians abuse our innocent memes. Pepe deserves better. And with your help, we can clear Pepe's name, and make him happy for once." They pointed fingers at politicians (not the media) for misappropriating *their* piece of culture, clearly demarcating and reinforcing the line between *them* and *us*, even though the *they* here were mainstream YouTube celebrities, not subcultural message board users. They encouraged their audience members to tweet #NotAllPepes, hoping to spark a movement to restore Pepe's good name. A quick search of the hash tag shows that the viewers responded in kind, still posting as of August 2017.

The idea of reclaiming meaning in remix culture, as mentioned, is a complicated one and poses several paradoxes. The underlying premise of remix culture is co-production of meaning on the part of a participating public, ideally allowing for marginalized voices to take part in public discourse. The built-in assumption is that meaning is unstable and fluid; it changes through de- and re-contextualization of a piece of cultural knowledge—in this case a cartoon character—connoting one thing to some and quite another to others.[66] In remix culture, such production of meaning does not stop, though it certainly favors some readings and interpretations as dominant and others as oppositional or marginal.[67] This is particularly true of Internet memes, whose very nature is rooted in intertextuality, replication and mutation through re-use.[68] Any effort to reclaim Pepe, however symbolic, seems to go against the very process that created him in the first place. The point of remix culture is to cut and paste and cut again to make sense of the world, much like Pepe's journey reflected in the hundreds of iterations over the years. It is not to insist on a singular interpretation and demand it of others.

Pepe also demonstrates that as much as meaning in remix culture is negotiable, memes do come to signify specific situations or encapsulate specific sentiments, feelings, and attitudes over time. That is, in fact, a major reason for their popularity and success. They gain cultural resonance because people who create and propagate them get the joke and intertextual references.[69] Although deployed to comment on various scenarios throughout the years, the Pepe meme's dominant function was as shorthand for a laidback attitude toward an event—far removed from white supremacy, anti-Semitism, and racism. One can, then, understand why Pepe devotees would lobby for a radical change in the public discourse in the media, especially that, as scores of Pepe meme creators and some journalists have pointed out, the hateful Pepes constituted a small fraction of the generally positive, "feels good, man" meme.

The process of reclamation brings forth the notion of content ownership, but not in a legal sense of copyright but in a philosophical sense of belonging. It ties to the already mentioned idea of territoriality online, especially among 4chan and Reddit users, both of whom have claimed Pepe as their own. Such claims of ownership also reveal the users' self-perception as a collective owner who has lost its cultural artifact to a rival and is unwilling to either abandon it or adopt the newly imposed meaning on Pepe as a bigot.

"PEPE IS OURS"

Along with the YouTube celebrities, at least three other groups launched reclaiming campaigns to recover Pepe in the wake of his public demonization: 4chan and Reddit users, and Pepe's creator himself. All three seem to have been driven by different motivations. As mentioned, the efforts of Redditors and 4channers largely coalesced around their opposition to mainstream culture, which, in their eyes, hijacked *their* symbol. The reclaiming campaigns therefore did not seem to be as much about Pepe's racist rhetoric as much as about Pepe's mainstreaming. Both board users acknowledged in their posts that outrageous iterations of memes are par for the course in remix culture; what bothered them was the loss of an artifact of *their* vernacular expression. A handful of journalists and 4chan users hinted in 2016 that turning Pepe into a Nazi might have been a strategic move on the part of subcultural trolls to reclaim the meme from pop culture.[70] The reverse logic of 4chan steeped in lulz was at work here: make a meme so vile that regular Internet users will not engage with it and leave it alone. As one anonymous 4channer concluded in a September 2016 post, that mission was accomplished: "well guys, it's official. Pepe is ours again, the normies find him too offensive."[71] But a fellow 4channer countered, suggesting that the efforts to take Pepe back failed because the frog was, in fact, not repulsive enough: "If r9k were actually trying to take pepe [sic] back they would have made him a misogynistic rapist. They were just in it for the dank" (r9k is a sub-board of 4chan).[72]

Shortly after Pepe's classification as a hate symbol, 4chan users engaged in long chats about Pepe's belonging, often referring to the frog as "ours." In one such conversation from September 2016, scores of anonymous users suggested that the meme had already been reclaimed; others wrote that Pepe did not need to be rescued because it belonged to 4chan all along. One anonymous user posed: "They may take our lives but they will never take our Pepes. Reeeeeee."[73] Another wrote, "It's even better this way; not only is Pepe not normie, his presence offends and triggers normiescum."[74] In a more thoughtful response, another anonymous 4channer chimed in, "I find these posts so stupid. Nobody has to 'take back' anything. All of the Pepes are made up of data. 0 and 1's. Nobody is going to be able to censor or stop Pepe. Unless you're a normie who think [sic] the internet revolves around normiebook and twitter [sic] you have no reason to worry."[75]

Reddit users still pondered the idea of Pepe's reclamation in June 2017 with user shoopdahoop22 posting a call to action: "Can we please start a movement to reclaim our beloved frog?"[76] The responses were mixed, with some Redditors ready to help and others ridiculing what they perceived as an absurd idea. One person suggested that no one dictated what Pepe meant and encouraged others to "keep meme-ing." Some of the chatter expressed anti-liberal and anti-progressive sentiments and deemed labeling Pepe a hate symbol a gross overreaction. Despite occasional proclamations of Pepe's ownership on both platforms, some 4channers recently expressed doubts about Pepe's cultural belonging. The answers to the June 20, 2017, question "Do you still like Pepe" varied. Some users said they were "over" the meme and the controversy while others staunchly defended the frog's legacy and asserted its cultural endurance over time. A few worried that Pepe has remained in the mainstream, affiliated now with their perceived ideological rivals, the normies. One anonymous user wrote, "Pepe is normie shit."[77] Another said, "normies . . . have started using him again, and its [sic] cringy, cringy, cringy But [sic] at some point they'll stop, and then pepe [sic] and kek will go back to being /ourguy/."[78]

The very explicitly territorial language that both board users deployed in their discussions to define Pepe's meaning and affiliations reflects a larger ideological battle that has been raging online in the last few years between subcultural platforms and the mainstream over Internet memes.[79] It has been fueled by *meme elitism*, an "online ideology rooted in the opposition to the popularization of memes among non-underground communities and the mainstream media."[80] Scores of memes have originated on platforms such as 4chan and Reddit over the years, branding them as meme incubators. In the words of 4chan founder Christopher Poole, the message board has been a "meme factory."[81] With the rise of social media, memes began to surface on platforms such as Twitter and Facebook, shedding the original contexts, language, and references of the subcultural community online behind.[82] One of the significant turns in such digital crosspollination was the launch of Know Your Meme, a site that catalogues memes and serves as a guide to meme culture for normies; that is, the public at large.[83] Memes have since become commonplace: accessible, available, and marketable, leaving members of 4chan disillusioned with such fast and vast cultural takeover. To add insult to injury, 4chan and Reddit users have expressed frustration over the loss of creativity, artistry, and rhetorical edge of contemporary pop culture memes, which they perceive as generic, tame, and boring.[84] Internet users now can create memes by using templates and meme-generating sites, often foregoing the creative process of designing and creating memes from scratch.

PEPE'S CREATOR WANTS HIM BACK

Meme enthusiasts on 4chan and Reddit were not alone in their quest to exonerate Pepe. The amphibian's creator, Matt Furie, wrote an editorial in *Time* magazine a few weeks after his cartoon character was classified a hate symbol, taking a stand against such association. He was still hopeful, he wrote, that the tide would change, and his "chill frog-dude"[85] would regain its old status as a "blissfully stoned frog"[86] that has been deployed by Internet users to comment on everyday life events. Furie suggested that the problem with Pepe was connected to signification power exerted by institutions such as the mainstream media, which have unprecedented access to the masses, defining Pepe's dominant meaning as a hate symbol for the public, the very paradox of meaning reclamation in remix culture mentioned earlier. Although unhappy about the anti-Semitic use of his character, Furie wrote:

> The problem with Pepe is that he's been stamped a hate symbol by politicians, hate groups, institutions, the media, and because of them, your mom. Before he got wrapped up in politics, Pepe was an inside-joke and a symbol of feeling sad or feeling good and many things in between. I understand that it's out of my control, but in the end, Pepe is whatever you say he is, and I, the creator, say that Pepe is love.[87]

For Furie, the reclaiming effort did not seem to be directly about subcultural territoriality, meme elitism, or the normie culture appropriating Pepe, the core complaints of 4chan and Reddit users. Here, the protest targeted the perceived extraordinary power of the dominant meaning-making machine oiled by politicians and mass media over the masses, leaving Pepe—and his enthusiasts—as casualties. In Furie's eyes, both the media and political figures exercised far-reaching influence over the mainstream culture and redefined meaning of a symbol that had already been well established online as the opposite of hate. Furie suggested that Pepe's accrued cultural capital was wiped out by the institutions of meaning production and subsequently replaced with a hate rhetoric as the meme circulated through news cycles. The narrative was accepted by regular people, such as "your mom," pointing once more to the powers of the vertical, top-down meaning making media institution and its gripping influence in remix culture.

To fight back, Furie launched the #SavePepe campaign in the fall of 2016, encouraging Pepe fans to produce positive images of his frog to counter the negative mainstream associations with hate groups. He said the iterations would become a part of the Peace Pepe Database of Love.[88] "We are in uncharted territory right now," Furie told the *Guardian* newspaper about his reclaiming efforts. "But I have to take some responsibility for him because he's like my kid or something. . . . I would like to get the frog off the hate database. It means a lot to me as he's an extension of myself."[89] By May 2017, Furie's enthusiasm for taking back his cartoon character seemed to fade. Pepe the Frog was put to rest in a new comic strip, lying in an open casket mourned by his friends. It was Furie's way, he wrote, of cutting off the hatred. The strip's publisher Fantagraphics issued a statement on Furie's behalf: "Having your creation appropriated without consent is never something an artist wants to suffer, but having it done in the service of such repellent hatred—and thereby dragging your name into the conversation, as well—makes it considerably more troubling."[90]

In a true lulz fashion, some on Reddit laughed. User futurestorms claimed that "you can't kill an immortal."[91] Redditor vassago77379 took down Furie and his perceived misguided efforts: "I love how nobody even knows who the guy is . . . Steps up all the sudden trying to 'kill' Pepe [sic] Bitch you lost control of pepe [sic] a long time ago, stop trying to act like what you say means anything."[92] A handful of tech and pop culture reporters echoed the sentiments, writing at the time that the idea of killing a meme in remix culture was impossible as Pepe did not belong to Furie anymore; he belonged to the Internet.[93]

Pepe did not remain dead long. As mentioned, Internet users on 4chan, Reddit, and social media have continued to talk about the frog and post the meme. Furie himself had a change of heart in June 2017. He and his brother launched a $10,000 Kickstarter campaign to bring Pepe back in a new cartoon series. By August 9, 2017, 367 people contributed to the cause, raising $34,757.[94] Furie's renewed enthusiasm for "reclaiming his status as a universal symbol of peace, love, and acceptance"[95] was back. The cartoon artist explained on the site that the hijacking of Pepe by white supremacists has been "a nightmare so I killed him off. We understand there's no way to fully control the internet or how people decide to use Pepe the Frog. Trying to control that would be a completely unreasonable goal. That said, the aim of this project is to positively resurrect Pepe,"[96] a mission that aims to achieve the unachievable by Furie's own admission.

FINAL THOUGHTS

Memes have often been trivialized in mainstream media as mere products of Internet humor—and scores of them undoubtedly are. Pepe the Frog may have started out as one, too, but it certainly did not end its life online on a chuckle. The silly cartoon character became a powerful and contested symbol on and offline, pitting ideologies and groups of people against one another, each deploying the icon to claim its ideas and assert their correctness. Pepe became a digital artifact of the 2016 U.S. presidential elections. The frog was vilified by Hillary Clinton who saw it as a stand-in for racism and a tool for her opponent to connect with those of Trump supporters who expressed alt-right sentiments through the use of the racist Pepe. Trump deployed it once before the controversy as a seemingly benign piece of pop culture that endorsed him as the next commander in chief, most likely relying on its potential appeal with the young and the like-minded. His son's subsequent use of the cartoon was in a retort to Clinton's "deplorables" comment as Pepe's meaning was beginning to be contested in the mainstream. The move ignited a media storm that, to some journalists, confirmed Trump's alliance with white nationalists, who, by then, had already been linked to the meme.

But Pepe's legacy as a meme and a symbol of hate has lingered beyond the Election Day as it continues to be referenced in mainstream media, dragging behind it the negative connotations. *New York Times Magazine*, for example, ran a cartoon that accompanied a July 11, 2017, story about the Trump presidency, placing Pepe outside the White House.[97] Although an artistic depiction, the illustration puts a cartoon character alongside the most prominent individuals in the administration and those in Trump's opposition, affording him the same importance and legitimacy as Trump's closest allies and his detractors. The scene perhaps prompts reflection on contemporary politics, when an imagined character and a hero of an Internet fad gets injected into a presidential campaign and stays in the limelight afterwards, taking over news cycles as if it were a political player in the presidential arena.

As it turns out, it was. Symbols, especially used in political context, are never neutral.[98] They index meanings that may not be obvious or inherent to the physical objects they embody, in this case a goofy cartoon frog that came to symbolize far-right nationalistic sentiments. They link individuals to larger political orders and ideas, synchronizing the meaning for the masses—in fact, engineering that meaning for them.[99] It should not be surprising, then, that Internet users who did adopt Pepe as a symbol of the alt-right used it as their avatar online, communicating via shorthand their political views and allegiances in light of the frog's newly established narrative. Others deployed the same symbol for lulz, as argued here, making distinctions between true hate and true lulz, challenging at times without additional context. The mainstream media and politicians were primarily the ones who manufactured the consent for this label, churning the alt-right association for months through news cycles. Although Pepe's legacy on 4chan and Reddit had been sealed a long time ago as a "stoner dude" who commented on life, it was effectively replaced by a much grimmer dominant discourse in the mainstream media and on social networking sites. The swap erased several years from Pepe's online resume and subsequently mobilized reclamation campaigns to take the meme "back," pointing to the contested readings of symbols in popular culture.[100]

PEPE, AGENDA-SETTING, AND THE MEDIA

A growing body of scholarship investigates such agenda-setting powers of mainstream media in remix culture as the traditional news outlets face competition from participatory public. Some have found that the grip of mainstream media as gatekeepers has loosened as more information bypasses and originates outside the vertical structures of meaning production through the participatory audience online.[101] This is particularly true in the day of mass self-communication,[102] when networked publics contribute to the production of news, challenging the "agenda setting monopoly"[103] of the traditional news outlets that have held the power to tell people what to think for decades.[104] In the contemporary hybrid media environment they increasingly take cues from social networking sites such as Twitter and Facebook, both of which have been considered by some as emerging sources of news and news cycle agenda-setters.[105]

But Pepe's rather swift and lasting meaning redefinition as a cultural symbol points to the still-enduring powers of mainstream media to set agendas for the masses in digital participatory culture. Why else would Zara withdraw a skirt with Pepe's likeness months after the election? The backlash from Twitter was immediate and so harsh that the fashion label dropped the frog almost overnight, distancing itself from the dominant reading of the meme in pop culture. The collaborative production of meaning certainly happened with the Pepe meme, as dozens of Pepe iterations surfaced online, doctoring the original to produce fresh veneers of interpretation—a Pepe "reversioning"[106] of sorts. But it died down considerably when the legacy media entered the cycle and took over the narrative from Internet fringes and social media platforms. It now established Pepe's new identity for the members of mainstream culture, many of whom had never heard of Pepe and only got the one—the prevailing—version of Pepe's meanings and uses.

The enduring agenda-setting powers of mainstream media were precisely at the root of Pepe creator's worry, and they also bothered some 4chan and Reddit users, who recognized the media's far-reaching grip into the mainstream. User CloudedGamer noted on Reddit shortly after the cartoon character was classified as a hate symbol:

> People who have never otherwise heard of Pepe are of course going to see that almost all of the media proclaims Pepe a hate symbol and come to the logical conclusions that it is. Whether people think pepe [sic] is a hate symbol or not actually makes no difference, but the general media's willingness to deliberately promote the idea is. It's why people like Anita come off as so infuriatingly absurd. Because it's not aimed at people who have a clue about the subject matter, it's aimed for people who don't have a clue and the fellow media buddies willing to promote it.[107]

As Pepe's racist legacy lingers—the poster that advertised the August 12, 2017, "Unite the Right" rally in Charlottesville, Virginia, portrayed dozens of Pepes as Nazi-looking soldiers—Furie's efforts to undo it continue. The cartoon artist has hired intellectual property attorneys and can now claim one legal victory over Pepe's racist appropriation. Furie settled a copyright infringement case in August 2017 with a self-published Texas author, whose children's book *Adventures of Pepe and Pede*, allegedly depicted the frog as an Islamophobic creature that wanted to make his "Wishington Farms" "great again."[108] Eric Hauser, a former assistant principal at a North Texas middle school, said he was not aware of Pepe's racist background when he wrote the book and meant no harm. His intent was, he said, to add a story with conservative themes such as honesty, truth, unity, pro-Americanism, and nationalism to the canon of children's literature. In the settlement, the author agreed that copyright infringement had taken place and was ordered to stop selling his book. He also agreed to donate all proceeds from the sale ($1,521) to the Council on American-Islamic Relations, a Washington, DC-based Islamic and human rights group.[109]

In a statement issued after the settlement, Furie's lawyers said that their client "wants one thing to be clear: Pepe the Frog does not belong to the alt-right."[110] Furie also vowed in the same statement that he would use further legal action "to end the misappropriation of Pepe the Frog in any way that espouses racism, white supremacy, Islamophobia, anti-Semitism, Nazism, or any other form of hate."[111]

But will he succeed? Perhaps—one self-published book author at a time. It is hard to imagine, though, how a single person, even with the help of lawyers, could manage to erase a specific meaning of a pop culture icon from the mainstream. The proposition becomes even more challenging online, where the sheer volume of content and anonymity of its producers could render this pursuit futile. How does one perform *damnatio memoriae* in the digital and social media era? Ancient Romans removed all reminders of condemned emperors by scratching out their likeness from paintings, frescos and sculptures, defacing coins that bore their faces, removing their names from public display, and oftentimes burning their writings. The punishment was harsh; it literally erased them from history. Doing the same to the racist iteration of Pepe the Frog—and preempting future attempts to restart the production—seems to border on miracle.

NOTES

1. Pepe creator Matt Furie did not grant permission to reprint the frog in this chapter. For examples of Pepe memes, please Google "Pepe the Frog meme."
2. Asaf Nissenbaum and Limor Shifman, "Internet Memes as Contested Cultural Capital: The Case of 4chan's /b/ Board," *New Media and Society* 19 (2017): 483–501. Ryan Milner, *The World Made Meme* (Cambridge: MIT Press, 2016). Limor Shifman, *Memes in Digital Culture* (Cambridge: MIT Press, 2014).
3. "Pepe the Frog" (Know Your Meme, 2015), http://knowyourmeme.com/memes/pepe-the-frog.
4. "Pepe the Frog" (Know Your Meme, 2015), http://knowyourmeme.com/memes/pepe-the-frog.
5. Julie Reinstein, "Wendy's Tweeted (and Quickly Deleted) a Pepe Meme" (BuzzFeed, January 4, 2017), https://www.buzzfeed.com/juliareinstein/wendys-pepe?utm_term=.ckQrqG8Z2#.fbyAOM487.
6. Jean Burgess, "Hearing Ordinary Voices: Cultural Studies, Vernacular Creativity and Digital Storytelling," *Continuum: Journals of Media and Cultural Studies* 20 (2006): 201–214. Mark Deuze, "Participation, Remediation, Bricolage: Considering Principal Components of a Digital Culture," *The Information Society* 22 (2006): 63–75. Lawrence Lessig, *Remix: Making Art and Commerce* (New York: The Penguin Group, 2009). Lev Manovich, *Software Takes Command* (2008), http://softwarestudies.com/softbook/manovich_softbook_11_20_2008.pdf.
7. Jean Burgess and Joshua Green, *YouTube: Digital Media and Society Series* (Malden, MA: Polity, 2009). Mark Deuze, "Participation, Remediation, Bricolage: Considering Principal Components of a Digital Culture," *The Information Society* 22 (2006): 63–75. Henry Jenkins, *Convergence Culture: Where Old and New Media Collide* (New York: New York University Press, 2006).
8. Axel Bruns, "Towards Produsage: Futures for User-Led Content Production," in *Proceedings Cultural Attitudes towards Communication and Technology*, ed. Fay Sudweeks, Herbert Hrachovec, and Charles Ess (Tartu, Estonia, 2006), 275–284.
9. Mark Deuze, "Participation, Remediation, Bricolage: Considering Principal Components of a Digital Culture," *The Information Society* 22 (2006): 63–75. Lawrence Lessig, *Remix: Making Art and Commerce* (New York: The Penguin Group, 2009). Lev Manovich, *Software Takes Command* (2008), http://softwarestudies.com/softbook/ manovich_softbook_11_20_2008.pdf.
10. Whitney Phillips, *This Is Why We Can't Have Nice Things: Mapping the Relationship between Online Trolling and Mainstream Culture* (Cambridge: MIT Press, 2015; e-book edition).
11. Gabriella Coleman, *Hacker, Hoaxter, Whistleblower, Spy: The Many Faces of Anonymous* (New York: Verso, 2014, e-book edition). Whitney Phillips, *This Is Why We Can't Have*

Nice Things: Mapping the Relationship between Online Trolling and Mainstream Culture (Cambridge: MIT Press, 2015; e-book edition).

12. Jean Burgess, "Hearing Ordinary Voices: Cultural Studies, Vernacular Creativity and Digital Storytelling," *Continuum: Journals of Media and Cultural Studies* 20 (2006): 201–214, 206.

13. Jean Burgess, "Hearing Ordinary Voices: Cultural Studies, Vernacular Creativity and Digital Storytelling," *Continuum: Journals of Media and Cultural Studies* 20 (2006): 201–214. Mark Deuze, "Participation, Remediation, Bricolage: Considering Principal Components of a Digital Culture," *The Information Society* 22 (2006): 63–75. Lawrence Lessig, *Remix: Making Art and Commerce* (New York: The Penguin Group, 2009). Henry Jenkins, *Convergence Culture: Where Old and New Media Collide* (New York: New York University Press, 2006).

14. Lawrence Lessig, *Remix: Making Art and Commerce* (New York: The Penguin Group, 2009), 6.

15. Jean Burgess, "Hearing Ordinary Voices: Cultural Studies, Vernacular Creativity and Digital Storytelling," *Continuum: Journals of Media and Cultural Studies* 20 (2006): 201–214. Jean Burgess and Joshua Green, *YouTube: Digital Media and Society Series* (Malden, MA: Polity, 2009). Mark Deuze, "Participation, Remediation, Bricolage: Considering Principal Components of a Digital Culture," *The Information Society* 22 (2006): 63–75. Lawrence Lessig, *Remix: Making Art and Commerce* (New York: The Penguin Group, 2009). Lev Manovich, *Software Takes Command* (2008). http://softwarestudies.com/softbook/manovich_softbook_11_20_2008.pdf.

16. Ryan Milner, *The World Made Meme* (Cambridge: MIT Press, 2016). Limor Shifman, *Memes in Digital Culture* (Cambridge: MIT Press, 2014). Limor Shifman, "The Cultural Logic of Photo-Based Meme Genres," *Journal of Visual Culture* 13 (2014): 340–358. Bradly Wiggins and Bret Bowers, "Memes as Genre: A Structurational Analysis of the Memescape," *New Media and Society* 17 (2015): 1886–1906.

17. Ryan Milner, "Pop Polyvocality: Internet Memes, Public Participation, and the Occupy Wall Street Movement," *International Journal of Communication* 7 (2013): 2357–2390.

18. Brian Spitzberg, "Toward a Model of Meme Diffusion," *Communication Theory* 24 (2014): 311–339, 312.

19. Jean Burgess, "All Your Chocolate Rain Are Belong to Us?" *Viral Video, YouTube and the Dynamics of Participatory Culture in Video Vortex Reader: Responses to YourTube*, eds. Geert Lovink and Sabine Niederer (Amsterdam, Netherlands: Institute of Network Cultures, 2008), 101–109.

20. Asaf Nissenbaum and Limor Shifman, "Internet Memes as Contested Cultural Capital: The Case of 4chan's /b/ Board," *New Media and Society* 19 (2017): 483–501, 485.

21. Gabriella Coleman, *Hacker, Hoaxter, Whistleblower, Spy: The Many Faces of Anonymous* (New York: Verso, 2014, e-book edition). Lee Knuttila, "User Unknown: 4chan, Anonymity and Contingency," *First Monday: Peer-Reviewed Journal on the Internet* 17 (2011). Ryan Milner, *The World Made Meme* (Cambridge: MIT Press, 2016). Asaf Nissenbaum, and Limor Shifman, "Internet Memes as Contested Cultural Capital," *New Media and Society* 19 (2017): 483–501. Whitney Phillips, *This Is Why We Can't Have Nice Things: Mapping the Relationship between Online Trolling and Mainstream Culture* (Cambridge: MIT Press, 2015, e-book edition). Limor Shifman, *Memes in Digital Culture* (Cambridge: MIT Press, 2014).

22. Gabriella Coleman, *Hacker, Hoaxter, Whistleblower, Spy: The Many Faces of Anonymous* (New York: Verso, 2014, e-book edition). Whitney Phillips, *This Is Why We Can't Have Nice Things: Mapping the Relationship between Online Trolling and Mainstream Culture* (Cambridge: MIT Press, 2015, e-book edition).

23. Asaf Nissenbaum and Limor Shifman, "Internet Memes as Contested Cultural Capital," *New Media and Society* 19 (2017): 483–501, 487.

24. Robert Hariman and John L. Lucaites, *No Caption Needed: Iconic Photographs, Public Culture, and Liberal Democracy* (Chicago: The University of Chicago Press, 2007). W. J. T. Mitchell, *Cloning Terror: The War of Images, 9/11 to the Present* (Chicago: The University of Chicago Press, 2011). David D. Perlmutter, *Photojournalism and Foreign Policy: Icons of Outrage in International Crises* (Westport, CT: Praeger, 1998). Barbie Zelizer, *About to Die: How News Images Move the Public* (New York: Oxford University Press, 2010).

25. Laurie Gries, "Iconographic Tracking: A Digital Research Method for Visual Rhetoric and Circulation Studies," *Computers and Composition* 30 (2013): 332–348. Laurie Gries, *Still Life with Rhetoric: A New Materialist Approach for Visual Rhetoric* (Boulder, CO: Utah State University Press, 2015). W. J. T. Mitchell, *Cloning Terror*. Barbie Zelizer, *About to Die: How News Images Move the Public* (New York: Oxford University Press, 2010).

26. Laurie Gries, "Iconographic Tracking: A Digital Research Method." Laurie Gries, *Still Life with Rhetoric*.

27. Ibid.

28. Gabriella Coleman, *Hacker, Hoaxter, Whistleblower, Spy: The Many Faces of Anonymous* (New York: Verso, 2014, e-book edition).

29. "Pepe the Frog" (Know Your Meme, 2015), http://knowyourmeme.com/memes/pepe-the-frog.

30. Abraham Riesman, "What Happens When Hillary Clinton Calls Your Cartoon Frog Racist" (*New York Magazine*, September 13, 2016). http://nymag.com/selectall/2016/09/pepe-the-frogs-creator-matt-furie-discusses-trump-memes.html.

31. "Pepe the Frog" (Know Your Meme, 2015), http://knowyourmeme.com/memes/pepe-the-frog.

32. Gabriella Coleman, *Hacker, Hoaxter, Whistleblower, Spy: The Many Faces of Anonymous* (New York: Verso, 2014, e-book edition). Asaf Nissenbaum and Limor Shifman, "Internet Memes as Contested Cultural Capital: The Case of 4chan's /b/ Board," *New Media and Society* 19 (2017): 483–501. Whitney Phillips, *This Is Why We Can't Have Nice Things: Mapping the Relationship between Online Trolling and Mainstream Culture* (Cambridge: MIT Press, 2015, e-book edition).

33. Whitney Phillips, *This Is Why We Can't Have Nice Things: Mapping the Relationship between Online Trolling and Mainstream Culture* (Cambridge: MIT Press, 2015, e-book edition), 126.

34. Olivia Nuzzi, "How Pepe the Frog Became a Nazi Trump Supporter and Alt-Right Symbol" (*Daily Beast*, May 26, 2016), http://www.thedailybeast.com/how-pepe-the-frog-became-a-nazi-trump-supporter-and-alt-right-symbol.

35. Jesse Singal, "How Internet Trolls Won the 2016 Presidential Election" (*New York Magazine*, September 16, 2016), http://nymag.com/selectall/2016/09/how-internet-trolls-won-the-2016-presidential-election.html.

36. Jared Taylor Swift (@JaredTSwift), tweet from January 13, 2016.

37. Jared Taylor Swift (@JaredTSwift), tweet from March 19, 2016.

38. David Williams (@NagatronTV), tweet from September 13, 2016.

39. Gabriella Coleman, *Hacker, Hoaxter, Whistleblower, Spy: The Many Faces of Anonymous* (New York: Verso, 2014, e-book edition). Whitney Phillips, "LOLing at Tragedy: Facebook Trolls, Memorial Pages and Resistance to Grief Online," *First Monday, Peer-Reviewed Journal of the Internet* 16 (2011). Whitney Phillips, *This Is Why We Can't Have Nice Things: Mapping the Relationship between Online Trolling and Mainstream Culture* (Cambridge: MIT Press, 2015, e-book edition).

40. Michael Barthel, Galen Stocking Jesse Holcomb, and Amy Mitchell, "Seven-in-Ten Reddit Users Get News on the Site" (Washington DC: Pew Research Center, *Journalism and Media*, 2016).

41. Ibid.

42. Reddit post by user Templar_Knight08, March 2017.

43. Reddit post by user FMantothemax, March 2017.

44. Reddit post by user State_, March 2017.

45. Gabriella Coleman, *Hacker, Hoaxter, Whistleblower, Spy: The Many Faces of Anonymous* (New York: Verso, 2014, e-book edition). Lee Knuttila, "User Unknown: 4chan, Anonymity and Contingency," *First Monday: Peer-Reviewed Journal on the Internet* 17 (2011). Whitney Phillips, *This Is Why We Can't Have Nice Things: Mapping the Relationship between Online Trolling and Mainstream Culture* (Cambridge: MIT Press, 2015, e-book edition). Jesse Singal, "How Internet Trolls Won the 2016 Presidential Election" (*New York Magazine*, September 16, 2016), http://nymag.com/selectall/2016/09/how-internet-trolls-won-the-2016-presidential-election.html.

46. Whitney Phillips, *Why We Can't Have Nice Things*. Jesse Singla, "How Internet Trolls Won."

47. Whitney Phillips, "LOLing at Tragedy: Facebook Trolls, Memorial Pages and Resistance to Grief Online," *First Monday, Peer-Reviewed Journal of the Internet* 16 (2011).

48. Whitney Phillips, *This Is Why We Can't Have Nice Things: Mapping the Relationship between Online Trolling and Mainstream Culture* (Cambridge: MIT Press, 2015, e-book edition), 25.

49. Gabriella Coleman, *Hacker, Hoaxter, Whistleblower, Spy: The Many Faces of Anonymous* (New York: Verso, 2014, e-book edition).

50. Lee Knuttila, "User Unknown: 4chan, Anonymity and Contingency," *First Monday: Peer-Reviewed Journal on the Internet* 17 (2011), 11.

51. Whitney Phillips, *This Is Why We Can't Have Nice Things: Mapping the Relationship between Online Trolling and Mainstream Culture* (Cambridge: MIT Press, 2015, e-book edition), 123.

52. Whitney Phillips, "LOLing at Tragedy: Facebook Trolls, Memorial Pages and Resistance to Grief Online," *First Monday, Peer-Reviewed Journal of the Internet* 16 (2011).

53. Tama Leaver, "FCJ-163 Olympic Trolls: Mainstream Memes and Digital Discord?" *The Fibreculture Journal* 22 (2013). Whitney Phillips, *This Is Why We Can't Have Nice Things: Mapping the Relationship between Online Trolling and Mainstream Culture* (Cambridge: MIT Press, 2015, e-book edition).

54. Tama Leaver, "FCJ-163 Olympic Trolls," 219.

55. Whitney Phillips, *This Is Why We Can't Have Nice Things: Mapping the Relationship between Online Trolling and Mainstream Culture* (Cambridge: MIT Press, 2015, e-book edition).

56. Reddit post by user ZorbaTHut, March 2017.

57. Jessica Roy, "Zara Pulls Denim Skirt after 'Pepe the Frog' Accusations" (*Los Angeles Times*, April 19, 2017), http://www.latimes.com/business/la-fi-zara-skirt-pepe-frog-20170419-story.html.

58. Jonah Bennett, "Here's How Two Twitter Pranksters Convinced the World That Pepe the Frog Meme Is Just a Front for White Nationalism" (*Daily Caller*, September 14, 2016), http://dailycaller.com/2016/09/14/heres-how-two-twitter-pranksters-convinced-the-world-that-pepe-the-frog-meme-is-just-a-front-for-white-nationalism/. Jesse Singal, "How Internet Trolls Won the 2016 Presidential Election" (*New York Magazine*, September 16, 2016), http://nymag.com/selectall/2016/09/how-internet-trolls-won-the-2016-presidential-election.html. Amelia Tate, "First They Came for Pepe: How 'Iconic' Nazism Is Taking Over the Internet" (*New Statesman*, February 16, 2017), http://www.newstatesman.com/science-tech/internet/2017/02/first-they-came-pepe-how-ironic-nazism-taking-over-internet.

59. Gabriella Coleman, *Hacker, Hoaxter, Whistleblower, Spy: The Many Faces of Anonymous* (New York: Verso, 2014, e-book edition).

60. Gabriella Coleman, *Hacker, Hoaxter, Whistleblower, Spy*. Whitney Phillips, *This Is Why We Can't Have Nice Things: Mapping the Relationship between Online Trolling and Mainstream Culture* (Cambridge: MIT Press, 2015, e-book edition).

61. Tama Leaver, "FCJ-163 Olympic Trolls: Mainstream Memes and Digital Discord?" *The Fibreculture Journal* 22 (2013). Whitney Phillips, *This Is Why We Can't Have Nice Things: Mapping the Relationship between Online Trolling and Mainstream Culture* (Cambridge: MIT Press, 2015, e-book edition).

62. Gabriella Coleman, *Hacker, Hoaxter, Whistleblower, Spy.*

63. Ibid.

64. Jonathan Bishop, *Transforming Politics and Policy in the Digital Age* (Hershey, PA: Information Science Reference, 2014), 155–173. Gabriella Coleman, *Hacker, Hoaxter, Whistleblower*.

65. Whitney Phillips, *This Is Why We Can't Have Nice Things: Mapping the Relationship between Online Trolling and Mainstream Culture* (Cambridge: MIT Press, 2015, e-book edition).

66. Laurie Gries, *Still Life with Rhetoric: A New Materialist Approach for Visual Rhetoric* (Boulder, CO: Utah State University Press, 2015). W. J. T. Mitchell, *Cloning Terror: The War*

of Images, 9/11 to the Present (Chicago: The University of Chicago Press, 2011). David D. Perlmutter, *Photojournalism and Foreign Policy: Icons of Outrage in International Crises* (Westport, CT: Praeger, 1998). Limor Shifman, *Memes in Digital Culture* (Cambridge: MIT Press, 2014). Limor Shifman, "The Cultural Logic of Photo-Based Meme Genres," *Journal of Visual Culture* 13 (2014): 340–358.

67. Stuart Hall, "Signification, Representation and Ideology: Althusser and the Post-Structuralist Debates," *Critical Studies in Mass Communication* 2 (1985): 91–114.

68. Ryan Milner, "Pop Polyvocality: Internet Memes, Public Participation, and the Occupy Wall Street Movement," *International Journal of Communication* 7 (2013): 2357–2390. Ryan Milner, *The World Made Meme* (Cambridge: MIT Press, 2016). Limor Shifman, *Memes in Digital Culture* (Cambridge: MIT Press, 2014).

69. Ryan Milner, "Pop Polyvocality." Ryan Milner, *The World Made Meme*. Limor Shifman, *Memes in Digital Culture*.

70. Olivia Nuzzi, "How Pepe the Frog Became a Nazi Trump Supporter and Alt-Right Symbol" (*Daily Beast*, May 26, 2016). http://www.thedailybeast.com/how-pepe-the-frog-became-a-nazi-trump-supporter-and-alt-right-symbol.

71. 4chan post by user Anonymous, September 28, 2016.

72. 4chan post by user Anonymous, September 28, 2016.

73. 4chan post by user Anonymous, September 28, 2016.

74. 4chan post by user Anonymous, September 28, 2016.

75. 4chan post by user Anonymous, September 28, 2016.

76. Reddit post by user shoopdahoop22, June 17, 2017.

77. 4chan post by user Anonymous, June 20, 2017.

78. 4chan post by user Anonymous, June 20, 2017.

79. Whitney Phillips, *This Is Why We Can't Have Nice Things: Mapping the Relationship between Online Trolling and Mainstream Culture* (Cambridge: MIT Press, 2015, e-book edition).

80. "Meme Elitism" (Know Your Meme, 2012). http://knowyourmeme.com/memes/cultures/meme-elitism.

81. Lee Knuttila, "User Unknown: 4chan, Anonymity and Contingency," *First Monday: Peer-Reviewed Journal on the Internet* 17 (2011), 3.

82. Whitney Phillips, *This Is Why We Can't Have Nice Things.*

83. Ibid.

84. Ibid.

85. Matt Furie, " Pepe the Frog's Creator: I'm Reclaiming Him. He Was Never About Hate" (*Time*, October 13, 2016). http://time.com/4530128/pepe-the-frog-creator-hate-symbol/.

86. Ibid.

87. Ibid.

88. Olivia Solon, "#SavePepe: Cartoon Frog's Creator Tries to Take Meme Back from Alt-Right" (*Guardian*, November 4, 2016). https://www.theguardian.com/technology/2016/nov/04/save-pepe-cartoon-frog-meme-matt-furie-trump.

89. Ibid.

90. Chris Neill, "Pepe the Frog Is Dead; Unfortunately, You Can't Kill a Meme" (*CBR*, May 9, 2017), http://www.cbr.com/pepe-frog-dead-pepe-meme-lives-on/.

91. Reddit post by user futurestorms, May 2017.

92. Reddit post by user vassago77379, May 2017.

93. Chris Neill, "Pepe the Frog Is Dead; Unfortunately, You Can't Kill a Meme" (*CBR*, May 9, 2017), http://www.cbr.com/pepe-frog-dead-pepe-meme-lives-on/.

94. "Save Pepe" (Kickstarter, 2017), https://www.kickstarter.com/projects/ 615106574/save-pepe.

95. Ibid.

96. Ibid.

97. Mark Lebovich, "This Town Melts Down" (*New York Times Magazine*, July 11, 2017), https://www.nytimes.com/2017/07/11/magazine/washington-dc-politics-trump-this-town-melts-down.html?mcubz=3.

98. Murray Edelman, *From Art to Politics* (Chicago: The University of Chicago Press, 1995). Charles Elder and Roger Cobb, *The Political Use of Symbols* (New York: Longman, 1983).

99. Charles Elder and Roger Cobb, *The Political Use of Symbols*.

100. Ibid.; Stuart Hall, "Signification, Representation and Ideology: Althusser and the Post-Structuralist Debates," *Critical Studies in Mass Communication* 2 (1985): 91–114.

101. Manuel Castells, *Communication Power* (Oxford: Oxford University Press, 2009). Henry Jenkins, *Convergence Culture: Where Old and New Media Collide* (New York: New York University Press, 2006). Max McCombs and Donald Shaw, "The Agenda-Setting Function of Mass Media," *Public Opinion Quarterly* 36 (1972): 176–187. Sharon Meraz, "Is There an Elite Hold? Traditional Media to Social Media Agenda Setting Influence in Blog Networks," *Journal of Computer-Mediated Communication* 14 (2009): 682–707. Ben Sayre, Leticia Bode, Dhavan Shah, Dave Wilcox, and Chirag Shah, "Agenda Setting in a Digital Age: Tracking Attention to California Proposition 8 in Social Media, Online News, and Conventional News," *Policy and Internet* 2 (12010): 7–32. Eli Skogerbo and Arne Krumsvik, "Newspapers, Facebook and Twitter: Intermedial Agenda Setting in Local Election Campaigns," *Journalism Practice* 9 (2015): 350–366.

102. Manuel Castells, *Communication Power*.

103. Sharon Meraz, "Is There an Elite Hold? Traditional Media to Social Media Agenda Setting Influence in Blog Networks," *Journal of Computer-Mediated Communication* 14 (2009): 682–707, 701.

104. Max McCombs and Donald Shaw, "The Agenda-Setting Function of Mass Media," *Public Opinion Quarterly* 36 (1972): 176–187. Sharon Meraz, "Is There an Elite Hold?"

105. Radim Hladik and Vaclav Stetka, "The Powers That Tweet. Social Media as News Sources in the Czech Republic," *Journalism Studies* 18 (2017): 154–174. Eli Skogerbo and Arne Krumsvik, "Newspapers, Facebook and Twitter: Intermedial Agenda Setting in Local Election Campaigns," *Journalism Practice* 9 (2015): 350–366.

106. Shaun Wilson, "Remixing Memory in Digital Media," in *Save as . . . Digital Memories*, eds. Joanne Garde-Hansen, Andrew Hoskins, and Anna Reading (New York: Palgrave Macmillan, 2009), 184–197, 185.

107. Reddit comment by user CloudedGamer, March 2017.

108. Liz Farmer, "Self-Published 'Pepe the Frog' Kids' Book Is Conservative but Not Alt-Right, Denton ISD Admin Says" (*Dallas Morning News*, August 10, 2017), https://www.dallasnews.com/news/education/2017/08/10/denton-isd-admin-published-childrens-book-pepe-frog-says-know-alt-right-symbol. Mark Frauenfelder, "Man Who Created Islamophobic Children's Book with Pepe the Frog Ordered by Court to Give Profits to Muslim Charity" (BoingBoing, August 30, 2017), https://boingboing.net/2017/08/30/man-who-created-islamophobic-c.html.

109. Mark Frauenfelder, "Man Who Created Islamophobic Children's Book."

110. Ibid.

111. Ibid.

Chapter Nine

Entertainment News and Satire in the 2016 Presidential Election

Joseph M. Valenzano III and Chad Painter

On June 15, 2015, the American political and comedic worlds experienced a seismic shift when Donald J. Trump announced his candidacy for president of the United States during an ostentatious press conference at Trump Tower in New York City. Many in the media and general public dismissed the real estate tycoon and media personality's bid for the presidency as a public relations stunt.[1] Although it's plausible the campaign started as a stunt, Trump's persistence and performance quickly dashed any expectations of his giving up pursuit of the highest office in the land. In fact, he only gained ground as sixteen other Republican candidates gradually fell by the wayside. Even still, reporters did not take his candidacy seriously; throughout the Republican primary, pundits derided him and claimed he had no chance of winning the nomination, let alone the general election. It took until mid-March 2016 for prominent Republicans to acknowledge Trump would likely become the party's standard-bearer, with conservative columnist Jonah Goldberg writing, "Republicans and commentators didn't believe [Trump] would run. They didn't believe he could be an attractive candidate to rational people, no matter how angry with 'the establishment' voters said they were. They—which includes me—were wrong."[2] Trump ultimately surprised everyone in the general election by defeating Democratic nominee Hillary Clinton despite numerous potentially campaign-killing gaffes.

One reason many thought Trump would not succeed was his chauvinistic statements and inability or unwillingness to apologize. Shortly after he announced his candidacy, he stirred controversy with *Fox News* reporter Megyn Kelly, describing her performance as moderator at a Republican primary debate thusly: "There was blood coming out of her eyes, blood coming out of her wherever."[3] Trump created several other firestorms throughout the campaign by not releasing his tax returns, by what Trump critics saw as asking supporters at rallies to pledge their loyalty to him with a salute reminiscent of Nazi Germany,[4] and by seeming to encourage violence at rallies while calling for security to remove protestors from the audience.[5] It seemed as though Trump could not go a day during the whole campaign without doing something that attracted negative media attention.

As mainstream journalists covered the "Trump Train" throughout the primaries, during the conventions, and into the general election, comedians salivated at the chance to satirize the Republican. For decades, the "not ready for prime time players" at *Saturday Night Live* (*SNL*) have taken it upon themselves to spoof presidential elections and candidates. Whether it was Chevy Chase playing up President Gerald Ford's clumsiness, Dana Carvey's iconic portrayal of the bookish President George H. W. Bush, Darrell Hammond's lampooning of President Bill Clinton, or the immensely popular rendition of President George W. Bush by Will Ferrell, *SNL* has led the way with its contemporaneous skewering of politicians, and the 2016 election was no different. In fact, they went outside their full-time cast and had Alec Baldwin portray Trump. *SNL* actually timed their forty-second season premiere (when Baldwin made his Trump debut) to occur on the weekend following the first general election debate between Trump and Secretary Clinton.[6]

Other comedies have taken up the model used by *SNL* to poke fun at politicians and celebrities. Some of the more popular of these depictions have been on shows such as *The Daily Show with Trevor Noah* and *Last Week Tonight with John Oliver*, which satirize news coverage of major events and government officials.[7] These shows share their appeal to a younger-skewing demographic but have become just as popular, and in some cases more so, as *SNL*. Nevertheless, these efforts, and those of *SNL*, have carved a meaningful role for comedy and satire of politics, one that influences contemporary audiences' attitudes and beliefs about the world around them.

In this chapter, we examine the role satire played in the 2016 presidential election. Specifically, we look at the episodes of *SNL* and *The Daily Show*, two of the more popular contemporaneous broadcast comedy programs that address political events, as well as the fictitious reporting conducted in the online publication *The Onion* that followed each of the three general election presidential debates. We approach satire as a type of humor—typically involving sarcasm, ridicule, irony, and exaggeration—used to expose, magnify, or criticize incompetence, stupidity, corruption, or wrongdoing.[8] This may include things such as "spoofing," "mocking," "poking fun," "parody," or other types of humor. We argue that satire has evolved from a mere genre of comedy to a refined way of exercising social responsibility and civic engagement. To illustrate this development, we first briefly describe the context surrounding the 2016 election broadly, paying particular attention to the context of each debate. We then provide an explanation of the concepts of social responsibility and satire, which we then use as a theoretical frame for analyzing the episodes of *SNL* and *The Daily Show* and the articles in *The Onion*. Finally, we provide some concluding thoughts on what these shows tell us about contemporary politics and news, as well as what responsibility comedians and satirists have to society during elections and important civic events.

A COMEDIAN'S DREAM: THE 2016 PRESIDENTIAL ELECTION

During election seasons, candidates often provide fodder for comedians to satirize in a variety of formats. The 2016 election proved to be a treasure trove of instances that invited mockery. Both Clinton and Trump had extensive public histories that comedians could mine for humor, and they provided voluminous amounts of new material throughout the primaries, conventions, and general election campaigns. In this section, we highlight aspects of that "new material," paying close attention to the representation of both candidates, the context surrounding the three general election debates, and the election itself.

AND IN THIS CORNER . . .

To understand how comedians parodied both candidates and the election, it is essential to understand how the public and world understood each of them. To best reflect these perceptions, we utilize both qualitative accounts from news outlets, as well as some quantitative polling data on the perceived attributes of both candidates. The focus of our effort here is to paint a picture of the two candidates' characteristics that potentially contributed to the parodies they received on television and in print.

The Pew Research Center conducted a survey in July 2016 that measured registered voters' perceptions of candidate traits and positions. Some of the findings are telling, depicting two deeply flawed candidates with glaring weaknesses that comedians would find appealing when designing jokes. Both Clinton and Trump were not seen as honest or truthful, while Clinton scored better than Trump on qualifications and judgment. Clinton also received higher marks when it came to voters understanding the candidates' positions and which candidate understood best the needs of voters. Interestingly, the majority of those polled believed Trump had a better chance of changing the culture in Washington, DC, but they also did not believe it would change for the better. Finally, those polled also indicated that the fact Clinton was the first female candidate for president by the Republican or

Democratic Party in American history would help, not hurt, her campaign.[9] Put succinctly, the survey indicated that Clinton was the favorite to defeat Donald Trump due to the latter's lack of experience, lack of understanding on issues and voter needs, and inability to improve politics in the capitol.[10]

Voters held misgivings regarding both candidates, and these doubts persisted even as the election drew nearer. In September, shortly before the first debate, the *New York Times* reported that only about half of those intending to vote held strong support for their candidate of choice while "the rest say that they harbor reservations about their candidate or that they are voting simply to thwart the other nominee."[11] Those reservations were fed by the actions of both candidates, from Clinton's troubles with the FBI to Trump's aggressive rhetoric and decision to release his tax returns, along with his "penchant for insults and provocations."[12] Voters, it seems, saw two candidates with significant shortcomings and gave no clear edge to either candidate.

Internationally, however, there was a clearer picture of the election from the beginning. This is relevant for two primary reasons. First, one of the hosts of the shows we examined is an international comedian (Trevor Noah). Second, and perhaps most importantly, in an era of global access and exporting of entertainment, the shows are no longer solely domestic in terms of audience. Even before the primaries for either party were complete, CNN crafted an anthology of sorts of international journalists and their perceptions on the race. Jonathan Kay, editor of *The Walrus* magazine in Canada, declared that the election elicited "nervous laughter" in his country due to the "naked religious bigotry, of race paranoia, of curdled nostalgia for mythologized 'greatness'" advocated by Donald Trump. In the same collection, Mikhail Fishman, editor-in-chief of the *Moscow Times*, stated that the Kremlin would celebrate if Trump won the Republican nomination. British and South African authors indicated clear support for Clinton over Trump, while several other countries focused more on issues than candidates.[13] That said, the depictions of Trump as a wild card and not a typical politician clearly emerged by this point in the international arena.

SHOWDOWN: HOFSTRA

The first presidential debate took place on September 26, 2016, at Hofstra University in New York. Billed in advance as what would be the most watched debate in presidential history, the first engagement between Clinton and Trump did not disappoint, reaching roughly eighty-four million viewers, topping traditional ratings juggernaut *Monday Night Football*.[14] Trump's behavior in this debate was consistent with his approach the entire campaign. CNN declared that he took to "repeatedly interrupting angrily or dismissively" his opponent's comments throughout the debate. Additionally, the outlet observed "he couldn't resist attacks, even when it was obvious they would backfire."[15]

Specifically, several statements and tactics by both candidates made headlines following the debate. For instance, news outlets and commentators reported that during the debate, Trump referred to not paying taxes as something that "makes me smart," and also reported that he refused to pay contractors who did work for his businesses.[16] At other points in the debate, Trump stretched the truth by denying he called climate change a hoax perpetrated by the Chinese and told moderator Lester Holt that his recitation of Trump's 2002 endorsement of the Iraq War was "wrong, wrong, wrong."[17] On this last point, Clinton made the highlight real when she declared Trump "has a long record of engaging in racist behavior."[18] Perhaps one of the oddest occurrences during the first debate was the repeated and excessive sniffing by Donald Trump.[19]

Clinton was also not without actions and stories ripe for satire. For example, she collapsed at a 9/11 commemoration and initially attributed the incident to "being overheated." Hours after that explanation, her campaign corrected itself and stated Clinton had been dealing with pneumonia for days leading up to the event. Officials argued that Clinton did not want to acknowledge the diagnosis and take a few days off the campaign because she wanted to "power through it" to demonstrate her drive, tenaciousness, and constitution.[20] All told, it was a strange, if not interesting, debate with plenty of material for comedians to mine. In fact, in addition to the debate itself, the coverage of the debate also drove the satirical representations that appeared on television during this time.

ROUND TWO: THE TOWN HALL TEMPEST

The second debate between Trump and Clinton on October 9 came on the heels of the release of a decade-old video where Trump made lewd statements about groping women, confirming for many his misogyny, lack of civility, and unfitness for office. This video seemed to be a damaging blow to Trump's campaign, especially because he was competing against the first major party female nominee for president. In fact, in advance of the debate but following the release of the video, the editorial board of the *Chicago Tribune* issued a projection that the video may very well have lost the election for the Republican nominee.[21] Trump was forced to issue a rare apology in the days leading up to the second debate, but even his apology was short and pivoted quickly to a condemnation of his opponent.[22] He further exacerbated the gender issue by inviting women who accused former President Bill Clinton of sexual misconduct to a press conference outside the debate hall.[23]

Clearly, one focus of the second debate would be the video and, by extension, Trump's fitness for office.

During the second presidential debate, Trump attempted to move past his statements in the video by referring to them as "locker room talk." Additionally, he attacked Secretary Clinton over her husband's sexual conduct while in office. He called Secretary Clinton "the devil," threatened to jail her if elected, and declared she had "tremendous hate in her heart." Clinton, for her part, awkwardly tried to use Abraham Lincoln as a justification for having a different public and private face, and saying different things to different audiences.[24] Trump also contradicted his running mate on policy toward Syria during the debate, claiming he disagreed with Pence and that they had not talked about the issue.[25] Finally, the town hall format did not appear to serve the Republican nominee very well, as he was accused of "stalking" Clinton throughout the debate by his opponents, supporters, and even across Twitter.[26] As with the first debate, there was plenty from this sordid second debate to poke fun at.

THE FINAL COUNTDOWN: THIRD DEBATE APPROPRIATELY IN SIN CITY

The third debate did not have the anticipatory excitement of the first, nor the high drama created by the release of Trump's lewd video that led into the second debate, but it did provide several notable elements in the final stretch of the campaign. In terms of topics, Chris Wallace of *Fox News*, who served as moderator, announced there would be six 15-minute topics in the third debate: debt and entitlements, immigration, economy, Supreme Court, foreign hot spots, and fitness to be president. Held on October 19 at the University of Nevada, Las Vegas, Trump and Clinton both pressed their cases to voters.

On the topic of immigration, one of Trump's central campaign issues, he used the Spanish slang term "hombres" to describe the type of illegal immigrants he sought to deport. The use of the term immediately chained out in social media, with nearly one hundred and thirty thousand tweets by the time the debate ended.[27] Additionally, Trump and Clinton accused each other of being puppets of Russian president Vladimir Putin and revisited attacking each other over sexual misconduct. Clinton also brought up the work of the Clinton Foundation, which Trump described as a "criminal enterprise,"[28] and Trump indicated he might not accept the election results if he did not win. This latter point, much like the "hombres" comment, became a major topic in post-debate coverage.[29] Ultimately, in what had become a trend across all three debates, the CNN/ORC poll regarding the final debate found Clinton "won" the event by a large 13-point margin.[30] It appeared that Clinton had momentum coming out of the third debate.

ELECTION SURPRISE!

Despite the expectation of an easy Clinton victory against Trump, the Republican contender walked away victorious when the actual votes were tallied. He won the electoral vote handily, taking 306 votes to Clinton's 232 while winning states that were seeming locks for Clinton such as Wisconsin, Michigan, and Pennsylvania. The popular vote was a different story, as Clinton won 48.5% of the vote to Trump's 46.4%, making Trump the second president in the twenty-first century to win the Electoral College but lose the popular vote.

Reactions to the election were as strong and strident as the rhetoric from both parties during the campaign. On the left, actors took to Twitter to express their shock at the biggest upset since Truman beat Dewey. Actor Joshua Malina wrote, "Somewhere tonight there's a little, racist, narcissistic, woman-hating, Jew-baiting kid who now knows he can grow up to be President." Chris Evans, star of Marvel's *Captain America*, tweeted, "This is an embarrassing night for America. We've let a hatemonger lead our great nation. We've let a bully set our course. I'm devastated." Trump had some celebrity supporters as well, though they were in the minority. Actor Stephen Baldwin tweeted, "God is moving . . . and America is speaking!" Others such as Kirstie Alley and Stephen Seagal tweeted their pleasure about the victory as well.[31]

The election, and the campaign that preceded it, provided a wide array of controversy, scandal, inflammatory rhetoric, and wild claims and accusations. It also represented one controversial and disliked figure defeating another controversial and disliked figure to ascend to the highest office in the land, a person who had made contentious comments regarding immigration and women, and who promised to build a wall along the Mexican border. The campaign, candidates, and charged atmosphere all created an opportunity ripe for satire. In fact, as we will demonstrate, it gave satirists more than just a humorous edge; they sought to promote their ideal of social responsibility through both politicians, especially Donald Trump, as well as journalists. As *Politico* reporter Shane Goldmacher wrote before the first debate, "Maybe it's going to take comedians to do the job that cable news has relinquished for so much of the campaign." This observation was augmented by the recognition Clinton campaign communication director Jennifer Palmieri provided in the same article that, "*Saturday Night Live* will certainly matter from now until the election a great deal."[32] We now unpack the concepts of satire and social responsibility that we use to examine the depictions of the first three debates and election in *SNL, The Daily Show,* and *The Onion.*

THE USE OF SATIRE IN POLITICAL HUMOR

There are two main types of satire: Horation and Juvenalian. Horatian satirists, who hold up human absurdities and follies to gentle and witty ridicule, comment on the ruling elite and macrolevel norms of social behavior.[33] Horatians, including most comedians and humorists in the current political satire environment, typically are optimists regarding humanity's willingness to overcome deficiencies once those faults are pointed out to them.[34] Juvenalian satirists savagely and mercilessly attack vice and error with contempt and indignation.[35] Juvenalians generally are pessimists who see no hope for a populace of "recidivist criminals . . . ineducable morons, and simian savages."[36]

Modern political comedy follows a long tradition of satire with deep roots stretching to the work of playwrights such as Aristophanes and Shakespeare, as well as farcical news vendors of seventeenth-century European country fairs.[37] Other historical examples include Jonathan Swift's *A Modest Proposal* (1729), writings by Benjamin Franklin and Mark Twain, and monologues by Will Rogers. Television examples include *That Was the Week That Was* (1962–1963 in England, 1964–1965 in the United States), *This Hour Has 22 Minutes* (1993–present), and *Saturday Night Live*'s Weekend Update (1975–present). Satire also has been an integral part of the work of political cartoonists such as Thomas Nast, Garry Trudeau's *Doonesbury*, and the artists at *Charlie Hebdo*.

People often laugh at surprising or odd occurrences, so fully understanding satire is not required for a satirical joke to be perceived as being funny.[38] However, audience members must have requisite knowledge of politics, civics, and current events to fully appreciate satirical humor.[39] Some scholars argue that viewers of political satire often are "political news junkies" who also consume traditional print and broadcast news sources, while others argue that greater effects are seen within political novices.[40] Still, political satire is well suited to the format of mock news for audiences that already know the politics, politicians, and political issues that serve as the underlying substance of the jokes through "real" news programming.[41]

Humor can be a tool used to enhance the salience of messages, increase learning and enjoyment of a subject matter, and heighten judgments of credibility, attitude change, and compliance.[42] However, humor at another's expense can have negative effects and, therefore, can be ethically problematic.[43] Satirists use humor "to diminish or derogate a subject and evoke toward it attitudes of amusement, disdain, ridicule, or indignation."[44] Humor during the 2016 presidential primaries was heavily negative and subversive, commonly incorporating obscenity, and distortions of a candidate's personal life and character.[45] Satire, however, is not used just for humor; it has a larger purpose regarding social and political life.[46] Traditionally, the humor used by *The Daily Show*, *Saturday Night Live*, and *The Onion* is "used much like the proverbial spoonful of sugar that helps the medicine go down; it keeps pointed criticisms from being perceived as being mean spirited by the audience."[47]

Further, satirists do not simply highlight the failings of politicians and political institutions, but highlight the gap "between vice and virtue, between good and bad, between what man is, and what he ought to be."[48] Satirists, therefore, often promote a disappointed idealism[49] or positive negativity[50] by balancing a pessimistic or critical outlook of the political process with an endorsement of an idealistic impression that citizens can redress these ills or follies. In practice, we cannot deny that one's own political ideology may influence his or her satirical product, however, there remains a long track record of humor that targets members of all political persuasions.

Social responsibility theory and entertainment programming

A press based on social responsibility is premised on the idea that freedom of expression is a positive freedom, or a freedom *to do* an action.[51] Expression is granted so the press can serve the public by promoting dialogue and pluralism while simultaneously seeking justice, covenant, and empowerment for constituent groups in a society.[52] The 1947 Hutchins Commission codified the theory of a socially responsible press, and its ideas have been incorporated in ethical codes created by the Society for Professional Journalists, as well as other mass communication organizations and individual newsrooms.

There is an ethical difference between news media and entertainment; however, public discourse about politics, news, religion, education, and commerce increasingly is mediated through entertainment programming.[53] All forms of political communication, including political satire, ought to be subject to normative theory[54] because the "boundaries between news and entertainment programming are falling fast."[55] The main goal of comedians and satirical news outlets is to entertain, but they also serve political and educational purposes that extend beyond mere humor. People create political understanding through the use of diverse political content, and this content gathering is obscured by unnecessary and untenable distinctions between news and entertainment.[56]

Few Americans rely exclusively on one news media source; the most knowledgeable and politically active citizens have a varied news diet that might include both the *NBC Nightly News* and the *Daily Show*.[57] Comedy programs with healthy doses of political satire also might serve as a gateway to increased audience attention to news and public affairs by providing basic knowledge and familiarity with traditional news topics[58]—if for no other reason than they can better understand the humor in their favorite programs. This gateway influence especially is true for males, younger adults, and less affluent viewers who are more likely to learn about presidential campaigns or candidates from entertainment programs.[59] This creates an inherent pressure of maintaining a measure of social responsibility while delivering entertaining content.

In social responsibility theory, an organization ought to act in a way that benefits society, either directly by advancing mainstream social goals or indirectly by avoiding socially harmful acts. The creators of any television series have an ethical obligation to their audience to be socially responsible in the pursuit of mainstream social goals. There are many historical and contemporary examples of creators shirking this obligation; however, there is a tradition of both self-regulation and an academic tradition of criticizing dramatists for unfavorable or problematic portrayals.[60] Communication, whether labeled news or entertainment, ought to:

> shape opportunities for understanding, deliberating about, and acting on the relationships among: (1) the conditions of one's day-to-day life; (2) the day-to-day life of fellow members of the community; and (3) the norms and structures of power that shape these relationships.[61]

Entertainment, like news, is covered by free speech protections. Government bodies, therefore, cannot force entertainers to adhere to any sort of ethical code. However, there is a distinction between law (what one can or cannot do) and ethics (what one ought to do). Entertainment portrayals also ought to serve an overriding public interest if there are foreseeable and substantial negative consequences to those portrayals.[62] Keep in mind, especially, that many of the foolish remarks attributed to politicians were actually made famous by comedians. For example, Tina Fey played Sarah Palin when the former suggested she could "see Russia from our house," and Will Ferrell made the comment "strategery" for which George W. Bush often gets mocked. On the more dangerous front, *Charlie Hebdo* staff became the target of terrorists in January 2015, killing twelve and injuring eleven others in response to cartoons depicting the Prophet Muhammad published by the outlet. The lesson is that comedians must take care with the power their work can have on the public perception of individuals. In the next section, we look at how this social responsibility and the act of satire played out in three major comedic outlets during the 2016 election.

ANALYSIS OF SATIRICAL DEBATE COVERAGE

Saturday Night Live

The October 1, 2016, *Saturday Night Live* episode began with mock debate between Clinton (Kate McKinnon) and Trump (Alec Baldwin), and moderated by Lester Holt (Michael Che). Jokes about Clinton focused on three themes. The first was her health, specifically a recent pneumonia diagnosis. Clinton entered the stage coughing and walking with a cane, and then stumbled and fell before taking the podium. The second theme was her lack of relatability and humanness. Clinton referred to "my own human father" who was "relatable, and I am, also, relatable" and pretended that she made up the obviously well-rehearsed line "Trumped-up trickle-down economics" off the cuff. The third theme was that she was overly confident that she already had won the election. At one point, she tells Holt, "[I] think I'm going to be president" and later, after a particularly ill-advised Trump line, asks if Americans can vote now instead of November 8.

Jokes about Trump also generally fell into three themes. The first was his lack of presidential temperament. Trump announced in his opening remarks that he was "going to be so calm and presidential that all of you watching are going to cream your jeans" before interrupting Clinton and Holt repeatedly with shouts of "wrong" and "shut up." The second, related, theme was that Trump is crazy. He loudly and constantly sniffed and snorted throughout the debate, and he accused Clinton and Barack Obama of taking his microphone to Kenya and breaking it. The third theme was that Trump is racist and sexist. He referred to Holt as "jazzman" and "Coltrane," and said that all Black people live on one street in Chicago "called Hell Street." When Clinton mentioned former Miss Universe Alicia Machado, who the real Trump publicly fat-shamed, he diverted by saying, "We should be talking about the important issues, like Rosie O'Donnell and how she's a fat loser." He later pivoted to the Bill Clinton-Monica Lewinsky affair, including a side remark that Lewinsky was "very heavy."

The second, town hall-style debate was satirized on the October 15, 2016, broadcast. The vast majority of jokes were at the expense of Trump, and those tended to follow the pattern set in the first debate. Trump once again was depicted as not being presidential, saying "I'm going to huff. I'm going to puff. And I'm going to blow this whole thing." He crazily stalked behind Clinton while the theme from *Jaws* played. When Trump saw a Black man stand to ask a question, his immediate response was "Oh no." He then called the man "Denzel." The debate followed the release of the infamous *Access Hollywood* tape where Trump talked about sexually assaulting women. Here, Trump said that his accusers needed to "shut the hell up." He then changed the subject to Bill Clinton's mistresses and tried to intimidate Hillary Clinton by saying that four of the mistresses were in the audience. Clinton faked crying before mockingly saying, "I'm made of steel. This is nothing. Hi girls."

Almost every joke about Clinton centered on her being an unhuman, unrelatable robot. She began the debate by saying that she would attempt "a casual lean" before falling awkwardly. After the first question, Clinton began her answer by saying, "Let me start by walking over to you like I practiced. Right. Left. Right. Left. Plant. Speak." Later, she quoted Michelle Obama, reused the economics line from the first debate, and said "just a couple of equally famous quotes from a couple of equally lovable women." The joke is that Michelle Obama generally was a well-liked and respected first lady, while Clinton is seen by Americans as being a cold policy wonk.

SNL continued the established themes of mockery in the third debate, which aired on October 22, 2016. Trump's caricature still represented him as an un-presidential, slightly unhinged racist and sexist. He began the fake debate by saying, "Tonight, I'm a sweet little baby Trump," and then started screaming after the first question. The sniffles resumed, as did long, rambling answers. He used the words "wrong" and "liar" so much that he affixed "trademark" after uttering them. He called the president of Mexico "Señor Guacamole," his wife "Taquito," and their daughters "chips and salsa." He then uttered the line, "Nobody has more respect for women than I do," which was followed by a montage of large groups of people laughing. The only real change was that Clinton came away virtually untouched in the third debate. There were light jabs about her unwillingness to discuss hacked emails, her exuberance at talking about her political record, and that her policies make her more of a Republican than Trump. However, all of the jokes came across more like good-natured ribbing among friends, especially when compared to the jokes about Trump that were much more personal in nature.

The Daily Show with Trevor Noah

The Daily Show's September 26, 2016, episode mocked both Trump and Clinton in its analysis of the first presidential debate, although the former was the punchline for a significant majority of the jokes. The Trump jokes mainly focused on his un-presidential demeanor. *Daily Show* host Trevor Noah called Trump an "asshole" and said "Trump was out of control" when he kept interrupting Clinton and Holt. He also argued that Trump only accidentally tells the truth about his relationship with the Black community, negative advertising, and his tax returns. After Trump said that not paying taxes "makes me smart," Noah compared him to O.J. Simpson for finding a loophole to get away with committing a crime. Noah also implied that Trump was committing a crime by saying that he "was sniffing a lot" before pretending to snort a line of cocaine off the anchor desk. Trump accused Clinton of fighting ISIS her entire adult life during the debate, and in response Noah commented that would make Clinton only twenty-six years old, which is impossible, he said, because "Trump wasn't hitting on her."

Jokes about Clinton typically lacked the venom reserved for Trump. Noah made two mild jokes about Clinton's cough, referencing Clinton's pneumonia. Noah accused Clinton of lying when she opened the debate by saying "Donald, it's good to be with you." Noah did call out Clinton for a lie about New York murder rates. However, he then gave advice on how to answer the question better, saying that the problem is not murder rates but stop-and-frisk police tactics. His jokes about Trump contained no advisory component after their delivery.

The October 10, 2016, episode of *The Daily Show* barely referenced the second debate. Instead, Noah spent the opening segment dissecting Trump's comments on the *Access Hollywood* tape, as well as the fallout broadcast on cable news. This segment depicted a clear change in tone regarding Trump on *The Daily Show*; Noah no longer saw Trump as a cartoonish buffoon but as a dangerous sexual predator. The only clip from the debate was a soundbite of Trump saying that his comments were "locker room talk." Noah then contradicted Trump, saying that he conflated "sex talk" with "sexual assault talk," and that "If you conduct locker room talk everywhere, it's not the locker room, it's you." Noah also showed the contradiction between Trump's words and actions by airing a clip from *The Apprentice* where Trump fired a contestant for talking crudely in his boardroom, saying, "It's not a locker room." This performance by Noah appeared to be more of an indictment of Trump than an effort to deliver political satire.

Noah spent the vast majority of his third debate analysis on October 19, 2016, again attacking Trump. The debate took place in Las Vegas, and Noah compared the debate to a bachelorette party, referring to Trump as the "giant novelty dildo." Later, Noah again referenced Trump's sniffling, insinuating that Trump had a runny nose because of possible cocaine use. After an exchange where Trump and Clinton accused each other of being Russian puppets, Noah joked that Trump thinks all women are puppets: "That's why he's always trying to stick his hand up them." Trump's sexism was a common element of Noah's analysis. He again mentioned the *Access Hollywood* tape, showed a faked photo depicting the thousands of women whom Noah said have accused Trump of sexual harassment, and played a fake voicemail of Trump apologizing to Lewinsky for calling her fat before saying that she looks "better now that you've lost the weight" and calling her a "total six."

Noah only made two mild jokes at Clinton's expense. He accused her of "defying the fashion police" by wearing all white after Labor Day before reversing course and saying, "She looks fly." Later, he joked that Clinton "defaulted to shifty mode" when asked about the substance of leaked emails. Noah also took time to say that Clinton destroyed Trump and "really spoke to all Americans" about sexual harassment. He then played a nearly minute-long clip of Clinton speaking during the debate before commenting, "Wow. That was power." Noah's performance indicated a clear candidate preference through his compliments to Clinton following mild jokes and intense personal criticism of Trump without any such compliments. More so than the more balanced depictions on *SNL*, *The Daily Show* spent most of its comedic time and resources attacking Trump.

The Onion

Between September 26–28, 2016, *The Onion* published eight articles and one video about the first presidential debate. The vast majority of jokes targeted Trump, typically about his temperament, ineptitude, and falsehoods. For example, one article stated that Trump was going to reference a made-up statistic about immigrants and crime as quickly as possible in order to gauge how many lies he could tell throughout the night. A fact-checking article mocked Trump for correctly knowing there are twenty-eight countries in NATO, stating that "You've got to give credit where it is due." The joke, of course, is that any presidential candidate should have basic knowledge of major U.S. partnerships, so Trump knowing this piece of information is only newsworthy because he is so ignorant regarding foreign and domestic policy. A "Highlights from the first presidential debate" video showed clips from the debate with jokes provided via chyron. One clip showed Trump repeatedly interrupting Clinton, with the accompanying chyron reading, "Report: Trump prepared for the debate by telling women to shut up his entire life."

Clinton's pneumonia also was the target of a joke during the "Highlights" video; a clip of Clinton walking onstage was greeted with the chyron "Hillary Clinton receives last-second chemo treatment before debate." Clinton also was mocked for dishonest statements, specifically that she was against the Trans-Pacific Partnership once negotiated terms were finalized. A fact-checking article labeled the statement false because Clinton only was against the TPP after "it was clearly electorally unviable."

The Onion covered the second debate with five articles and one video published between October 9–10, 2016. Most jokes again targeted Trump, although the outlet did mock Clinton for her dishonesty. In fact-checking the debate, Clinton's statement that she wants a Supreme Court that will continue to favor marriage equality was labeled true "as of 2013." The joke is that she favors marriage for same-sex couples because it helps her politically, not because she thinks it is the right thing to do.

Like *The Daily Show* coverage, *The Onion*'s jokes became more mean-spirited toward Trump following the release of the *Access Hollywood* tape. For example, in the October 9 article "Anderson Cooper begins debate by giving Trump opportunity to explain what the fuck is wrong with him,"

Onion writers, in the voice of Cooper, say that Trump is "not a mentally well person" and that "there is something very, very wrong with you on the most basic and fundamental level." Similarly, in the highlights video of the second debate, Trump says "It's just words" while referencing his statements to Billy Bush; the chyron reads "It's just sexual assault." In the same piece, *Onion* writers reference Trump's alleged connections to Russian president Vladimir Putin, writing that Trump silenced a Putin phone call during one of Clinton's answers. *The Onion* also made its first reference to Clinton being an almost surefire winner in the "Highlights" video, writing "Trump: 'If I were president—and thank God I won't be.'" The implication is that even Trump knows that he has lost the election.

Trump was the almost exclusive object of humor in the fake news outlet by the third presidential debate. Between October 19–20, 2016, *The Onion* published six articles and one video about the debate. Themes developed in earlier debates were reused and reexamined. For example, in a fact-checking article, Trump's claim that Clinton is "such a nasty woman" was followed by the statement that it is unclear whether Trump was referring to the Democratic nominee or "one of the women who have accused him of sexual assault, or one of the millions of other American women he has serially insulted and disrespected." The video highlights included the chyron that "Putin, Assad clink wine glasses while watching the debate in Moscow," another reference to Trump's alleged campaign ties to the Russian, and by extension Syrian, dictator. Another joke focused on Trump's strained ties with the larger Republican Party apparatus in that Republicans would have two minutes to distance themselves from Trump following each of his responses. They could "use the time either to condemn the candidate's remarks outright or to explain again to voters that the values of Trump do not reflect those of the party." The punchline, however, is that Trump "reportedly spent the GOP's entire speaking time talking over them and loudly accusing them of lying," a reference to Trump's actions during Clinton's speaking times during the debate.

CONCLUSION

Of the three satires examined here, *SNL* provided a somewhat more balanced critique of the two candidates than did *The Onion* or *The Daily Show*. Consistent across the platforms, jokes targeted Trump's perceived loose association with the truth, his seeming racist and sexist comments and actions, and what some saw as his general unfitness for office. Satirical representations of Clinton took aim at her propensity for political expedience, dishonesty, and scripted nature. There was a clear disparity evident in that type of satire used toward each candidate as well, especially beginning with the second debate that occurred shortly after the release of the *Access Hollywood* video where Trump was recorded making lewd comments regarding women. Satire aimed at Trump was more of the Juvenalian form, treating him as an irredeemable moron with no hope for recovery or improvement. On the other hand, the satire toward Clinton was more Horatian in form, in that it pointed out faults in the candidate but in a way that invited improvement and did not portray her as a moron or criminal. Clearly, these outlets had a position in the election and understood their role as providing more than simply humor. Instead, they engaged in political activism in the name of humor.

HAVE YOU NOT BEEN ENTERTAINED?

Political campaigns, in particular presidential elections, have long been a source of humor and satire in American popular culture. The election of 2016 was no different, with several successful humorists taking aim at the candidates and the election for significant portions of their programming and publication. Supposedly, these are simply attempts to entertain the public, but recent research has illustrated that political satire, the likes of which *SNL, The Daily Show*, and *The Onion* employed during the 2016 election cycle, serves the purpose of more than simply amusing the public—they also educate and influence their audiences. Given that impact, these humorists and outlets have a responsibility to society that goes well beyond being funny. In the case of some actors and writers in the texts we analyzed, they understood their social responsibility as trying to shift their audience toward one particular candidate—the one they saw as less offensive. Some may argue that advocacy is a misapplication of the concept of social responsibility; however, some media ethicists insist that subjectivity and even partisanship can be consistent with a socially responsible press.[63] However, this practice raises some significant issues that we will now explore.

On a conceptual level, the issue of the impact satire can have on an election or the public's impression of a person seems to be more related to the type of satire employed, rather than the volume. Although when aggregated, the prevalence of jokes across the three sources we analyzed seemed to indicate more jokes targeting candidate Trump, the type of satire was also clearly different. We are not suggesting that volume of jokes is unimportant, but rather that if the volume of satirical representations about an individual are of the Juvenalian form, they will have a greater impact than if they were of the more benign Horatian form. A high number of jokes portraying someone as being a moron beyond redemption can have more of an impact than those that leave room for corrective action. Then again, given that candidate Trump went on to win the election, the issue here is not settled and deserves further exploration.

The use of Juvenalian satire in a political election is also something with which the American Republic should be concerned. It appears from our analysis that comedians may use Juvenalian humor as a means of exerting some influence that is more like political activism than something based in their understanding of social responsibility. In other words, when they see their conceptions of social boundaries and norms violated in the public sphere, they employ Juvenalian forms of satire in an effort to eliminate the violator. On those who, in their estimation, "play by the rules," they utilize Horatian satire, thereby seeming to go "softer" on that candidate or person. The fact remains, however, without a code of ethics to somehow govern entertainment personalities and humorists in their use of satire, this judgment actually can damage public perceptions of social institutions and public figures.

For instance, an extensive use of Juvenalian satire that attacks an individual or group in a mean-spirited manner may do more damage to the cause of the comedian than the target. Because Juvenalian satire is a much nastier way of laughing at someone else's expense, it may come across as mean-spirited, and thus not be as supported by an audience, as well as coarsen the moral sensitivities of the audience members who support the general position of the satirist. There is, however, a lingering question on this point in that comedians must reconcile what they may see as their responsibility with an audience's potentially negative reception to the jokes.[64]

There is also a danger with modeling Juvenalian satire without a clear exposition for the rationale behind it. In seeing excessive implementation of biting personal jokes at a person's expense, it may lead to the presumption by an audience that such behavior is acceptable without understanding any parameters for its use. This presumption may prove counterproductive in a culture that has become increasingly concerned with things such as cyberbullying, aggression, and harassment. Perhaps one of the core elements of a code of ethics for entertainment personalities should include some form of guidance for the proper use of satire and the role comedy can play in shaping behavior in the broader public.

In an era where the public, the private, and the comedic are indelibly linked, and where many citizens get their news from a variety of sources, including satirists and comedians, it is important as a society that we pay attention to the ethics of comedy, especially comedy that takes on politics, public affairs, and newsmakers. Media ethicists increasingly are exploring the implications of entertainment and amusement, which now constitute nearly 90 percent of produced content.[65] Entertainers have few legal standards to hold them accountable; however, there are ethical standards that society expects them to follow.[66] In other words, there is not a codified ethical standard similar to the Hutchins Commission. Entertainment programming, however, needs a positive code of ethical conduct because it helps inform citizens by raising questions, offering incisive observations, and voicing marginalized perspectives.[67] Indeed, entertainers "can benefit by an articulation of aspirations, duties, and responsibilities."[68]

Democracy depends on an independent and trusted press, and comedic efforts that employ dark satire of news organizations can damage that trust; the same type of efforts toward public officials also can damage trust in public institutions and the democratic process. It is important that entertainment personalities recognize this role and find a balance between appropriate ethical conduct, social responsibility, and effective humor. It is also imperative that those that present the news as satire do so with an acknowledgment that what they do is not news or news programming because the more an audience believes that *The Daily* Show, for instance, is news, the more blurred the line between real and fake news becomes. This blurred line can exacerbate the degradation of public trust in the social institutions that serve as the glue in a democratic society. If the news is the fourth estate of government, then entertainment that engages public matters and people might be residential grounds on that estate.

NOTES

1. Jose A. DelReal, "Donald Trump Announces Presidential Bid," *Washington Post*, June 16, 2015; Annie Karni and Adam B. Lerner, "Trump Says He's Running for President, Really," *Politico,* June 16, 2015.
2. Jonah Goldberg, "Donald Trump Spells the End of the Republican Party as We Know It," *Chicago Tribune,* March 23, 2016.
3. Holly Yan, "Donald Trump's 'Blood' Comment about Megyn Kelly Draws Outrage," *CNN,* August 8, 2015.
4. Nick Gass, "Trump Defends Loyalty Oaths: 'We're Having Such a Great Time,'" *Politico*, March 8, 2016.
5. Avi Selk, "The Violent Rally Trump Can't Move Past," *Washington Post,* April 3, 2016; Monica Davey and Julie Bosman, "Donald Trump's Rally in Chicago Canceled after Violent Scuffles," *New York Times,* March 11, 2016.
6. Shane Goldmacher, "Will 'Saturday Night Live' Take Down Trump?" *Politico*, September 29, 2016, http://www.politico.com/story/2016/09/saturday-night-live-trump-228874.
7. See, for example, Ryan E. McGeough, "The Voice of the People: Jon Stewart, Public Argument and Political Satire," in T. Goodnow (Ed.), *The Daily Show and Rhetoric*, Lanham, MD: Lexington Books, 2011, 113–127.
8. Gilbert Highet, *The Anatomy of Satire*, Princeton, NJ: Princeton University Press, 1962; Charles A. Knight, *The Literature of Satire*, Cambridge, UK: Cambridge University Press, 2004.
9. Pew Research Center, "Candidate Traits and Perceptions," July 7, 2016, http://www.people-press.org/2016/07/07/5-candidate-traits-and-perceptions/.
10. This Pew Research Center poll did oversample Hispanics and Democrats.
11. Patrick Healy and Dalia Sussman, "Voters' View of a Donald Trump Presidency: Big Risks and Rewards," *New York Times,* September 15, 2017, https://www.nytimes.com/2016/09/16/us/politics/hillary-clinton-donald-trump-poll.html.
12. Ibid.
13. "From Nervous Laughter to Trump-Supporting Kremlin: How World Sees U.S. Vote," *CNN*, January 29, 2016, http://www.cnn.com/2016/01/28/opinions/presidential-election-international-views-roundup/index.html.

14. Merrit Kennedy, "Clinton-Trump Showdown Was the Most-Watched Presidential Debate Ever," *NPR*, September 27, 2016, http://www.npr.org/sections/thetwo-way/2016/09/27/495692196/clinton-trump-showdown-is-most-watched-presidential-debate.

15. Eric Bradner, "6 Takeaways from the First Presidential Debate," *CNN,* September 27, 2016. http://www.cnn.com/2016/09/27/politics/winner-presidential-debate-takeaways/index.html.

16. Ibid.

17. Ibid.

18. Ibid; Alex Seitz-Wald, "6 Key Moments of the First 2016 Presidential Debate between Trump and Clinton," *NBC News,* September 27, 2016, http://www.nbcnews.com/storyline/2016-presidential-debates/6-key-moments-first-presidential-debate-between-trump-clinton-n655121.

19. Alex Seitz-Wald, "6 Key Moments."

20. Amy Davidson Sorkin, "Clinton's Sick Days," *The New Yorker,* September 26, 2016, http://www.newyorker.com/magazine/2016/09/26/clintons-sick-days.

21. Editorial Board, "Editorial: Donald Trump May Have Lost the 2016 Election in 2005," *Chicago Tribune,* October 9, 2016.

22. "Transcript of Trump Video Statement to Lewd Remarks about Women," *Reuters*, October 8, 2016.

23. Jeremy Lott, "Donald Trump Holds Press Conference with the Clinton's Accusers," *Washington Examiner,* October 9, 2016.

24. Eric Bradner, "7 Takeaways from the Second Presidential Debate," *CNN,* October 10, 2016. http://www.cnn.com/2016/10/10/politics/presidential-debate-takeaways/index.html.

25. Leigh Ann Caldwell, "Six Takeaways from the Second 2016 Presidential Debate," *NBC News,* October 10, 2016, http://www.nbcnews.com/storyline/2016-presidential-debates/top-six-moments-second-presidential-debate-n663371.

26. Alastair Jamieson, "2016 Presidential Debate: Trump Accused of 'Stalking' Clinton on Stage," *NBC News,* October 10, 2016, http://www.nbcnews.com/storyline/2016-presidential-debates/presidential-debate-trump-accused-stalking-clinton-stage-n663516.

27. *Fox News,* "The Top 9 Moments of the Third Presidential Debate," October 19, 2016, http://www.foxnews.com/politics/2016/10/19/top-9-moments-third-presidential-debate.html.

28. Ibid.

29. Stephen Collinson, "Trump Refuses to Accept Election's Outcome," *CNN,* October 19, 2016. http://www.cnn.com/2016/10/19/politics/presidential-debate-highlights/index.html.

30. Jennifer Agiesta, "Hillary Clinton Wins Third Presidential Debate According to CNN/ORC Poll," *CNN*, October 20, 2016, http://www.cnn.com/2016/10/19/politics/hillary-clinton-wins-third-presidential-debate-according-to-cnn-orc-poll/index.html.

31. For a collection of various celebrity tweets in response to the election, see: Lawrence Yee, "Election 2016: Hollywood Reacts to Presidential Results," *Variety,* November 8, 2016, http://variety.com/2016/biz/news/election-2016-results-reactions-hollywood-hillary-clinton-donald-trump-1201913001/.

32. Goldmacher, "Will 'Saturday Night Live' Take Down Trump?"

33. Gilbert Highet, *The Anatomy of Satire*.

34. Highet, 1962; R. Lance Holbert, John M. Tchernev, Whitney O. Walther, Sarah E. Esralew, and Kathryn Benski, "Young Voter Perceptions of Political Satire as Persuasion: A Focus on Perceived Influence, Persuasive Intent, and Message Strength." *Journal of Broadcasting and Electronic Media* 57, no. 2 (2013): 170–186.

35. Charles Sander, *The Scope of Satire*, Glenview, IL: Scott, Foresman, 1971.

36. Gilbert Highet, *The Anatomy of Satire*.

37. Julia R. Fox, "Wise Fools: Jon Stewart and Stephen Colbert as Modern-Day Jesters in the American Court," in *The Stewart/Colbert Effect: Essays on the Real Impacts of Fake News*, 136–148, Jefferson, NC: McFarland & Company, Inc. Publishers, 2011.

38. Jörg Matthes and Adrian Rauchfleisch, "The Swiss 'Tina Fey effect': The Content of Late-Night Political Humor and Negative Effects of Political Parody on the Evaluation of Politicians," *Communication Quarterly* 61, no. 5 (2013): 596–614.

39. Fox, 2011; R. Lance Holbert, Jay Hmielowski, Parul Jain, Julie Lather, and Alyssa Morey, "Adding Nuance to the Study of Political Humor Effects: A Study of Juvenalian Satire Versus Horatian Satire," *American Behavioral Scientist* 55 (2011): 187–211; Patricia Moy, Michael A. Xenos, and Verena K. Hess, "Communication and Citizenship: Mapping the Political Effects of Infotainment," *Mass Communication and Society* 8 (2005): 111–131; Dannagal Goldthwaite Young, "The Privileged Role of the Late-Night Joke: Exploring Humor's Role in Disrupting Argument Scrutiny," *Media Psychology* 11 (2008): 119–142; Dannagal Goldthwaite Young and Sarah E. Esralew, "Jon Stewart as Heretic? Surely You Jest: Political Participation and Discussion among Viewers of Late-Night Comedy Programming," in *The Stewart/Colbert Effect: Essays on the Real Impacts of Fake News*, 99–116. Jefferson, NC: McFarland & Company, Inc. Publishers, 2011.

40. Xiaoxia Cao, "Hearing It from Jon Stewart: The Impact of *The Daily Show* on Public Attentiveness to Politics," *International Journal of Public Opinion Research* 22 (2010): 26–46; Dannagal Goldthwaite Young and Russell M. Tisinger, "Dispelling Late-Night Myths: News Consumption Among Late-Night Comedy Viewers and the Predictors of Exposure to Various Late-Night Shows," *Harvard International Journal of Press/Politics* 11, no. 3 (2006): 113–134; Moy, et al., "Communication and Citizenship," 2005; Dannagal Goldthwaite Young, "The Privileged Role of the Late-Night Joke: Exploring Humor's Role in Disrupting Argument Scrutiny," *Media Psychology, 11* (2008): 119–142.

41. Holbert, et al., "Adding Nuance to the Study of Political Humor Effects," 2011; Robert T. Tally Jr., "I Am the Mainstream Media (And So Can You!)," in *The Stewart/Colbert Effect: Essays on the Real Impacts of Fake News*, 149–163, Jefferson, NC: McFarland & Company, Inc. Publishers, 2011.

42. Michael Nitz, Allison Koehn, and Hayley McCarron, "Too Early to Be Funny? An Analysis of Late Night Comedy during the 2016 U.S. Presidential Primaries," in *Political Campaign Communication: Theory, Method, and Practice*, 103–122, Lanham, MD: Lexington Books, 2017.

43. Chad Painter and Louis Hodges, "Mocking the News: How *The Daily Show with Jon Stewart* Holds Traditional Broadcast News Accountable," *Journal of Mass Media Ethics* 24, no. 4 (2010): 257–274.

44. Megan R. Hill, "Developing a Normative Approach to Political Satire: A Critical Perspective," *International Journal of Communication* 7 (2013): 324–337, p. 329.

45. Nitz et al., "Too Early to Be Funny?"

46. Leonard Feinberg, *Introduction to Satire*, Ames, IA: The Iowa State University Press, 1967; Megan R. Hill, "Developing a Normative Approach to Satire," 2013.

47. Painter and Hodges, "Mocking the News."

48. Dustin Griffin, *Satire: A Critical Reintroduction*, Lexington: University Press of Kentucky, 1994, p. 36.

49. Jeffrey P. Jones, *Entertaining Politics: New Political Television and Civic Culture*, Lanham, MD: Rowman & Littlefield, 2005.

50. Charles E. Schutz, *Political Humor: From Aristophanes to Sam Ervin*, Rutherford, NJ: Fairleigh Dickinson University Press, 1977.

51. Isaiah Berlin, *Liberty: Incorporating Four Essays on Liberty*, Oxford, UK: Oxford University Press, 2002.

52. Clifford G. Christians, John P. Ferré, and P. Mark Fackler, *Good News: Social Ethics and the Press*, Oxford, UK: Oxford University Press, 1993; Clifford G. Christians, Theodore L. Glasser, Denis McQuail, Kaarle Nordenstreng, and Robert A. White, *Normative Theories of the Media: Journalism in Democratic Societies*, Urbana: University of Illinois Press, 2009; John C. Nerone, *Last Rights: Revisiting Four Theories of the Press*, Urbana: University of Illinois Press, 1995.

53. Mark K. McBeth and Randy S. Clemons, "Is Fake News the Real News? The Significance of Stewart and Colbert for Democratic Discourse, Politics, and Policy," in *The Stewart/Colbert Effect: Essays on the Real Impacts of Fake News*, 79–98, Jefferson, NC: McFarland & Company, Inc. Publishers, 2011; Neil Postman, *Amusing Ourselves to Death: Public Discourse in the Age of Show Business*, New York: Penguin Books, 1985.

54. Megan R. Hill, "Developing a Normative Approach to Political Satire."

55. Clifford G. Christians, Kim B. Rotzell, Mark Fackler, Kathy Brittain McKee, and Robert H. Woods, *Media Ethics: Cases and Moral Reasoning*, Boston: Pearson, 2005, p. 240.

56. Angharad N. Valdivia, "What Can We Get Away With? The Ethics of Art and Entertainment in the Neoliberal World," in *The Handbook of Mass Media Ethics*, 189–200, New York: Routledge, 2008; Bruce A. Williams and Michael X. Delli Carpini, "Unchained Reaction: The Collapse of Media Gatekeeping and the Clinton-Lewinsky Scandal," *Journalism* 1, no. 1 (2000): 61–85; Young and Tisinger, "Dispelling Late-Night Myths."

57. Jody C. Baumgartner and Jonathan S. Morris, "Stoned Slackers or Super Citizens? *The Daily Show* Viewing and Political Engagement of Young Adults," in *The Stewart/Colbert Effect: Essays on the Real Impacts of Fake News*, 63–78, Jefferson, NC: McFarland & Company, Inc. Publishers, 2011; Lauren Feldman and Dannagal Goldthwaite Young, "Late Night Comedy as a Gateway to Traditional News: An Analysis of Time Trends in News Attention among Late-Night Comedy Viewers during the 2004 Presidential Primaries," *Political Communication* 25 (2008): 401–422.

58. Matthew A. Baum, *Soft News Goes to War*, Princeton, NJ: Princeton University Press, 2003; Xiaoxia Cao, "Hearing It from Jon Stewart: The Impact of *The Daily Show* on Public Attentiveness to Politics," *International Journal of Public Opinion Research* 22 (2010): 26–46; Lauren Feldman, Anthony Leiserowitz, and Edward Maibach, "The Science of Satire: *The Daily Show* and *The Colbert Report* as Sources of Public Attention to Science and the Environment," in *The Stewart/Colbert Effect: Essays on the Real Impacts of Fake News*, 25–46, Jefferson, NC: McFarland & Company, Inc. Publishers, 2011; Feldman and Young, 2008.

59. Michael A. Xenos, Patricia Moy, and Amy B. Becker, "Making Sense of *The Daily Show*: Understanding the Role of Partisan Heuristics in Political Comedy Effects," in *The Stewart/Colbert Effect: Essays on the Real Impacts of Fake News*, 47–62, Jefferson, NC: McFarland & Company, Inc. Publishers, 2011.

60. Rebecca M. Chory-Assad and Ron Tamborini, "Television Exposure and the Public's Perceptions of Physicians," *Journal of Broadcasting and Electronic Media* 47, no. 2 (2003): 197–215; Alice Hall, "Film Reviews and the Public's Perceptions of Stereotypes: Movie Critics' Discourse about *The Siege*," *Communication Quarterly* 49, no. 4 (2001): 399–423; Chad Painter and Patrick Ferrucci, "Unprofessional, Ineffective and Weak: A Textual Analysis of the Portrayal of Female Journalists on *Sports Night*," *Journal of Mass Media Ethics* 27, no. 4 (2012): 248–262; Chad Painter and Patrick Ferrucci, "'His Women Problem': An Analysis of Gender on *The Newsroom*," *The Image of the Journalist in Popular Culture* 6 (2015): 1–30; Chad Painter and Patrick Ferrucci, "Gender Games: The Portrayal of Female Journalists on *House of Cards*," *Journalism Practice* 11, no. 4 (2017): 493–508.

61. Bruce A. Williams and Michael X. Delli Carpini, "The Eroding Boundaries between News and Entertainment and What They Mean for Democratic Politics," in *The Handbook of Mass Media Ethics*, 177–188, New York: Routledge, 2008, p. 183.

62. Mark Cenite, "Ethical Learnings from *Borat* on Informed Consent for Make Benefit Film and Television Producers," *Journal of Mass Media Ethics* 24, no. 1 (2009): 22–39.

63. Christians et al., "Normative Theories of the Media," 2009; Theodore L. Glasser, "Objectivity and News Bias," in *Philosophical Issues in Journalism*, 176–185, Oxford, UK: Oxford University Press, 1992; Stephen J. A. Ward, *The Invention of Journalism Ethics: The Path to Objectivity and Beyond*, Montreal: McGill-Queen's University Press, 2006.

64. To this end, a clearer understanding of the demographic characteristics and political affiliations of the audience members for each show may change some of the ways in which this data would be interpreted.

65. Lee Wilkins, "Foreword," *Journal of Mass Media Ethics* 27, no. 4 (2012): 219.

66. Jason T. Peifer, "Can We Be Funny? The Social Responsibility of Political Humor," *Journal of Mass Media Ethics* 27, no. 4 (2012): 263–276.

67. Ibid.

68. Ibid.

Chapter Ten

Journalistic Hegemony of "Blue Privilege"

Tracing the Use of Identity Politics Toward a Political Economy of News Coverage

Ben Voth

Among the most esteemed rhetorical tools of contemporary moral judgment as offered by the epistemic community of academia is "white privilege." This moral rubric provides a basis for essentializing race and securing various advantages of interpretation for those who understand white privilege best. This notion is arguably the central axis of a larger panoptic gaze in intellectual life toward human identity.[1] Michel Foucault borrowed from Jeremy Bentham's idea of a tower within a prison—called a panopticon—to suggest the all-seeing nature of authority. The sight of superior intellectual authorities over human bodies constitutes a *biopower* understood as identity politics. Today people can easily lose public standing, employment, income, and more when they are found guilty of determinations of discriminatory conduct regarding identity politics. The unique membership and ascendancy of individuals into this community of judgment constitute blue privilege. They are the educated set of individuals that constitute a network of institutions that make these determinations. This essay focuses on one such institution: journalism. The capacity and privilege to interpret who is and is not racist, sexist, homophobic, or variously pathologically discriminatory is substantially managed within a political economy[2] of interpretation held by an intellectual community. Journalists represent an important subset within the intellectual community and function as important gatekeepers of public information. For instance, Feminism represents an important innovation in intellectual thinking with regard to sexism. The systemic pejorative description of conservative women such as Sarah Palin, Michelle Bachman, Ann Coulter, Sarah Huckabee, or Melania Trump point to an irony to the presentation of feminism in journalistic coverage. The burning of Sarah Palin's church one month after President Obama's election in 2008 and anemic coverage of the political hate crime is iconic of the journalistic manipulation process with regard to identity politics. These manipulations[3] represent a substantial improvement and efficiency over the crude propaganda designs described by Jacques Ellul in the twentieth century.[4] This more contemporary political economy of identity politics is developed by Cass Sunstein.[5] Ellul's notion of propaganda was associated with the more primitive technological features of information distortion as imagined by public relations practitioners such as Edward Bernays. His work was an outgrowth of understanding propaganda as utilized in World War II. Sunstein is building upon this knowledge with a more keen awareness of twenty-first century technology seen as social media. The idea of "nudging" suggests that public relations practitioners can reach more intimately into the personal lives of individuals in the effort to achieve influence. Nudging alludes to the subtle micro targeting of persuasion that can be accomplished through social media and the comprehensive awareness of user preferences within the Internet. This chapter examines a number of important components of journalistic management of blue privilege: defining what is blue privilege, examining empirical data on journalistic blue privilege, blue privilege and the Trump phenomena, journalistic coverage of the presidential primaries for 2016, and finally the general presidential election as a public backlash.

WHAT IS BLUE PRIVILEGE?

Of course, blue is nowhere in the rainbow of understood persons of color. Red, brown, yellow, black, and white are all reductionist color metaphors often used to describe the far more complex world of human ethnicity. Blue in an American context today refers to the red and blue maps of politics—whereby blue denotes the Democratic Party and its followers while red denotes the Republican Party and its followers. On an international level blue may denote the United Nations and the fantasy of sovereign global governance. In many respects blue is a useful metaphor for the true and highest world of discursive privilege extended from the halls of academia to the peacekeeping forces of the United Nations.

As a domestic matter for the United States, blue privilege is tied to the interpretivist class that decides matters of political significance. The simple dichotomy of a two major party system shared between Democrats and Republicans is often signified by the colors blue and red. Until the 1990s, the journalistic community interpreted Red as being the color of Democrats and

Blue being the color of Republicans. This assignment was apparent in the visual display of electoral results in presidential elections. States were shaded red or blue based on which party earned the greatest amount of votes. The switch from original denotation was determined by journalists and indicates their unique powers in the interpretivist class. There was apparent anxiety that red was connoted as socialism—comparable to Soviet Red Communism and the "Red Scare." Blue was seen as less pejorative.[6] This is an essential characteristic of blue privilege—not simply a political or ideological preference but the capacity to draw the terministic boundaries.[7]

Blue privilege is approximately an ideological preference for the Democratic Party. It nonetheless involves more in the drive for a stronger centralizing state and public respected authoritarian control. Founding civil rights hero James Farmer Jr. referred to the activists within these ranks as "Jacobins"—an allusion to the French revolution.[8] The blue privilege is a cycle of interpretive cynicism pressing power away from the individual and toward an idealized state government.

EMPIRICAL DATA ON JOURNALISTIC BLUE PRIVILEGE

The public sense of distortion surrounding the journalistic community is apparent in polling of the public. The public does not trust journalism today and this low ebb of trust follows decades of decline. When Gallup first began asking about public trust for the television press in 1993, 19 percent of the public had very high trust in the television press and 16 percent had very little trust. Today in June of 2016, 8 percent of the public has very high trust and 38 percent have very little trust for the television press.[9] Television press are among the least trusted institutions surveyed in the United States by Gallup and includes institutions such as the military and the church. Gallup measures continued to find plummeting confidence during the election of 2016. A study in September 2016 found that while the long standing trend of reduced trust continued, among Republicans it plummeted in one year from 32 percent to 14 percent.[10] The drop stands out notably from the trend and demonstrates a collapse. It is difficult to overstate the public hostility to journalists and the smaller community of television journalism.

Such trends are amplified by journalism schools on college campuses that have accentuated the ideological delivery of news in the twenty-first century. Party affiliation of journalists remains decisively one-sided—favoring the Democrats by more than 14 to1 in almost all newsrooms.[11] A mutual fantasy theme[12] between the political party of favor (Democrats) and journalists is that this political collaboration is morally justified as part of a broader agenda of protecting the weak from the ravages of inequality.[13] The formal aspects of such collaboration are indicated by incidents such as Donna Brazille's role with CNN in feeding questions to candidate Hillary Clinton or George Stephanopholus's transition from Clinton campaign advocate to television news analyst for ABC news. Donald Trump, who has a long tradition of supporting the Democratic Party—including Hillary Clinton as recently as 2012—was helped tremendously in his campaign to be the Republican National Committee (RNC) nominee, against more conservative Republican candidates.[14] Journalistic efforts to focus on Trump backfired from an ideological standpoint and accelerated Trump's rise to the top of the Republican field. Journalists highlighted the strong Trump attacks against the RNC heir apparent in Jeb Bush. The attention was almost certainly motivated by an ideological goal on the part of journalists to create a spectacular implosion of the Republican Party. This proved to be a profound miscalculation on the part of Jacobins within the journalistic community.[15] These Jacobin-styled arguments seek to displace individual liberty in favor of state managed equality (under the guise of fighting inequality) and convinced journalists to approach their craft with a clearer unrepentant ideology that interrogates one party defending established interests (Republicans) and the opposing party (Democrats) as being an inherent insurgency against those established interests. A growing social justice ethic common to the pedagogy of journalism sympathizes with the needs of the state to intrude upon individuals in order to achieve more egalitarian ends such as the elevation of the poor. The public is overwhelmingly convinced that these distortions are real and destructive to their trust of the original social contract found in the First Amendment assuring a free press. For Republican voters, a bright line was crossed and all trust in the media was lost during election 2016.

The public believes that the media is profoundly biased, and they believe journalists dramatically distort the information they receive and then transmit to the public.[16] Those trends have accelerated to unprecedented levels of public anger. The rhetorical framing of news stories is vital to the persuasive processes surrounding the rhetorical presidency.[17] The American presidency represents an important distillation of ideological contests within the public. It is certainly the most well-known and far ranging participation of the public in a political question. Tens of millions of Americans listen to journalistic communication studying the "horse race" of presidential election. Once elected, the president is the senior executive and the most visible icon of federal power. Study of reporting on the presidency helps us better understand how blue privilege is at work. Ending the presidency is the most powerful invocation of the terministic screens provided by the media. Theodore H. White wrote in *The Making of the President, 1972*, "The power of the press is a primordial one. It determines what people will think and talk about—an authority that in other nations is reserved for tyrants, priests, parties, and mandarins."[18] Gatekeeping a conversation about either violently removing a president or using the constitutional mechanisms such as impeachment can be a point of symbolic order in news stories. The ideological preferences of blue privilege are apparent in the news stories featuring these themes from 2001 until 2017. In this time, two Republican presidents and one Democratic president served in office. Stories using the president's name within one sentence with the verbiage of killing or impeaching the president were queried in the LEXIS/NEXIS database that reviews a comprehensive set of major newspapers. This limited study of newspaper texts will serve as an example of blue privilege at work in current coverage of President Trump in comparison to previous presidents.

The variations within the first six months of these presidents provides a compelling data point for how the demise of the president is framed within blue privilege. In the first six months of the Bush presidency—a Republican president—the media used the sentence of impeach and Bush 1,037 times (see table 10.1). In the first six months of the Obama presidency—a Democratic president—the media used the sentence of impeach and Obama 438 times. In the first six months of the Trump presidency—a Republican president—the media used the sentence of impeach and Trump 3,053 times. This dataset provides a rather stark indication of how deeply ideological journalism has become.

Impeachment is a term of political art and typically involves ideological opponents of the president joining in the forum of the House of Representatives to endorse articles of impeachment. The act is rarely accomplished in American civic history but often discussed. The occasions where the journalists indulge the conversation in public print is an important rhetorical basis for encouraging the potential impeachment of the president. An unusual anomaly in this data set is that more than 90 percent of President Bush's mentions took place in the first month of his presidency. It is quite likely that Bush's impeachment discussion was closer to 60 total rather than 1037. The impeachment of President Clinton in 1998 was an important prelude to Bush's close election in 2000. It is apparent that Clinton's impeachment was discussed by journalists in relation to Bush's election within the same sen-

Table 10.1. Terms of Impeachment

Impeach w/s president	**Total**						
President/ Month	**T otal**	January	February	March	April	May	June
Bush 2001	**1037**	991	15	4	4	15	8
Obama 2009	**438**	276	63	30	36	23	10
Trump 2017	**3053**	275	368	202	191	1302	715

Source: Lexis-Nexis, 2017.

tence during the month of January. A high percentage of references also related to impeachment arguments surrounding an Illinois governor's role in selling President Obama's former senate seat. There are few mentions in the first six months of President Obama's presidency. President Obama also had a smaller January surge that may have been tied to apprehensions that Americans would not accept an African-American president. There does appear to be a declining indulgence to discuss the possibility of impeachment as the Obama presidency enters the sixth month. The discussion of Trump's impeachment was relentless and escalating. President Trump was not accepted as president by journalists and the high numbers for every month were exponentially higher than the monthly number of Obama and Bush. Journalists would argue that they are only reporting these incidents and/or that the president deserved these numbers. It is however important to recognize that this interval is typically defined by journalists as the honeymoon period or "first 100 days"—an interval where the president's recent election earns the president extra political credibility, power, and influence. Journalists believed they had saddled the Republicans with the worst conceivable candidate by the end of the RNC nominating process. This led Hillary Clinton to wonder in September why she was not fifty points ahead. She was in an ideological echo chamber constructed by an increasingly Jacobin journalistic community that saw the election as predetermined by their own persuasive goals. That is clearly not the relationship between President Trump and the current journalistic community. Journalists were completely blindsided by his election in 2016 and there were almost no predictions that he would win.

A further indication of blue privilege among the journalists is how the discussion of "killing" and the president was reported by journalists (seen in Table 10.2). The respective totals for sentences containing the president and a verb about killing were: Bush—1,280, Obama—2,608, and Trump—7,890. There were twice as many discussions of 'kill' regarding President Obama as with President Bush. This points to an escalating partisan atmosphere and may also indicate an effort to amplify the popular journalistic meme that the president's opponents were so racist that they wanted to "kill the President." This would amplify sympathy and empathy for the president. There are three times as many discussion of "kill" and President Trump as President Obama. Killing the president is an absolutely criminal and treasonous act. Discussions will in many cases result in a visit from the Secret Service and possible prosecution. Of course, all language can be used metaphorically. Perhaps the Congress "killed" President Trump, Obama, or Bush's agenda. Nonetheless, the metaphor is an effective barometer of political intensity and a clear negative symbolic valence directed at the president. The clear escalating rhetorical trend suggests confirmation for the increasing partisan divide and deep energies of both sides. It does suggest an overriding hostility toward President Trump compared to previous presidents.

BLUE PRIVILEGE AND TRUMP PHENOMENA

As previously noted, the election of Donald Trump to the presidency was largely unpredicted by journalists and associated pundits. It was arguably among the biggest upsets in presidential election history and it staggered political prognosticators. Moreover, the evidence is clear and compelling that journalists favored Trump's opponent—Hillary Clinton—in an overwhelming fashion. Journalists who often maintain the mantra that the public should "follow the money" did follow the money of journalist donations to political candidates. What they found was that 96 percent of all political donations by journalists in 2016 went to Democratic Party candidates.[19] Though journalists moderated all of the presidential debates, they found that President Trump lost all three televised debates. Though the public reported that the October 2016 debates were highly influential to their thinking and decision making for the election, the public did not reach the expected conclusion that Hillary Clinton would be made president. The pattern of media coverage in election in 2016 is rather important to our current understanding of blue privilege in the journalistic community. The unusual pattern of coverage uncovered by a Harvard study reveals the depths of a spiral of cynicism now anchoring the blue privilege of journalistic practice. The Shorenstein study provides hard empirical data for the pervasive blue privilege surrounding coverage of the most powerful political position in the world: the American presidency.[20]

COVERING THE PRESIDENTIAL PRIMARY PROCESS

Between 2015 and 2016 the two major parties were rather uniquely compelled to pursue a vigorous primary challenge process to elect and select their nominee prior to the general election. More than twenty major candidates sought the nomination—five on the Democratic side and sixteen on the Re-

Table 10.2. Terms of Kill

Kill! w/s president	**Total**						
President/ Month	**Total**	January	February	March	April	May	June
Bush 2001	**1280**	131	161	161	162	143	168
Obama 2009	**2608**	433	537	308	631	259	440
Trump 2017	**7890**	1331	1591	1114	1760	1153	941

Source: Lexis-Nexis, 2017.

publican side. This does not include third party candidates such as Jill Stein and libertarian candidate Gary Johnson. The 2016 election was unusual because the two-term president was ineligible to run as a candidate again and his vice president did not choose to become a major nominee. Journalistic coverage of the candidates is imperative to the maintenance and ultimate election of these candidates. Public craving for impartial forums likely drove an unusual high level of public participation and viewership for the primary debates. These debates regularly involved the participation and arguments of five or more candidates in the respective parties. These debates hosted by journalists attracted audiences of five to twenty million people. Republican debates tended to be twice as large in audience as Democratic debates—another clue the journalists chose to ignore is how Republican enthusiasm would likely overwhelm the Democratic nominee in the general election.

Various aspects of the long chronology for selecting the nominees over a period of months demonstrate the salience and power of blue privilege in the journalistic community. On the Democratic side, it was rather evident that presumptive nominee Hillary Clinton, was being favored by journalists. Speaking times and speaking opportunities in the debate reflected this preference. Three democratic presidential candidates complained after the first debate that the events were providing them with an unequal opportunity to offer their advocacy. A Democratic National Committee (DNC) official was disciplined for publicly arguing that the primary debates were designed to favor Hillary Clinton. In fact, some commentators complained that DNC debates were scheduled against popular sporting events to discourage viewership.[21] After the election, evidence emerged that former DNC chair Donna Brazille was feeding questions in advance of town hall debates to Hillary Clinton exclusively. She was fired from her position at CNN in relation to this charge. In 2017, evidence has continued to pile up on a multitude of fronts that the DNC orchestrated an effort to elect Hillary Clinton rather than Bernie Sanders.

On the Republican side, public interest was approximately twice as large as indicated by viewing sizes that were often over twenty million. There were many more debates and many more candidates. There were so many debaters that the media had to create what were termed "undercard" debates wherein low polling Republican candidates squared off in early broadcast events that were then followed by the "main event" debates of the higher polling candidates. Some contemporary academic viewers have defended journalists against charges of bias by pointing to the generous amount and tone of coverage for candidate Donald Trump. The Shorenstein study is clear on this point.[22] Trump received quantitatively larger amounts of coverage than other candidates. In fact, rival candidates regularly complained about this for months. The debates were a fascinating indicator of how this trend tended to work. In Republican primary debates, journalists formed a rule requiring that anyone attacked by name during the debate be allowed to have an additional thirty seconds to respond. This tended to result in Donald Trump getting several additional turns answering argument. In more than ten debates, Trump was almost always the largest consumer of airtime and analysts conceded that Trump was garnering billions of dollars in free advertising from the debates. Trump supplemented his advantages in the debates by using the social media form of tweeting. This allowed him to bypass traditional media channels to reach the public outside editorial controls. This style of tweeting and using the debates led to the profound paradox that both in the primaries and the general election, the candidate who raised and spent the most campaign money did NOT win—obliterating one of the most central premises of many on the ideological left committed to the overturning of *Citizens United*—a Supreme Court decision gutting campaign finance reform aimed at limiting campaign spending by candidates. As the Republican debates wore on and candidates began to drop out, candidates such as Ben Carson began to beg during the live debates, "would someone please attack me?" Half jest and half sincere concern, the question exposed a paradox that turned the outsider, Trump and radical populist, into an unstoppable political rocket. The more controversy was engendered by candidate Trump, the more coverage he received. The more coverage he received, the more his polls accelerated upward. It was not long before the establishment favorite—Jeb Bush—was compelled to retire from the primary race early in the process. Bush outspent Trump in an exponential fashion, to no avail.

The Shorenstein study also shows that coverage was not only quantitatively higher but also more qualitatively positive. This is perhaps the key irony for analysts seeking to defend the journalistic community against charges of ideological distortion. Academics—who also affiliate at an incredibly high rate with Democratic Party politics[23]—tend to rationalize the distorted coverage of the press in elections such as 2016 by explaining that Trump received high coverage and positive coverage during the primary process. There are at least three key ingredients that tend to deny this rationalization. First, the positive treatment of Trump came at the profound expense of the Republican Party. It is not a stretch to argue that many of Trump's arguments against his rivals were scurrilous and personal. A debate between Trump and Marco Rubio about whose hands were larger was an unsubtle discussion about male genitalia.[24] Trump verbally ran Bush out of the race on continuous charges that Bush lacked energy. Trump's peculiar carnival style populist personal attacks against the Republicans burnished the general journalistic notion that Republicans were at worst, as bad as Trump suggested or at best, the RNC was a spectacular circus of clowns who could not defeat the amateurish efforts of Donald Trump the TV entertainer. The media moderators appeared to visibly enjoy and encourage the barn burning escapades of Donald Trump who gave every indication of rhetorically burning down the Republican establishment and the RNC process that would inevitably select Jeb Bush, just as the DNC was selecting its more moderate alternative in Hillary Clinton. Months of escalating rhetorical warfare on the Republican side tended to confirm two premises of the cynical premises journalists were holding about the Republicans: 1) any candidate emerging from the RNC process would be severely damaged by the primary process and ripe for campaign ads featuring prominent verbal attacks on the nominee from a fellow Republican and 2) if Trump won the nomination he would be the easiest candidate for Hillary Clinton to defeat because he was so clearly extreme in his rhetoric.

This second factor is an important reason why the journalistic community affirmed the candidacy of President Trump. He appeared to be the best candidate to face off against Hillary Clinton. His boorish antics in debates were thought to provide an easy masculine caricature of sexism that the first major female candidate for president would knock out of the political park in the general election. Commentators were genuinely shocked with candidate Trump, who retaliated against this framing by inviting alleged sexual assault victims of President Clinton to attend a press conference prior to one of the general debates.[25]

This key axiology is confirmed again by the data of the Shorenstein study. Once the nominations were complete in August, Trump's coverage factors reversed. Clinton got more coverage and more positive coverage. Trump received less journalistic coverage and more negative coverage. The sharp change in tack by the journalists suggests that there was an underlying motive in elevating Trump throughout the primary process for the Republicans. Media attacks and coverage in the primary process tended to sabotage the party's efforts to control their own nomination and substituted one of the wildest political wild cards of the past one hundred years. Few analysts thought Trump could win the general election.[26]

More interesting was the sharp uptick in negative coverage as the campaign entered the final phase between August 8 and the election on November 8. The study found that interval dominated by 77 percent negative coverage and only 23 percent positive coverage in relation to Trump. In the primary campaign for the Republican nomination, Trump's coverage was almost neutral at 56/44 in the positive/negative ratio.[27] The 21 percent uptick in negative coverage suggests that the media helped Trump arrive at the nomination during the primary process—defeating more than a dozen Republican rivals and then dramatically increasing negative coverage after the nomination in order to help Hillary in the final push toward the election. In fact, Clinton got 13 percent more positive coverage in the closing general election phase than Trump. Yet in the overall election coverage Trump had 6 percent more favorable coverage than Clinton. These statistics clarify that in the two major phases of the election—nomination and general election—

there were very different ideological agendas at work. In the nomination phases, Jacobins within the journalistic community sought to elevate the candidate Trump with positive coverage. That favoritism was so significant over the much longer period of nomination that even with 13 percent more favorable coverage than Trump in the general election phase (the period between the party nomination and the final election in November), Trump still had net favorable coverage for both periods. A good specific example of this problem in the coverage ratios for the week of October 2. That was roughly one month before the election and took place as the presidential debate season was beginning. This is a phase where undecided voters begin to engage in a study of candidates that may lead to a decision for a candidate. In that week, Clinton had a positive/negative coverage ratio of 53/47. It is highly unusual for any candidate to have a positive ratio during a general election period. By comparison, in that same week, Trump had a positive/negative ratio of 23/77.[28] This means there was a thirty-point gap in positive coverage. This rather impressive disparity was nearly replicated in the week of October 23 when the Clinton/Trump ratios were 48/52 and 91/9. This means that the positive coverage gap two weeks before the election was 43 points in favor of Clinton. The fact that these massive gaps did not add up to net negative coverage for Trump for all election coverage suggests a sharp ideological course change by journalists after the conventions. Journalists worked to have the weak candidate of Trump nominated for the Republicans and then savaged him in the shorter general election phase. That ideological project apparently backfired. The fact that on average Trump had more favorable coverage when data from the primaries nomination phase is included points to the profound reversal of coverage that existed from August 8 to November 8. In a three month interval of coverage, the media reversed sharply. This is a rather dramatic reversal in coverage between the primary and the election. The negative coverage of Trump in the fall hit a crescendo in the week of October 16 when 96 percent of the coverage was negative.[29] Of ten different news outlets analyzed, Fox had the most positive tone of coverage for Trump—though more than 70 percent was negative.

By contrast, Clinton press coverage in the presidential debate period was relatively positive. In the week of October 2, Clinton's total coverage actually went net positive—which rarely happens in elections. She was close to that same positive mark three weeks later on October 23. Press coverage in the closing month of the election was incredibly positive for the Clinton campaign.[30] The *Los Angeles Times* was her most favorable outlet while *Fox News* was her least favorable outlet. The Shorenstein study tends to demonstrate that journalists were exercising blue privilege during the primaries—trying to push Hillary further to the ideological mark of Bernie Sanders. As a self-identified socialist, Sanders represents the bluest shades of democratic party advocacy. Once Sanders lost the nomination, the media did switch coverage paths and offered high negative coverage of Trump and high positive coverage of Clinton to produce the bluest result possible in America's political life.

Debate press coverage was a key ingredient in this overall problem. Coverage was overwhelmingly positive for Clinton with regard to the debates and overwhelmingly negative for Trump. 65 percent of stories about the presidential debates were positive for Clinton whereas 18 percent of stories about the presidential debates were positive for Trump. For the month of October when most of the debates happened, the primary focus of news was the presidential debates.

THE BLUE PRIVILEGE KIDNAPPING OF REPUBLICAN AFRICAN AMERICAN ALAN KEYES

The power of journalistic framing and management of a political economy of identity politics managed by this community is well illustrated by a contrasting incident from the presidential election of 1996. A powerful example of how far off from a free press we have gone can be found in a Republican primary debate of 1996. Not unlike 2016, Republicans had a number of candidates seeking the nomination to run against incumbent president Bill Clinton. Among them was a surprising upstart by the name of Alan Keyes. Keyes is an African American and in 1996 his oratorical skills were greatly admired and he finished strongly in the Iowa and New Hampshire Presidential Republican caucuses. That set up a televised candidate debate in 1996 at an Atlanta TV station. Keyes was invited to attend by the Atlanta Press Club. About a week before the event, the station had second thoughts about hosting Keyes, but Keyes remained adamant that he had an invitation and other candidates said the original plan should be honored. A month before the debate, the sponsors made a decision to invite only the top four polling candidates: Dole, Alexander, Buchannan, and Forbes.[31] All of those candidates agreed that Keyes should have been allowed on the stage. That set the stage for a rather incredible incident. On the night of the debate, Keyes arrived along with dozens of supporters for the televised debate. As Keyes approached the venue, the station called Atlanta police to the site. In front of television news crews recording the event, Alan Keyes was handcuffed and pushed into the backseat of a police car. He was driven to the edge of Atlanta and released on the top of a parking garage while the television debate went on without him. At no time was Alan Keyes charged with a crime. He was simply handcuffed by officers and forcibly removed from the property of the station and driven away. It sounds like something from a distant authoritarian government. The next day, the democratic mayor of Atlanta, Bill Campbell, apologized for Keyes's mistreatment, saying "this is not usually how we treat our guests in the city." That was the end of the conflict. No lawsuits were filed. No other apologies were made. One of the nation's first serious African-American presidential candidates was handcuffed in Atlanta and kidnapped from a televised public debate. Imagine for a moment if in 2008, presidential candidate Barack Obama had shown up for a democratic primary debate and instead of entering the studio, was met by police officers, forcibly detained, and driven off-site until the debate was over. America's epistemological communities would have rallied Jacobin forces to powerful results—immediately. Epistemological voices would have thundered against the outrageous racial slur inherent in such actions. It is impossible to reconcile the events that happened to Keyes—and still viewable today on YouTube[32]—without understanding that the journalistic community believes that the concept of racism is a malleable ideological construct. It demonstrates rather forcefully that journalism exists as service for these ideological interests and not for the political interests of individual liberty as embodied in Alan Keyes's free political speech rights and political arguments. Moreover, it is not unimportant that Keyes challenged Barack Obama for the Senate seat of Illinois in 2004. Journalists did not suggest at any point in this election that Barack Obama's "white privilege" played a role in the overwhelming defeat of African-American Keyes in Illinois. As noted previously in the case of "white Hispanic" George Zimmerman (see note 3), the journalistic community has the power to strip individuals of ethnic identity and confer a blank erasure denoted by the word "White." Journalism today continues to serve limited political interests. This raw display of biopower is vastly more diffused today twenty years later as "good" and "bad" ethnic political players are managed by smear campaigns like those sexistly exerted against Sarah Palin in election 2008 where she was withered by the scathing humor of Tina Fey depicting her as a dimwitted fool dangerous to American politics. The sophistication of the political economy managing election outcomes within journalistic practices has escalated to our present circumstances. The primaries conveyed the conventional trajectory of this political economy, but a bubble pops this massive political economy in November of 2016.

THE GENERAL ELECTION: PUBLIC BACKLASH

In the general election debates, journalists misunderstood the results of the debates they moderated and reported upon, leading to the unexpected election of Donald Trump. The *Washington Post*'s journalist Chris Cizilla was surprised at how many voters thought Donald Trump won the debates journalists scored as universal and strong wins for Clinton:

> People didn't think Trump lost the debates as badly as I did. I named Clinton the winner in each of three presidential debates—and I didn't think any of the three were particularly close. Lots of people who voted Tuesday did not agree with me. *Among the 64 percent who said the debates were an "important" part of their vote for president, Clinton won by a narrow 50 percent to 47 percent margin over Trump. Of the 82 percent of people who said the debates were a "factor" in their decision for president, Trump took 50 percent to 47 percent for Clinton.*[33]

Cizilla's analysis was based upon exit data on Election Day asking voters what factors were at work in the decisions in the voting booth. Cizilla's confession and the larger dataset indicate that journalists are skewing presentations of deliberative functions, like debates, so much that they cannot discern their own role in the rhetorical production.

Taken in sum, all of this data points to a rather profound epistemological result. The public chose Trump as a symbolic act of defiance against the political economy of identity politics managed by journalists. The public was warned repeatedly by journalists that Trump was violative of almost every conceivable moral notion affirmed by the journalistic community: the integrity of facts, the esteem of American identity politics as embodied in Obama and Clinton, the respect for conventional political agendas over personal attacks, a reverential sense of immigration's role in the positive American character, and the respect earned in acts of public service such as Clinton's role as Secretary of State. The public could have chosen more than a dozen more conventional candidates on the Republican side—most with traditional political trajectories from the Congress or governorships. The selection of Trump in the primaries and again in the general election pointed to a desire to reframe political debate in the United States and a concerted effort to break and even shatter the rhetorical framework built over decades in the contemporary journalistic practices of the media established since Watergate. In the words of public commentator Michael Moore, the election of Trump was an "f" "u" to everything we know about politics.[34]

The public rejection of the media frame built around the rejection of sexism embodied in the contest between the "boorish" Trump and the "intellectual" and "sophisticated" feminine Clinton was attacked by the public—not because the public sought to endorse racism, sexism, or any of the –isms ideologically managed by the journalistic community to suit their own interests. Public affinity for equality as an American principle transcends the notion of ethnic categories. Americans tend to affiliate with Martin Luther King, Jr.'s notion of being judged by the content of their character and not the color of their skin. The journalistic coverage of ethnicity is so politically strategic that it tends to undermine this deeply held civic conviction. The rejection of Clinton was an affirmation of the equal non-ideological application of discrimination discernment. The charges of sexism and racism should be reported in a manner that could equally indict all persons whether they were a Democrat or Republican. This still obscured reality of the election lies at the heart of a public repudiation of blue privilege as operated by an interpretive elite contained within conventional American journalism. Moore was right—it was a dramatic rejection like never before seen in the world. Current efforts to rationalize the result falsely assert narratives surrounding events such as Charlottesville wherein all Trump supporters are implicated as members of the Nazi Party, the KKK, or White Nationalist organizations. Though these members are actually closer to less than ten thousand,[35] the fantasy theme of believing that all Trump supporters are involved in various political iterations of ethnic supremacism remains salient among those with blue privilege. The dialectic is an escalation of the rhetorical frame voters rejected in 2016 but underscores the contemporary refusal of some journalists to accept the present ideological defeat and seek to sustain the political economy dictating how identity politics can be managed for desired ideological outcomes.

CONCLUSION

Plato's intellectual fantasy in *The Republic* that societies might be led by philosopher kings is in fact a continual reality of political sovereignty. Those who interpret the ongoing political order and the meanings forming the basis for action do hold the ultimate sway over human affairs. Bombs and bullets fly as the result of meanings and not vice versa. Consequently, the innate concern of individuals about their own relation to vulgar communication practices such as propaganda lie at the heart of any reasonable resistance to authoritarianism. Contemporary America and its associated political orders dependent upon a free press are an essential point of reflection in the interest of individual human freedom. President Trump's shocking election represents a rupture in the political economy of identity politics as managed by this contemporary group of philosopher kings. Among Jacobins schooled in methodologies like thinkers such as Saul Alinsky, cynicism about American ideals reigns supreme. The ideological capture of so much major media journalism into the Jacobin orbit presented a critical test of their epistemological power. Communication theorist, Kathleen Hall Jamieson has observed for decades now the "spiral of cynicism" pervading election media coverage.[36] A referendum on the spiral of cynicism appears to suggest that Trump's election is a repudiation of the epistemological hold of this Jacobin ethic disseminated by radicals such as Saul Alinsky. Blue privilege is an interpretive ethic of cynicism about American idealism. A cynicism about cynicism now appears to spin back in the public sphere against the journalistic handlers and minders. This cynicism about cynicism emanates from a "forgotten man"[37] of the American public that believes in traditional American idealism repudiated as "racist" and variously "-phobic" by journalistic interpreters of American political culture. The rupture of blue privilege is arguably an important extension of the American public's desire for preserving individual liberty. Blue privilege as an effort to consolidate state power against individualism remains in an escalating rhetorical stance that indulges more radical political solutions like the beheadings of the Jacobins. Killing the president is frequently trafficked in the public's discussion and apparent in examples such as comedian Kathy Griffin who offered Trump's beheaded visage to earn public acclaim. After a visit from Secret Service, she recanted her Jacobin fantasy and apologized. More recently, she reports that she no longer apologizes for the action.[38] This suggests the stable presence of a public media sphere that allows the contemplation of beheading the president as without moral transgression. The blue philosopher kings continue to seek a coup and return to public power. The subversion of the blue philosopher kings by the American public in election 2016 points to an idealistic reformation of civil ideals. The efforts of individuals to continually interrogate the basis of social meanings as offered by journalists remains vital to the civic processes of the United States that have ideally enacted the promises of the First Amendment—including the freedom of press. The implications of this journalistic collapse for the future are significant: 1) the emergence of a new press, 2) the entrenchment of a spiral of idealism, and 3) the demise of Jacobin politics.

Initially, new journalistic options are forming in the midst of this election and going forward. The Internet opens a new frontier of counter ideological resistance to the blue privilege community. Breitbart is the most evident and clear example of this trend. Smaller but apparent examples like Tomi Lahren are indicative of how individuals from an almost blog-like stance will be able to command exponential followers to a resistance to conventional media recognized by outlets such as the *Washington Post* and the *Los Angeles Times*. Entire channels from the Internet will allow viewers less ties to cable television norms to evade the ideological channels dredged for them in the past.

Secondly, President Trump will tend to amplify the calling out of traditional institutions. This will be highly significant for the two major political parties. Trump's unusual emergence as an independent fighter against traditional politics will prove most problematic for Democrats. Already, Democrats find themselves at one of their worst national and local election positions in more than one hundred years. Not since the 1920s, have Republicans held so many elected positions. The continued ascendancy of more radical ideological characters such as socialist Bernie Sanders portends a party that sees itself as needing to up the ideological ante rather than back down in the face of the shocking 2016 loss. Special elections since 2016 tend to confirm the trend that Democrats are losing the national dialogue. Echo chambers like conventional television and movies create sensations that they are winning. From the Emmy awards to NFL broadcasts, the public is walking away from the Jacobin street theater directed at the president. Unable to understand or adapt to this public reaction, the Democrats appear likely to endure further severe losses in election 2018. The Republicans are not exempt from this cynicism about cynicism. Conventional Republican senators will find themselves subject to primary challenges that may jeopardize the conventional wisdom that Senate incumbents tend to win. This will be the critical question approaching the ideological makeup of the Senate in 2018. The litmus tests surrounding illegal immigration and the Affordable Care Act suggest that the rebellion of 2016 is not over and that not all of the future victims will be Democrats. Some will be traditional Republicans.

Thirdly, Jacobin politics as initiated by key practitioners like Saul Alinsky and Stokely Carmichael may be burning itself out. The radical notion offered by black power advocates like Carmichael may finally yield to the enduring idealism of men like James Meredith. African American race politics burns brightest in America today with regard to what the future of Jacobin politics may be. California academic radical, Dr. Frank Wilderson, also urges students to "burn it all down."[39] But what happens when we are surrounded by those hollowed out and de-institutionalized scenes? A renaissance of beloved community more sincere to American ideals and traditions will likely provide a positive completion to Martin Luther King Jr.'s letter from a Birmingham Jail:

> One day the South will recognize its real heroes. They will be the James Merediths, with the noble sense of purpose that enables them to face jeering and hostile mobs, and with the agonizing loneliness that characterizes the life of the pioneer. . . . One day the South will know that when these disinherited children of God sat down at lunch counters, they were in reality standing up for what is best in the American dream and for the most sacred values in our Judaeo Christian heritage, thereby bringing our nation back to those great wells of democracy which were dug deep by the founding fathers in their formulation of the Constitution and the Declaration of Independence.
>
> Never before have I written so long a letter. I'm afraid it is much too long to take your precious time. I can assure you that it would have been much shorter if I had been writing from a comfortable desk, but what else can one do when he is alone in a narrow jail cell, other than write long letters, think long thoughts and pray long prayers?
>
> If I have said anything in this letter that overstates the truth and indicates an unreasonable impatience, I beg you to forgive me. If I have said anything that understates the truth and indicates my having a patience that allows me to settle for anything less than brotherhood, I beg God to forgive me.
>
> I hope this letter finds you strong in the faith. I also hope that circumstances will soon make it possible for me to meet each of you, not as an

> integrationist or a civil-rights leader but as a fellow clergyman and a Christian brother. Let us all hope that the dark clouds of racial prejudice will soon pass away and the deep fog of misunderstanding will be lifted from our fear drenched communities, and in some not too distant tomorrow the radiant stars of love and brotherhood will shine over our great nation with all their scintillating beauty.[40]

King's dream remains alive today and fiercely patriotic heroes such as James Meredith, who is also still alive, are ignored by epistemological communities drowning in cynicism. Meredith served in the U.S. Armed forces and he remains a fierce ideological defender of American constitutional patriotism. Throughout the Civil Rights era, he patiently disagreed with racial activists—even Martin Luther King Jr.—about how to best fulfill the end of racial segregation. He believed in a fierce patriotic strain of individualism now ascendant in contemporary politics. The Afro-pessimist vision of "burn baby burn" may be replaced by Afro idealists like James Farmer who rebutted Carmichael's phrase with "learn baby learn." The long nightmare, which began in the mid-1960s by radicals dedicated to abolishing rather than reforming the American dream, may have finally encountered the moral exhaustion of their cause. All of this could signal a fast approaching day where we are all no longer judged by colors such as red, blue, brown, black, and white but by the "content of our character." The end of blue privilege and a decentralization of epistemological order into individualistic hands stands to disrupt the ideological cynicism so presently entrenched in our social praxis. This end could portend the emergence of a more idealistic America.

NOTES

1. See Michel Foucault, *Discipline and Punish: The Birth of the Prison*, trans. A. Sheridan (New York: Pantheon Books,1977).
2. Robert Gilpin, *Global Political Economy: Understanding the International Economic Order* (Princeton, NJ: Princeton University Press), 2001.
3. For example, *New York Times*, when covering the important racial struggle over the killing of Trayvon Martin, referred to his killer, George Zimmerman, as a "*white* hispanic." That distortion was designed to impugn the ethnicity of the individual defending himself from Martin's assault. For a full discussion of this and further examples of blue privilege see Ben Voth, "Blue Privilege," *American Thinker*, July 11, 2013, http://www.americanthinker.com/articles/2013/07/blue_privilege.html.
4. Jacques Ellul, *Propaganda: The Formation of Men's Attitudes* (New York: Random House, 1965).
5. See Richard Thaler and Cass Sunstein, *Nudge: Improving Decisions about Health, Wealth, and Happiness* (New York: Penguin Books, 2009).
6. Jodi Enda, "When Republicans Were Blue and Democrats Were Red," *Smithsonian Magazine*, October 31, 2012, http://www.smithsonianmag.com/history/when-republicans-were-blue-and-democrats-were-red-104176297/.
7. See Kenneth Burke, "Terministic Screens," in *Language as Symbolic Action*, 45, (Cambridge, UK: Cambridge University Press, 1966) and Catherine Helen Palczewski, Richard Ice,

and John Fritch, "Terministic Screen," in *Rhetoric in Civic Life*, (State College, PA: Strata Publishing, 2012), 39.

8. Ben Voth, *James Farmer Jr.: The Great Debater*, (Lanham, MD: Lexington Books, 2017).

9. Art Swift, "Americans' Trust in Mass Media Sinks to New Low," *Gallup*, September 14, 2016, http://www.gallup.com/poll/195542/americans-trust-mass-media-sinks-new-low.aspx.

10. Ibid.

11. Chris Cilliza, "Just 7 Percent of Journalists are Republicans. That's Far Fewer Than Even a Decade Ago," *Washington Post*, May 6, 2014, http://www.washingtonpost.com/news/the-fix/wp/2014/05/06/just-7-percent-of-journalists-are-republicans-thats-far-less-than-even-a-decade-ago/.

12. Ernest Bormann, "Fantasy and Rhetorical Vision: The Rhetorical Criticism of Social Reality," *Quarterly Journal of Speech*, 58, (1972): 396–407.

13. See Lars Wilnat and David H. Weaver, "The American Journalist in the Digital Age," 2014, http://archive.news.indiana.edu/releases/iu/2014/05/2013-american-journalist-key-findings.pdf; and the research by Thomas E Patterson from the Shorenstein Center demonstrating biased coverage in election 2016; Thomas E. Patterson, "Research: Media Coverage of the 2016 Election," Shorenstein Center, Harvard University, September 7, 2016, https://shorensteincenter.org/news-coverage-2016-general-election/. Further, a study by the Center for Public Integrity finds that journalists gave more than 96 percent of their political donations to causes supporting Hillary Clinton during election cycle 2016. This is important because of a central journalistic maxim that abuses of power can be traced by "following the money." For journalists, the money leads to Hillary Clinton: "Buying of the President: Journalists Shower Hillary Clinton with Cash, Far Fewer Making Contributions to Donald Trump, Analysis Shows," Center for Public Integrity, October 17, 2016, https://www.publicintegrity.org/2016/10/17/20330/journalists-shower-hillary-clinton-campaign-cash.

14. Thomas E. Patterson, "Research: Media Coverage of the 2016 Election," Shorenstein Center, Harvard University, September 7, 2016, https://shorensteincenter.org/news-coverage-2016-general-election/.

15. I predicted that Hillary Clinton already lost the 2016 election in September based upon the ideological miscalculations of Jacobin epistemological communities—including journalists. The essay was originally written in past tense to indicate that the election was already lost by early fall. Editors at *American Thinker* modified the verbiage to make the essay more of a question. See Ben Voth, "Is Hillary Clinton losing the 2016 Election," *American Thinker*, September 25, 2016, http://www.americanthinker.com/articles/2016/09/is_hillary_clinton_losing_the_2016_election.html.

16. See Jim A. Kuypers, *Partisan Journalism: A History of Media Bias in the United States*, (Lanham, MD: Rowman & Littlefield, 2014).

17. See Jeffrey Tulis, *The Rhetorical Presidency* (Princeton, NJ: Princeton University Press, 1987).

18. Theodore White, *The Making of the President, 1972,* (New York: Bantam Books, 1973).

19. Dave Levinthal and Michael Beckel, Center for Public Integrity, "Buying the President 2016: Journalists Shower Hillary Clinton with Campaign Cash/Far Fewer Making Contributions to Donald Trump, Analysis Shows," October 17, 2016, https://www.publicintegrity.org/2016/10/17/20330/journalists-shower-hillary-clinton-campaign-cash.

20. Thomas E. Patterson, "Research: Media Coverage of the 2016 Election," Shorenstein Center, Harvard University, September 7, 2016, https://shorensteincenter.org/news-coverage-2016-general-election/.

21. Gabriel Debenedetti, "Disappointing Debate Ratings Spark Democratic Campaign Complaints: The DNC Comes Under Fire for Saturday's Low Viewership Figures," *Politico*, November 15, 2015, http://www.politico.com/story/2015/11/democratic-debates-cbs-clinton-sanders-omalley-215909.

22. Patterson, "Research: Media Coverage."

23. Just recently *Washington Times* reported twelve Democrats for each Republican in higher education. Bradford Richardson, "Liberal Professors Outnumber Conservatives Nearly

12 to 1, Study Finds," *Washington Times* (October 6, 2016), http://www.washingtontimes.com/news/2016/oct/6/liberal-professors-outnumber-conservatives-12–1/.

24. Gregory Krieg, "Trump Defends the Size of His Penis," *CNN*, March 4, 2016, http://www.cnn.com/2016/03/03/politics/donald-trump-small-hands-marco-rubio/index.html.

25. Ben Kamisar, "Trump Appears Alongside Bill Clinton Accusers before Debate," *The Hill*, October 9, 2016, http://thehill.com/blogs/ballot-box/presidential-races/300120-trump-appears-alongside-bill-clinton-accusers-before.

26. Josh Katz, "Who Will Be President?" *New York Times*, November 8, 2016, https://www.nytimes.com/interactive/2016/upshot/presidential-polls-forecast.html?mcubz=3. This aggregation of data suggested Clinton had an 85% chance of victory prior to the election.

27. Patterson, "Research: Media Coverage."

28. Ibid.

29. Ibid.

30. Ibid.

31. Susan Baer, "Excluded from S.C. Debate, Keyes Begins Hunger Strike Anti-Abortion Candidate Says He Won't Be Silenced," *Baltimore Sun*, March 1, 1996, http://articles.baltimoresun.com/1996–03–01/news/1996061101_1_lamar-alexander-hunger-debate.

32. "Alan Keyes Barred from Presidential Debate and "Kidnapped" by Atlanta Police—1996," *YouTube*, 2015, https://www.youtube.com/watch?v=SehAtMQPNmQ.

33. Chris Cizilla, "The Thirteen Most Amazing Findings in the Exit Polls," *Washington Post*, November 10, 2016, https://www.washingtonpost.com/news/the-fix/wp/2016/11/10/the-13-most-amazing-things-in-the-2016-exit-poll/?utm_term=.01b23d4e2bee. Emphasis mine.

34. Michael Hains, "Trump Victory Would Be the Biggest F*** You Recorded in Human History," *Real Clear Politics* (October 26, 2016), https://www.realclearpolitics.com/video/2016/10/26/michael_moore_trump_victory_would_be_the_biggest_fk_you_recorded_in_human_history.html.

35. Megan Trimble, "The KKK Is Still Based in 22 States in the U.S.," *U.S. News and World Report* (August 14, 2017), https://www.usnews.com/news/best-states/articles/2017–08–14/the-kkk-is-still-based-in-22-states-in-the-us-in-2017.

36. Joseph N. Capella and Kathleen Hall Jamieson, *Spiral of Cynicism: The Press and the Public Good* (New York: Oxford University Press, 1997).

37. Amity Shlaes, *A New History of the Great Depression: The Forgotten Man* (New York: Harper Collins, 2007).

38. Andrew Park, "Kathy Griffin Says She Won't Apologize Anymore for Trump Beheading Photo," *CBS News* (August 30, 2017), https://www.cbsnews.com/news/kathy-griffin-says-she-wont-apologize-anymore-for-trump-beheading-photo/.

39. Colin Jenkins, "Burning Down the American Plantation: An Interview with the Revolutionary Abolitionist Movement," *Truth Out*, September 16, 2017, http://www.truth-out.org/opinion/item/41931-burning-down-the-american-plantation-an-interview-with-the-revolutionary-abolitionist-movement.

40. Martin Luther King Jr., Letter from a Birmingham Jail, April 16, 1963, https://www.africa.upenn.edu/Articles_Gen/Letter_Birmingham.html.

Chapter Eleven

Sports Figures, Social Commentary, and the Role of Sports Journalism During the 2016 Presidential Election

Erin Whiteside

During the 2016 U.S. presidential election, it was not uncommon to hear individuals lament the non-stop news coverage, barrage of political advertisements, and the seemingly oppressive deluge of social media posts among friends arguing the drawbacks and merits of each candidate. So, it was perhaps unsurprising when a sports columnist for a prominent newspaper opined for a "break" from politics and their related social issues when he turned his attention to sports. As he wrote, "When I go to the bank, I don't want the teller to lecture me on global warming. I just want him or her to cash my check. When I watch a game, I want to escape the real world for a couple of hours, not to be reminded of all its problems."[1] That notion of escapism has long underpinned an argument for the value sports bring to society; indeed, their perceived ability to transcend divisions and connect diverse individuals in pursuit of a common goal is often touted as evidence of sports' progressive social contribution.[2] The notion of escapism is a driving force for both fan attendance and also the consumption of mediated sports content and so when individuals violate that implicit agreement, they often face a backlash.

Thus, despite working for news organizations, sports journalists operate within a framework where the definition of sports as politically neutral has in turn shaped the norms and values that govern their coverage. Over time, those work routines have increasingly shifted journalistic standards in sports further from its news counterpart, and created an accepted standard of professionalism that has been critiqued as not much different from entertainment and celebrity journalism.[3] Occasionally, however, the boundaries of typical sports coverage are exposed for their limitations, forcing fans, sports reporters, and the news industry itself to confront the idea that sports does not operate separately from news, politics, and culture, but is a product of it, and a platform for negotiating cultural norms and values.[4]

In these moments, sports journalists face questions about their civic responsibilities as journalists to the communities they serve. Sports journalists encountered such a moment during the 2016 election cycle; politics and sports intersected in several ways, including through the practice of sports figures using their cultural status to campaign for candidates and speak out on pressing social issues that were simultaneously being debated in the election. On the latter point, perhaps no statement resonated as strongly as that made by National Football League player Colin Kaepernick when he began refusing to stand during the national anthem, a political act that generated much attention both within and beyond the sports world. The San Francisco 49ers quarterback told reporters that his activism was in support of the broader Black Lives Matter movement, and a statement against the U.S. government's oppressive policies toward Black communities.[5]

The Black Lives Matter movement was a wedge issue in the 2016 presidential campaign and each candidate sought to align themselves with key demographic bases on each side of the debate. Those differing stances became especially clear at the national conventions. As one *Chicago Tribune* reporter noted, "the second day of Hillary Clinton's Democratic National Convention could have been subtitled 'Black Lives Matter.'"[6] Conversely, at the Republican convention Milwaukee County sheriff, David Clarke, opened his speech by "declaring, 'Blue Lives Matter!'" and later criticized the Black Lives Matter movement.[7] And in his acceptance speech, Donald Trump asserted that he was the "law and order candidate," a phrase imbued with racial undertones, which some critics suggested were meant to hint at crackdowns on minority communities.[8]

Given that such issues were at the forefront of the election, and that Kaepernick's protest cast the bright light of sports upon them, sports journalists were presented with the opportunity to shape discussions about the state of contemporary racial politics and ideas of nationalism among the sports media-consuming public and beyond. To explore that idea, this chapter addresses the question of the civic responsibility of sports journalists by evaluating the intersection of sports and politics during the 2016 election cycle with a focus on sports coverage among California-based news outlets in response to Kaepernick's actions. I begin this chapter by arguing that sports be understood as a powerful political space and that sports journalists have typically played a role in stabilizing a set of values and norms that uphold a conservative ideology. Then, I provide a brief history of politics and sports before focusing on the political discourse stemming from one of the biggest sports stories of the year.

SPORTS, POLITICS, SOCIAL ISSUES AND SPORTS JOURNALISM

Sport as a Prominent Political Space

Sporting events are imbued with symbolism that performs powerful ideological work with material political consequences. For example, critical sport sociologists argue that one reason competitive sports resonate so strongly with Americans is that they appear to showcase American ideals of meritocracy, where one's race, nationality and even prior criminal records have no bearing in determining one's sporting success.[9] Ultimately, the belief that the best players achieved their status through simple hard work aligns with conservative views of the American dream, in which social mobility is equally accessible to all.[10] Other media scholars have documented the ways in which mediated sport reflect and uphold racial hierarchies through representations that associate innate athleticism with Blackness and superior intelligence with Whiteness.[11] Critical sports sociologists Mary McDonald and David Andrews argue such characterizations are grounded in racist assumptions once "used to justify the institution of slavery and Social Darwinist constructions of White supremacy."[12] Other examples of the ideological work of sporting discourses are evident in the pre-game festivities in many American sports, which often feature "feverish displays of nationalism, patriotism, and militarism";[13] The National Football League has a history of especially using the vehicle of football to promote a pro-U.S. military agenda in a series of "carefully orchestrated productions that have since made such activities seem normal."[14] These expressions are often knitted into the accepted ritual of sport in a way that is transparent—so much so, that sports are often understood in popular media as apolitical spaces and symbols of social progress that unite individuals across racial, class, and gender lines. Thus, when athletes or sports figures speak out on social or political issues, they are often labeled as "being political," in a way that the organization of sport is not.

Sports Figures and Politics

Given the accepted notion of sports as apolitical, it is somewhat unusual for current athletes and sports figures to endorse candidates and speak out politically.[15] Doing so may result in serious consequences, such as alienating "chunks of their fan base, [and] cutting into their endorsement potential"; thus renowned sports agent Leigh Steinberg has historically advised his clients to avoid wading into political waters.[16] As NBA legend Michael Jordan is quoted as explaining to reporters why he declined to endorse an African-American Democratic Senate candidate in his home state of North Carolina, "Republicans buy shoes, too."[17] Still, some of recent history's most notable political acts were made by athletes and in sporting spaces. Muhammad Ali declined to enter the draft during his boxing prime as a statement against U.S. military policy; track athletes Tommie Smith and John Carlos are famous for donning black gloves and raising their fists while on the Olympic medal podium in protest of U.S. civil rights abuses at the 1968 Games. All three athletes faced severe initial backlash, and the personal risks among athletes for speaking out on social or political issues remain a powerful silencing force.

Athletes and Politics during the 2016 Presidential Election

In 2016 both Hillary Clinton and Donald Trump sought to align themselves with various sports figures, a practice that makes the candidates appear likeable and accessible.[18] Most notably for Trump was his February endorsement by NASCAR CEO Brian France; the candidate then went on to inflate the news, explaining to supporters at a rally in North Carolina that "NASCAR endorsed Trump, can you believe that?" (France reportedly reached out to the campaign to assert that he did not want the sport to be associated with the candidate and that the endorsement was solely a personal choice.) Several other sports figures also endorsed Trump, including former collegiate men's basketball coach Bobby Knight, several University of Iowa football and wrestling players—who endorsed the candidate at a rally on campus and appeared with him on stage—and Ultimate Fighting Championship (UFC) President Dana White, who also spoke at the Republican National Convention.[19] Prominent athletes also publicly supported Hillary Clinton, perhaps none as famous as National Basketball Association all-star LeBron James, who campaigned on her behalf and appeared with her at a rally in the swing-state of Ohio two days before the election, in hopes of motivating the African-American vote in that state.[20] U.S. Soccer star Megan Rapino worked on policy development with the Clinton campaign and was a vocal supporter of the candidate. Jason Collins, the first openly gay NBA player, spoke at the DNC convention and Mike Tomlin, the Pittsburgh Steelers head coach, hosted a fund-raiser for Clinton at his home. Mark Cuban, the owner of the Dallas Mavericks was perhaps the most vocal, tweeting often about his distaste for Trump and support of Clinton.

The Work Routines and Governing Norms of Sports Journalism

Sport occupies a unique location among the wider news and broadcasting industry as its journalists and reporters are simultaneously valued and belittled by their non-sports news colleagues. On one hand, sports are a driving force behind subscriptions and readership in print and digital, especially among the lucrative male demographic,[21] and a major draw to cable subscriptions among customers.[22] Ultimately, the revenue potential of sports makes them critically valuable to a wider news organization's profit potential. On the other hand, sports are "not generally seen as prestigious within the culture of news and journalism" and sports reporters are often described as working in the so-called "toy department" of the wider newsroom, a disparaging moniker meant to convey sports journalism's perceived less-than-virtuous approach to the craft.[23] These low opinions are in part a function of media's symbiotic relationship with sport itself. Providing visibility and a vehicle to develop attachments to teams and leagues among fans is a contribution sports journalists provide to the teams and leagues they cover; subsequent growth among those teams and leagues leads to demand for more content, ultimately tying the two industries' fortunes together.[24] Thomas Horky and Barbara Stelzner describe this relationship as a "dependency trap," one of a series of threats to quality journalism they argue exist as a function of accepted sports journalistic ethical practices.[25] For instance, sports, "with its highly affective content and its large degree of personal involvement—provokes an emphasis on emotions."[26] That emphasis in turn negates reasoned, insightful analysis. Other norms that threaten the production of quality sports journalism include "boosterism," or the practice of privileging the home team in coverage, and what the authors call "thematization," or the pressure to generate content that produces ratings, an expectation that results in homogenous news lacking in an investigative tone. The lack of investigative journalism is but one result stemming from accepted standards that diverge from those who cover news-related beats; reporters who develop personal relationships with sources, or become personally vested in their team's success may avoid stories that cast those teams or athletes in a negative light; such was the case with performance enhancing drugs in sports, for instance. "Doping," has long been a part of elite sports, but "few sports journalists cover this issue," in part, because doping turns off viewers.[27] The risks associated with sports journalism's work standards are also reflected in coverage that focuses largely on in-game action and a belief system that sports reporters should privilege their role in becoming an expert on the game itself over situating their work "at the centre of wider political, economic and cultural factors."[28] Part of the intense focus on in-game action is the role sports journalists play in constructing the mediated version of sports in which certain narratives tend to prevail, such as heroes and villains, nationalism, clichés, and stereotypes.[29]

Reimagining Sports Journalism

In their work evaluating the role of sports journalism in society, Raymond Boyle, David Rowe, and Garry Whannel write that sports journalists are "key cultural narrators," thereby reminding us of the cultural power sports journalists wield. Drawing from that point, critical sports scholars have argued that sports reporters should move toward a more civic-minded approach as a way to better serve their communities; adopting a more reflexive approach to the practice of sports journalism, for instance, may transform sports coverage into a genre that enables thoughtful and insightful social analysis, and ultimately aligns with typical journalistic standards.[30] Among those standards is a focus on public service journalism, especially that which "implies a concern with civic issues and inequality."[31] Similarly, Boyle and colleagues argue that sports journalists should embrace the watchdog role, ask questions that concern their audiences, and pursue stories that hold sports organizations accountable to their wider communities.[32] This type of sports reporting might also be achieved through what Rowe calls a "problem-oriented" approach to journalism, or the practice of treating every identified problem as the opportunity to provide an answer, through context, explanation, and depth reporting.[33] Doing so would enable sports reporters to connect events to larger socio-political issues, thus redrawing the boundaries of where sports reporting begins and ends, and in turn diversifying what it can accomplish as a voice in the public sphere.

Yet, such shifts may not be without consequence; sports media giant ESPN has faced backlash in conservative and libertarian circles for its increased engagement with social issues and political commentary, which are viewed as left leaning and biased.[34] Thus, media organizations that produce sports content may face a difficult dilemma between depth engagement among their sports reporters that highlights social inequities and civic issues, with the risk of alienation among fans, who wish to escape those realities when consuming sports content, or see those conversations as biased.

ANALYSIS: A POLITICAL CONVERSATION THROUGH COLIN KAEPERNICK

There are numerous ways to assess media texts, and I am approaching sports journalism in this chapter through the lens of its ability to contribute to political discourse. To accomplish that goal, I first explore the questions sports journalists asked during the Colin Kaepernick story, and the answers and context they in turn provided; I specifically focus on local sports journalists in California, who possess both the source connections to Kaepernick, his then-team of the San Francisco 49ers, and the NFL, as well as ties to specific communities, two key ingredients for contextual, public-minded journalism.[35]

Local sports coverage of Colin Kaepernick's political stand was in many ways as diverse as the state of California itself. Coverage included stories that overtly praised Kaepernick's social justice motives, others that ridiculed and demonized the athlete and still others that provided insight in less polarizing ways.[36] Regardless of political stance on the issue, though, sports journalists encountered the opportunity to contribute to political discourse in ways that perhaps have never happened before; the collision of Kaepernick and the election thus transformed sports journalists into industry gatekeepers who faced the question of evaluating the boundaries of acceptable sports journalism. I argue that the boundaries did in fact change, and in ways that aligned with a conservative agenda, Donald Trump and the NFL in general; these narratives were particularly potent in their relation to shared assumptions about nationalism, racial politics, and the simultaneous (and contradictory) allegiance to the idea that sports are—and should be—an apolitical space. Moreover, such shifts were a product of accepted ways of practicing sports journalism, as well as specific choices journalists made in providing context beyond the boundaries of sports.

CONNECTING SPORTS TO POLITICS

Almost immediately after the story broke on August 27, sports reporters contributed to moving it beyond the confines of sports. Among the first reactions included by sports reporters was a comment from the White House via spokesman Josh Earnest who said in part, "as objectionable as we find his perspective, he certainly is entitled to express it."[37] That day Kaepernick also criticized both Donald Trump and Hillary Clinton, comments that were reported in the sports section in outlets as varied as the *Lake County Record Bee*, *Marin Independent Journal*, and the *San Jose Mercury News*.[38]

By August 30, sports stories were including comments from then-candidate Donald Trump, who told a radio host that he thought Kaepernick's protest was "a terrible thing. Maybe he should find a country that works better for him. Let him try. It won't happen."[39] Democratic vice president candidate Tim Kaine responded in a September 1 televised interview with ABC on the topic, explaining that although he would "do it differently," we must "respect people's abilities to act according to their conscience."[40] Curiously, no California news site/newspaper included his comments in sports stories at any point in the time sampled, nor through the date of the election.[41]

With the story grounded in its relationship to the campaigns and key political figures, as it continued to grow, much coverage went beyond reporting simply what was happening, and began exploring the question of what does refusing to stand for the flag *mean*? The most obvious sports angle is what his actions meant to his playing status, but the NFL quickly resolved this question by releasing a statement that read in part, "Players are encouraged but not required to stand during the playing of the National Anthem."[42]

Once it was clear Kaepernick was not violating policy, reporters then broadened their analysis beyond sport-focused implications, in turn implicitly embracing the opportunity to contribute to wider conversations on nationalism and racial politics that were simultaneously happening among the presidential candidates.

KAEPERNICK AS FOIL TO POLICE AND MILITARY

Coverage of Colin Kaepernick echoed the prominent nationalistic rhetoric emanating from the Trump campaign, narratives that were a function of source selection and choices about color and detail sports reporters made in their role as storytellers. The combination of these practices ultimately juxtaposed Kaepernick to conservative ideals of nationalism, while simultaneously questioning the broader Black Lives Matter movement.

Source Selection as Vehicle for Amplifying Voices on the Right

As sports reporters worked to contextualize the story, they likely sought out sources that would provide reaction to the non-sports story of what refusing to stand for the national anthem meant, but would also "make sense" in a sports story. As a consequence, many of the sources who sports journalists quoted were connected to sports, the military/police, or both. For instance, eleven different outlets in California referenced NASCAR racer Tony Stewart's tweet on the subject, which read that Kaepernick should "Learn the facts about police before running his (expletive) mouth!"[43] Reporters similarly amplified an equally provocative statement from major league baseball player Aubrey Huff, who strongly asserted that standing for the anthem should go without question when he tweeted, "Wow, the amount of people who agree with sitting during the national anthem is truly disturbing! We wonder why our country is in the toilet?!"[44] A Minnesota Vikings player added that he felt failing to stand for the flag was tone deaf in its disrespect for the military, saying to a reporter, "We're out here playing a game, making millions of dollars. People are losing their life, and you don't have the common courtesy to do that. That just drove me nuts."[45] Quarterback Drew Brees was probably the most prominent NFL player to speak out, and told ESPN he "wholeheartedly" disagreed with Kaepernick, describing his fellow quarterback's actions as "being disrespectful to the American flag"; these comments were widely repeated in local California coverage.[46] Others provided simultaneous support for Kaepernick's right to sit during the anthem, while still condemning the act itself, a sentiment summed up by one of Kaepernick's teammates, who said "We have real issues in society that need to be addressed. That was his way of standing up for it. I respect his right. Again, whether I agree with what he did or not—that's not something I would do, but he did it."[47] Another player was quoted as explaining that change is important, but "shaming the country, is unpatriotic."[48]

Reporters also consulted NFL players, and sports figures in their communities who had served in the military, a choice that may reflect sports reporters' awareness of the scope of the story. An Associated Press article, for instance, included comments from Pittsburgh Steelers player Alejandro Villanueva, who played at Army and served in Afghanistan and was quoted as saying he would "stand proudly" for the anthem and was "thankful to be in this country."[49] Another localized the story by speaking with community members, including a high school basketball coach who was quoted as saying "I am in law enforcement. They pick law-abiding citizens. I watch [Kaepernick] on the news, and he seems idiotic with his statements."[50] Reporters similarly interviewed fans who had served in the military, some of whom provided harsh commentary on the story; as one said, "I busted my ass for 20-plus years and he sits on his ass? I'm not fond of that method. I believe he's been ill-informed on some of his statements."[51]

The only sports figures to provide unqualified support during this period who were also covered by the California sporting press were Tommie Smith and John Carlos, the track stars most noted for standing on the Olympic podium in 1968, with their fists raised, in defiance of civil rights abuses in the United States. The (now) iconic athletes endorsed Kaepernick's stand, with Smith quoted as saying "I support him because he's bringing the truth out—regardless of how (it's) done. If it's not done violently, at least he should be heard."[52] Carlos similarly publicly supported the football player, offering an answer to the oft-repeated critique that Kaepernick, a multimillionaire, should be grateful for all that the country has provided him.[53] He told reporters that Kaepernick was giving a voice to members of the Black community, before posing a radical question: "Who's speaking for them if he doesn't speak for them?"[54] Finally, reporters also widely shared an excerpt from NBA great Kareem Abdul-Jabbar, who wrote an op-ed piece in the *Washington Post* and who also, like Smith and Carlos, moved beyond thinking about whether refusing to stand for the flag is disrespectful:

> What should horrify Americans is not Kaepernick's choice to remain seated during the national anthem but that nearly 50 years after Ali was banned from boxing for his stance and Tommie Smith and John Carlos's raised fists caused public ostracization and numerous death threats, we still need to call attention to the same racial inequities. Failure to fix this problem is what's really un-American here.[55]

But sports reporters did not rely solely on current and former athletes and coaches or fans; consulting a broader array of voices to comment on the issue signaled a choice by those reporters to broaden the discussion beyond sports. Those sources, though, represented a population that enjoys a close relationship with the NFL: military and police officers. The San Francisco Police Officers Association, for instance, sent a letter to the NFL which described Kaepernick's actions as "ill-advised," showing a "total lack of sensitivity" toward police, while accusing the quarterback of having "an incredible lack of knowledge" about officer-related shootings; sports reporters, in turn, widely repeated the statement.[56] Some included additional context, including the emotional pain and suffering police officers endure after what was described in the letter as a "fatal encounter." As one story explained to readers through and including comments from the letter, "Some [police officers are] so affected they never return to the streets.[57] Others noted the letter's assertion that Kaepernick had an "incredible lack of knowledge" about police shootings.[58] The inclusion of sources outside the sports world further helped amplify the notion that Kaepernick's protest was disrespectful, thus positioning the athlete as un-American.[59] As one military veteran explained to a reporter, Kaepernick should "[g]o ahead and stand against what you want to stand against, but not America."[60]

Color and Storytelling as Vehicle for Juxtaposing Kaepernick and Patriotism

Reporters are fond of saying that sometimes "stories write themselves," which may have been the case on September 2, when the 49ers played the Chargers on "Salute to the Military Night" in San Diego. Indeed, conflict functions as a governing principle in journalism, one around which reporters often make news judgments; there was no shortage of it in this story, given Kaepernick's visual protest, and his vocal critics. The San Diego game, however, further cast the opposing sides into view. In setting the scene for readers, sports reporters drew from emotion-laded narratives of hero vs. villain, implicitly assigning Kaepernick to the latter. One writer narrated that the "blend of patriotism and protest" at the game felt "straight out of a 'Rocky' movie" and then when Chargers player Chris Swain, a U.S. Navy reserve, leapt into the end zone for a touchdown in the second quarter, "it was only fitting."[61] In both previewing and reviewing the game, narratives and analysis achieved through the inclusion of color and detail set Kaepernick opposite of the military being honored that night. For instance, before first reminding readers that Kaepernick would be sitting for the anthem, one reporter then explained that the player can "expect boos when he runs onto the field."[62] Another started his story as such: "Colin Kaepernick will sit. And San Diego will salute."[63] Other reporters provided unusual detail about the spectacle of the national anthem itself, thus humanizing unspoken ideas of nationalism; In a *San Jose Mercury News* story, a reporter noted that "Once Naval Petty Officer 1st Class Steven Powell sings the National Anthem, Kaepernick figures to rise up and take the field against the Chargers in his first start since Nov. 1."[64] Others described the flags themselves, or the feeling in the stadium during those nationalistic displays. A lead to one story began by telling readers that "While a naval officer sang the first notes of 'The Star Spangled Banner' and dozens of military members unfurled an oversized flag on the football field, Colin Kaepernick and Eric Reid dropped to one knee on the San Francisco 49ers' sideline." That story later provided color in the way of describing a sign held by a fan reading "You're an American, Act like one," and quotes from a fan who told the reporter that "I was in the Navy and I saw men and women bleed and die for this flag."[65]

KAEPERNICK AS PROXY FOR BLACK LIVES MATTER

Kaepernick was explicit in stating that he saw his actions as part of the larger Black Lives Matter movement, and a political statement on White-on-Black police violence in the United States. He gave a lengthy interview shortly after the news broke, and was largely praised in response for his patience and frankness during that conversation.[66] Given that connection, in evaluating what refusing to stand for the flag meant, reporters also contextualized Kaepernick himself, who in many ways became a visible symbol of Black Lives Matter during that time, a movement that the conservative right has in many ways sought to delegitimize. That same process was manifest in evaluations of Kaepernick himself, both through opinion writing, and the inclusion of quotes from both official and non-official sources. For instance, while some praised his patience following one interview, others hinted at condescension. One described Kaepernick as *lecturing* reporters on his hopes of bringing awareness and helping people "realize what's really going on in this country."[67] Another called him "a snippy and at times rude rising star" who is now "an aggrieved QB."[68] One openly mocked the player, setting a scene for readers: "There Colin Kaepernick was Sunday afternoon in the 49ers locker room, a backup quarterback discussing racial injustice in America. Being the focal point of the locker room and of the team. Funny how that works. He sits on his duff during the national anthem and he becomes national news."[69]

Reporters at times suggested he was naïve, even through praise; for instance, as a writer for the *Sacramento Bee* stated: "While an admirable stance for someone to take, you have to wonder if Kaepernick truly understands the crapstorm he created for himself."[70] Reporters echoed the notion of Kaepernick as naïve in other ways, speculating that his protest was empty and would accomplish nothing. "By taking a knee," one writer opined, "Kaepernick will not solve police misbehavior or murderous weekends in Chicago. Neither will his call for 'awareness' because, Lord knows, we're aware."[71] Others belittled his protest, with one describing it as a "misguided one-man war vs. the national anthem"[72] and another simply calling him an "idiot."[73] One reporter mockingly asked, "This was your grand plan to change the national conversation?"[74] A local high school basketball coach and law enforcement official was quoted at length describing his feelings, saying in part that he believed Kaepernick was purposely creating a firestorm as a way to get "out of the Bay Area."[75] Finally, Kaepernick's right to speak out was cast under scrutiny through references to his wealth. As one reporter explained, "I don't think it's racist to argue that he's a millionaire who hardly is living a struggle."[76] Another quoted a player who also made this point: "I understand that people aren't getting justice, but when you have a $100 million contract, you could have taken out a whole commercial and said, 'Hi, I'm Colin Kaepernick, and I'm against this.'"[77]

Finally, conversations about Kaepernick's supposed naiveté and known wealth dovetailed in a way that suggested activism on behalf of the disenfranchised—especially among the privileged—is fraught with risks and, ultimately, not worth it. As one writer explained, Colin Kaepernick was "rusty" as a player "and now he's a social activist who refused to stand during the national anthem. Is he trying to get the 49ers to release him?"[78] After detailing Kaepernick's activism, another opined, "I sincerely hope Kaepernick enjoyed his time as a professional athlete."[79] Kaepernick was, indeed, in a fight to make the team's roster, and articles regularly reminded readers that head coach Chip Kelly had plainly said that Kaepernick's actions had not hindered his ability to make the roster.[80] While a pressing question for sports fans, connecting the two in this way inevitably invites readers to consider the consequences of activism rather than its benefits.

DISCUSSION: THE LIMITS OF SPORTS JOURNALISM

At a recent meeting of the Associated Press Sports Editors, yahoosports.com columnist Dan Wetzel spoke on a panel about the intersection of sports and politics. As a successful sportswriter who has covered myriad investigative stories, Wetzel cautioned his fellow sportswriters from moving too far from sports, especially when it comes to politics. As he explained, "I don't see a lot of value in it. No one is looking for my opinion on that stuff, and it can only turn people away."[81]

The polarizing nature of politics was especially potent in 2016, and it was not hard to, as Wetzel said, turn people away by sharing political views with someone who might not share the same position. That sentiment may have been at work in sports coverage of the Kaepernick story; although Kaepernick publicly stated that his actions were inspired by the Black Lives Matter movement, and that he was speaking out on the issue of police violence, reporters did not address those issues head-on, beyond simply quoting Kaepernick himself and providing the transcripts of his interview on the topic to readers unfiltered. Such decisions may have been a function of sports journalists trying to avoid politicizing the situation and maintain a "neutral" stance. However, the context, color, and nuance they did provide in the form of description and the inclusion of military and sports sources underscored nationalistic and pro-military rhetoric, in line with conservative positions on such topics. Importantly, these positions are accepted and understood as inherently *non-political* in sporting spaces, making the consultation of military sources, for instance, appear part of the apolitical tone of sports, while the inclusion of comments from, say, a Black Lives Matter leader, seem reflective of an ideological agenda. These ideas further helped define social critique within the context of sport as unpatriotic and unwelcome; moreover, when sports reporters connected social activism to its risks, rather than its benefits, the subsequent meaning reflected a conservative agenda that eyes socio-political movements like Black Lives Matter with skepticism.

Defying the flag in such a radical way created an emotional response, which amplified the "emotional risk" sports reporters face in covering a topic with heightened personal involvement among audience members.[82] The result of that risk is coverage that relies on clichés and "meaningful" images that resonate with readers, as opposed to reasoned, thoughtful analysis. That phenomenon was manifest in how sports journalists turned their attention to contextualizing what Kaepernick's protest meant. Subsequent coverage generally focused on the *what* and the *how*—two questions that were answered with highly-charged imagery of the flag and taken-for-granted definitions of patriotism, narratives that were amplified when a practically "ready-made" conflict story presented itself with the 49ers game against San Diego on "Salute to the Military Night." The outcome was stories that cast Kaepernick as exploiting his platform for political ends, narratives that contribute to guarding the NFL's status quo—the "feverish displays of nationalism, patriotism, and militarism" that are a regular part of everyday games, spectacles like the SuperBowl and corporate social responsibility campaigns—as politically neutral.[83]

Outliers can help illustrate the potential of media in a given context, and one article in particular stands out for its focus on the *why*. An investigative reporter for the Bay Area News Group, Thomas Peele, wrote an op-ed praising Kaepernick shortly after the story commanded national attention. Although the unequivocal support diverges sharply from the general sentiments reflected in the coverage, he argued his point by focusing on why Kaepernick was kneeling, in doing so naming Black victims of police violence, and providing context on the issue for which Kaepernick is so passionate; three news outlets posted the story, including *The Daily News* in Palo Alto, California, the only one to feature it in its sports section.[84] This is not to say that every article on the topic should include information to contextualize Kaepernick's reasoning, but the overall absence of such information stands in stark contrast to the overwhelming amount of context provided in focusing on the *what*. It is, perhaps, not a surprise that this piece was written not by a sports reporter, but by an individual on the news desk.[85] Similarly, Abdul-Jabbar's comments urging Americans to move beyond critiquing Kaepernick's actions and begin considering the issues that motivated them is also notable for its physical location; certainly it earned high visibility in the *Washington Post* news op-ed section, but as a news story, it leaves in place assumptions about where conversations must happen when sports and politics intersect.

As the story continues to unfold and others like it present themselves, sports journalists should adopt a reflexive approach to their reporting. Consulting current players about their reaction to Kaepernick may make journalistic sense, but given the political economy of sports, and the intense corporate pressure to resist speaking out politically among athletes, it is perhaps not surprising that few, if any, athletes were initially willing to either voice their support for Kaepernick or, more importantly, comment on issues important to the Black Lives Matter movement. Similarly, choosing military veterans to speak out on the issue may appear unbiased in a sporting context, but using those sources elevates the pro-military stance that is part of the fabric of the NFL. The outcome of these choices explains why the *what* and the *how* were privileged over the *why*. And in doing so, sports journalists thus contributed to a process cementing an existing value system that stabilizes existing power arrangements, where the inclusion of pro-military rhetoric is considered objective while the presence of alternative voices, especially those that challenge racial hierarchies as those affiliated with Black Lives Matter do and continue to do, are considered political.

Those outcomes were further amplified via sports reporters' role as storytellers, in observing information and providing it to readers in the form of color and detail. NFL games are staged to reflect a nationalistic and pro-military position; flyovers, flags and other nationalistic displays are so ubiquitous that they have become transparent, resulting in a shared understanding of such displays as apolitical. In simply describing the imagery as a backdrop to Kaepernick's protest, sports journalists engaged in a new version of "boosterism"; instead of aligning coverage from the point of view of the home team, coverage of Kaepernick was aligned with the interests of the NFL, its relationship with the U.S. military, and a value system where the acceptance of such displays is inherently mandatory.

Broadening source selection and story scope are not easy suggestions for sports journalists to adopt. As part of media organizations, they in part provide a product to fans who in many ways demand an "escape" from reality when consuming sports and sports media, and, as the columnist from my introduction reminds us, do not want to hear about politics when engaging with sports media. Yet leagues and teams have manufactured a space that normalizes conservative ideology as objective. Further complicating matters are sports media's relationship with the teams and leagues themselves; the two entities' fortunes are intertwined, and thus criticism among sports journalists may harm the larger media organization's interests. Ultimately, the Colin Kaepernick story highlights the conflicts of interest in sports journalism and its limits in fully contributing to public discourse on civic issues.

CONCLUSION: COVERING THE POLITICAL IN SPORT

Colin Kaepernick is not the only contemporary athlete to speak out on sociopolitical issues, and there is evidence that successful professional athletes may be challenging a system that asks for noncommitment on such issues in exchange for wealth and status. A month before Kaepernick's protest, four all-star National Basketball Players spoke out at the ESPY awards, calling for awareness and action on issues central to the Black Lives Matter movement and beyond. As one of the players, Carmelo Anthony, said:

> The racial profiling has to stop. The shoot-to-kill mentality has to stop. Not seeing the value of black and brown bodies has to stop. But also, the retaliation has to stop. The endless gun violence in places like Chicago, Dallas, not to mention Orlando, it has to stop. Enough. Enough is enough.[86]

As we move into an era where athletes may be more inclined to speak out, sports journalists will play an increasingly powerful role in shaping the conversation on socially relevant issues. Sports journalists will likely continue to debate Kaepernick's actions, and their work will play a major role in shaping the way we define patriotism, activism, and the role of sports in serving as a platform for social change. Ultimately, a willingness to make visible what is transparent, and take risks in redefining the expectations of sports journalism are required actions for sports journalists to more fully contribute to the public discourse on these topics, and fulfill their journalistic role to the communities they serve.

NOTES

1. David Whitley, "Let's Put a Kip on Sports Protests," *Orlando Sentinel*, September 3, 2016, http://www.orlandosentinel.com/sports/os-cheap-seats-david-whitley-0903–20160903-column.html.
2. Stanley D. Eitzen, "Classism in Sport: The Powerless Bear the Burden," *Journal of Sport and Social Issues* 20, no. 1 (1996): 95–105.
3. David Rowe, "Sports Journalism: Still the 'Toy Department' of the Media?" *Journalism* 8, no. 4 (2007): 385–405.
4. Many sports sociologists have made this argument. A straightforward introduction to the topic of culture and sports can be found here: Richard Giulianotti, *Sport: A Critical Sociology* (Cambridge: Polity Press, 1996).

5. On August 28, 2016, Kaepernick gave an 18-minute interview to reporters in front of his locker in which he discussed his protest and what he felt needed to change. Among his comments included the following statement: "People of color have been targeted by police. So that's a large part of it and they're government officials. They are put in place by the government." See the following citation for the full interview transcript: Eric Branch, "49ers' Colin Kaepernick Transcript: I'll Continue to Sit," *San Francisco Chronicle*, August 28, 2016.

6. Dahleen Glanton, "Hillary Clinton Isn't Afraid to Say Black Lives Matter," *Chicago Tribune* (Chicago, IL), July 27, 2016, http://www.chicagotribune.com/news/columnists/ct-clinton-black-lives-matter-glanton-20160727-column.html.

7. Nick Gass, "Milwaukee Sheriff at RNC: 'Blue Lives Matter,'" *Politico.com*, July 18, 2016, http://www.politico.com/story/2016/07/rnc-2016-sheriff-dave-clarke-225768.

8. Geoff Nunberg, "Is Trump's Call for 'Law and Order," a Racially Coded Message?" *NPR,* July 28, 2016, http://www.npr.org/2016/07/28/487560886/is-trumps-call-for-law-and-order-a-coded-racial-message.

9. Jonathan Gayles, "Steroids and Standardized Tests: Meritocracy and the Myth of Fair Play in the United States," *Educational Studies,* 35, no. 1 (2009): 1.

10. Kevin Hylton, *"Race" and Sport,* (New York: Routledge, 2009), 31.

11. Toni Bruce, "Marking the Boundaries of the 'Normal' in Televised Sports: The Play-by-Play of Race," *Media, Culture and Society* 26, no. 6 (2013): 861–879.

12. Mary G. McDonald and David L. Andrews, "Michael Jordan," in *Sports Stars: The Cultural Politics of Sporting Celebrity*, eds. David Andrews and Steven Jackson (New York: Routledge, 2001), 25.

13. Adam Rugg, "America's Game: The NFL's 'Salute to Service' Campaign, the Diffused Military Presence, and Corporate Social Responsibility," *Popular Communication* 14, no. 1 (2016): 27.

14. Michael L. Butterworth, "Militarism and Memorializing at the Pro Football Hall of Fame," *Communication and Critical/Cultural Studies* 9, no. 3 (2012): 246.

15. Des Bieler, "LeBron James Introduces 'President Hillary Clinton' at Cleveland Rally," *washingtonpost.com*, November 6, 2016, https://www.washingtonpost.com/news/early-lead/wp/2016/11/06/lebron-james-introduces-president-hillary-clinton-at-cleveland-rally/?utm_term=.eb6c761d3cda.

16. Bill King, "Political Playbook," *Street and Smith's SportsBusiness Journal* 10, no. 37: 10.

17. Kwame JA Agyemang, "Black Male Athlete Activism and the Link to Michael Jordan: A Transformational Leadership and Social Cognitive Theory Analysis," *International Review for the Sociology of Sport* 47, no. 4: 437.

18. Bill King, "Political Playbook," *Street & Smith's SportsBusiness Journal* 10, no. 37: 10.

19. "Which Sports Figures Are Supporting Hillary Clinton, Donald Trump or Gary Johnson?" *Sports Illustrated*, September 26. 2016, https://www.si.com/more-sports/athlete-presidential-endorsements-donald-trump-hillary-clinton-gary-johnson.

20. Bieler, "LeBron James."

21. David Rowe, "Sports Journalism: Still the 'Toy Department' of the News Media?" *Journalism* 8, no. 4 (2007): 385–405.

22. Brian Stelter, "Rising TV Fees Mean All Viewers Pay to Keep Sports Fans Happy," *New York Times*, January 25, 2103.

23. Raymond Boyle, David Rowe, and Garry Whannel, "Controversy? Questions for Sports Journalism," in *The Routledge Companion to News and Journalism*, ed. Stuart Allen (New York: Routledge, 2010), 245.

24. Sut Jhally, "The Spectacle of Accumulation: Material and Cultural Factors in the Evolution of the Sports/Media Complex," *Insurgent Sociologist* 12, no. 3: 41–52.

25. Thomas Horky and Barbara Stelzner, "Sports Reporting and Journalistic Principles," in *Routledge Handbook of Sports Communication*, ed. Paul Pedersen (New York: Routledge, 2013): 125.

26. Ibid.

27. Ibid, 123.

28. Raymond Boyle, *Sports Journalism: Context and Issues* (London: Sage, 2006), 28.

29. Horky and Stelzner, "Sports Reporting," 124.
30. Gavin Weedon, Brian Wilson, Liv Yoon, and Shawna Lawson, "Where's All the 'Good' Sports Journalism? Sports Media Research, the Sociology of Sport, and the Question of Quality Sports Reporting," *International Review for the Sociology of Sport*, 4, ttps://doi.org/10.1177/1012690216679835.
31. Ibid, 7.
32. Boyle, Rowe, and Whannel, "Controversy?" 252.
33. Rowe, "Sports Journalism," 389.
34. See, for example, Will Racke, "Report: ESPN's Left-Wing Politics Are Driving Away Viewers," *The Daily Caller,* April 28 2017, http://dailycaller.com/2017/04/28/report-espns-left-wing-politics-are-driving-away-viewers/.
35. The analysis included sports coverage from local news outlets in California from August 27, 2016, to September 5, 2016. The sample included 157 articles from a variety of news sources. The time frame was chosen after first evaluating the coverage and determining that there was an initial spike in articles as sports journalists likely worked out how to cover the issue. I chose to look only at California coverage because the news event itself included a local sports figure, as well as a game in that time frame between the San Francisco 49ers and San Diego Chargers, which yielded additional coverage and opportunities to address the Kaepernick story. Finally, with regular access to Kaepernick, I surmised that local reporters had the opportunity to use their existing sources to develop angles to the story, thus potentially producing more and varied coverage.
36. Several examples of such coverage include: Thomas Peele, "Kaepernick Is First Amendment Hero," *Daily News* (Palo Alto, CA), September 2, 2016; Lowell Cohn, "49ers' Colin Kaepernick Ignores the Contradictions of His Outrage," *Press Democrat* (Santa Rosa, CA), August 28, 2016.
37. Janie McCauley, "Kaepernick's Decision to Sit through Anthem Scrutinized," *Associated Press*, August 29, 2016.
38. Various versions of the same story reported on by Bay Area News Group reporter Cam Inman appeared in multiple outlets that reach diverse demographics and communities. The three examples referenced here include: Cam Inman, "Kaepernick Protests Sparks Strong Reactions," *Lake County Record Bee* (Lakeport, CA), August 30, 2016; Cam Inman, "49ers' Colin Kaepernick Says Why He Won't Be Standing for National Anthem: To Bring Justice to America," *Marin Independent Journal* (San Rafael, CA), August 29, 2016; Cam Inman, "Kaepernick Says He'll Keep Sitting for Anthem," *San Jose Mercury News* (San Jose, CA), August 29, 2016.
39. Cam Inman, "Kaepernick Protest Sparks Strong Reactions," *Monterey County Herald* (Monterey, CA), August 30, 2016. See also: Press Democrat Staff, "Donald Trump to Colin Kaepernick: Find a New Country," *Press Democrat* (Santa Rosa, CA), August 29, 2016.
40. The interview can be found at: Jessica Hopper, "Donald Trump a 'Diplomatic Embarrassment,' DEM VP Tim Kaine Says," *ABC News*, Sept. 1, 2016, http://abcnews.go.com/Politics/donald-trump-diplomatic-embarrassment-dem-vp-candidate-tim/story?id=41792986.
41. This assertion is based on my research using the Newsbank database. I used a combination of key words and phrases from the interview along with Tim Kaine's name (both in combination with interview excerpts and alone) but could not find a single search result in which comments from the interview were included in a sports story in California news.
42. Cam Inman, "The 49ers Quarterback Is Protesting Minority Rights and Racial Injustice," *Orange County Register* (Santa Ana, CA), August 28, 2016.
43. "It's a Blast from the Past at Darlington," *San Diego Union-Tribune* (San Diego, CA), September 4, 2016. Also: Cam Inman, "Backlash Hits Kaepernick Full Force," *Mercury News* (San Jose, CA), August 30 2016. A version of the article written by Cam Inman of the Bay Area News Group, also appeared in the *Monterey County Herald, Daily Democrat, Times Herald, Santa Cruz Sentinel, Lake County Record Bee, Chico Enterprise-Record, Red Bluff Daily News, Marin Independent Journal* and *Vacaville Reporter*.
44. This tweet appeared in both the *Orange County Register* and the *San Jose Mercury News*, two of the larger newspapers in California. See: Cam Inman, "The 49ers Quarterback is

Protesting Minority Rights and Racial Justice," *Orange County Register* (Santa Ana, CA), August 28, 2016.

45. Eric Branch, "Harbaugh on Kaepernick: 'I don't Respect the Motivation or the Action,'" *San Francisco Chronicle*, August 29, 2016.

46. "Football World Reacts to Anthem Protest," *Redding Record* (Searchlight, CA), August 31, 2016. These comments were repeated in small outlets like the Redding Record, and larges ones, including the *San Jose Mercury News* and the *Chico Enterprise-Record.*

47. Eric Branch, "What They Said: 49ers Discuss Colin Kaepernick," *San Francisco Chronicle*, August 28, 2016.

48. Eric Branch, "Eagles Jenkins: Kaepernick's Stance Will Inspire More Discussion about QB," *San Francisco Chronicle*, (San Francisco, CA), August 28, 2016.

49. Janie McCauley, "Kaepernick's Decision to Sit through Anthem Scrutinized," *Associated Press*, August 29, 2016.

50. "Local Figures React to Kaepernick," *Bakersfield Californian* (Bakersfield, CA), August 30, 2016. Another example: Michael Gehlken, "Sitting on a Huge Topic: Varied Takes from Vallejo Veterans, Football Coaches, Players on Kaepernick," *Times Herald (*Vallejo, CA), September 4, 2016.

51. Gehlken, "Sitting on," September 4, 2016.

52. Daniel Mano, "Quarterback Receives Credit for His Courage," *Mercury News* (San Jose, CA), September 1, 2016.

53. Cohn, "Kaepernick Ignores," August 28, 2016. As the writer opined, "Kaepernick has benefited from our miserable, rotten society—the one he says fails so many people. Who has benefitted more than Kaepernick? . . . He lives a privileged life."

54. Daniel Brown, "Anthem Protest—Sports Activists Back Kapp—Olympian Carlos, Other Crusaders Support Protest," *Santa Cruz Sentinel* (Santa Cruz, CA), August 31, 2016.

55. Kareem Abdul Jabbar, "Insulting Colin Kaepernick Says More about Our Patriotism Than His," *Washington Post,* September 1, 2016.

56. Cam Inman, "Kaepernick Protests Spark Strong Reactions," *Monterey County Herald*, (Monterey County, CA), August 30, 2016.

57. Janie McCauley, "Kaepernick's Decision to Sit through Anthem Scrutinized," *Associated Press*, August 30, 2016.

58. Cam Inman, "Kaepernick Protests Spark Strong Reactions," *Daily Democrat,* (Woodland, CA), August 30, 2016.

59. Gus Thomson, "Patriot Games: What Will You Do When the National Anthem Plays?" *Loomis News*, September 2, 2016.

60. Eric Branch, "Sports," *San Francisco Chronicle* (San Francisco, CA), Sept. 1, 2016.

61. Michael Gehlken, "On a Night Focused on 49ers QB Kaepernick, Chargers Rookie and Navy Reserve Officer Scores Fitting Touchdown," *San Diego Union-Tribune* (San Diego, CA), September 2, 2016.

62. Matt Barrows, "Kap Turns Preseason Finale into Intriguing Contest," *Sacramento Bee,* (Sacramento, CA), September 1, 2016.

63. Connor Letourneau, "Starting QB Choice Could Come Friday," *San Francisco Chronicle,* (San Francisco, CA), August 31, 2016.

64. Cam Inman, "Kaepernick Assures No Routine Exhibition," *Mercury News*, (San Jose, CA), September 1, 2016.

65. Greg Beacham, "Kaepernick, 49ers Teammate Kneel during National Anthem," *Associated Press*, September 2, 2016.

66. Kaepernick is known as being somewhat surly with the media. His interview on the topic was reported as different from his usual demeanor.

67. Cohn, "Kaepernick Ignores," August 28, 2016.

68. Tim Kawakami, "Kap Stands Up for His Sit-Down Stance," *Mercury News*, (San Jose, CA), August 28, 2016.

69. Cohn, "Kaepernick Ignores," August 28, 2016.

70. Marek Warszawski, "Farewell Colin Kaepernick the 49ers QB: Hello Kaepernick the Political Pinata," *Fresno Bee* (Fresno, CA), August 27, 2016.

71. Mark Whicker, "Kaepernick Shielded by Flag He Won't Honor," *Orange County Register* (Santa Ana, CA), August 30, 2016.
72. Mike Waldner, "Stadium Debut Highlights Busy Week at ECC," *Daily Breeze* (Torrance, CA), August 30, 2016.
73. Lew Brewster, "Random Thoughts," *Inland Valley Daily Bulletin* (Ontario, CA), August 30, 2016.
74. David White, "Colin Kaepernick, What Exactly Were You Thinking?" *Fresno Bee* (Fresno, CA), September 4, 2016.
75. "Local Figures React to Colin Kaepernick," *Bakersfield Californian*, (Bakersfield, CA), August 30, 2016.
76. Kawakami, "Kap Stands Up."
77. "Local figures," August 30, 2016. Another examples includes: Cohn, "Kaepernick Ignores," August 28, 2016,
78. Grant Cohn, "Chip Kelly's 49ers Worries Are Many, and They Are Large," *Press Democrat* (Santa Rosa, CA), August 27, 2016.
79. Warszawski, "Farewell Colin Kaepernick."
80. Josh Dubow, "As Anthem Controversy Simmers, Kaepernick Prepares to Play," *Associated Press*, August 31, 2016.
81. Wetzel's comments came at the annual meeting of the Associated Press Sports Editors, in June, 2017.
82. Horky and Stelzner, "Sports Reporting," 125.
83. Rugg, "America's Game," 27.
84. Thomas Peele, "Kaepernick Is First Amendment Hero," *Daily News* (Palo Alto, CA), September 2, 2016.
85. A second notable article that stands out as an outlier was also written by someone outside the sports realm. In her piece historicizing the national anthem and its role in sporting events, an Associated Press news reporter illuminated the political ends of such practices. Her piece was put out on the sports and news wire by the Associated Press: Errin Haines Whack, "AP Explains: National Anthem Is Icon of Patriotism, Protest," *Associated Press,* August 31, 2016.
86. For a full transcript of the speech, see Melissa Chan, "Read LeBron James and Carmelo Anthony's Powerful Speech on Race at the ESPY Awards," *Time,* July 14, 2016, http://time.com/4406289/lebron-james-carmelo-anthony-espy-awards-transcript/.

Index

4chan, 156; anonymity of members on, 158; description of, 155; Pepe legacy on Reddit and, 172–173; Pepe reclamation and, 168–170; on Pepe as white supremacy symbol, 165–166; sub-board of, 169
60 Minutes Overtime, 12

ABC News, 20, 119; worldview response to Trump, D., speech, 105, 108
abcnews.com.co, 12, 26n2
Abdul-Jabbar, Kareem, 231
Access Hollywood tape, 67–70, 193, 194–195
ad hominem tactics, 48
ADL. *See* Anti-Defamation League
ads: "Mirrors", 148; primary debates as free, 211; "Role Models", 144, 148; Russian, 27n15; "Speak", 144; "What's at Stake", 147–148, 148
advocacy journalism, 13, 24, 196
agency: agent conflation with, 112–115; agent-scene worldview, 105–106, 116–117; construction of Clinton, H., 112–115
agenda building, on Twitter, 58
agenda-setting, media, 173–174
agenda-setting theory, 58
Alexy, Robert, 48
Ali, Muhammad, 226
Alinsky, Saul, 217, 219
American dream, 5, 140–141, 143, 225
American Psychological Association, 46
American Republic, 124–125, 197
American Society of Newspaper Editors, 119
Anthony, Carmelo, 237
Anti-Defamation League (ADL), 163–164, 166, 167, 174; Pepe creator protest against, 170–172
Antifa, 49
Assange, Julian, 23
Associated Press Media Editors Statement of Ethical Principles, 119
Associated Press Sports Editors, 234
athletes: 2016 election and, 226; Black Lives Matter speech by NBA, 237; characterization of Black, 225; politics and, 225–226
The Atlantic, 18, 123
audio tapes, Clinton, H., on Palestinian election, 122
authoritarianism, 44, 217
Azari, Julia, 57

Bachman, Michelle, 204
Baker, Gerard, 3
Baldwin, Alec, 182, 191
Baldwin, Stephen, 187
Bannon, Steve, 101, 102, 124
basket of deplorables, 35, 120, 162
Bay Area News Group, 235

bias, media, 1–2; before and after election campaign, 118–122; confirmation, 19, 22; donations to Clinton, H., example of, 119, 120, 122, 221n19; election coverage and, 78–81; framing bias, 15; Lippman on, 79; negative coverage and, 83–84, 91, 91–92, 93, 119; primary coverage charges of, 210; pro-Clinton/anti-Trump actions by all networks, 119–122; subtle forms of, 79; types of, 80; worldview expression as, 5. *See also* blue privilege; cable news coverage, of 2016 election; worldviews

Biden, Joe, 110

Black Lives Matter, 224, 230, 234–235; Kaepernick as proxy for, 233–234; NBA athletes ESPY speech on, 237

Blackness, athleticism and, 225

Blow, Charles, 45

blue privilege, 7; 1996 Republican primary debate and, 214–215; backlash against, 215–217; contemporary propaganda and, 204, 220n3; definition of, 204–205; empirical data on journalistic, 205–208, 221n11, 221n13; impeachment and, 206–208, 207; Jacobins and, 205, 206, 213, 219, 221n15; Keyes kidnapping and, 214–215; "killing" term reporting and, 208, 209; media donations to Clinton, H., and, 221n19; party affiliation of journalists and, 205–206, 221n11, 221n13; philosopher kings and, 217, 218; in primary process coverage, 209–214; racism, sexism and identity politics, 216–217; Trump, D., phenomena and, 209; White, T. H., on power of press and, 206

boosterism, 227, 236

Boy's Club, 155

Brazile, Donna, 79

Brees, Drew, 230

Breitbart, 218

Burke, Kenneth, 102–103, 116

Bush, Billy, 67

Bush, George H. W., 107, 182

Bush, George W., 136; Ferrell and, 190; impeachment term and, 207

Bush, Jeb, 206, 211

BuzzFeed, 3–4, 11, 27n18; study limitations, 17; study validity, 15–17

By Any Means Necessary, 49

cable news coverage, of 2016 election: candidate mentions, 88, 90; candidates covered in, 86; coverage tone, 86–87, 91; designating networks, 85; fairness study results for, 87–90; hypotheses about, 84, 90; intercoder reliability scores, 87; measures, 85–87; media personality types, 86; method of studying, 84–85; negative tone or content, 83–84, 91, 91–92, 93; network with most coverage, 91; objectivity of, 88, 90–91, 92; partisan choices of network, 93–94; public perceptions and, 95; pundits use in, 88, 90, 94; purpose of studying, 78; ratings, 97n23; reliability assessment, 87; research questions for studying bias in, 80–81, 87–88, 89–90; study limitations, 94–96

campaign narratives: intimate spaces for, 136, 151n13; Lewis on best, 136, 140–141, 150; narrative theory and, 136; power of, 136; Reagan and, 136, 141, 145; social media and, 5–6, 136–137, 149

campaign narratives, Clinton, H., 135, 139; American dream in, 143; announcement speech and, 141–143, 152n32; concession speech, 133–134; decentering nature of, 139; early communications and, 138–139; female achievement, 134; Fighter storyline, 139–141, 144, 150; gender issue, 137–138, 149, 152n23; Internet and, 135–137; lack of clear, 147; lack of compelling, 134; MAGA contrasted with, 134, 141, 145, 150; narrative-in-response tactic, 134–135, 149; Stronger Together, 145, 147, 150; Trump, D., attack strategy in, 146, 147, 148–149, 149–150; videos, 139–141, 147–149; "What's at Stake" ad, 147–148, 148

Campbell, Bill, 214–215

Carlos, John, 231

Carmichael, Stokely, 219

Carrey, Jim, 43, 45

Carson, Ben, 211
CBS, 119, 123; on "I alone" agent, 126n32
Chadwick, Andrew, 57, 69–70
Charlie Hebdo, 190
Che, Michael, 191
Chicago Tribune, debate coverage in, 185
Chomsky, Noam, 82
Christie, Chris, 36
Citizens United, 211
Cizilla, Chris, 215–216
Clarke, David, 224
Clinton, Hillary: advance notice of questions given, 78–79, 206; agency and, 112–115; announcement speech, 141–143, 152n32; athletes endorsement of, 226; basket of deplorables comment of, 35, 120, 162; blue privilege and, 212; concession speech of, 133–134; consubstantiality with, 117–118, 123, 124–125; *The Daily Show* on debates and, 193–194; donations to, 119, 120, 122, 221n19; exaggerated claims made by, 21–22; Jacobin miscalculations and, 221n15; journalists as favoring, 210; Kaepernick criticism of Trump, D., and, 229, 239n38; narrative-in-response tactic of, 134–135, 149; *New York Times* and *Washington Post* endorsement of, 1–2; predicted loss of election by, 221n15; press worldview response to acceptance speech, 110–115; pro-Clinton/anti-Trump bias actions, 119–123; *SNL* satire of Trump, D., and, 191–192; terministic screens and, 115; Trump, D., use of Twitter compared to, 56, 59, 60; worldviews in nomination speech, 104–105. *See also* campaign narratives, Clinton, H.; debates, presidential
Clinton, William Jefferson (Bill), 135, 145, 191; impeachment and, 207–208; Trump, D., on, 68
CNBC, 121
CNN, 15, 22, 69, 77; bias samples, 120, 121, 122; in bias study, 84, 91; candidate mentions on, 88, 90; candidates discussion percentages for, 87–88; DNC videos played by, 120; firing of Brazile, D., 78–79; Trump, D., othering by Zakaria, 42; worldview response to Clinton, H., nomination speech, 110–111, 111; worldview response to Trump, D., acceptance speech, 106–107, 107–109, 110, 127n60
CNN Money, 12
CNN Reality Check, 109
code of ethics, entertainment and, 197
Colbert, Stephen, 44, 45
Collins, Jason, 226
comedians: candidate flaws and, 190; main goal of, 189; presidential elections satirized by, 182, 183; satire, social responsibility theory and, 187; Trump, D., othering by, 43–45
Comey, James, 21–22
concession speech, Clinton, H., 133–134
confederate flag, 43
confirmation bias, 19, 22
conservatives: belief in fake news by, 18–20; sports and sports journalism and, 236–237; Trump, D., denounced by, 37, 47
consubstantiality, with Clinton, 118, 123; accountability and, 124–125
Conway, Kellyanne, 21
Coulter, Ann, 204
credibility, media: pundits and, 95–96; ratings, 2–3
Cruz, Ted, 21, 66, 66–67

Daily Beast, 120, 164; on Nazi Pepe, 161
The Daily Show with Trevor Noah, 6–7, 182–183, 184, 189; Clinton, H., and, 193–194; debates satirized on, 192–194
Dale, Donald, 21
dance of the dunces, 39
Danish election coverage, 81
Darrow, Clarence, 117
David Letterman Show, 55
deaths, uninvestigated, 122
debates, presidential, 67, 122; advance notice of questions in, 78–79, 206; satire potential and media coverage, 184–186; satirical coverage of, 191–195; second, 69; viewership, 184; voter perceptions of winners, 215–216

debates, primary, 210; of 1996, 214–215; free advertising from, 211; ideological distortion charges during, 211; response time and attack rule, 210–211
deep state, 40
democracy: fake news and, 24; Obama, B., on Clinton, H., and, 145–146; pundits and, 83, 94; satire potential damage to, 198
Democratic National Convention (DNC): Black Lives Matter and, 224; blue privilege and, 210, 212; deaths after, 122; video coverage, 120
Democrats: color association with, 204–205; losses and difficulties for, 218–219; news network chosen by, 93–94
DNC. *See* Democratic National Convention
Dole, Bob, 214
donations, to Clinton, H., 119, 120, 122, 221n19
doping, in elite sports, 227

Earnest, Josh, 229
election, 2016 presidential: as backlash against blue privilege, 215–217; disconnect between voters and media, 77–78; election results and response, 187; fairness and balance in coverage of, 78–81, 91–93; fake news examples, 11; hybrid media use, 57–58, 69–70; international perceptions of, 184; Internet impact on, 135–137; media coverage and bias during and after, 119–123; media donations to Clinton, H., 119, 120, 221n19; minority voters in, 150n5; Pepe the Frog meme in, 162–164; pundits role in coverage of, 81–84; rhetoric of, 34, 47, 48; rough nature of, 31; social media importance in, 136–137, 149, 151n17; sports-politics intersection during, 224–226; unusual features of, 40. *See also* cable news coverage, of 2016 election; campaign narratives; debates, presidential; framing, of nomination acceptance speeches
email, 135
entertainment programming: code of ethics importance in, 197; free speech and, 190; satire in, 6–7; social responsibility theory and, 189–190
escapism, sports journalism and, 223
ESPN, 228
ESPY awards, 237
Evans, Chris, 187

Facebook: *BuzzFeed* report on fake news and, 11, 15, 17, 27n18; engagement, 16; Russian ads on, 27n15; shares, 16–17, 23
fact-checking, 20, 125, 194–195
fake news, 2; abcnews.com.co example of, 12, 26n2; *The Atlantic* on, 18; belief in, 16–21, 27n19; *BuzzFeed* survey on, 3–4, 11, 15–17, 27n18; confirmation bias and, 19, 22; conservative media definition of, 13–14; conservatives belief in, 18–20; democracy and, 24; election campaign examples of, 11; interview quotes and, 13; Ipsos Public Affairs study on, 17, 18; liberal and conservative media differences in, 14–15, 27n12, 27n14; liberals and, 20–21; mainstream definition of, 12–13, 14; on NASA, 12; not newsworthy sense of, 13, 14; party affiliation and belief in, 17; political discourse and, 12; poverty reports and, 29n42; Rich death and, 23; Russian interference issue and, 14–15, 20, 22; stereotypes, 18; on transgender suicides, 20–21; Trump, D., and, 1, 21, 22, 28n32, 101; under-reporting and, 22; ways to deal with, 26
Fallon, Jimmy, 149
Farenthold, David, 67
Farmer, James, 220
FBI, 120, 121
feminism, 203–204
Ferrell, Will, 190
Fessler, Daniel M. T., 18
Fey, Tina, 215
Fighter storyline, Clinton, H., narrative as, 139–141, 144, 150
Fisher, Walter, 136
FN. *See Fox* News

Foreign Policy, 39–40
Foucault, Michel, 203
Four Theories of the Press (Siebert, Schramm, Peterson), 79
Fox News (FN), 20, 181–182; balanced coverage of acceptance speeches, 118; in bias study, 84, 91; candidate discussion and mentions on, 87–88, 88, 90; candidate favored by, 80; negative coverage and, 92, 213; *Washington Post* on, 15; worldview response to Clinton, H., nomination speech, 110–111, 111–112; worldview response to Trump, D., nomination speech, 105, 126n32
framing, of nomination acceptance speeches, 101–102, 125n5; terministic screens and, 102–103. *See also* worldviews
framing bias, 15
France, Brian, 226
Francis, Pope, 11
Franklin, Benjamin, 188
free press, 24, 218
free speech, 49
Furie, Matt, 155, 163; *New York Magazine* interview with, 160; protest against ADL classification, 170–171; Reddit user response to, 171

Gallup, on trust in media, 28n26
gatekeeping bias, 80
gender, Clinton, H., campaign narrative issue of, 137–138, 149, 152n23
Goldwater rule, 46–47
Goodwin, Michael, 2–3
Google Trends, 63
Griffin, Kathy, 45, 218
The Guardian, 20, 171

Haas Institute for a Fair and Inclusive Society, 33
Habbo Hotel, trolling raid, 166
Habermas, Jürgen, 48
Handler, Chelsea, 44
Hannity, Sean, 13–14, 23
Harvard-Harris Poll, 17
Hayward, Steven, 42
Herman, Edward, 82
The Hill, 17
Hofstra University, debate at, 184–185
Holt, Lester, 122
Horation satire, 188, 195–196
Huffington Post, 78, 120
humor, purpose of satire and, 188–189
Hutchins Commission, 189, 197

I alone agent, worldview of Trump, D., as, 124, 126n32
iconographic tracking, Pepe the Frog, 157–159
idealism: rhetoric and, 116; terministic screens and, 117
identity politics: blue privilege and contemporary propaganda in, 204, 220n3; contemporary philosopher kings in, 217, 218; racism, sexism and, 216–217
immigration, 121; fake news and, 18–19; hombres comment on illegal, 186; media on legal and illegal, 24–25; number of legal immigrants, 24–25; Trump, D., nomination acceptance speech and, 107–108
impeachment, 206–208, 207
The Intercept, 121
intercoder reliability scores, 87
Internet, 135–136, 151n13, 218; Habbo Hotel trolling raid, 166; voter use of, 137, 151n18. *See also* social media
Internet memes: battle over, 169–170; definition of, 155; elitism, 169–170; metamorphoses of, 160; normies and, 169–170; participatory culture surrounding, 157; remix culture and, 156–157; trolling and, 161. *See also* lulz logic; Pepe the Frog meme
Ipsos Public Affairs, 17, 18

Jacobins, 205, 206, 213, 219, 221n15
James, LeBron, 226
Johnson, Gary, 210
Jordan, Michael, 225
journalism: advocacy, 13, 24, 196; press agents and, 81. *See also* blue privilege; sports journalism
journalists: choice of candidate, 212; as philosopher kings, 217, 218. *See also*

pundits
Juvenalian satire, 188, 195, 196–197

Kaepernick, Colin: as Black Lives Matter proxy, 233–234; Clinton, H., and Trump, D., criticized by, 229, 239n38; as foil to police and military, 230–233; locker room interview, 238n5; national anthem protest of, 224, 229–230, 230; sports coverage analysis, 228–234, 239n35, 239n38; tweets on, 230, 239n44
Kagan, Robert, 45
Kaine, Tim, 229
Kelly, Chip, 234
Kelly, Megyn, 181–182
Kelsey, Richard, 46
Keyes, Alan, kidnapping of, 214–215
killing, reporting on use of term, 208, 209
King, Andrew, 117
King, Martin Luther, 219–220
Knight, Bobby, 226
Know Your Meme, 159, 169
Koppel, Ted, 13–14
Kristof, Nicholas, 41–42
Kristol, Bill, 38, 40
Kurtz, Howard, 123
Kuypers, Jim A., 79, 92, 116–117

Las Vegas, debate in, 186
Lewinsky, Monica, 191
Lewis, William, 136, 140–141, 145, 150
liberals, fake news and, 20–21
Lippman, Walter, 79, 81
locker room talk, 69, 186, 193
Los Angeles Times, 16, 19, 34, 35, 144, 213; Internet challenge to, 218
Lowry, Rich, 37
lulz logic, 160, 161, 164, 165–166; lulz economy, 164; Nazi Pepe and, 166, 166–167

Maddow, Rachel, 14
mainstream media (MSM): bias actions during and after election campaign, 119–123; Pepe the Frog entry into, 159–164, 172–173; trolls symbiotic relation with, 165
Make America Great Again (MAGA), 148; Clinton, H., narratives contrasted with, 134–135, 141, 145, 150; Twitter and, 145
Malina, Joshua, 187
Manjoo, Farhad, 120
materialism, in agent/scene worldview, 116–117
McCain, John, 67
McGeough, Ryan Erik, 117
McIver, Meredith, 65, 66, 67
McKinnon, Kate, 191
media: accountability and consubstantiality, 124–125; agenda-building theory of, 58; agenda setting by, 58, 173–174; bias actions during and after election campaign, 119–123; categorizing outlets of, 27n12, 27n14; credibility ratings, 2–3; cultivated views in, 82; disconnect between voters and, 77–78; donations to Clinton, H., 120, 221n19; editorial and opinion distinctions in, 95; engagement with Trump, D., tweets about, 62–63; free speech and, 49; Furie on dominance of, 170–171; Hutchins Commission on, 189, 197; hybrid system of, 57–58, 69–70; on legal and illegal immigration, 24–25; liberal dominance of, 24; mistrust in, 23–24, 28n26, 71, 77–78, 205; Monmouth study on partisan reporting and, 19–20, 28n26; *New York Times* on objectivity challenge in, 50; objectivity tenets, 49–50; poverty reports and, 29n42; predictions, 5, 212; pundits role in election coverage and, 81–84; reliance of varied sources of, 189–190; Trump candidacy announcement response in, 181; uncivil discourse in, 93; ways to judge reports in, 26; *why* focus in, 235. *See also* bias, media; debates, presidential
The Media Research Center, 80
memes. *See* Internet memes
Meredith, James, 219, 220
meta-beliefs theory, 19
military, patriotism, Kaepernick and, 230–233
Miller, Alice, 49

Minaj, Nicki, 155–156
minority voters, 150n5
"Mirrors" ad, 148
mistrust, of media, 23–24, 28n26, 77–78, 205; hostility trend, 205–206; party affiliation of journalists, 205–206, 221n11, 221n13
Monmouth University Polling Institute, 19–20, 28n26
Moore, Michael, 216, 217
The Moscow Times, 184
Mother Jones, 68
Moyer, Bill, 123
MSM. *See* mainstream media
MSNBC, 20; in bias study, 84, 91; candidate discussion and mentions on, 87–88, 88, 90

NASA, 12
NASCAR, 226, 230
Nast, Thomas, 188
national anthem. *See* Kaepernick, Colin
National Basketball Association (NBA), 225, 226, 231; athletes speaking out on Black Lives Matter, 237
National Football League (NFL), 228, 229; national anthem guideline, 229; player opposition to Kaepernick, 230–231; pro-military stance of, 225, 236
National Review, 36–37, 37, 161; "Against Trump" issue of, 36, 37; Trump, D., opposition stance of, 36, 36–37
NATO, 22
Nazi Pepes, 160–161; *Daily Beast* article on, 161; lulz logic and, 165–166, 166–167
NBA. *See* National Basketball Association
NBC, 112, 114, 119
NBC Nightly News, 189
negativity, in election coverage, 83–84, 91, 91–92, 93, 95, 119; comparing primary with general election, 212–213; conceptualizations of, 95; Obama, B., percentages for, 123; toward Republicans, 92
New York Magazine, Furie interview in, 160
New York Times (NYT), 19, 57, 121, 123; candidate favored by, 80; Clinton, H., endorsement by, 2; Clinton Foundation donation not reported by, 120; on elite and media, 77; Kristof on Trump, D., supporters, 41–42; media partisanship opinion piece in, 50; Pepe the Frog meme cartoon in, 172–173; worldview response to Clinton, H., nomination speech, 113, 114–115; worldview response to Trump, D., speech, 105, 106, 110
the *New Yorker*, 120, 133; Remnick's anti Trump, D., editorials, 38–39, 41
NFL. *See* National Football League
Nixon, Richard M., 101, 108
Noah, Trevor. *See The Daily Show with Trevor Noah*
Nolte, John, 3
nomination acceptance speeches, 101–102; FN balanced coverage examples, 118; press worldview in response to Trump, D., 105–110, 126n32, 127n60; Trump, D., on immigration, 108–109; worldviews in, 103–105
nostalgia, 141
NYT. *See New York Times*

Obama, Barack, 58, 108, 145–146; as first social media president, 136; impeachment and, 207, 208; Keyes and, 215; positive-negative coverage percentages, 123
Obama, Michelle, 61, 65, 145
objectivity: cable news study of, 88, 90–91, 91, 92; conservative ideology as, 236–237; by media personality, 92; *New York Times* on challenge of, 50; tenets, 49–50
The Onion, 6–7, 182; on *Access Hollywood* tape, 194–195; debate satire in, 194–195
othering: contemporary usage of, 32–34, 34; definition of, 4; original meaning of, 32, 34; sociologists use of otherness, 33
Othering & Belonging: Expanding the Circle of Human Concern, 33
othering, of Trump, D., 31; bare-knuckle politics and, 48; Clinton, H., basket of deplorables comment as, 35; CNN and,

42; comedians and, 43–45; confederate flag image as, 43; by conservative pundits, 37–38; contradictory nature of, 49; "dance of the dunes" phrase, 39; during early months of Trump administration, 38–42; *Foreign Policy* piece as, 39–40; free speech and, 49; Goldwater rule violations in, 46–47; Habermas ideal discourse and, 48; ideal discourse and conduct rules perspective, 48–49; media objectivity tenets and, 49–50; media partisanship and, 49–50; *National Review* and, 36–38; #NeverTrump, 36, 38, 47; *New York Times* readers and, 41–42; in the *New Yorker*, 38–39; on personality and state of mind, 45–47; in popular culture, 43; Remnick and, 38–39, 41; on Twitter, 42–43
outrage discourse, 83

Palestinian election, Clinton, H., audio tape on, 122
Palin, Sarah, 190, 203–204, 215
panopticon, 203
partisanship: blue privilege and, 208; cable network choices and, 93–94; Monmouth study on reporting and, 19–20, 28n26; othering and, 49–50; socially responsible, 196
party affiliation: of academics, 211, 221n23; color association with, 204–205; fake news and, 17; of journalists, 205–206, 221n11, 221n13
patriotism, Kaepernick and, 232–233
pay-for-play schemes, 121
PBS, 120
Peace Pepe Database of Love, 171
Pepe the Frog meme, 6; comic strip on death of, 171–172; creation of, 155; in election campaigns, 162–164; Furie protest against ADL classification, 170–172; hate symbol classification of, 163–164, 165–166, 167, 169, 174; iconographic tracking and, 157–159; journey and use of, 155–156, 156; lulz logic and, 165–166, 166–167; mainstream appropriation of, 159–164, 172–173; as media agenda setting example, 173–174; racist legacy of, 174; reclaiming of, 167–168, 168–170; remix culture function of, 168; social justice warriors and, 161; trolling and, 164–165; as white supremacy symbol, 159, 161, 162–163, 164–167
Perry, Katy, 155
Peterson, Wilbur, 79
phenomenology, emergence of Other concept and, 32
philosopher kings, 217, 218
Pittsburgh Steelers, 231
plagiarism scandal, Trump, M., speech and, 61, 62
Plasser, Fritz, 82
Plato, 217
Podesta, John, 23, 133–134
police: Kaepernick as foil to military and, 230–233; violence, 234
political cartoonists, 188
political satire, educational role of, 196
Politico, 78, 144, 187
politics: athletes and, 225–226; connecting sports to, 229–230, 239n38; polarizing nature of, 234–235; sports journalism intersection with, 224–226; sports as neutral on, 223–224, 229. *See also* identity politics
polls, 77; Harvard-Harris, 17; media mistrust in responses to, 77–78; Monmouth, 19–20, 28n26; public mistrust in, 78, 124–125, 205; voter perceptions of candidates, 183–184
Poole, Christopher, 170
populism, 150n5
poverty, media reports on, 29n42
Power Line blog, 42
presidential elections: 2016, 215–217; honeymoon period of, 208; Jacobin miscalculations in 2016, 221n15; results of 2016, 187; satire and, 182, 183. *See also* election, 2016 presidential
primaries: blue privilege and, 209–214; blue privilege in debate coverage, 210–211; coverage ratios, 213–214; media predictions and, 212; number of candidates at start of, 209
"produsers", 156

ProPublica, 77
Psychological Science, 18
Psychology Today, 19
PTSD, Trump quote on soldiers and, 13, 26n7
pundits: campaign coverage use of, 88, 90, 94; critical perspective on, 82–83; democracy and, 83, 94; election campaign coverage role of, 81–84; media credibility and, 95–96; outrage discourse and, 83; reliance on, 78; in television news, 82
Putin, Vladimir, 195

racism: Pepe the Frog and, 174; racial profiling, 237; sexism, identity politics and, 216–217
Radutzky, Michael, 12
Reagan, Ronald, 136, 141, 145
Reddit: ADL classification protest on, 163–164; anonymity of members on, 158; *The _Donald* and, 160; Pepe legacy on 4chan and, 173; Pepe negative connotation and, 165–166; Pepe reclamation by 4chan and, 168–170; remix culture and, 156; user response to Furie campaign, 171
Reid, Eric, 233
Reign of April, 42–43
remix culture, 6; Furie on media influence in, 170–171; Internet memes and, 156–157; misunderstanding about, 163; Pepe meme function in, 168; premise underlying, 167–168; "produsers" in, 156; Trump, D., Pepe the Frog and, 160
Remnick, David, 38–39, 41
Republican National Convention (RNC), 211–212; Blue Lives Matter theme in, 224
Republicans, 124, 206; color association with, 204–205; fake news belief and, 17; Keyes kidnapping and, 214–215; negativity toward, 92; news network chosen by, 93–94
rhetoric: idealism, 116; narrative theory and, 136; pro-military, 236; white privilege, 203
rhetoric, election campaign, 47; Alexy conduct rules and, 48–49; boundaries between attack and acceptable, 48; recent trend in, 50; typical, 34, 48; unusual feature of 2016, 34
Rich, Seth, 23
RINOs, 36
RNC. *See* Republican National Convention
Robinson, Eugene, 45
Rogers, Will, 188
"Role Models", 144, 148
Romney, Mitt, 58, 59, 150n5
Roosevelt, Franklin Delano, 25, 108
Rothenberg, Stuart, 43
Rountree, Clarke, 103
Rowling, J. K., 43
Rubio, Marco, 152n32, 211
Russian interference issue, fake news and, 14–15, 20, 22; Russian ads on Facebook, 27n15

"Salute to the Military Night", 232, 235
San Francisco 49ers, 228, 232–233, 235
San Francisco Police Officers Association, 232
satire: audience reception and, 197, 201n64; comedians and, 187; debate coverage use of, 191–195; debates as source for, 184–186; democracy and, 198; educational role of political, 196; entertainment programs and, 6–7; historical examples of, 188; Horation, 188, 195–196; Juvenalian, 188, 195, 196–197; presidential elections and, 182, 183; purpose of humor and, 188–189; social responsibility theory and, 6–7, 187; types of, 188; viewers of political, 188
Sanders, Bernie, 79, 145, 213–214, 218
Saturday Night Live (SNL), 6–7, 187; as balanced critique of candidates, 195; debates satirized on, 191–192; past candidates satirized by, 182
Scarry, Eddie, 2
Schramm, Theodore, 79
self/other dichotomy, 32–34, 40
sexism, racism, identity politics and, 216–217
sexual misconduct, as satire material, 185–186
Shakespeare, William, 188

Shapiro-Wilk test, 62, 63
Shields, Tyler, 45
Shorenstein study, 209, 210, 211, 212
Siebert, Frederick, 79
Simpson, O. J., 192
SJWs. *See* social justice warriors
Smith, Tommie, 231
SNL. *See Saturday Night Live*
Snopes, 20–21
social justice warriors (SJWs), 161
social media: campaign narratives and, 5–6, 136–137; election campaign importance of, 136–137, 149, 151n17; first president to use, 136; Internet memes on, 170; traditional view of, 55
social responsibility theory: advocacy misapplication of, 196; entertainment programming and, 189–190; satire and, 6–7, 187
Society of Professional Journalists (SPJ), 119, 189
sociology, otherness in, 33
Soros, George, 11
"Speak" ad, 144
Spicer, Sean, 65
spiral of cynicism, 217
SPJ. *See* Society of Professional Journalists
sports journalism, 7–8; conflicts of interest in, 237; connecting sports to politics, 229–230, 239n38; cultural power of, 227–228; emotional risk of reporters, 235; escapism and, 223; Kaepernick coverage analysis and, 228–234, 239n35, 239n38; limits of, 234–237; low view of, 227; patriotism, Kaepernick and, 232–233; political neutrality and, 223–224, 229; politics intersection with, 224–226; proxy for as Black Lives Matter, 233–234; reimagining, 227–228; Right-oriented source selection and, 230–232; sport as political space, 225; *what* focus of, 235–236; *why* focus lacking in, 235; work routines and norms of, 226–227
statement bias, 80
Stein, Jill, 20, 210
Steinberg, Leigh, 225
Stelter, Brian, 77
Stewart, Tony, 230
Streisand, Barbara, 35
Stronger Together motto, 145, 147, 150; as narrative-in-response, 134–135
suicides, transgender, 20–21
Sunstein, Cass, 204
Swift, Jonathan, 188

Television Explorer, 84
television news, pundits role in, 82
The Television News Archive, 84, 85
terministic screens: agent/agency worldview and, 117–118; idealism and, 117–118; Trump, D., and Clinton, H., reflected, 115; worldviews and, 102–103, 115
thematization, in sports journalism, 227
TMZ, 45
Todd, Chuck, 114
Tomlin, Mike, 226
transgender suicides, fake news on, 20–21
trolls, 157, 164–165; Habbo Hotel raid, 166; memes weaponized by, 161; symbiotic relation with mainstream, 165
Trudeau, Garry, 188
Trump, Donald: blue privilege and, 209; Bush, J., and, 211; candidacy announcement, 181; Clinton, H., ads in response to, 144, 147–149; Clinton, H., attacks on, 146, 147, 148–149, 149–150; on Clinton, B., 68; *The Daily Show with Trevor Noah* satire on, 192–194; Democrats and, 218–219; on fake news, 1, 101; "false claims" of, 21, 22, 28n32; firestorms created by, 181–182; I alone agent worldview, 124–125, 126n32; impeachment term used by media, 207, 208; journalists choice of, 212; Kaepernick criticism of Clinton H., and, 229, 239n38; Knight endorsement of, 226; Kristof article on supporters of, 41–42; media bias and, 2; NASCAR CEO endorsement of, 226; *National Review* stance against, 36, 36–37; negative coverage of, 93; Pepe the Frog association with, 159–160; press worldview response to, 105–110, 126n32, 127n60; pro-Clinton/anti-

Trump bias actions from all MSM sources, 119–123; PTSD quote of, 13, 26n7; response to Kaepernick, 224; Rubio and, 211; Russian hacking issue and, 14–15, 20; *SNL* satire of Clinton, H., and, 191–192; tax returns and, 14; terministic screens and, 115; Todd interview of, 114; worldview expressed in nomination acceptance speech of, 103–104; worldviews in speeches of Clinton and, 5. *See also* debates, presidential; othering, of Trump, D.; Twitter, Trump, D., use of
Trump, Melania, plagiarism scandal and, 61, 62; statement issued by, 68; Twitter case study, 64–67
Twain, Mark, 188
Twitter: as agenda-building medium, 58; election responses to election by actors on, 187; iconographic tracking of Pepe on, 159; Kaepernick-related tweets on, 230, 239n44; #MAGA motto on, 145; #NeverTrump position on, 36, 38, 47; othering of Trump on, 42–43; Pepe the Frog and, 161–162; Romney use of, 58, 59; space allowed on, 55
Twitter, Trump, D., use of, 4; *Access Hollywood* tape and, 67–70; analysis conclusions, 70–72; analysis overview, 56–57; archive, 60–61, 61; "bot" accounts and, 72; Clinton compared to, 56, 59, 60; communication style, 56, 70; content and strategy, 59–60; election campaign tweets, 60–63; engagement with tweets about media, 62–63; first tweet, 55; hybrid media campaign, 57–58, 69–70; media attack tweet percentages, 70; media coverage and, 63–64, 64, 70; most retweeted and favorited tweets, 61–62; number of followers, 55; number of tweets during campaign, 61; Pepe the Frog tweet on, 160; personal nature of, 56; plagiarism scandal and, 61, 62; rules broken by, 70; sample time frame, 61; study limitations and implications for future research, 72; top tweets, by retweets, 63; traditional social media view and, 55; Trump, M., plagiarism case study, 64–67; trust in media undermined by, 71; tweet sources, 56; unfiltered nature of tweets, 56, 70

Ultimate Fighting Championship (UFC), 226
uncivil discourse, 93
undercard debates, 210
USA Today, 14–15
U.S. Navy, 232
US News & World Report, on fake news, 12–13

videos, 120, 139–141, 147–149
voters: candidate traits and positions perceived by, 183–184; debate winners perceived by, 215–216; disconnect between media and, 77–78; Internet use by, 137, 151n18

The Wall Street Journal, 3, 16
The Walrus, 184
war, meanings as cause of, 217
Warren, Elizabeth, 145
The Washington Post (WP), 68, 121; *Access Hollywood* article in, 67; candidate favored by, 80; on concession speech, 133–134; on Fox News, 15; Lowry interviewed by, 37; media bias and, 2, 79–80; on voter perceptions of debate winners, 215–216; worldviews in response to Clinton, H., acceptance speech, 110, 111, 114; worldviews in response to Trump, D., speech, 105, 106–107
The Washington Times, 122
Watergate, 28n26
Weekly Standard, 38
Wehner, Peter, 37, 40
Wells, Chris, 57
Wetzel, Dan, 234
"What's at Stake" ad, 147–148, 148
White, Dana, 226
White, Theodore H., 206
white privilege: Obama, B., and, 215; as rhetorical tool, 203
white supremacy, Pepe the Frog and, 159, 161, 162–163, 164–167
Wikileaks, 120, 122

Williamson, Kevin D., 36–37
working class, 25
worldviews, 5; agent/agency, 112–115, 117–118; agent-scene, 105–106, 116–117; in Clinton, H., nomination acceptance speech, 104–105; consubstantiality with Clinton, H., 118, 123, 124; definition of, 102; I alone agent, 124–125, 126n32; purpose and act interanimation of, 103–104; in response to Clinton, H., 110–115; in response to Trump, D., 105–110, 126n32, 127n60; terministic screens and, 102–103, 115; in Trump, D., nomination acceptance speech, 103–104. *See also specific news networks*
WP. *See The Washington Post*

xenophobia, 24

Zakaria, Fareed, 42
Zephoria Digital Marketing, 16

About the Contributors

Abe Aamidor (MA, Journalism, Southern Illinois University—Carbondale) is a veteran daily newspaper reporter (retired) who has worked at the *St. Louis Globe-Democrat*, the *(Champaign-Urbana) News-Gazette*, and the *Indianapolis Star*, where he also served as union president. His major journalism honors include twice a finalist in the Missouri Lifestyle Journalism Awards and twice first place in the Associated Press Managing Editors (Indiana) feature series category. He is the author, coauthor, or editor of six books, including the biography, *Chuck Taylor, All Star: The True Story of the Man Behind the Most Famous Athletic Shoe in History* and *Media Smackdown: Deconstructing the News and the Future of Journalism*. His novel, *Letting Go*, will be published in October 2018.

Stephen D. Cooper (PhD Rutgers) is professor emeritus in the Communication Studies Department of Marshall University. In addition to various journal articles and book chapters, he is the author of *Watching the Watchdog: Bloggers as the Fifth Estate* and coauthor of *Organizations and Unusual Routines: A Systems Analysis of Dysfunctional Feedback Processes*.

Katherine Haenschen (PhD University of Texas at Austin) is an assistant professor of communication and social analytics in the Department of Communication at Virginia Tech. Her research focuses on the intersection of digital media and politics, and has appeared in the *Journal of Communication*. She has been recognized with the Kyoon Hur Best Dissertation Award from the Mass Communication Division of ICA and a paper award from the Political Communication Interest Group of the Association for Education in Journalism and Mass Communication. Prior to joining the academy, she worked as a digital media consultant and political campaign manager.

Michael Horning (PhD Penn State University) is assistant professor of multimedia journalism in the Department of Communication at Virginia Tech. He is also an affiliate with Virginia Tech's Center for Human Computer Interaction. Before entering the academy, he was a general assignment news reporter for a community newspaper in Southwest Virginia where he regularly covered government and politics. His research interest includes how emerging media technologies influence audience experience and response to news, and how such technologies shape journalistic practices. His published research examines topics as varied as how audiences responded to the use of YouTube in the 2008 election debates, how mobile devices impact audience interest in news content, and how journalistic norms and value influence political cartoonist's coverage of sensitive political topics. Horning is also recipient of the Association in Journalism and Mass Communication's top research award in new media and politics.

Jim A. Kuypers (PhD Louisiana State University) is professor of rhetoric and political communication at Virginia Tech. He is the author, editor, or coauthor of twelve books, including *Purpose, Practice, and Pedagogy in Rhetorical Criticism* (winner of the Everett Lee Hunt Award for Outstanding Scholarship) and *Partisan Journalism: A History of Media Bias in the United States* (a Choice Outstanding Academic Title for 2014). He is a former coeditor for the *American Communication Journal*. He is the recipient of the American Communication Association's Outstanding Contribution to Communication Scholarship Award, the Southern States Communication Association's Early Career Research award, and Dartmouth College's Distinguished Lecturer Award. His research interests include political communication, media bias, meta-criticism, and the moral/poetic use of language.

Stephanie A. Martin (PhD University of California) is assistant professor of communication and public affairs at Southern Methodist University. She specializes in the public rhetoric of conservative evangelicals, especially in relation to economic issues, the American dream, American exceptionalism, and the American welfare state. Martin is also interested in the American presidency, and how presidents since Franklin D. Roosevelt have used new media to advance their economic agendas. She is the editor of *Columns to Characters: The Presidency and the Press Enter the Digital Age*, and has published a growing collection of well-received journal articles and book chapters.

Natalia Mielczarek (PhD University of Iowa) is assistant professor of communication in the Department of Communication at Virginia Polytechnic Institute and State University in Blacksburg. Her work has appeared in edited books and journals such as *Visual Communication Quarterly* and *Journal of Arab and Muslim Media Research*. Her research interests include visual rhetoric, iconicity, Internet memetics and instrumentalization of images in digital participatory culture. She is a former print journalist.

Chad Painter (PhD University of Missouri) is an assistant professor of communication at the University of Dayton, where he teaches courses in journalism and mass communication. He studies media ethics with emphases on the depiction of journalists in popular culture, the alternative press, and diversity studies. Currently, he serves as the head of the AEJMC Media Ethics Division and is coauthoring the next edition of *Media Ethics: Issues and Cases*. He has eight years of professional experience as a reporter, editor, and public relations practitioner for print and online publications.

Andrea J. Terry (PhD Texas A&M University) is an instructor of communication at California Polytechnic State University, San Luis Obispo. Her research investigates the contentious and complementary interactions between political and religious discourse, both on national and local levels. Dr. Terry's work has earned national recognition from the Religious Communication Association and can be found in publications such as the *Journal of Communication and Religion*, *Communication Inquiry*, and the *Journal of Religion, Media, and Digital Culture.*

Joseph M. Valenzano III (PhD Georgia State University) is associate professor and chair of the Department of Communication at the University of Dayton. His research specializes in the intersection of politics, religion, and the media. He has published in journals such as *Communication Monographs*, *Communication Quarterly, Communication Education,* and the *Journal of Communication and Religion*. He has coedited a book on civil religious rhetoric, coauthored a book on religious television programming, and coauthored three textbooks.

Ben Voth (PhD University of Kansas) is associate professor and director of speech and debate in corporate communication and public affairs in the Meadows School of the Arts. Voth is the author of three academic books regarding the role of political rhetoric in American and global affairs, and has published more than twenty-five academic book chapters explaining how communication and argument shape society. He worked as a consultant with Holocaust survivors at the U.S. Holocaust Memorial Museum in Washington DC; human freedom advocates from North Korea and Burma at the Bush Institute in Dallas, Texas; as the Debate Fellow for the President Calvin Coolidge Foundation in Plymouth Notch, Vermont. His teaching and research mission is to equip individuals to have their voice. His expert opinions appear in the *Dallas Morning News*, NPR radio affiliates across the nation, *Fortune Magazine*, and the online political magazine *American Thinker*. He is a leading national scholar on debate, and recently travelled to Rwanda to apply his communication work toward further assisting their government in overcoming the history of genocide in that nation.

Erin Whiteside (PhD Penn State University) is associate professor of journalism and electronic media at the University of Tennessee. Her work explores the intersection of sports, media, and culture and she is primarily interested in diversity and ethics in the sports media workplace, discourses of gender and sexuality in sports media, and processes of cultural meaning-making through sports media consumption. Her recent work has focused on the cultural negotiation over issues related to gender equity and Title IX, and she has published on that topic in *Journalism* and *Communication and Sport*.